The War in Vietnam

Moral Argument and the War in Vietnam

A COLLECTION OF ESSAYS

Edited and Introduced by Paul T. Menzel

AURORA PUBLISHERS INCORPORATED

NASHVILLE/ LONDON

COPYRIGHT © 1971 BY
AURORA PUBLISHERS INCORPORATED
NASHVILLE, TENNESSEE 37219
LIBRARY OF CONGRESS CATALOG CARD NUMBER: 79-143721
STANDARD BOOK NUMBER: 87695-123-X
MANUFACTURED IN THE UNITED STATES OF AMERICA

Contents

IV. CAN ETHICS, IDEOLOGY, AND HISTORY MEET?

Acknowledgments

Permissions for all the reprinted articles are noted at the bottom of the first page of each selection. I thank all the authors and publishers who have cooperated in my task of procuring reprint permissions. (Footnotes in all the excerpted selections have been renumbered to fit the present volume, and omissions from the original are indicated by dots in the text.)

Several individuals have been of considerable assistance to me in putting this volume together. First among them is Dr. Charles Scott of the philosophy department at Vanderbilt University, who suggested the volume to me in the first place. Back further may I acknowledge the many persons, far too numerous to mention, who have stimulated me to think about the war.

Preface

Another book on Vietnam?!? The abundance of printed material on the war may by this time seem to have relegated to insignificance all but the most uniquely scholarly or up-to-date new writing on the subject. Those on all sides of the debate are largely tired of this war. We want to move on to other things, to discussions of domestic problems and of Cambodia and Laos.

I share in these sentiments myself. Yet the war in Vietnam continues. It is still, realistically if not psychologically, the dominating present-day issue of our foreign policy. Arguments about it may be hashed out again and again, yet there is room to spare for clear thought and conviction amidst confusion. In fact, confusion about the war is still prevalent in all sectors of our society. This past year many confused arguments from both sides were being presented during the fall 1969 Moratorium and the spring 1970 Cambodian crisis. Basic issues and facts were often ignored, and arguments missed the relevant points. In this light this volume may be seen to have a legitimate purpose, the clarification of moral argument about the war. It happens also to constitute a useful collection of many of the outstanding articles on the war in the past half decade.

I should comment on the broad scope of "moral" in my conception of the book. I take the moral sense of how we "should" and "ought" to act to be the most ultimate sense in which we ask these questions. When used in this way it is senseless to ask, after admitting what is *morally* required, whether that should in fact be done. Anyone who uses "moral" and still asks that question reveals that he is using the word narrowly and has some other more ultimate conception of what should be done which is his disguised moral principle. Thus, if a point of view on this war claims to shun moral questions and seriously asks us to act on conflicting nonmoral criteria, I still take it to be offering a moral argument, only moral in its own terms and not necessarily based on usual moral criteria of the society. There is no purely nonmoral view of what United States policy should be. Thus the scope of "moral argument" in this book is very broad.

At the same time let me mention some limits I have placed on the discussion in this book.

Readers will note the absence of much discussion of the war as a possible "prudential mistake": purely for its own interest the United States should (or should not) have intervened in Vietnam, and for the same reason it should not (or should) now extricate itself as quickly as possible. I do not deny that there is a moral dimension to "self-interest" and "prudence." I only presume that in most contexts we do separate it from morality. We have criteria both for self-interest and

Moral Argument and the War in Vietnam

for morality. And we may regard this war as in or against the nation's own interests yet realize that that is not necessarily a judgment for or against the morality of the war. That may be a *good* reason for having gotten in and for not getting out, or a good reason for the opposite, *especially* in the absence of other definitive reasons. But it is not a *moral* reason, and those who offer this criticism or defense of the war do not usually offer it as such.

I do not become directly involved in the question, Can moral criteria be applied to wars at all? I presume they do apply, and then proceed to ask whether this war is moral. There are, of course, many ways in which any sense could be denied to applying moral predicates to wars. By saying that "morality does not apply to war" we might mean that in fact moral criteria are not dominant influences on states' decisions to enter or not enter wars. We might also be making a moral claim itself: states should not use moral criteria in their own conscious decisions about war. Or we might mean that moral predicates are just not conceptually appropriate to things like states and wars, and where they are applied it is out of an outdated metaphorical, anthromorphic view of wars and states. Or we may mean that *all* moral predicates are a sham.[1] But I observe that people do in fact use moral predicates in judging wars. I shall simply assume that the business of using them that way does make some sense.

I will focus on the morality of the Vietnam War itself, the policy that got us in and keeps us in and the policy that might get us out. I do not touch many other important moral judgments related to the war: the morality of using specific weapons (e.g., napalm), the morality of different tactics used to try to protest and stop the war, and the personal moral blame that specific individual leaders in our society may face if the war is judged to be immoral. Neither will I discuss pacifism or the morality of war in general. I intend to focus on *this war itself,* not on *war itself.*

Furthermore I do not intend the analyses of the war presented herein to be factually definitive. Selections have been chosen primarily because they speak to specific moral issues and can be viewed as illustrating certain kinds of moral arguments about the war. Usually the most detailed and definitive factual descriptions of a given subject will have to be found in other writings. This is not to say that the presentation of facts is not important to the volume. It certainly is, and there is much of it herein, for moral argument is itself a complex interrelationship of factual claims and moral principles.

Important facts about the situations in Cambodia and Laos are noticeably absent. These situations have become increasingly important

---

1 These various meanings are distinguished by Richard A. Wasserstrom, "On the Morality of War: A Preliminary Inquiry," in Wasserstrom (ed.), *War and Morality* (Belmont, Calif.: Wadsworth, 1970, pp. 79-82.)

within the last year. Unfortunately, the best analysis of situations is usually not made until after they become centers of crisis. Although there are some important and informative writings on these areas, I have not felt myself qualified to put together a volume, or part-volume, on them. Besides, many of the arguments in this volume will be applicable to Cambodia and Laos.

Neither do I intend the discussion herein to be philosophically definitive. The articles and editorial comments are not meant to be technical, academic philosophy, though at points the importance of broader, abstract, "philosophical" issues will be clear. The book may be quite useful in providing a springboard for certain philosophical discussions, but it is not itself philosophically rigorous.

Finally, I will frankly mention that my own moral position is strongly against United States involvement in Vietnam. However, this book need not therefore be tainted in its purpose (and I hope not in its execution), which is to clarify moral arguments about this war from all sides. I need to guard against accusations from two sides. On the one hand my political opponents to the right may detect a predominance of antiwar views in the selections (thirteen out of twenty, by one count) and a bias in my editorial introductions. To them I may point out that any war is bound to stimulate fewer eloquent moral analyses for it than against it; the war itself is a fact of the status quo; it probably has come about at least in part through circumstances and the force of events and not through moral reflection, and its supporters will be less pressed to articulate moral arguments to keep it going than its opponents will be to stop it. Then, too, if in the end moral analysis seems to weigh more heavily toward one side than the other, this may be due more to the nature of the war itself than to any bias of its analysts. On the other hand, some of my friends on the left may wonder how I can even pretend to present "analysis" rather than polemic at a time when it is imperative to stop the war. Of course, as a moral agent there are many points at which I forsake academic analysis and assume a very political stance. But in that process, clarity of moral reflection can be crucial, both for one's own ability to formulate and articulate a political position and for one's ability to persuade others. Confusion, as I said earlier, is prevalent in some sectors of the antiwar movement. To keep from being co-opted or from being immobilized by confusion induced by an articulate opponent, it is important to know the arguments on which one's position stands. Then, too, it just may be that this war *is* so morally atrocious that "analysis" of it will not turn out to be politically neutral. To say this is to suggest neither that detailed argument and analysis is the most effective way of changing things in our society nor that such argument and analysis can never become a delusion along the road to political change

Nashville, Tennessee, February 1971

Part I

A Just War?

A Just War?

Introduction

The theory of the "just war" has a long and distinguished tradition. Formulated first by St. Augustine early in the fifth century, it has since been developed in many forms, primarily by Christian theologians and ethicists. Contemporary thought and society have called it into serious question, so much so that perhaps some readers will wonder why a section on just war stands at the beginning of this volume. To be sure, the theory has encountered genuine difficulties in its application to modern wars. And among other things, non-Christian readers may find rather distracting the overtly Christian language which appears in it here and there. Yet let us look at the major questions which the theory poses, for example those taken up by Mr. Little in his initial paper: (1) Is the government in whose defense the war is being waged a legitimate government? (2) Has aggression been committed against that government by the wartime enemy? (3) Has the decision to wage the war been made by the legitimate procedures? (4) Does the war effort discriminate between combatants and noncombatants in its targets? (5) Do the benefits to be derived from fighting the war outweigh its evils and costs? I think most of us find that these are some, if certainly not all, of the standard moral questions we wish to ask about any particular war. To ask whether the Vietnam War is a just war is thus a convenient and enlightening but hopefully not binding framework in which to carry on moral discussion.

A major defect of the theory has been its use historically to emphasize only the justness of wars. In the past the theory has often operated in practice as an assumption that a war was just, unless there was overwhelming evidence to the contrary.[1] The theory has seemed to contend that a certain kind of war is just, without emphasizing equally, or perhaps more strongly, that wars not sanctioned by the theory are unjust. But this is more an historical defect than one ingrained in the theory itself. Indeed, the whole theory might be rephrased as the "unjust war theory," whose operating maxim is, "A war is unjust, unless it can reasonably be shown to fulfill all five (or however many we may end with) of the following conditions. . . . "

The impression that just war theory functions largely to condone wars may also be conveyed by the fact that at times its primary task has been to devise rules for the conduct of war. From the late seventeenth century until the League of Nations in 1919, many rules for legitimate conduct within a war were spelled out, but little was done to develop

Moral Argument and the War in Vietnam

and apply criteria for the justness or unjustness of a war itself.[2] However, the bulk of the theory directs itself to the latter issue. Obviously the first three questions mentioned deal with the justness of a war itself, and even the fourth and fifth may also do so. The distinction between combatants and innocent noncombatants may, of course, be made in evaluating a specific tactic within a war whose larger justness is assumed (the World War II obliteration bombings of German cities and atomic bombings of Nagasaki and Hiroshima are often thus debated). The distinction may also be made in a larger context: if modern wars nearly always take place between nations as wholes—with all their economic, human, and political resources—then perhaps most supposed "noncombatants" are seldom genuinely "innocent," or even "noncombatants" at all, and thus in turn we should doubt the morality of any modern state's policy of war. If, also, a given state must of necessity kill large numbers of noncombatants to be even minimally "successful" in its war effort, then one can question whether that state can morally pursue that war at all. The last possibility can also be raised for the fifth question (the "proportionality" of good over evil): A person may not wish simply to argue how to minimize the evils of a war, but to contend that the war cannot in practice be fought at all without producing much more evil than good.

Perhaps all the questions of just war theory lose their traditional clarity when applied to Vietnam. Yet they remain crucial to consider. Take, for example, the question of the *legitimacy and sovereignty* of the state allegedly aggressed against. The Geneva Accords, as the discussion between Mr. Little and Mr. Ogle indicates, do anything but grant *clear-cut* status of sovereign statehood to the government in Saigon. Even if they did, the debate over the sovereign or unsovereign character of the Saigon government would not be settled. The question remaining is the larger "sovereignty" of that government, not simply in legalistic relation to the Accords, but in the context of historical character and origin.[3] The critic of United States policy might argue that the choice of Diem to head a government was neocolonial and clearly at odds with the fact which lay behind the whole Geneva conference: the historical movement for general independence from the French had won the war in 1954.[4] "Legitimacy" becomes so complex in Vietnam in recent decades that traditional just war criteria lose their clarity. Yet, undoubtedly, it remains relevant to consider the legal status, the actual political origin, and the degree of popular support of the Saigon government. These are important in terms of democratic ideals, international stability and rule of law, and continuity of historical and national development.

The "aggression" issue, too, changes its traditional character. In Vietnam we are certainly not dealing with a clear armed invasion.[5] The debate is rather over the character of the *revolution within* South Vietnam. Was it stimulated by the violence and trust-breaking of the Saigon authorities against the people, so that it was a spontaneous and defensive revolution? Or, despite some local elements, was its impetus largely imported from the North, and from Thai and Laotian rebels? If the program for the revolution was "imported" in some sense, might the conditions of the revolution nevertheless be so largely indigenous, and the program such, that the revolution is nevertheless justified?[6] These questions are relevant, for most of us feel inclined to accept the assumption that "violence is most clearly justified when those whose own lives are at stake make the decision on whether the prize is worth dying for."[7] That assumption is needed by a supporter of the war to give moral force to his claim that the revolution against the Saigon government is not truly indigenous. Yet it will itself throw doubt on the morality of United States policy—we are a nation at a distance, technologically, socially, geographically—unless one can argue that the people (not on the enemy side) who are bearing the brunt of the deaths in South Vietnam have themselves "made a decision" (in the relevant sense) to bring our military force to bear within their nation.

Whether the United States government has made its decision to enter the war through legitimate decision-making procedures is equally as complex an issue in the contemporary situation. From Mr. McDermott's article a large number of questions about the usual simplicity of a "constitutional" decision begin to appear: If the Johnson administration withheld the truth, and even lied, about its policies during the presidential election of 1964, did the American public have the chance to make a constitutional decision to prosecute the war with American ground troops? Did it perhaps, in voting so decisively for Johnson over Goldwater, even make an explicit decision against such a policy? Were the ideological similarities of the Pentagon and the White House so similar that *in effect* there was little civilian control over the military in this decision making process? Does some structure here carry over into decisions made by any administration, even the most war-critical one? The actual processes of authorization in a modern state are often so complex that the criteria for "legitimate" authorization become fluid and confused.[8] Certain formal criteria may render the Vietnam War properly authorized, but it is possible that more complex realities may either deny that propriety outright or at least force the just war theory to be recast and detailed at this point.

A general suspicion that "means" are ultimately reducible to "ends" may underlie a suspicion of all just war criteria. One can view those means which are ordinarily thought to limit pursuit of ends as only disguised reconsiderations of ends: we take means into account just because "ends are contingent and uncertain (the results of the war depend in large part upon the ways in which it is fought), and . . . there are other ends in the world besides the ones we have most recently chosen."[9] Means are important simply because they figure into any comprehensive and ultimate assessment of ends. Now if that should be a correct analysis of the relation of means to ends (whether it is

Moral Argument and the War in Vietnam

is highly debatable—at least philosophically), it may be thought that the first four points of just war theory become irrelevant; everything would depend on the fifth point, the weighing of resulting goods and evils. But that is not quite correct. Indeed everything would in the end depend on weighing the sum total of goods and evils, and that would mean that any one of the theory's first four points could be outweighed by some other end; thus we could no longer interpret the theory as requiring a war to satisfy *all* five points in order to be just. But the theory's first four points would not thereby become irrelevant: they might in fact be relevant precisely because they enable us to more "wisely" judge the total goods and evils. War, for instance, with "Victory!" as its only cry narrowly focuses on only some ends. In fact this interpretation of means and ends seems very realistic in light of the experience of Vietnam. A critic of the war can claim that the failure of United States policy to satisfy the first four points of the theory is the best causal explanation of why United States policy has not in fact been able to achieve its goals.

As the first selection of this section, the debate between Mr. Little and Mr. Ogle covers all five questions we have mentioned. This debate may well be thought, in readers' final impressions, to put most of its energy into the first two questions. Mr. Lacouture's article relates most directly to the second, and will at one point (p. 32) suggest a reversal of just war predicates to North Vietnam's decision to aid the rebels in the South. Mr. McDermott deals, as mentioned, with the third question. The other questions are left largely to later parts of the book. The fourth will be discussed from a slightly different angle in Section II on genocide; Section IV will indirectly consider the fifth, especially the end of international stability, which Mr. Little strongly emphasizes (p. 21).

Notes

1 Donald A. Wells, *The War Myth* (New York: Pegasus, 1967), p. 34.

2 Wells, *The War Myth,* p. 38

3 An interesting philosophical discussion of "lawful government" is somewhat relevant to this point. R. M. Hare has contended that the phrase "sovereign (or lawful) government" is normally used performatively to proclaim the speaker's allegiance to a particular government, not to designate certain descriptive characteristics (including purely "legal" ones) of that government. See his article, "The Lawful Government," in Peter Laslett and W. G. Runciman (eds.), *Philosophy, Politics, and Society: Third Series* (New York: Barnes and Noble, 1967).

4 See in this connection the comments by Gabriel Kolko in his introduction to the NLF's Ten Points, p. 168.

5 For instance, even Secretary of Defense McNamara testified before Congress that even as late as 1966, only 15,000 (6.5 percent) of the 235,000 enemy troops in South Vietnam were N. Vietnamese regulars. Revealed by Sen. Joseph Clark, *Congressional Record,* March 21, 1966. Even clearer figures were given by Sen. Mike Mansfield, from Pentagon sources: only 400 N. Vietnamese soldiers were among an enemy force of 140,000 in South Vietnam

in 1965 when the sharp escalation of United States military involvement began. See Draper, p. 192, footnote 12.

6 See, in some considerable connection here, the selection in Section IV by John McAlister and Paul Mus. See also the Oglesby selection in that section, pp. 220-222.

7 Howard Zinn, "Vietnam: Setting the Moral Equation," *The Nation,* January 17, 1966.

8 Wells makes this point in "How Much Can 'The Just War' Justify?" *Journal of Philosophy,* LXVI, No. 23 (December 4, 1969), pp. 821-822.

9 Michael Walzer, "Moral Judgment in Time of War," in Richard Wasserstrom (ed.), *War and Morality* (Belmont, California: Wadsworth, 1970), p. 61.

Is the War in Vietnam Just?*

By David Little

Professor Roland Bainton, in his very helpful book, *Christian Attitudes Toward War and Peace*, divides traditional Christian positions on war into three camps: pacifists, just war theorists, and crusaders. It is difficult to know what insight a conviction of pacifism can bring to the problem of evaluating whether or in what way a particular war ought to be conducted since the pacifist is opposed in principle to the use of military force. Correspondingly, the proponent of the holy war seems to possess only one criterion of evaluation, namely whether or not a war serves a holy end.

From my point of view, neither pacifism nor a crusade theory is of much help in examining the initiation and conduct of war because of their respective forms of inflexibility. I wish to hold military action open as at least one possible instrument of good, without at the same time running the great danger of sanctifying a resort to arms. Consequently, the just war tradition seems the most hopeful means for developing a useful set of moral standards in regard to the problem of war.

The traditional Christian just war theory has sought to translate Christian norms like love and fidelity into appropriate guidelines for military activity. In Augustine's words, "Love does not preclude a benevolent severity," and yet, presumably, it does modify and control severity. When wars meet certain general standards, Augustine argued, the Christian may be obliged to countenance them. "Those wars may be defined as just which avenge injuries," and by that Augustine meant defensive action waged either in self-defense or for the purpose of recovering something wrongfully expropriated. Furthermore, wars are just only if they are waged under the auspices of a legitimate authority, and conducted according to the principle of discrimination (the moral immunity of noncombatants from attack); all torture, looting and wanton violence are excluded. Augustine also felt that abiding fidelity to treaty obligations was an important aspect of the just war theory. Finally, the principle of proportionality (that the good intended be at least as clear and as great as the evil done) has attached itself to the just war tradition.

Since there is so much talk about the patent 'immorality' and 'injustice' of the Vietnam War, it may be useful to raise just-war questions about what is going on there. I should not think we have posed all the moral

*This article, the subsequent reply by Mr. Ogle, and the rejoinder by Mr. Little first appeared in *Reflection: A Journal of Opinion at Yale Divinity School*, Volume 64, Nos. 1-3 (November, 1966 through March, 1967). Reprinted by permission of the editor. For a much more detailed version of many of the arguments presented by Mr. Little here, see his later book, *American Foreign Policy and Moral Rhetoric: The Example of Vietnam* (New York: Council on Religion and International Affairs, 1969).

Moral Argument and the War in Vietnam

problems involved in the Vietnamese situation when we have asked these questions. But perhaps we will have introduced some kind of coherent moral framework into a discussion that has not been distinguished by much care or precision.

Let us put four questions to ourselves which raise some salient aspects of the just war theory so far as the Vietnam conflict is concerned. 1) Is the Republic of South Vietnam, under whose auspices the allegedly defensive action was initiated, a legitimate authority? 2) Has the Republic of South Vietnam been 'injured' (aggressed against) by a foreign state? 3) Has the United States effort there been initiated by the president in a legitimate way? 4) Is the war being conducted according to the principles of discrimination and proportionality?

1. South Vietnam as Legitimate Authority

Many critics of the administration are in the habit of arguing that the Diem-Ky succession is plainly an illegal and illegitimate government. However, the extensive and carefully documented legal brief, "The Lawfulness of United States Assistance to the Republic of South Vietnam," prepared by John Norton Moore and James Underwood in collaboration with Professor Myres McDougal of the Yale Law School, makes it very difficult to sustain that point of view any longer. It is, of course, a popular assumption that according to the Geneva Accords of 1954, South Vietnam was rendered "merely a temporary zone not even qualifying politically as a state," and that, therefore, any alleged aggression by the North is only in the nature of a civil war between two zones.

Actually, as the brief makes clear, "the language about the zones was intended to preserve the existing claims to sovereignty to all of a united Vietnam by both [North Vietnam] and [South Vietnam]" (13. Page references to the McDougal brief will be given in parentheses henceforth). At various times since the Accords, nations such as Great Britain, France, Sweden and even Russia have acknowledged the independent sovereignty of South Vietnam. As Dr. B.S.N. Murti, an Indian scholar associated with the International Control Commission put it:"[Since] the Geneva Agreement, two independent sovereign states . . . came into existence in Vietnam and the division of the country seems permanent. . . . Both the states are completely independent with full-fledged governments of their own owing no allegiance to the other" (29).

Moreover, South Vietnam has by now been recognized as an independent state by about sixty nations, and it has twice nearly been admitted to the U.N. "The history of the U.N. resolutions and debates

8

on the status of the two Vietnams after the 1954 Geneva Accords leave no doubt that the Republic of Vietnam is recognized as an independent state under international law and some of the debates lend support to the proposition that there are now two independent states in Vietnam" (28). (Incidentally, in order to conform to the recognized standards of legitimacy, a state must have a territory, a government, a people and a capacity to enter into relations with other states. The government of South Vietnam meets these standards.

But what of the Geneva Accords, which guaranteed unification by means of elections? As ought to be common knowledge, neither the U.S. nor S.V. signed the Accords, and for that reason could hardly be bound by them. What is still more significant, however, are some of the problems with the Accords, particularly on the point of elections. The crucial matter of elections was not carefully considered nor were provisions or stipulations in any way laid down. "This cavalier treatment of the political settlement problems must be considered a major weakness of the Accords and suggests that the parties were aware of the possibility of an extended partition in Vietnam unless, of course, they contemplated unification other than by elections" (165). Certainly, there is no basis for the argument that failure to live up to these very vague references to elections by S.V. left only one course of action open to the North, namely armed intervention.

It is frequently contended that while the Diem-Ky succession may be *legally* legitimate, the Vietcong really represent the people, and ought, therefore, to be recognized as the true political authority. While it is true the Ky administration is not representative, there is, to my knowledge, little evidence to substantiate the conclusion that the Vietcong command anything like majority support. Douglas Pike's study, "How Strong Is the NLF?" in the *Reporter* (February 24, 1966) finds the actual political support for the Vietcong in the neighborhood of 10 percent of the population.

So far as I am concerned, however, the most convincing evidence for strong anti-Vietcong sentiment is found in a revealing interview held in April, 1966 with Thich Tri Quang, the radical Buddhist leader who opposed Ky so vigorously. "Q. What do you think of the Vietcong movement? A. This is mostly a matter of semantics to me. People try to separate North Vietnamese Communists from South Vietnamese Communists. No such separation exists. They are both Communists. And . . . as a religious man, the ideology they possess is much more dangerous than the guns they possess" (*Time* April 22, 1966). In the *New Haven Register* (June 9, 1966), a similar report appeared regarding a Buddhist statement on peace talks with the Vietcong: "The statement by the Unified Buddhist Church denied any neutralist tendencies among the estimated .5 million Buddhists it represents. It said the presence of American troops in the nation of 15 million 'is obviously needed, temporarily.' "

Moral Argument and the War in Vietnam
2. The Question of Communist Aggression

If it could be demonstrated that the war in Vietnam was initiated exclusively in the South, and was historically unrelated to the activities of the government in the North, then the U.S. would be completely out of order. As a matter of fact, however, there is no question whatsoever about the impartial evidence for vigorous aggressive activity launched by the North across an internationally recognized territorial boundary. The information compiled in the legal brief from non-United States sources like the I.C.C. is far too massive to be quoted in detail here.

There is, of course, the well-known affirmation issued by the I.C.C. on June 2, 1962: "There is evidence to show that the [North Vietnamese] have allowed the Zone in the North to be used for inciting, encouraging and supporting hostile activities in the Zone in the South, *aimed at the overthrow of the administration in the South.*" Even more interesting is the report published by the Canadian member of the I.C.C. Legal Committee on February 13, 1965: "[The hostile activities of North Vietnam] are in direct and grave violation of the Geneva Agreement, and *constitute the root cause of general instability in Vietnam . . .* The cessation of hostile activities by North Vietnam is *a prerequisite to the restoration of peace in Vietnam as foreseen by the participants of the Geneva Conference of 1954*" (35).

No one need contend that the war is the exclusive result of external aggression to be able to show that a legitimate government has been 'injured.' The record is clear on the variety of sources for the conflict. As Richard N. Goodwin writes in *Triumph Or Tragedy,* "the reality is there is aggression and there is also civil war" (25). Nevertheless, if the Vietcong gain in effectiveness because of their association with the North, they must also take the serious international consequences of that association. Had the Vietcong succeeded in remaining genuinely independent of the North (if that were possible), the U.S. would be faced with quite a different situation. As things stand, S.V. would appear to be fully within its rights in asking the U.S. to come to its aid.

3. The President's Initiative

While critics of the administration attack President Johnson's manner of involving U.S. troops and resources in Vietnam as unconstitutional and therefore illegitimate, their criticisms are odd. American history is replete with examples of 'presidential discretion' in foreign affairs, from the war with France in 1798, to Korea in the 1950s, to Lebanon in 1958, to the Cuban missile crisis in 1962.

Furthermore, the Congress has by no means been without opportunity for participation in the decision-making process. On August 7, 1964 Congress passed the Gulf of Tonkin Resolution, whose "language . . . coupled with the record of the congressional debates as a whole

10

strongly indicates that it was the congressional intent to authorize the use of armed force if necessary, as the president should determine, to assist the Republic of Vietnam in combating aggression . . ." (106). Some of the congressional discussion over the Resolution is most instructive.

"MR. SCOTT: 'I support the resolution. I was glad to hear the chairman say there is nothing in the resolution which limits the right of the president to repeal any attack or prevent further aggression within the areas described in the resolution.' MR. FULBRIGHT: 'That is correct.' MR. COOPER: 'Then, looking ahead, if the president decided that it was necessary to use such force as could lead into war, we will give that authority by this resolution?' MR. FULBRIGHT: 'That is the way I would interpret it. . . . In the old days, when war usually resulted from a formal declaration of war—and that is what the Founding Fathers contemplated when they included that provision in the Constitution—there was time in which to act. . . . Under modern conditions of warfare, . . . it is necessary to anticipate what may occur. . . .' MR. COOPER: 'But the power provided the president in section 2 is great.' MR. FULBRIGHT: 'This provision is intended to give clearance to the president to use his discretion.' " (See Brief, 102-7.)

A careful reading of this discussion indicates very clearly that the Congress knew what it was doing by passing the resolution, and that, for several reasons, it was concerned not to tie the hand of the president to a formal declaration of war.

4. The Conduct of the War

To show that the Vietnam War passes the tests of discrimination (noncombatant immunity) and proportionality (that the good intended to be at least as clear and as great as the evil done) is by far our most difficult task. However, it is important to see that the reasons why the task is difficult are not simply American malevolence and hardheartedness. The difficulty is the result of a combination of the character of the war in Vietnam and American shortsightedness and lack of imagination.

Let us examine, first, the very grave problem of noncombatant immunity in the war. As Professor Paul Ramsey rightly says in his essay, "Can Counter-Insurgency War Be Conducted Justly?": "The use of our advanced technology as a way of avoiding a decade of counter-guerrilla warfare on the ground is bound to occasion the greatest qualms of conscience in anyone who knows that the conduct of the war should be both discriminating and proportionate if it is to be a barely human and a politically purposive enterprise."

In the light of the staggering reports of civilian casualties, who could help agreeing with Ramsey? Yet as he and others have pointed out, the character of insurgency warfare itself makes impossible any clear distinction between combatant and noncombatant. A guerrilla war involves by definition the *in*visibility of the combatant, the indistinguishability of soldier and civilian. Furthermore, the prime objects of guerrilla activity, at least in the initial stages of the war, are nonmilitary personnel, such as political and community leaders. In other words, insurgency thrives on, and could not succeed without, the elimination of the combatant-noncombatant distinction. It is not, therefore, too harsh to conclude that in principle a great share of the moral onus for civilian casualties rests with these who initiate an insurgency war.

However, in face of the effects of extensive U.S. bombing in South Vietnam, it is hard to relieve one's conscience quite so easily. Surely the only option open to the U.S. is not the intensified use of weapons such as napalm and 'lazy dog' bombs, weapons that are bound to injure civilians. One would hope, for example, that stepped-up American troop commitments with an increased emphasis upon holding and pacification operations, such as Arthur Schlesinger, Richard Goodwin and others have been calling for, would mean decreasing reliance upon B—52's. It is very important, in my judgment, that public discussion center around *live* alternatives to the preponderant emphasis upon bombs. To keep such a war as this at least "barely human" is the anguishing but necessary task of the Christian moralist.

The Principle of Proportionality

Along with the principle of discrimination, the principle of proportionality raises a number of perplexities with respect to U.S. policy in Vietnam. The whole reason for the great uncertainty over our policy is precisely the difficulty one has in convincing himself that the benefits are worth the costs in suffering to the people of Vietnam as well as costs in energy, money and resources to the people of the United States. Unquestionably, the most serious problem for even the most loyal administration supporter is the nagging uncertainty over whether the country for which we are paying such a price *can* survive if and when insurgency is stopped. One can imagine the degree of 'backlash' if some years hence in a pacified Vietnam, political maneuvers produce a Communist takeover. That is clearly a risk we run and must face.

Like everyone else, I am sure that had we not become involved in S.V. in the first place, it would hardly be 'proportional' to get involved (in the light of what we now know). In my judgment, the benefits nowhere nearly match the costs. But it is the fact of our involvement there that makes a critical difference, that introduces a new set of considerations to be calculated in the balance. Now the question is not simply: 'Has S.V. any chance of self-determination?' but also: 'Can the U.S. assure that it shall be given that chance?'

There is little doubt in my mind that from 1954 on, the U.S. thought that S.V. had a good chance of developing viability. Moreover, the U.S.

was prepared to assure that chance against outside pressure, even though there was then no clear understanding of the lengths to which our government would go in making good that assurance. In its formal declaration at the end of the Geneva Accords, the U.S. was plainly disturbed by the possibility of Northern subversive activity. "[The U.S.] would view any renewal of the aggression in violation of the aforesaid Agreements with grave concern and as seriously threatening international peace and security. . . ." That concern was reaffirmed by President Eisenhower in 1954 and then again in 1957, and several more times by President Kennedy.

That is not, of course, to say that prior to Johnson's decision to commit combat troops in the spring of 1965 anyone understood the U.S. assurance as entailing such a decision. If I read the record aright, no one ever seriously imagined such a step would be necessary. As Goodwin puts it, "More important than any other single factor was the hopeful expectation, the wish, . . . that victory might come easily and with little pain. . . . At every step, it seemed to many that the struggle was almost won" (28-9). The whole story of Vietnam is a tragic story of miscalculation regarding *what it would in fact cost* to give the South a chance against the hostile designs of the North.

But that the assurance was repeatedly and publicly declared to be important for us, that the U.S. often warned the North against resting that assurance, cannot, I believe, be denied. The McDougal brief seems accurate when it states: "The present U.S. assistance to the Republic of Vietnam is entirely consistent with the expectations created by U.S. actions at the Geneva Conference of 1954" (81).

As a result of our involvement and our repeated declarations regarding the importance of giving S.V. a chance against outside arbitrary interference, special benefits have to be weighed against the costs. There is a good deal more at stake here than mere national prestige or pathological anticommunism (though these elements have played an unfortunately large role in the administration's rhetoric). The issue is whether in face of clear I.C.C. evidence of aggression, the U.S. could fail to measure up to the set of expectations it had been developing over the course of ten years, particularly when the combined activities of the Vietcong and North Vietnamese gave immediate promise of totally overturning S.V. In this specific, but important, context, Johnson's decision does not seem to have badly violated the principle of proportionality.

Again, one is faced with the dilemma: what if the very military action that is designed to protect S.V. ends up destroying it? At this level, proportionality becomes very fuzzy. I can only urge, once more, that the existence of this dilemma is one good reason for doing all we can in S.V. to minimize the use of bombs and other devices that so obviously undermine whatever civilian fabric that still exists there. On balance, the substantial increase of ground forces in S.V. for holding and pacification purposes seems preferable to the continuance of bombing at

Moral Argument and the War in Vietnam

the present rate (in the South as well as in the North). Though I have barely scratched the surface of the complex moral, legal and political problems that make up the Vietnam War, I have at least suggested one possible framework for sorting out and responding to some of the problems. The use of this (truncated) version of the just war theory, together with the line of argument I have developed, will no doubt strike many as heartless and legalistic. Where is the passion, the indignation, the sense of condemnation? My only defense is that there is perhaps room in a moral community for division of labor. We have not been at a loss for passion, indignation and condemnation so far as Vietnam goes. But perhaps we have lacked attempts to line out some criteria for making moral judgments, as well as attempts to see the criteria through in relation to the facts.

Actually, my hopes for this undertaking are simple: that as a result of it, moral rhetoric will not be applied quite so indiscriminately to Vietnam.

Mister Little—The Answer Is 'No!'

By Arthur Bud Ogle

Professor David Little's article, "Is the War in Vietnam Just?" (*Reflection*, Nov., 1966) evokes a strong rejoinder. Mr. Little justifies his exercise by purportedly introducing a coherent moral framework. His conclusions seem rather to reflect a convenient moral rationalization. . . . I shall analyze the four points upon which Little's argument is based. . . .

One Vietnam or Two?

First, is South Vietnam a legal and legitimate authority? Obviously the southern sector of Vietnam has achieved international recognition—so have Red China and East Germany. The point is not whether recognition has been achieved, but how and why. The United States, having assumed France's role of protector and supervisor, has established and "legitimated" the government of South Vietnam. The U.S. and France supported the Japanese-appointed emperor Bao Dai. We brought Diem back to Vietnam from a U.S. seminary. We established and financed his regime. At the same time, our military forces were being defeated by the "liberation" army of the Democratic Republic of Vietnam.[1] Our actions have been within the confines of international legality. But our Machiavellian international politics has done everything but promote a just peace. As James Reston has said, "Our commitment was to a 'legitimate government,' and what we have now in Saigon is neither 'legitimate' nor a 'government.' Our promise was to help South Vietnam, not to destroy it." [2] In order to understand this statement, it is necessary to look again at the development of U.S. involvement in Vietnam.

All parties at the Geneva Conference of 1954 were apprehensive about the U.S. position at that time. The Viet Minh relinquished conquests south to the twelfth parallel (to move back to the seventeenth) and west to half of Laos in the face of France's pledge for internationally controlled reunification elections. France unwillingly gave up its Indochinese claims. The South Vietnamese government recognized diplomatic defeat.[3] The International Control Commission certainly expected to implement reunification as their reports make evident. At the conference table

Moral Argument and the War in Vietnam

the United States seemingly even agreed to the reunification of Vietnam by 1956.[4] But we obviously had no intention of keeping the cease-fire and reunification programs agreed to there. Rather than negotiate claims and establish legitimate interests the United States reserved for itself the role and right to be the unilateral arbiter and judge of the situation. We subsequently violated the international trust of Britain, France, Cambodia, Laos, China, Russia, and the Democratic Republic of Vietnam even though our careful phrasing again protected us from outright fabrication. The machinations at that time and the subsequent developments bear eloquent testimony to our sole interest—protection of U.S. policy objectives in Asia.

Our policy evidently has been to secure the permanence of two Vietnams. This is directly contrary to international agreement and territorial integrity. Mr. Little's frequent citations of the McDougal brief[5] merit careful examination here. McDougal readily admits that all parties at the Geneva Conference recognized that Vietnam was one independent country.[6] The only question was who ought to be the legitimate ruler. Recognition of the state of Vietnam meant that there was one political territory of Vietnam but did not deny the possibility of two contending governmental units. The fact that two representatives from Vietnam were present at Geneva in no way proves that there were two states of Vietnam but only two contending parties—one supported by France and one fighting for independence. McDougal's own sources indicated that originally the struggle in Vietnam was a political civil war (e.g., Professor Friedman's note 119, p. 172). The participants at Geneva decided there should be a temporary partition and reunification by 1956. Obviously this did not happen. There are now two clearly distinct governments. But this is a result only of our interference and accomplished only upon our instigation.[7] McDougal contends that the Geneva Conference is responsible for the permanent division of Vietnam. He refers to the "cavalier treatment" of election provisions at Geneva as an indication that the parties involved did not really believe reunification was possible. It is important to note that his only supporting reference is Bernard Fall, who in the same book[8] points out that the cavalier treatment of the entire problem was primarily the fault of the United States.

Another argument Little presents is hard to understand. He tries to show that not everyone in South Vietnam likes the Communists. Who has argued that they all did? Little quotes Douglas Pike, a U.S. government employee whose statistics disagree with those of every other reporter in the field, that "actual political support of the Vietcong [is] in the neighborhood of 10 percent of the population." But the phrase "actual political support" is a misleading one. Mr. Little himself admits that, by the same standard, Premier Cao Ky's "actual political support" would probably be less than 5 percent. Takashi Oka's study[9] indicates a large and growing trend toward the Viet Cong. But this is not the essential point. While Thich Tri Quang does not favor a Communist

16

takeover, as Mr. Little reminds us, his opposition to U.S. presence and control in Vietnam is even stronger.[10] One wonders if Mr. Little ever considered the possibility that the people of Vietnam do not want Cao Ky, the Viet Cong, or an American war. Perhaps they want peace.

Who Are The True Aggressors?

Second, the question of Communist aggression. There is little argument that the war "was initiated exclusively in the South." From the time Diem was established in power there was constant sparring and open battle with various political and religious sects. Finally with the establishment of the National Liberation Front, a "representative" group of nationalists, Buddhists, Catholics, Communists, business and labor leaders, and mountain tribesmen,[11] the present civil war began. These people were South Vietnamese. It is of interest that not a single member of Diem's original government came from "South Vietnam"[12] and that the seven most powerful men in the Ky cabinet are from the north.[13]

As of 1956 the United States had already been giving illegal military aid to South Vietnam. By 1960 U.S. soldiers were in charge of training and supervising all South Vietnam's military. Either Mr. Little is seeking to avoid the issue of responsibility with regard to the "Northern invasions" or is deliberately misreading the evidence. There is incontrovertible evidence that by 1962 there had been some northern aggression. But Mr. Little never addresses himself to placing the responsibility for such aggression. Perhaps the north was only "avenging injuries" in a just cause.

While the South Vietnamese delegate accepted the resolutions at Geneva with slight reservations and accepted, although not with full cooperation, the Joint Commissions and the International Control Commission established there, South Vietnam did not take the agreements seriously. But whether or not South Vietnam agreed with Geneva she obviously broke what North Vietnam took to be a trust. Mr. Little does not refer to the deliberate and illegitimate rice embargo enforced by the south in 1954.[14] He does not mention the constant provocations and refusals to cooperate.[15] He does not refer to the 1957 International Control Commission Report which says, "the major part of its difficulties has arisen in South Vietnam." Nor does he refer to the I.C.C. reports of 1958, 1960, 1961. Instead he waits until June 2, 1961 to cite only one paragraph of a report which also stresses that "the establishment of a U.S. Military Assistance Command in South Vietnam as well as the introduction of a large number of U.S. military personnel beyond the stated strength of the MAAG amounts to a factual military alliance which is prohibited under Article 19 of the Geneva Agreement.[16] Mr. Little discounts these violations because they do not refer to overt aggression of the U.S. or South Vietnamese in North Vietnam. His insensitivity to the real guilt of a provoking country is disturbing. South

Moral Argument and the War in Vietnam

Vietnam and the United States have provoked the north to aid the National Liberation Front. Can we then hold them guilty for responding? And can there be any doubt that with our present daily devastation of the north we are in fact the true aggressors?

In Search of Presidential Discretion

Third, the president's initiative. Mr. Little's point is granted. Obviously the president has the authority to engage the United States in limited war. But that in no way justifies such action. Even after we committed ourselves to Diem and refused the innumerable offers of reconciliation offered by North Vietnam between 1954 and 1958, [17] we should have known when to stop. It does not seem too much to ask our president to use discretion in choosing where and how we will use our support. It is long past time that the U.S. recognize our loyalties and commitments should not go automatically to stable, secure, anti-Communist governments no matter how undemocratic they are. George Kennan has said, "There is more respect to be won in the opinion of this world by a resolute and courageous liquidation of unsound positions than by the most extravagant or unpromising objectives." [18]

It is imperative that the U.S. stop using double talk and outright lies. If we seriously want peace why did we refuse U Thant's proposal of August-September 1964 which had already been agreed to by the North Vietnamese? If we truly seek peace, why did Adlai Stevenson have to wait for six months only to receive at last a negative reply from Washington to U Thant's prearranged top-secret conference with Hanoi and the National Liberation Front? [19] Why did we reject Ho Chi Minh's offers via Charles de Gaulle in October 1963 and December 1964.[20] If a just peace is our aim why did we resume bombing in May 1965 even knowing that Hanoi had expressed a willingness to negotiate without prior U.S. withdrawal?[21] Why were the LaPira-Fanfani overtures from Vietnam answered with bombardment of Haiphong in December 1965?[22] Why has the government refused to answer the charges that the United States has accelerated the war effort in response to peace feelers from the other side at least ten times in the past three years?[23]

The president certainly has the power to get us into the war. But when he is mistaken or has acted in bad faith, as the above examples indicate, it is imperative that Christians unite in the strongest possible protest of the president's actions.

The Conduct of the War

Fourth, the conduct of the war. In 1966 we have dropped more bomb tonnage on Vietnam, a land substantially smaller than Japan, than we did in the entire Pacific campaign of World War II—638,000 tons of bombs.[24] That is four and one-half tons of bombs per square mile—in

18

one year. We systematically destroy 10,000 acres of farmland and kill at least 1,000 innocent civilians per month in the southern sector alone.[25] Our pilots fly over 25,000 sorties weekly against Vietnamese targets. But the 1,700 tons of bombs[26] and $7 million worth of bombs and bullets we distribute daily in Vietnam[27] are very impersonal figures. Devastated villages, burning babies, fourteen-year-old prostitutes, armless grandfathers, blinded mothers, orphaned children—these are the witnesses to our military presence. We continue to make political and military mistakes while the people of Vietnam are forced to bear their costs.

We certainly must disagree with Mr. Little that the conduct of the war is "by far our most difficult task." It is indeed difficult to decide how to go about killing innocent civilians in the most Christian way possible. But actually our task is to get out of the hell we ourselves have created and leave with a minimum of suffering.

Mr. Little blames much of the suffering and desolation on the Viet Cong. They are at fault, because they initiated an insurgency war. But placing part of the onus on the VC in no way changes what *we* are doing in Vietnam. Little should know that a counter-insurgency war has never been won in open battle but only by eliminating the insurgent's base of support. The United States seems to have chosen the obliteration of the entire country—north and south—in order to destroy this base for the National Liberation Front. If their support depended upon territorial strongholds we would win. But perhaps the base of support is the Vietnamese people. The NLF could not operate such an "invisible" war without at least the tacit support of the peasants. While that support for the NLF continues, we cannot win no matter how vast a military arsenal we build. As McNamara said on February 18, 1964, "A counter-guerrilla war can be won only by the Vietnamese themselves."[28] Perhaps we ought to reexamine our policies in light of McNamara's own admissions that while the South Vietnamese army loses 12,000 deserters per month[29] the NLF are able to recruit 6,000 new soldiers per month.[30]

Standard of Proportionality?

Fifth, the principle of proportionality. It is incredible that Mr. Little can conclude that our war effort "does not seem to have badly violated the principle of proportionality." Marine Corps sources indicate that the civilian-Viet Cong kill ratio is sometimes as high as 6 to 1[31] and that it takes from $100,000 to $400,000 for every Viet Cong killed.[32] We spend 2.7 billion dollars per month[33] for the war, Vietnamese prices rise upwards of 10 percent per month,[34] less than half of the children of Vietnam even get two days of school per week.[35] One wonders what Mr. Little and Mr. McDougal use for a standard of proportionality. While millions starve around the world we spend close to $34 billion in destroying rich and fertile farmland. While U.S. poverty programs shrink, Vietnamese brothels and black markets flourish. While the U.S. mili-

Moral Argument and the War in Vietnam

tary-industrial complex prospers, the Vietnamese villagers fight and hide and cry and die. The argument that we had to rise against the "hostile designs of the North" is bogus. We violated international trust first, we helped provoke the north Vietnamese attacks, we supported a regime which alienated 80 percent of the population. . . .

Notes

1 Robert Shaplen, *The Lost Revolution.*
2 *New York Times,* May 18, 1966.
3 Bernard Fall, *Viet-Nam Witness.* Tran Vo Do's telegram to Ngo Dinh Diem, July 22, 1954. p. 62.
4. M. E. Gettleman, *Vietnam.* Mr. Walter Bedell Smith's declaration of the U.S. government position, July 21, 1954. pp. 156 f.
5 Myres S. McDougal, *The Lawfulness of United States Assistance to the Republic of Viet Nam.*
6 *Ibid.,* pp. 13, 151.
7 Philippe Devillers, *China Quarterly,* January-March, 1962, p. 4. D. D. Eisenhower, *Mandate for Change,* pp. 371 ff.
8 Bernard Fall and M. G. Raskin, *The Viet-Nam Reader.*
9 *New York Times Magazine,* July 31, 1966. See also Walter Lippmann, *San Francisco Chronicle,* January 2, 1966.
10 Jean Lacouture, *Vietnam: Between Two Truces,* pp. 219-222.
11 *Viet-Nam Witness,* p. 241.
12 *Ibid.,* p. 60.
13 *Washington Star,* October 16, 1966.
14 *Viet-Nam Reader,* p. 93.
15 *Ibid.,* p. 93.
16 *Vietnam,* pp. 166-190.
17 *Vietnam: Between Two Truces,* p. 68. *Vietnam,* pp. 161 f.
18 *New York Times Magazine,* September 18, 1966.
19 *New York Review of Books,* November 17, 1966.
20 Felix Greene, *Vietnam, Vietnam,* p. 158.
21 Shurmann, Scott, Zelnik, *The Politics of Escalation in Vietnam,* pp. 83-88.
22 *Ibid.,* pp. 96-107.
23 This is the main thesis of *The Politics of Escalation in Vietnam,* a very frustrating and revealing book.
24 Robert S. McNamara, *New York Times,* April 21, 1966.
25 Neil Sheehan, *New York Times Magazine,* October 9, 1966.
26 *New York Times,* April 21, 1966.
27 *San Francisco Chronicle,* May 12, 1966.
28 *New York Times,* February 19, 1964. See also Richard N. Goodwin, *Triumph or Tragedy.*
29 *New York Times,* May 1, 1966.
30 *New York Times,* August 10, 1966.
31 Congressman C. J. Zablocki, *Congressional Record,* March 17, 1966.
32 *Saturday Review,* October 29, 1966. Or *New York Times,* July 5, 1966.
33 Reinhold Niebuhr, *Christianity and Crisis,* October 17, 1966. Wayne Morse, Newsletter, September, 1966.
34 *Vietnam, Vietnam,* p. 135. See also, *New York Times,* November 20, 1966.
35 William Pepper, "Senator Morse Reports," September, 1966. He summarizes a government report.

A Just War or Just A War?

By David Little

. . . The Use and Abuse of Power

Among the comments and criticisms regarding my application of just war theory, the principle of proportion assumes a primary place. In general, there is an arbitrary selectivity about the "price list" of Mr. Ogle. He bears down very heavily upon the *dis*values of U.S. action, while either neglecting or slanting some of the values which must be weighed in the balance. At this point, [we need to emphasize] . . .the worth of a system of international expectations regarding the use and abuse of power. Crucial to the maintenance of such a system is the development of predictable and reliable arrangements among nations that prevent arbitrary and aggressive behavior.

Were such patterns developed in the international community toward the GVN (South Vietnam), and were they infringed in such a way as to place in jeopardy the broader set of expectations throughout Southeast Asia? Despite Mr. Ogle's version of the history of U.S. relations with Vietnam, I believe the answer is yes. We have not learned anything spectacular or necessarily nefarious when Mr. Ogle asserts that in becoming involved in Vietnam, the "sole interest" of the U.S. was the protection of its policy objectives in Asia. What else would it have been doing there? In 1954 U.S. policy objectives were to introduce some stability and reliability into an area that had just felt the force of Communist expansionism in the Korean war. That event coupled with U.S. experience throughout the Stalinist period (which ended in 1953) lent an air of reality to Western fears about international communism, regardless of the pathologies of McCarthyism.

There is no need to construe U.S. policy as having excluded the apparent interests of the majority of the Vietnamese people. Even though Ho Chi Minh had succeeded during the war with the French in rubbing out most of the leadership of the VNQDD, the non-Communist nationalist party,[1] the spirit of non-Communist nationalism certainly existed in 1954. After all, nearly one million people "voted with their feet" by leaving the DRV (North Vietnam) after 1954. Thus, there were good grounds for U.S. support of the GVN: there was a reasonable chance of permitting indigenous non-Communist nationalism to develop and to help stabilize Southeast Asia against arbitrariness and aggressiveness in international affairs.[2]

21

Moral Argument and the War in Vietnam

It ought to be firmly understood that the Geneva Accords, which were supposed to spell out international expectations, were an incredible set of "non-agreements." Victor Bator is certainly right when he calls the unsigned Final Declaration (providing for elections, temporary partition, etc.) "a skillful make-believe."[3] There are aspects of irreducible uncertainty about the Accords, and therefore room for elasticity of interpretation, although Mr. Ogle's observations are some of the more exotic I have encountered.

Despite their ambiguity, the Accords produced some common understanding. Bator suggests that the great time and effort spent by the parties on the demarcation line implied that "the innocent-sounding text of the final agreement must have signified something of greater import."[4] That was the strong possibility of a divided Vietnam, as subsequent diplomatic attitudes attested. Thus the U.N. delegate of the U.S.S.R. (a co-chairman of the Geneva Convention) claimed but three short years after the Accords that "in Vietnam two separate states existed." It is unlikely the U.S. could have forced the U.S.S.R. to come to such a judgment. On the contrary, for its own reasons the U.S.S.R. was voluntarily articulating the general set of international expectations that surrounded Vietnam.

As to the question of the infringement of international expectations even Mr. Ogle surprisingly concedes the "incontrovertible evidence that by 1962 there had been some northern aggression." We may note that aggression means "a first or unprovoked attack." If the U.S. was really responsible for provoking the DRV, then there was no aggression. But if there was aggression, as Mr. Ogle admits, then by definition the DRV was responsible. However, there are more important problems here than an unsophisticated use of language. These problems are posed by Ogle's references to the indigenous character of the NLF's insurgence. Is the NLF primarily the product of a spontaneous and "representative" revolutionary uprising, or is it to a significant degree the product of a wider Communist pattern of subversive and aggressive behavior that has deep connections with the DRV?

Who Are the Viet Cong?

Harrison Salisbury in a recent article[5] called for a fresh and careful appraisal of the NLF. We have such an appraisal in Douglas Pike's exhaustive study, *Viet Cong: the Organization and Technology of the National Liberation Front of South Vietnam.*[6] Pike confirms what many people have suspected, that the NLF is not "simply a hammer in the long arm of the DRV."[7] There have been a variety of non-Communist groups represented in it, though groups like the Buddhists, the Cao Dai and the Montagnards abruptly dissociated themselves as the true character of the organization became apparent.[8] Furthermore, Pike naturally concedes that there was considerable hostility to the Diem regime throughout South Vietnam. But one of the central and persuasive theses of the study is the *separability* of diffused resentment from the program and organizational techniques of the Communist center of the NLF.[9]

> The NLF was not simply another indigenous covert group, or even a coalition of such groups. It was an organizational steamroller, nationally conceived and nationally organized, endowed with ample cadres and funds, crashing out of the jungle to flatten the GVN. It was not an ordinary secret society . . . It projected a social construction program of such scope and ambition that of necessity it must have been created in Hanoi and imported. A revolutionary organization must build; it begins with people suffering genuine grievances, who are slowly organized and whose militancy gradually increases . . . Exactly the reverse was the case with the NLF. It sprang full-blown into existence and then fleshed out. The grievances were developed or manufactured almost as a necessary afterthought.[10]

After close examination of the policy objectives of the DRV and the NLF, Pike concludes that there probably is some strain within the NLF between the Northern and Southern Communist leadership around the question of annexation. But there is no tension as to the goal of exclusive Communist domination in South Vietnam, and there is no serious interest in the neutralization of South Vietnam, let alone in the neutralization of the DRV.

Finally, Pike's analysis helps us to see striking parallels between the organization and activity of the NLF and that of North Vietnamese cadres in Laos and Thailand.[11] In other words, there *is* a pattern of subversive and aggressive behavior in Southeast Asia that threatens the stability of the area. This is undoubtedly why diplomatic representatives of the Philippines, Malaysia, Thailand, South Korea, and other Asian countries recently raised some questions about U Thant's version of the Vietnam War.[12] There seems to be very little evidence that U.S. action has alienated any of these governments, or those of Australia and New Zealand. On the contrary, there is general support for U.S. policy, and the character of Thai, Australian and South Korean involvement is not insignificant.

Is the Game Worth the Candle?

But even if we calculate realistically the dangers of tolerating aggressiveness in Southeast Asia, people will continue to ask whether the game is worth the candle in Vietnam. There is simply no easy means for arriving at an answer to that question. The best we can do is make marginal judgments, though I still believe that good reasons can be given for siding, in general, with the administration's policies. Some of those reasons stem from a dissatisfaction with the critics' appraisal of the situation in Vietnam.

Moral Argument and the War in Vietnam

A) One does not come away from Pike's book with any great confidence in the desire of either the DRV or the NLF to negotiate, except on terms vastly in their favor. It must not be forgotten that they were within a hair's breadth of winning South Vietnam. Why they should have wanted to concede anything at all up until rather recently eludes me.

B) The manifest intention of the Communists in the NLF to dominate any coalition government in South Vietnam dictates the necessity for a greatly strengthened International Control Commission to prevent a takeover. That will not eventuate if the U.S. unilaterally evacuates everything but pious hope, as Mr. Ogle suggests. Nor can we put much trust in the fact that Communists in South Vietnam have a relatively small hard core political base. A small measure of popular support does not usually impede Communist activity.

If some system of controls is adequate, then a genuine coalition government may be possible, along with the neutralization of South Vietnam and Laos (there is no hope for neutralizing the DRV). Indeed, obtaining such a system of controls should be the primary goal of a negotiated settlement, *for on enforceable controls everything else depends*. Unfortunately, success in this regard must wait upon a more secure military stalemate than we have yet. But without controls, there is no hope of protecting what is now clearly a substantial portion of non-Communist sentiment in South Vietnam. What is more, without proper guarantees there is little assurance that the DRV will mind its international manners.

C) Though it is notoriously difficult to judge the trends of morale in South Vietnam, it is not clear that the NLF has the future on its side. At the end of 1966, Viet Cong defections were found to be proportionately higher than those of the GVN army.[13] In addition, Denis Warner recently reported that the possibility of political stability in South Vietnam is not completely illusory: "politics has come to Vietnam, and, for the first time, there is at least the hope that some day not far off the men and women in paddy fields . . . will be able to identify themselves with the government in Saigon."[14] If these bits of evidence do little to make us sanguine, they do at least show how hard it is to be certain that there is *no* reasonable chance of success in Vietnam.

D) There are at least four types of attitude toward the present level of killing and devastation in Vietnam. One attitude finds no good reasons for U.S. action in Vietnam and, therefore, understandably regards all the suffering caused by the U.S. as completely reprehensible (Ogle). A second attitude grants some plausibility to U.S. involvement, but overall sees the costs in suffering to be too great to justify involvement. A third attitude regards as a necessary evil the level of suffering caused in the defense of worthy goals. A fourth attitude (my own) finds good reasons for fighting, concedes that fighting entails necessary evils, but wishes to reserve judgment on the kind of weaponry and strategy used by the U.S. I should wish to take into account . . . the "shape of the war" in order to determine the most morally efficient weapons in counter-insurgence, i.e., those weapons that accomplish maximum military benefits with minimum injury and risk to civilians. Simply making sure one is *aiming* at military targets may not satisfy the requisites of discrimination in a guerrilla war.

Some Particular Objections To Mr. Ogle's Account

I have no space to list and document all my objections to Mr. Ogle's interpretations. A few points will illustrate [them]. . . . 1) Along with the U.S., *both* France and Great Britain recognized the GVN as "the only legal government of Vietnam" (in the words of the British delegate) *before, during and after* the Geneva Convention. The U.S. did not itself create international recognition of the GVN. The Communist countries, of course, recognized the DRV as the only legal government. When after the Accords *two* legitimate governments gained fairly wide international recognition, that was simply an acknowledgment of *an existing fact*: two regimes were respectively legitimate in the eyes of a substantial number of countries. (*This* is what fn. 119, p. 172 of the McDougal brief says.) As Bator puts it: "The pretense that a single Vietnam was being dealt with [at the Geneva Conference] was a weird diplomatic evasion" (*op. cit.,* p 49).

2) The U.S. and the GVN could not have made the official positions toward the Accords clearer. There was a remarkable lack of deceptive phrasing. The U.S. was not "a party to nor bound by the decisions taken at the conference," as President Eisenhower stated publicly on the final day of the conference. The U.S. said only that it would not disturb the Accords by threat or use of force, which it did not do. As for the GVN, Mr. Ogle's allegations are wondrous. He states that the delegate of the GVN "accepted the resolutions at Geneva with slight reservations." In reality, the GVN delegate registered a harsh and lengthy protest against the manner in which the conference was conducted as well as the conditions. At the end of the conference he resigned on the spot in personal protest. It is hard to know how under these conditions any "trust" was broken after the conference. Which is worse: publicly to accept agreements and break them (as did the DRV), or publicly to reject them and break them?

3) As to elections, both the U.S. and the GVN urged from the beginning that the U.N. be invested with power to supervise a plebiscite in 1956. The refusal to include this provision was one reason both governments rejected the agreements. Without any controls or guarantees (except those of the feeble ICC), it seems unreasonable to have asked the GVN to enter into elections in 1956. That was a period when, by General Giap's own admission, things were exceptionally repressive in the DRV.

Moral Argument and the War in Vietnam

Therefore, hopes for free elections were fatuous. That fact coupled with the sizeable numerical superiority of the North made elections, to which the U.S. and the GVN had never agreed anyway, highly questionable. Great Britain, for example, never held that the GVN was "legally obliged" to hold elections. Furthermore, Anthony Eden pointed out: "There can be little doubt that the brief two years allowed by the Geneva Agreements [for elections] was altogether too short. Some of us thought so at the time . . ." (*Harper's*, August, 1966, p. 42). Nor did the U.S.S.R. show any interest in elections. "In 1955 the Americans were given to understand in no uncertain terms that there were not going to be any free elections in North Vietnam, North Korea or East Germany. There could be no elections in Vietnam in the Western sense of the term, despite the language of the Geneva declaration" (Kenneth T. Young, *Asia, 4* [Winter, 1966], p. 121). Though this is foggy business at best, the international expectations were by no means unequivocally on the side of the enforcement of elections. Solemn denunciations of the U.S. for "breaking trust" put a strain on the facts.*

4) As to the question of "aggression" and responsibility, Mr. Ogle confuses legal and moral arguments. In the face of the legal morass which is the Geneva Accords, where it is so hard to say clearly who has rights to do what, it is unusual to imply that because arrangements that were not agreed to were not fulfilled, the "offended" party has a legal right to cross an internationally recognized cease-fire line and subvert the "offending" government. Even when legal obligations are clear, there is common agreement in international law that "acts of economic, ideological and indirect aggression . . . may not be justified by any considerations of a political, economic or strategic nature" (McDougal brief, p. 48). It could, of course, be argued that a given regime had become so unjust that another government had a "higher obligation" to overthrow it. Then, however, we are well beyond the realm of legal rights, as in the case of Vietnam. A clean moral rationale for "just aggression" is a knotty affair at best.

Actually, if anything "provoked" the DRV it was not the failure of the GVN to live up to obligations it clearly repudiated from the start. It was the continued existence of the GVN at all. It is probable that the only reason the DRV accepted terms at Geneva was the anticipation of a ready and imminent collapse of the South. That that did not occur was undoubtedly a bitter pill for the North. However, for the reasons we have reviewed, the existence of the GVN as a recognized, legitimate entity was a fact of international life. Such a fact of life did not imply that the DRV might arbitrarily and unilaterally decide the fate of the GVN as it saw fit, because it judged itself aggrieved. By that logic, the West German Republic, for example, might rightfully subvert the DDR because it felt itself "provoked" by the DDR's existence.

*Editor's note: For an opposing view on the 1956 elections, see George McT. Kahin and John W. Lewis, *The United States in Vietnam* (Delta Books, 1967), pp. 52-57, 80-87.

Vietnam is a tangled and frustrating situation, the sort of situation that begets intemperance. It was predictable that men of good will would, in their frustration, seek to lay blame on someone like the president for a state of affairs it was his cruel fortune to inherit rather than create. It was also predictable that the president would, in turn, over-react to his critics and occasionally say and do preposterous things. There is need in this case to live with frustration in such a way that we neither underrate the reasons for fighting a limited war in Vietnam nor exaggerate them, that we say neither too little nor too much about why we are there. That does not exclude serious disagreement over aspects of our policy. It does discourage the temptations of intemperance: to grasp too quickly at straws.

Notes

1 See Hoang Van Chi's grisly account of the ruthlessness of Ho Chi Minh's regime *From Colonialism to Communism.*

2 I still question whether strategically it would not have been more prudent to bank on Thailand. By 1965, however, that was merely an academic question.

3 Victor Bator, "Geneva, 1954: The Broken Mold," reprinted in *Vietnam: Why,* a collection of essays from *The Reporter,* p. 49. See Bator's *Vietnam: A Diplomatic Tragedy.*

4 *Ibid.,* p. 50.

5 *New York Times,* Jan. 16, 1967.

6 MIT Press, 1966.

7 *Ibid.,* p. 326.

8 *Ibid.,* pp. 201ff.

9 "No long-run threat to the NLF loomed larger than the formation in Saigon of a popular, participational, democratic government," *ibid.,* p. 163.

10 *Ibid.,* p. 76.

11 See Seymour Topping, "Next on Peking's Hit Parade?" *New York Times Magazine,* Feb. 20, 1966. Incidentally, there is also ICC evidence of several thousand North Vietnamese troops in Laos supporting the Pathet Lao, contrary, of course, to the Geneva Agreements of 1962 which the DRV *did* affirm; *New York Times,* Aug. 23, 1966.

12 See *New York Times,* Jan. 14, 1967.

13 *New York Times,* Dec. 18, 1966. Cf. *New York Times,* Feb. 24, 1966, when the story was the other way around.

14 Denis Warner, "South Vietnam's Political Awakening," *The Reporter,* Nov. 17, 1966, p. 42.

Charlie's Long March*

by Jean Lacouture

On the battlefield the GI's call them "Charlie"; at headquarters in Saigon, the "V.C." In the conservative papers they're the Viet Cong and in the liberal press, the "NLF." In the East they are "the Front" or "our glorious comrades of the Vietnamese liberation army." In the West one would prefer not to call them anything. One fights them without knowing them.

Seen from Washington they were at first a fiction. Now, they are merely a faction. In the beginning it was a form of Red banditry, a mélange of folkloric agitation and fanatical refusal to obey the decent laws of the good Mr. Diem. Later one saw them as the advance guard of an invasion of free South Vietnam by a North Vietnam likened to Nazi Germany. This assumed a historical resemblance between Ho Chi Minh and Hitler which impressed at least Mr. Rusk.

Today it is a matter of different "groups" manipulated by the North but only representing, according to Mr. Goldberg or Mr. Ball, and according to the time of day, from one half to one and one half per cent of the population. A feeble proportion, but so active, it would appear, that with the support of Northern elements estimated at 25,000 men, it has prompted the shipment to Vietnam of hundreds of thousands of U.S. soldiers, supporting a "nationalist" army of more than 600,000. Accursed little groups, who are not content with being tough in combat, but who have lived to see themselves acknowledged "the major factor on the South Vietnamese political scene" by George Carver, a CIA agent and learned spokesman for the most conservative circles of the administration, in a major article in *Foreign Affairs* (April 1966).

We can understand neither the nature nor the present behavior of the "Viet Cong" without recalling several stages in its historical development. For revolution is not a new phenomenon in South Vietnam—it is a "long march."

It begins in the early 1930s with the formation of the Communist Party of Indochina (CPI), the appearance of powerful Trotskyist groups in Saigon, and the growth of politico-religious sects and the Vietnam Quoc

---

* Originally printed in *Ramparts,* vol. 5, no. 2 (July, 1966), pp. 11-14. Copyright Ramparts Magazine, Inc., 1966. Reprinted by permission of the editors.

Moral Argument and the War in Vietnam

Dan Dang, the Vietnamese Kuomintang, more active in the North but present also in the South.

A second stage, opening in 1945, is the anticolonial insurrection against France, which ends in 1954 with the Geneva compromise. The revolutionaries of the South foot the bill, for the South is left in the conservative hands of Mr. Diem. The third stage in the history of the movement is Saigon's refusal to implement the Geneva Accords (and to a lesser degree Hanoi's), touching off the formation of a *maquis* of rebels in places like Quang-Ngay, Zone D and the Plain of Joncs. During the fourth stage, the North becomes aware of the agitation in the South and seeks to harness this revolutionary force which will serve its objectives of reunification and socialization. And in the fifth stage, Hanoi comes out openly in support of the revolts in the South and gives its sponsorship to what is now officially called the National Liberation Front of South Vietnam.

From here we see the radicalization of the movement. It starts in 1961 after the creation of the People's Revolutionary Party (PRP), the Communist section inside the "Front." At the same time there is competition between the autonomous "Southern" tendency in the NLF and the growing influence of Hanoi, due to escalation of the war and the increasing numbers of North Vietnamese troops and cadres in the South.

Revolution in South Vietnam is an old story. It is not an import from the North. In fact, political life under French colonial rule is always more violent in the South than in the North. The avowedly colonial regime imposed on the South (the North is a mere protectorate) leaves Saigon and its hinterland more open to modern and progressive influences. And while nationalism is developing at Hue and Hanoi, diverse revolutionary tendencies are making themselves felt in Saigon and the backcountry. In the sizable French colony, largely composed of working class whites, leftist ideas gain currency, particularly after 1935, with a corresponding influence on the Vietnamese elites. The system of land distribution, much more feudal in the South, favors the flowering of radical movements, as does the growth of a proletariat in the urban area around Saigon. The CPI, created at Haiphong in 1930 at the instigation of Ho Chi Minh (then known as Nguyen ai Quoc), has a strong section in the South. And the Trotskyists are strong enough in 1932 to win four or five seats in the Saigon municipal election.

The Trotskyists owe much of their success to an exceptional leader, Ta Thu Tau, a popular figure known for his fiery oratory. The Communists have a competent leadership—Dr. Thach, Duong Bach Mai and Tran Van Giau—but they suffer, up to 1941, from the conservative directives of their French "brother" party, then hogtied by its support of the Popular Front government of Leon Blum. During the war the Communists are persecuted, and several dozen of them are sent to the prison at Poulo-Condors, an island in the Indian Ocean still considered to be "the university of the revolution."

If the Trotskyists are powerful in Saigon, the Communists are doubly so in the countryside. In 1941 a vast dragnet operation is launched in the Mytho region, fifty miles south of Saigon in the Plain of Joncs, resulting in the arrest of 3,000 Communists—which gives some idea of the party's strength in the area. The Plain of Joncs is to become a stronghold of the Viet Minh, and later of the Viet Cong. Few rural areas in the world of that time contain so many avowed Marxists.

The elimination of the French administration by the Japanese in 1945, followed by the collapse of the Japanese, creates a vacuum which gives an extraordinary impetus to the Communists. Ho Chi Minh marches on Hanoi with the guerrillas he has been training for four years in southern China and seizes power, with a sense of timing and a genius for tactical alliances reminiscent of Lenin in 1917. But in the South, the Communist high command, obsessed by its rivalry with the Trotskyists, loses valuable time, devoting its energies to ill-directed violence and repression (Ta Thu Tau is assassinated) French units, freed from Japanese prisons and assisted by the British regiments of General Gracey, seize the occasion and take power. The responsibility for the ineffectiveness of the Communists can be laid to Tran Van Giau, whose fanaticism and taste for violence leave him soon isolated and unpopular.

Defeated, the Communists of the South take to the *maquis,* applying the strategy of alliances with the nationalists so well defined by Ho Chi Minh at the time of the creation of the Viet Minh Front and the dissolution of the Communist party. Of the twelve members of the Committee of Nam-Bo (South), Marxists hold only two posts (interior and economy). Military affairs are directed by a nationalist, the famed Nguyen Binh, who is to be liquidated in 1952, probably on the orders of the North Viet Minh high command.

The war against the French expeditionary corps is never as hot in the South as in the North. But the battle in the South has more political overtones and gives to the Communists, more than to their allies, the opportunity to train the population. They work the peasants "in depth," initiating an agrarian reform which succeeds better than in the North and wins them a great prestige among the peasants. As the war draws to a close in 1954, the Viet Minh controls wide areas of South Vietnam— more than half the Mekong Delta, the Camau peninsula in the far south and Quang-Ngay, along the fourteenth parallel.

Nevertheless the Geneva powers—including the Russians, Chinese and Viet Minh—decide to divide Vietnam at the seventeenth parallel, which will deprive the revolutionaries of several millions of their partisans, about a fourth of the population they formerly controlled. Viet Minh partisans are to be regrouped into five zones, and then move north. By and large the order is obeyed. The Communists order about 100,000 men north, leaving 5,000 as cadres for agitation, for the future. In carrying out the Geneva formulas, the Communists have to put considerable pressure on their nationalist allies, less ready than they to

Moral Argument and the War in Vietnam

respect a treaty guaranteed by Messrs. Molotov and Chou En Lai. Once again, as in the years 1936-40, the Communists acquire a reputation as moderates and opportunists, a reputation they will try to live down later.

Thus, in 1954, the revolutionary movement in the South is delivered to the mercies of Mr. Diem. The Geneva Accords provide that no one may be prosecuted for his activities during the war. But the Diem regime respects the rule even less assiduously than the authorities in the North. Pro-Viet Minh partisans in the South, Communists and nationalists alike, are soon to be the victims of a witch hunt. Feeling betrayed, they will not be very good citizens of South Vietnam; nor will the survivors of the sects crushed by Diem in 1955.

The underground begins to take form in 1956, in the west, around Chaudoc and Long-Xuyen, and in the northwestern plantation zone, near the Caodaiste center of Tayninh. The categorical refusal of the Saigon government to hold the elections called for in the Geneva documents and the growing severity of the repression push the revolutionaries into violent opposition.

Throughout the first phase of the revolt, it remains purely "Southern." The cadres left behind by the Communists play rather a moderating role, the watchword from Hanoi being "respect of the Geneva Agreements," in accord with the then Moscow-and-Peking line. It is only slowly that Marxists begin to penetrate the anti-Diem movement. By this time the movement is anti-American as well, in view of Washington's unequivocal support of the Saigon government and the reinforcement of the U.S. military mission. As early as 1959 the revolt has already assumed sufficient magnitude for Diem to say on receiving the Gaullist vice-president Antoine Pinay, in Saigon: "We, too, have our Algerian war . . . ."

Still Hanoi guards its reserve, but emissaries sent South report that the rebels are beginning to denounce the cowardice of the Northern regime. The Central Committee of the Lao-Dong (Communist party reconstituted in 1952) studies a report presented by Le Duan, deputy secretary general and veteran of the war in the South. Le Duan recommends that North Vietnam give its total support to the anti-Diem movement, arguing that the Geneva Accords no longer have any validity after the violations committed in the South. About this time Diem pushes through a law permitting the execution of suspects, and nullifies the landslide election to parliament of Dr. Dan, an outspoken but firmly anti-Communist opposition leader.

It is only in 1960 that Hanoi clearly assumes its responsibilities. But is not without considerable soul-searching. The "Viet-Cong" (abbreviation of Vietnam Cong San, or Vietnamese Communists), as Messrs. Diem and Nhu like to call them, have at this time only a small minority of Communists in their ranks. Ho Chi Minh and his advisors note, however, that the anti-Diem nationalists are redoubling their activity—the solemn appeal of eighteen leaders in April calling for a return to democracy; feverish intrigue in the army that will result in the abortive coup of November 1960. Diem's regime appears to be tottering, and the Communists fear being outdone by the nationalists, fear the nationalists will be the beneficiaries of the coming victory over Diem.

Then, at the Third Congress of the Lao-Dong, September 1960 in Hanoi, in the presence of a strong Soviet delegation, Le Duan pushes through a program of energetic support for the revolutionary movement in South Vietnam. More important still, he is elected secretary-general of the party, replacing Ho Chi Minh, who retains the presidency. Thus the partisan of intervention in the South is at the controls. He circulates to his comrades in Hanoi the text of an appeal made the previous March by "a group of veterans of the South Vietnamese resistance," which says the time has come for a general insurrection against the "My-Diem" dictatorship ("My" means American). Ho Chi Minh and his comrades now intend to act swiftly to take control of this movement.

It is thus with their open support that the creation of the NLF is announced in December 1960, grouping together the forces which have struggled against Diem for four years. To all appearances, Communists are in the minority. And the ten-point program announced by the NLF might be that of almost any agrarian nationalist party of the Third World, except, perhaps, for the denunciation of American "imperialism" and "monopolies." The insistence on neutralism, on independence for the South, on the necessary alliance with Cambodia and Laos, gives the impression that the movement seeks the help of a variety of allies and prefers not to antagonize anyone but Saigon.

If Hanoi has surely approved the simple formula of an organization that will serve as cadre and high command for the uprising, it feels at the same time that this type of Front (as in the time of Nguyen Binh, in 1950), gives the nationalists an unnecessary predominance. These misgivings prompt the formation, early in 1962, of the People's Revolutionary Party, a resurrection of the Southern section of the CPI. This time the language is clearly Marxist, and the job of this hard Communist cell is to channel and control the activity of the Front.

Curious, but we don't find the old chieftains of the Southern CPI at the head of the PRP, neither Dr. Thach, who has become minister of health in Hanoi, nor Duong Bach Mai, nor Tran Van Giau, purged for ultra-left adventurism in 1945 and consigned to an honorific post in Hanoi. The key figures in the PRP seem to be Vo Chi Cong, vice-president and, it is believed, acting secretary-general of the NLF, and General Trung, reputed to be a pseudonym for Nguyen Son, a top aide of Viet Minh General Giap at the time of Dien Bien Phu.

The injection of the PRP inside the NLF—a spine, so to speak—is one of the factors in the radicalization of the Front. But this is not due simply to calculations of Hanoi. The realities of the extension of the war inevitably give priority to elements that are the most battle-trained,

Moral Argument and the War in Vietnam

most experienced in organizing, closest to Hanoi and thus most capable of making liaison with Northern units operating on Southern soil. These are estimated at 25,000 soldiers and specialists, comprising about 10 percent of the revolutionary forces. But more than anything else, it is the U.S. bombings, North and South, that strengthen the PRP position inside the NLF and give it authority among the people.

Recent reports from "V.C." controlled zones show two startling developments:

1. That PRP strength has grown in four years from 7,000 to nearly 100,000 partisans.

2. That PRP cadres are less inclined to use ruses with the population, and tend to present themselves more and more as Communists.

It is hardly astonishing that from the point of view of the interests of the party, a prolonged war is desirable. What is more astonishing is to see this opinion shared by Dean Rusk.

The long march of the "Viet Cong" is not finished. Everything indicates that as long as the war lasts, the movement's orientation will move more and more toward the left. But there is one other reality we must keep firmly in mind, and that is the profoundly Southern character of the movement. None of the fighters of the NLF, certainly, would deny that their goal is as much the reunification of Vietnam as its independence. But the program of the Front, and the comments of its spokesmen on the need for a long breathing period before reunification, show that the Front is still deeply marked by the original history of the revolutionary movement in South Vietnam. The sects, the secret societies, the Communists, the nationalists are still there, and to believe that they will blindly accept dictation from the North is to falsify their history and present development.

Crisis Manager*

John McDermott

The decision to escalate the Vietnam War was not made in 1965. It was made in 1964. It was certainly made within six months of President Kennedy's death. It may even have been made within six weeks of his death.

Several writers have speculated that the Johnson Administration decided to send ground troops against the South and fighter bombers against the North long before either the Tonkin crisis of August, 1964 or the Pleiku raid of February, 1965. Franz Schurmann found a hint to this effect in Johnson's 1964 New Year's message to the South Vietnamese Government, and I. F. Stone has gradually assembled an impressive case that the fundamental decisions were made in the same year.[1] But even Stone's material, persuasive though it is, rested ultimately on the debatable belief that events which appeared on the surface to be linked in a deliberate pattern of escalation were in fact so linked by the Government.

We need no longer doubt it. Roger Hilsman, Assistant Secretary of State for Far Eastern Affairs, 1963-4, self-confessed member of the Kennedy "inner circle" and the latest of the JFK entourage to commit his public service to the public record, tells us more even than we need to know in order to clinch the case.

According to Hilsman's account the Kennedy administration was fundamentally divided by the crises in Laos and Vietnam. One faction— Harriman, Hilsman, the State Department (minus Rusk), the president himself—favored what Hilsman calls the "political" approach. As did their "military" opposite numbers, these men believed that the insurgencies in South Vietnam and Laos were ultimately attributable to North Vietnamese direction, arms, and personnel. But they believed nevertheless that this threat could best be curbed by limiting the application of American power within the borders of Laos and South Vietnam. In Laos this meant using the neutralist faction led by Souvanna Phouma and the international community led by the Soviet Union to keep the left-wing Pathet Lao at bay. This "political" approach did not prohibit the use of American "advisers" in the Lao Army and Air Force nor

*This article originally appeared as a review of Roger Hilsman's *To Move a Nation* (New York: Doubleday, 1967), in the *New York Review of Books*, Volume IX, Sept. 14, 1967. Copyright John McDermott, 1967. It is reprinted here by permission of the editors and the author.

Moral Argument and the War in Vietnam

did it even preclude sending regular U.S. units to fight within the Kingdom of Laos; it merely hoped, in the event U.S. soldiers had to be sent, to limit their numbers to a few thousand and their mission to protecting the Mekong River system.

The same emphasis on limited objectives and limited use of American forces carried over to Vietnam. Because South Vietnam had no Souvanna Phouma that Washington was aware of—never having looked for one—different tactics had to be used. The favored policy was to give unlimited political support to the governmental apparatus of South Vietnam while trying to limit our support of Diem and his entourage. Since Diem countered by placing the administrative reins more and more in his own, and Nhu's hands Washington's policy of splitting its support never quite worked out. In any case our military effort was to be limited to South Vietnam, US soldiers were to be limited to an "advisory" role, and US fliers on combat missions were to have only limited visibility to the public. If US units had to be sent to keep South Vietnam "free," their numbers and their role, as in Laos, were to be limited as well.

The "military advocates" within the Kennedy administration were more numerous by far than their opposites and, as we have since learned to our dismay, more long-lived as well. They included Secretaries Rusk and McNamara, the Joint Chiefs of Staff led by their Chairman Maxwell Taylor, presidential assistant Walt W. Rostow, and the then Vice President, Lyndon Johnson. With Rostow as their ideologue they insisted that the Indochina crisis was attributable to North Vietnamese aggression, and that it could be resolved only by meeting Hanoi head on, accepting the naked challenge with an open American response, and by striking directly at the "source of aggression." Thus they constantly urged the introduction of regular American forces, bombing of the North, and a policy which promised to obscure what Hilsman and his colleagues thought were the critical differences between the internal situation of Laos and South Vietnam.

There were other views within the Kennedy administration, but they never gained sufficient support to constitute a faction. The Undersecretary of State for Economic Affairs, George Ball, opposed even the limited involvement pressed by the "political" faction and stressed the danger that the US would be sucked into a major intervention in Vietnam. The principal Undersecretary of State, Chester Bowles, had the temerity at one point to suggest that all of Southeast Asia be neutralized. Ball's advice was considered and rejected by both factions but Bowles's proposal was dismissed as "imaginative," "far-seeing," and premature, and Bowles himself, who wasn't considered tough-minded enough for the higher levels of the Kennedy administration, was later exiled to a lesser post.

The dispute opened in April, 1961 when Johnson returned from an Asian inspection trip and recommended "a major effort" in South Vietnam. "Essentially the same" recommendations were put forward in October of the same year by the Taylor-Rostow mission to Vietnam. Taylor proposed sending a force of 10,000 U.S. regulars to fight in South Vietnam as the vanguard of an expeditionary corps which, he foresaw—and accepted—even then, would possibly have to exceed 300,000 men. Rostow proposed bombing North Vietnam " . . . a course of action for which [he] was a responsible advocate on this and subsequent occasions." President Kennedy rejected the qualitative changes being proposed, just as he had in April, but did direct that plans be prepared to introduce US troops in the event it proved necessary. He also accepted the Taylor-Rostow recommendations for increases in aid to Diem and for a build-up of American advisers.

For almost two years the Kennedy administration remained in this compromise stance. The dispute between the two factions was muted by the success of US-sponsored counter-insurgency tactics in Vietnam and by the collaboration of the Soviet Union in leading the Pathet Lao to join in a coalition regime with the neutralists and the right-wing. But in late 1963 these gains began to wear thin, especially in Vietnam, as first the NLF and then the Buddhists started to succeed in their assaults against the Diem regime. After Diem's murder on November 2, 1963 the NLF commenced several months of vigorous campaigning which rapidly undid its earlier losses.

Definitive evidence of this change in fortune had not yet begun to reach Washington when President Kennedy was murdered on November 22. Nevertheless, Hilsman points out, " . . . Walt Rostow presented to the new president a well reasoned case for gradual escalation and soon thereafter a proposal was put forward by the Pentagon and CIA for a program of low level reconnaissance over Laos and for a program of increased military pressure against the North." Included in this combination of proposals—Hilsman does not specify the source—was the recommendation that US air attacks within South Vietnam be stepped up and that a bombing offensive commence against the North. The key element in all of the proposals was the now familiar "military" conclusion that the Indochina crisis could be undone only by striking at North Vietnam.

Even the recommendation for low-level reconnaissance over Laos was built upon this view. Its proponents, Hilsman is careful to point out, envisioned that US aircraft would be fired upon by the Pathet Lao and we could then justifiably respond by striking at the infiltration routes along the Laotian-Vietnamese border. Harriman and Hilsman fought back, arguing that the adoption of the proposals would both undo the Laotian Accords and increase rather than diminish North Vietnamese assistance to the Viet Cong. They suggested instead that the small-scale infiltration then being carried on by the North Vietnamese could best be frustrated by assigning South Vietnamese forces to ambush duties within Laos.

The dispute within the new administration was not resolved but merely

Moral Argument and the War in Vietnam

postponed once again by the suggestion that McNamara return to Saigon to investigate the general state of affairs and especially the question of infiltration. His trip was announced on December 9; President Kennedy had been dead only seventeen days. The defense secretary spent the 19th and 20th in Saigon and on his return, still uncertain of the importance of North Vietnamese infiltration,[2] refused to join with those who wanted to bomb the North but did recommend that a list of targets be readied should the decision to bomb be made later.

At this point in the narrative Hilsman ends his chronological account, and turns, in the very next paragraph, to his own decision to leave the government. By January 20, 1964, Hilsman decided to resign his post " . . . sure that the United States under [President Johnson's] direction . . . was obviously going to take the military path—even though it climbed the ladder of escalation slowly and deliberately." He gives no details and no explanation of what had happened in the month between McNamara's indecisive return from Saigon and this decision. It matters little, however, for he has given us enough information already to place the events of the next several months in accurate perspective.

By February 6, 1964, it became clear for the first time what the "program of increased military pressures against the North" included when the St. Louis *Post-Dispatch* revealed that commando operations by South Vietnamese troops against North Vietnam had been significantly increased. Similar stories in the *Wall Street Journal* of March 6 and, especially, in the April issue of *Aviation Week* linked the step-up to the decision made within the administration that it was impossible to win the war by confining it within South Vietnam's borders.

In the same period rumors of other warlike moves began to filter out of official Washington. On February 16 *The New York Times's* usually well-informed Military Editor, Hanson Baldwin, stressed the likelihood that US ground troops would be sent to South Vietnam: and Wayne Morse, whose value in warning against escalation in this period cannot be overemphasized, all but explicitly confirmed the news on March 4 after a secret briefing by Dean Rusk. On March 30 the Washington *Star* reported even the normally guarded McNamara as saying "privately on Capitol hill" that the war would likely be extended within the next few months.

The first "hard" news of the changes in store came on April 19 when the American-financed right-wing Lao Army overturned the government of Souvanna Phouma. In spite of strong Chinese pressure to restore the provisions of the 1962 Accords and the evident willingness of the Pathet Lao to return to the coalition, Phouma instead returned to office on May 2 as head of a new coalition which excluded the Pathet Lao. An important address by Rusk, on the 22nd, for the first time publicly linked South Vietnam and Laos into a single military theater of operations: on the 27th, the new Lao government was sent a shipment of fighter aircraft. Shortly afterward, Souvanna Phouma "surprised"

Washington by asking that US aircraft carry out low-level reconnaissance against the Pathet Lao. By June 6 and 7 several US aircraft had been duly shot down, and Washington felt free to announce, on the 8th, that retaliatory air attacks had commenced against Pathet Lao territory.

In Vietnam, events moved almost as rapidly. The US aid program was increased on April 23: General Westmoreland, the Army's rising star, was sent to take command in Saigon on the 25th; additional fighter aircraft were sent on May 12 and troop reinforcements on the 14th. A major strategy conference was held in Honolulu on June 1, and on June 23, the president announced that Maxwell Taylor would take over as Ambassador to Saigon. It would be difficult to believe that Taylor went to Saigon to carry out any other program than that which we had been urging within the government since October, 1961. In confirmation of this, events began to move still more rapidly. On July 10 Air Marshal Ky announced still another increase in commando raids against the North[3] and this was followed on July 14 by the announcement that 600 more US troops would be sent to Vietnam. On the 27th it was announced that still another 5,000 troops were being sent, increasing the US force by almost 50 percent, and on the same day the destroyer *Maddox* began her slow voyage up the North Vietnamese coast.

On August 2 while South Vietnamese naval vessels shelled North Vietnamese radar installations on the islands of Hon Me and Hon Nghu the *Maddox* lurked between three and eight miles off the same coast and was shortly thereafter driven off by North Vietnamese gunboats. Immediately after a high-level White House meeting on the 3rd the president threatened retaliation against the North if the attack were repeated. Within hours a new attack was reported in Washington—and denied by Hanoi—and on August 4 the first retaliatory raids were carried out against a wide range of strategic targets in North Vietnam.[4]

Then, in testimony which was withheld from the public for more than two years, Secretary McNamara reported to the Senate Foreign Relations Committee on August 6 that a series of steps had already been taken to move large numbers of US forces into Southeast Asia. These included the readying of Army and Marine ground forces for duty with South Vietnam and the dispatch of US fighter bombers to Thailand, which was to become the major launching point for the raids on North Vietnam when they were resumed the following year. The prologue was complete and the stage was set for the February, 1965 escalation: but first a bothersome election against the irresponsible Goldwater had to be gotten out of the way.

When did the administration "decide," i.e., irrevocably commit itself, to escalate the war? Certainly by June 23, 1964 when Taylor was appointed to Saigon: probably by April 19, 1964 when our clients in Laos drove the Pathet Lao from the governing coalition. Hilsman seems by his own actions to believe that the "decision" had been made by January

Moral Argument and the War in Vietnam

20. In some sense, of course, the escalation had been decided on November 22, 1963, for President Kennedy's death placed the "military" in control and ensured at least the slow erosion of the restraints he had so far accepted upon our Indochina policy.

Hilsman does not attempt to hide his disdain for the "military" faction which brought about the escalation and especially for the heavy-handed and simple-minded types he finds in the higher reaches of the Pentagon. A year and a half ago—January 20, 1966—I. F. Stone wrote a perceptive review of Curtis LeMay's autobiography in these pages and, interestingly enough, many of the ideas found in that review can be found scattered through Hilsman's book. For Hilsman, as for Stone, the higher leadership of the armed services is blind to the requirements of nuclear age diplomacy, absurdly overconfident of the efficacy of military techniques, especially strategic bombing, and thoroughly immersed in petty interservice rivalries. Moreover, both perceive that the "military" faction extends far beyond the boundaries of the uniformed services. Dean Rusk, Walt Rostow, Nixon, or, for that matter, Johnson may wear civilian clothes, but it matters very little. Their views are a direct extension of the interests of one or more of the armed services; they are "military." As far as the results of policy are concerned, they are pretty much interchangeable with Curtis LeMay.

Nevertheless, even with this addition to our understanding, the relationship of the two factions is not clearly delineated. Hilsman and, to a lesser extent, Stone portray the "political" and "military" factions as serious antagonists in national policymaking, which is not at all so. I suspect they do so partly because they are thrown off by the frequently crude and colorful language of the "military" faction. Roger Hilsman, for example, does not speak of "Whiz kid liberals," of "frying cities to a crisp" or even of "nailing the coonskin to the wall." He has never fallen in love with a B-17, never dreamt—as Barry Goldwater has phrased it so wonderfully—of dropping ICBM *nukes* into the Kremlin men's room. "Political" language is cooler, more abstract; it prefers euphemism to metaphor. It is closer to the language of an Ivy League faculty club than to that of the officers' mess.

The language difference is not unimportant. It represents a difference of emphasis on many questions ranging from when to use the Bomb, to the relative merits of Boeing's and General Dynamics' version of the F-111, to whether civilian casualties in Vietnam are merely "body-count" or are also "regrettable." But a difference in emphasis is all it represents. Pentagonese and academic coolspeak translate into each other too readily for one to think otherwise. Maxwell Taylor is fluent in both. Both languages are so closely related that one can move from one to the other without quite noticing it, just as the country moved from Kennedy's War to Johnson's War in 1964. The truth of the matter is that the two factions are not pressing mutually exclusive courses of action: they do not represent alternative national policies or leadership.

This phenomenon may at first appear surprising and at variance with the facts. We know, for example, that Hilsman's public assessment of the "military" faction in Government is mild compared to the judgments which "political" men like himself will render in private. On a number of occasions I have raised this issue with officials in Washington who never fail to tell me that the Pentagon—and other Washington establishments as well—is filled with "madmen" and "fools," people who really want to use the Bomb in Vietnam or, because of Vietnam, people who are simply out of touch with reality. Such frank—and private—interviews are a common experience in Washington and among higher level university foreign-policy consultants. Hilsman reports that at one point in the Kennedy administration an official prepared a mock account of a high-level meeting on Vietnam in which Averell Harriman ". . . stated that he had disagreed for twenty years with General Krulak [of the Marine Corps] and disagreed today, reluctantly, more than ever; he was sorry to say that he felt General Krulak was a tool and had always thought so." Harriman probably did think Krulak a fool. So, apparently, did President Kennedy who, shown the fictitious account, roared with laughter. What kind of men are these who describe their associates as "madmen" and "fools," but who nevertheless assign charge over nuclear weapons to "madmen" and give major troop commands, here and abroad, to "fools"?

Roger Hilsman is an able and articulate member of a relatively new class of men in American life. He is a Crisis Manager, one of the men who have held and continue to hold the handful of positions in the National Security apparatus. It is their job to manage the still youthful crisis—only twenty-three years old—which we call the cold war. Hilsman himself represents the newer breed of Crisis Managers, as tough minded as Acheson but not so "military," and as subtle as McCloy but not so closely connected with the older and European-oriented Wall Street business community. Like so many of the younger Crisis Managers he is an intellectual and a Kennedyite, is mildly liberal, and maintains a base within the university establishment. He is not a typical member of his class, but he is perhaps typical of the best of his class and this is the value of *To Move A Nation.* It is a portrayal and a defense of liberal, "political," intelligent, and responsible Crisis Managers and of their struggles against the "madmen" and the "fools." In short, it shows us the Crisis Managers at their best. It is not a reassuring sight.

The Crisis Managers face a peculiar problem in dealing with the armed services and the services' allies within the civil apparatus. They have assigned themselves the task of presiding over a vast military bureaucracy—and its supporting institutions—in a period in which changes in technology have forced revolutionary changes in the military art. With the exception of one or two like Hilsman (a graduate of West Point), they generally lack military training and yet somehow must try to maintain direction over the efforts of their always restive military technicians.

Moral Argument and the War in Vietnam

Under such circumstances they have become the most ideological of men. Without the presumed superiority of an almost infallible conception of the National Interest they could not hope to force grudging acquiescence from their more technically skilled military subordinates.

Their outlook is a peculiar one and is shaped by this need to keep the military in check. What makes them particularly vulnerable to the pressures of the armed services is the fact that they are themselves ideological militarists as well. Unlike their uniformed subordinates the Crisis Managers do not believe in uniforms and medals, the glories of the service academy circa 1930, and the moral superiority of the military life. But just like their subordinates within the military they perceive international reality almost exclusively in military and strategic ways; their faith in coercion, and while they use political language often enough, in the end they rely on the military devices which they possess in such great profusion.

At one point in *To Move A Nation* Hilsman is confronted with the necessity to explain why Laos is worth a major military adventure. His answer is both revealing and characteristic, especially for a self-styled "political." There is a road, he tells us, or rather the latent possibility of a road, which follows the tortuous course of the Mekong River from southwestern China, through more than a thousand miles of mountain, jungle, and swamp, to southern Laos and Cambodia. It is a line of communication, he argues using a military terminology that neatly marches along the page, and it must be denied the Chinese. No strong or suggestive evidence is offered that China wants to or is able to undertake this tedious excursion. Hilsman does not even see that that is an issue; instead America's overseas imperatives can be read directly from an unmarked military map.

The Crisis Managers are anti-Communist, more so even than the service chiefs, but there is no ethical content to their hatred of Bolshevism, nor any sense at all of how they themselves may appear to Communist leaders. The Communists—a capitalized epithet usually lacking distinction as to faction, era, or nationality—are said to have no respect for people or their values, practice terror, possess an insatiable appetite for power. But by Hilsman's own description the US, in the decade 1954-64, committed every imaginable perfidy in Laos. Governments were toppled, international agreements trampled upon, elections fixed, political parties created out of nothing, the Army placed on a monthly stipend, the economy distorted and corrupted, and several varieties of military adventurers encouraged in their aimless depredations against the long-suffering Lao people. Hilsman is quite firm in insisting, however, that the villains of the game are the Pathet Lao because of their "intransigeance and duplicity," their "vicious" and "ruthless" opposition to free world influence in Laos.

A liberal of sorts, Hilsman naturally finds McCarthyism depraved; a moral man, he was appalled by the "unspeakable" practices found in

Diem's prisons. Yet he was among the earliest and most persistent enthusiasts for the Strategic Hamlet Program, which forcibly removed several million South Vietnamese from their homes and livelihood into what used to be called concentration camps. Still a proponent of the forced deportation of civilians, Hilsman criticizes the history of the Program only from a technical standpoint. There were never enough political police to prevent rebels—excuse me, Communists!—from infiltrating the Hamlets and Ngo Dinh Nhu "corrupted" the Program by pushing it too rapidly.

Consider once more the significance of the Strategic Hamlet Program or, for that matter, any of the resettlement programs which preceded it or followed it, including the current pacification program. These programs aim at forcing most rural South Vietnamese in disputed areas into government-controlled detention camps where they can be kept under exceptionally close surveillance by police and military authorities. Any person who remains outside the camps is assumed to be Viet Cong and may be killed on sight or by means of saturation bombardment in the "free fire" zones, i.e., the areas outside the camp. (The report on "The Village of Ben Suc" in the July 15 *New Yorker* gives a careful account of this process.) It is necessary to ask whether any Communist government has ever undertaken so inclusive a program of detention and terror. Even Stalin's collectivization of the Thirties assumed only a minority of the peasantry were enemies of the regime. In South Vietnam every peasant is a potential *kulak* and is treated accordingly. "Political" officials like Hilsman are perfectly serious in defending these programs as an essential means of saving the population from Communist totalitarianism. Such behavior on the part of civilized men is difficult to explain. It does indeed seem to be anticommunism of a particularly pathological kind. One gets the impression that the Crisis Managers conjure up a diabolical caricature of the Communists and then, to demonstrate how hard-nosed and realistic they are, try to go the caricature one better.

The Crisis Managers are defined by their relation to power. They want power but power of a peculiar kind. They are not interested in power as a form of personal adornment, such as the image of Mussolini recalls, nor do they seek power primarily as a means to chosen ends. They call themselves pragmatists (and moderates, always) intending to convey by this overused term that they are interested primarily in means taken by themselves, that is, in relative isolation from the ends they bring about. In Hilsman's book, as in so many Crisis Manager tracts, this leads to a preoccupation with the process of decision-making. Decisions normally have both antecedents and consequences, but Crisis Managers are not particularly concerned with these. They are interested in the process: who made the decision, when and where, who was consulted and who wasn't, who was cool and who agitated, who comes out of it looking good, and who will be the goat in the next round of memoirs.

Moral Argument and the War in Vietnam

The Crisis Managers' relation to power is not mechanical, however, and it is not, *prima facie,* frivolous. They want power in its most immediate forms, power today, power to decide, to move and manipulate now, this moment. But their relationship to the power which they seek so assiduously is pictured in a grimly serious way. The telephone calls in the night, the immense influence of the institutions they control, and the knowledge that they deal always with life and death issues—all these produce in the Crisis Managers a portrait of themselves as lonely and heroic men never quite free of the heavy burdens of their high office, burdens of which lesser and more carefree men, like you and me, are blessedly ignorant. The language of this portrait—an immediate relation to reality, historical significance, self-chosen loneliness, suffering for others, the burden of decisions, confrontation with the issues of life and death—suggests the "existential" idiom of writers like Colin Wilson: Chapter thirty-two of Hilsman's book, for example, bears the now familiar expression, "The Agonies of Decision." This usage is quite deliberate.

Agonies reach their climax during crises and, like most Kennedy memoirists, Hilsman has a long and loving section on the Cuban Missile Crisis of 1962. That crisis was naturally the high point in the lives of those Crisis Managers who happened to be working that year. Then, at the height of the crisis, for the first and only time perhaps in history, the fate of all mankind—all the significant power over that fate and all the significant decisions—was in the hands of a few men. Historical reality had been reduced to them, to their actions. For those few heady hours all events seemed obedient to the conscious will of a handful of intimates. Their engagement was complete, their every action was bent to the common task, where they went, what they said, whom they saw, how they appeared to others—all of this counted for those few magic hours. It was a truly beautiful moment.

This curious aspect of Crisis Manager ideology is revealed in a very sharp way. In his treatment of Kennedy's behavior during the crisis, Hilsman subtracts every morsel of substantive political significance and finds himself, ultimately, reduced to writing in a way that is frightening in its triviality. The late president's earlier and inexcusable tolerance of administration threats to destroy the Castro regime—even after the Bay of Pigs—is largely ignored, even though this contributed to the crisis in the first place. The fact that Kennedy brought all mankind to the brink of unfathomable suffering, partly in order to save face, while rejecting the compromise proposals of U Thant, Walter Lippmann, and others, is clear enough from Hilsman's account of these events, but he takes no direct notice of it. Perhaps most important, Hilsman passes over the disastrous legacy of Kennedy's victory—the belief that the Soviets backed down out of fear and weakness. True or not, this was precisely the conclusion which freed Kennedy's successor to chance the Vietnam escalation two years later. As Walt Rostow wrote last February:

A Just War?

If the Cuba missile crisis was the Gettysburg of the Cold War, Vietnam could be the Wilderness; for indeed the Cold War has been a kind of global civil conflict. Vietnam could be made the closing of one chapter in modern history and the opening of another. . . .

Having thus reduced the scope of his interest, what else can Hilsman say? Kennedy's behavior during the crisis itself was "exquisite."

Crisis represents reality at its best for liberal Crisis Managers like Hilsman, and this simple insight gives us the key to their relationship with the maligned military and "military" types. The Crisis Managers are the moderates between two extremes, peace and war. Their stake is in cold war, of which they are both children and progenitors. Unlike the generals they have no stake in active war. They don't like war partly for the same reasons you and I don't like war, but also because in war the power to make decisions escapes to the generals and that is anathema for liberal Crisis Managers.

It is, then, only by contrast to Curtis LeMay or Walt Rostow that our liberal Crisis Managers appear as sane and reasonable men, just as "advisers" in Laos appear a sane alternative to "nukes" in Peking. Without the terrifying backdrop of the Pentagon, and without the distorting influence of a swollen military establishment in our national life, the Crisis Managers would have too few crises to manage and their true role would emerge more clearly, perhaps even to themselves. Their half-disguised militarism, unprincipled anticommunism, and a bizarre, pretentious, and sometimes comic mystique of power are fully as antagonistic to a stable peace as is the ultimate faith in strategic bombing—in fact more so. Perhaps without knowing it, they have made cold war manipulation and military coercion in foreign countries a kind of noble calling. It is understandable that the process of making money or enlightening undergraduates should become for them tame business compared to life and death confrontation with the Bomb, the task of policing and redeeming the Third World, smiting Marx and Mao with fistfuls of pragmatism and moderation—as they put it—and of getting the whole of mankind moving again. Thus the Crisis Managers are addicted to cold war. They cannot do without it. They are the moderates who protect us from the twin evils of Dr. Spock and Dr. Strangelove.

This is why Hilsman did not go to the public in January, 1964. He resigned because the "fools" and the "madmen" had won control of the government. He *knew* escalation was coming. An insider with the facts at his command and an experienced and respected policymaker, had he moved to attack the administration publicly in 1964, it is conceivable that the war might not have been escalated, especially if some of those who agreed with him had joined him. But Crisis Managers don't go to the public. The public really has no right to meddle in foreign policy. An informed opinion on foreign affairs". . . like blue cheese . . . [is] an acquired taste" and the public has never acquired it. But

Moral Argument and the War in Vietnam

more important by far than any contempt the Crisis Manager may feel for the public, is his own commitment to "existential" decision-making. Managing crises is the privilege of a Crisis Manager as managing securities is the privilege of a portfolio manager. To go to the public is unthinkable, it is to exercise a deadly threat against the existence and prerogatives of one's own class (not to mention one's own future as a member in good standing). One simply does not do such things. Hilsman's book is a treatise on the politics of policymaking within the foreign-affairs apparatus, not an *exposé* to rally a dormant public. Academic shoptalk has it that it may also be a ticket to the next Kennedy administration. It is also an often touching and obviously genuine tribute to the memory of John Kennedy.

In reviewing books like *To Move a Nation* it is fashionable to touch on the familiar abstract conflict between something called the national interest and something else called the public's right to know. Calm, serious, and brief attention to the merits of both sides generally suffices to get the reviewer through this particular ritual. But times have changed.

January, 1964 was the beginning of an election year. The national administration had committed itself to a course of war, which even now has not expanded to its full limit. A responsible official within the administration was so appalled by the prospect that he resigned. But he kept silent. We must assume there were others who knew as he knew and who felt as he felt but they too kept silent.

In 1960, during the famous Kennedy-Nixon televised debates, candidate Kennedy proposed that the US assist anti-Castro exiles to invade their homeland. The proposal was attacked as irresponsible by Nixon, even though it was already the policy of the Eisenhower administration, a policy initiated and championed within the administration of Nixon himself. Eventually Kennedy too revealed a different face; his prepresidential skepticism of the scheme's worth was expressed in his hesitations during the Bay of Pigs affair.

As a *system* our political institutions broke down in 1960 and 1964. The complex of institutions which comprise that system—the parties, the press, the Congress, the private organizations, the ethics of responsible government—has no political justification save its capacity to subject government to periodic informed consent; and this is precisely what it failed to do in its last two attempts.

In 1960 and 1964 the Crisis Managers held out the illusion of alternatives to the public, and while we played in their proffered sandbox, they simply went ahead with the real world decisions or, as with Hilsman, let others go ahead with them, without public hindrance. The point to understand is that they carried out this fraud not out of malice or caprice, but because they were Crisis Managers. The whole significance of the Crisis Manager system is that they are—as a class—a perpetual conspiracy against the right of the public to self-government. Public indifference cannot be listed as an excuse. Nineteen-sixty and 1964 were not random years; they were election years, years when public figures are charged by our ethic to break through indifference and cause the public to make judgments on public business. What Kennedy, Nixon, and Hilsman did cannot be excused as a matter of protecting the national interest from the Russians, the Cubans, or the North Vietnamese. The other side knew what we were planning in these places.[5] What Kennedy, Nixon, and Hilsman were doing was protecting the Crisis Manager system against the public.

It should be added that this is precisely the significance of the CIA, a significance which has been largely overlooked in the recent controversies surrounding the agency. Critics of the CIA charge that its activities escape scrutiny by the president and his top advisers. Its defenders, including the last three presidents, counter that the charge is not true and then proceed to defend the agency's existence and influence as necessary if certain governmental activities are to escape the scrutiny of our enemies. But the Russians and the Chinese and the Cubans and the rest know far more about the operations of the CIA than does the American public. This is as it should be, for it is perfectly evident that the primary function of the CIA is to conduct that great part of our foreign policy which, for good reasons and bad, must escape the scrutiny of the American public. CIA spokesmen acknowledge this in defending the secrecy of their relationship to the NSA; such secrecy was necessary in the Laos and Vietnam programs[6]—and is necessary in Greece today. It is the essence of the Crisis Manager system that a large part of public policy be carried out in hiding from the public. The CIA is the institutional reflection of that system.

Nineteen-sixty-eight . . . [was] an election year. Much of the country . . . [was] strongly persuaded that the Vietnam War should be terminated, but . . . [was] able to do precious little to bring it to an end. . . .

. . . [In 1967] I had a long conversation with a leading university consultant to the State Department and a major bureau chief of one of the big news magazines. Both had previously and strongly supported administration policy in Vietnam. Now, the former wished for nothing more than a face-saving withdrawal and the latter merely hoped that "something could be done." Both agreed the war was hopelessly stalemated, both thought Nixon would win the nomination in 1968 and run on a more-war program. Both agreed Johnson would win and both agreed that the war would either go on indefinitely or lead to war with China. Both agreed nothing could be done.

Through his magazine the bureau chief had good intelligence on the more political segments of the business community, especially among those who had balked at Taft in 1952 and forced the GOP to provide Eisenhower as an alternative. What about them? They . . . [had] lost all confidence in Johnson, he reported. They . . . [thought] him a "madman" and . . . [saw] no limit to how far . . . [he'd] go. "What are they doing about it?" I persisted. "Nothing," he replied, "there is

47

Moral Argument and the War in Vietnam

nothing that can be done."

Perhaps he . . . [was] wrong but his mood reveals the final and most deadly legacy of the Crisis Manager system. The "military" are in the saddle and the revelations of "politicals" like Hilsman have no political effect. We have lived so long with Hilsman's system that we have forgotten how to act. Others are actors and we are only spectators. This state of affairs is now a durable feature of American political life.

Notes

1 Schurmann in *The Politics of Escalation* and Stone in *I. F. Stone's Weekly,* April 27, June 8, and October 12, 1964, May 17 and December 6, 1965, and September 26, October 24, and December 5, 1966.

2 As has been widely reported in the press, Hilsman reveals that the North Vietnamese were not then infiltrating into South Vietnam, that there had been no recent increase in infiltrees, and that those who had already come were southerners returning from the 1954 regroupment. Regular North Vietnamese units did not enter South Vietnam until the fall of 1965, several months after the bombing of the North and the arrival of American units in the South.

3 Saigon *Post,* July 10, 1964. The irrepressible Stone found this item and published it in his September 12, 1966, *Weekly.*

4 The late Bernard Fall made this point in an analysis published in the Washington *Post* on August 9. The targets had been officially described as "gunboats and their supporting facilities" but included the coal mines at Hong Gai.

5 In the Vietnamese case, an East-European source reports that he saw the first emplacement of antiaircraft artillery in Hanoi and Haiphong while on a visit in March, 1964.

6 The CIA maintained a special and often dominant relationship to the American Vietnam project at least until Henry Cabot Lodge's appointment as Ambassador in June, 1963. During the early part of the program, roughly March, 1955 to June, 1959, the CIA had been especially concerned to develop Vietnam's internal security services, primarily the political police or *Sûreté* which Saigon had inherited from the departed French colonial authorities. The Michigan State University Advisory Group (MSUG) was used as a cover for this activity.

Wesley Fishel, former Chief Advisor (director) of MSUG and currently Professor of Political Science at MSU, has recently chosen to dispute this, writing, for example, to the *New York Review* (June 29, 1967) that ". . . there was never at any time any overt or covert connection between MSU and the CIA; there was no contract nor even an informal relationship." In the same letter Fishel acknowledged that MSUG trained what he calls "civil police" but denies that it had anything to do with "secret police" and he denied as well that MSUG had engaged in any " 'spying' activities."

His colleagues within the MSUG project tell quite a different story. Guy Fox, like Fishel a former Chief Advisor to MSUG (1961-2) and Robert Scigliano, Assistant to the Chief Advisor during Fishel's term of office in that post, report that in mid-1959 the U.S. Aid Program ". . . absorbed . . . the CIA unit that had been operating within MSUG; the University group refused to provide cover for this unit in the new contract period" (Scigliano and Fox, *Technical Assistance in Viet Nam: The Michigan State University Experience,* Praeger, 1965, p. 11). As for " 'spying' activity," the two merely report that MSU's technical assistance activity in Vietnam was harmed by its ". . . somewhat forced hospitality as organizational cover for certain intelligence functions of the American government until mid-1959" (*ibid.,* p. 60).

Fishel's distinction between civil and secret police is a puzzle. The MSUG's *Final Report* (Saigon, 1962, mimeographed) lists only three different police forces in Vietnam, the Municipal Police, the Civil Guard, and the *Sûreté.* Most of MSUG's assistance went to the *Sûreté.* The latter had been the colonial secret political police and was widely feared and hated by Vietnamese nationalists. If the *Sûreté* ceased being a secret police in 1955 there is no record of it. In any case the repressive role the *Sûreté* played within South Vietnam during the Diem—and Fishel—period is very clear and it did not change a bit when Fishel had it renamed the Vietnamese Bureau of Investigation.

Part II

Genocide?

Genocide?

Introduction

Is United States policy in Vietnam an act of genocide against the people of that country? The question cuts through any debate on the subject of ends justifying means. If there is any means in war which cannot conceivably be justified by ends, genocide is certainly the foremost candidate. Genocide—the intentional extermination of a national, ethnic, or racial group—seems so atrocious that human communities would cease to retain their humanity if it were morally permissible. Furthermore, the means-ends distinction does not seem to produce anything here: can any end, even if we are permitted to balance it against genocide, outweigh the evil of (and resulting from) intentionally exterminating a nation, race, or ethnic group? Other ends seem to pale by comparison. While "justifiable homicide" is a sensible term, "justifiable genocide" seems deeply incoherent. Thus the charge of genocide cannot possibly be accepted (no matter how regretfully) by a defender of United States policy, only to be circumvented by other factors and perspectives. "Well, for the credibility of the non-Communist bloc, we just had to commit genocide," is not a plausible moral argument. Politics, no matter how "realistic," cannot be that callous. Thus the debate over the charge of genocide is squarely centered on whether the United States has actually committed it in Vietnam.

That debate is over both the *factual* consequences of United States policy in Vietnam and the *conceptual* character of genocide. It asks, How massive is the destruction caused by the United States? and, Should the description "genocide" be applied to those facts? Often in moral discussions we are fairly clear on what a given concept demands in order to be applied; then we argue whether the facts are such that the concept can be applied to the case in question. But in other instances our concepts are not that clear; we may agree on the facts but still argue whether a certain concept should be used to describe them. In the genocide charge both facts and concepts are at issue, but it is application of the concept which undoubtedly occasions the most serious disputes.

Perhaps all parties could agree on the following toll of civilians in South Vietnam: 29,000 have been killed by the revolutionaries and North Vietnamese since the war began, and Allied fire (mainly bombs) has caused over 200,000 casualties and 60,000 deaths in 1970 and at least 1.2 million casualties and 360,000 fatalities from 1965 to 1971.[1] Accord-

51

Moral Argument and the War in Vietnam

ing to Defense Department figures, over 3 million tons of bombs were dropped on North and South Vietnam from 1965 to 1969; the bombing rate over South Vietnam in March 1969 was 130,000 tons a month. Over 9 million tons of air, ground, and naval explosives were used by Allied forces from 1965 to 1970; in the same period the NLF and North Vietnam used 17,500 tons. Four million acres of forests and 500,000 acres of cropland were defoliated through 1968 (Rhode Island is 500,000 acres in area). Through 1968 two million of South Vietnam's 9 million population were refugees from within South Vietnam.[2] All parties might also agree that the cultural and historical character of Vietnamese society has been considerably altered (destroyed, some would say) by the massive United States presence.[3]

But then the debate will rage heavy: Does this constitute genocide? We are just not used to handling the concept. It has not been a familiar concept in our moral vocabulary, and it is defined as an *intentional action*, a matter (philosophically at least) of much ambiguity, confusion, and controversy. The mere actual consequences which result from an action are not sufficient to establish that these consequences have been intentionally brought about.

The concept of intentional extermination of a national group is broader than a narrower one with which it is often confused. It does not entail that the extermination of the group, say the Jews in Germany, is carried on "simply because they are Jews." The latter characterization implies that genocide must have the extermination of the Jews as its intrinsic and ultimate goal; we could then not ask further why Jews were to be exterminated, or, if we persisted in doing so, the *only* answer would be, "because they are Jews." Historically it may be true that the Nazis slaughtered the Jews out of sheer, ultimate, racial prejudice, slaughtered them "*simply* because they were Jews." That need not be true of genocide in general. It is required of genocide only that it be *intentional* and not accidental. Means of action as well as ends can be intentional. Thus genocide may be an instrumental means to something else. In fact, by saying it was a "means" and not merely a coincidental circumstance or side effect, we would be saying it was intentional. Any means which one takes to his chosen end is intentional.[4] It may not be "the main intention" of the action, but it is nevertheless intentional. (If we keep this in mind we will not be misled when Sartre, e.g., says the Nazis killed a Jew "simply because he was a Jew."[5] In stressing the character of genocide by that remark, he can only be reflecting the fact that means to ends are intentional and that it therefore is natural to say we perform them because they are what they are. That is not to say that the national group in question could not be exterminated in turn for other ends. In fact in that same paragraph, Sartre describes genocide as "a political means."

Presumably we are not dealing with a case of genocide as an end in itself when we are discussing United States war policy in Vietnam.

This might have been true of Nazi treatment of the Jews, but it is certainly not plausible to say that the sufficient and ultimate reason for United States policy is to wipe the Vietnamese nation and culture from the face of humanity. The charge is rather that the United States is using genocide against the Vietnamese as a means to whatever other foreign policy ends it has. That, in the abstract, at least, is surely conceivable. A nation can use genocide as a means to ward off certain threats. If one is to map out the charge in detail, one will have to spell out just what end it is toward which genocide is a means, and why. Both Sartre and Chomsky attempt to do this in their selections. Sartre's interpretation in particular rests on a far-reaching analysis of the nature of United States foreign policy: it is fundamentally neocolonial toward the Third World, and the example of genocide against anti-American revolution in Vietnam serves major ends of United States policy toward the rest of the Third World. Just as American hydrogen bombs are designed to deter Soviet attack, so also the extinction of Vietnam as a historical and cultural entity will deter attacks on American policies in all underdeveloped and formerly colonial nations.[6]

Sartre's and Chomsky's explanations that genocide is fitted to be a means of United States policy are not in themselves, however, sufficient to establish that the United States has committed that crime against Vietnam. Before one can call the massive American killing of civilians in Vietnam a "means" (in the sense relevant for intentional action), one must be prepared to claim for United States policy certain other characteristics necessary to qualify the massive killings as intentional. Here the discussion explodes with philosophical controversies. I will here consider some of the complexities created by two such alleged characteristics of intentional action: (1) *Foreknowledge* of the results caused by an action does not always render those results intentional. (2) For a result to be intentional requires the agent to have had some *conscious, subjective purpose* to produce it. Suppose these points are correct. Then a defense of United States policy against the charge of genocide could claim that the massive destruction of Vietnam is not a *conscious* purpose of United States policy and thus, that though indeed the destruction might have been *foreseen*, it is not *intentional*.

The distinction between foreknown and intended results is known as the principle of "double effect."[7] Mr. Ramsey defends it by pointing to the example of abortion: the debate there is whether the taking of the life of the fetus is intended, and, he implies, the person favoring an abortion will have to say that it is not an *intentional* killing of the fetus, though of course he *foresees* the death he would cause.[8] Two important kinds of responses are stimulated by the way Mr. Ramsey makes this distinction. The first concerns the merits of the distinction itself; the second concerns his application of the distinction to moral questions about war.

(1) To foresee a result and bring it about because it is *necessary*

53

for achieving some goal of a larger action always qualifies that result as intentionally brought about.[9] Then the killing of a fetus, for example, becomes intentional, though we may subsequently decide that it is "justifiable" or "excusable." [10] Genocide, of course, might subsequently never be judged to be justified or excused. Regardless of that, however, we should note that genocide can be applied to Vietnam under this conception of intention only if we claim that the actual extensive destruction is a *necessary* means to the goal of United States policy. That claim is hotly debated. It is denied by Messrs. Little and Ramsey; both surmise that the United States could have fought, without large, indiscriminate weapons, a counter-guerrilla war in Vietnam which still could have been successful in terms of the goals of United States policy.[11] On the other hand, the claim is defended very explicitly by both Sartre and Chomsky.

(2) Even if all foreseen results of personal actions are not necessarily intentional, it does not follow that there is a moral distinction between "foreseen extermination" and "(intentional) genocide." Perhaps the state action of exterminating a national-cultural-ethnic group is such a moral abomination in its own right that foreseeing it is sufficient to establish guilt. Chomsky comments that the American government may only have been "experimenting" with massive destruction when it went into the war full scale.[12] Perhaps such massive destruction is so abhorrent morally that it is not excused by only foreseeing it and not intending it, or by only experimenting with it and not literally foreseeing it. Foreknowledge may also become more and more evidence for intention when the same policy with the same foreseen results is used again and again, as Chomsky now claims we are repeating in Laos and Cambodia. Such repetitions are evidence that these results are foreseen as effective and necessary means for achieving certain goals, and that renders them criminal.

Some would claim that results must be "consciously, subjectively intended" and not merely foreseen as necessary means, in order to be described as intentional. Ramsey can in part defend United States policy against the charge of genocide because he requires such a subjective purpose in order to describe an action as intentional.[13] However, "conscious, subjective purpose" is itself a problematic notion. Miss Anscombe notes that the principle of "double effect" has been abused by a very narrow, Cartesian, private notion of "conscious mental event," so that all you have to do to disclaim intention is to make "a little speech to yourself: 'What I mean to be doing is. . . .' " [14] Such little inner rationalizations may not alter the description either of what actually *happens* or of what I really *do*. The reason, in turn, may be either because immediate subjective consciousness is too narrow a conception of consciousness, or because consciousness in any form is not required for intention. And thus it is possible that, just as we might demonstrate the *pattern* of a person's behavior to reveal his action as intentional despite the disclaimers of his immediate consciousness, we might also demonstrate the *pattern* of a state's behavior to reveal it as intentional despite the disclaimers of the immediate consciousness of its leaders and policymakers. In any case it is questionable whether such a conscious element is required for intentional *state* action. If states are not the kinds of entities which are "conscious" in the literal sense, and if we still want to retain some sense for intentional *action* by a state (so that, among other things, it makes sense to hold states *morally blameworthy)*, then perhaps asking for "conscious purpose" is asking for too much. The ways we describe how a state *acts* at all will have to be considered in formulating a notion of genocide.

Mr. Ramsey applies the distinction between foreseen patterns of behavior and the immediate intentional thrust of an action to situations of guerrilla warfare. The notion of genocide rests in part on the distinction between combatants and noncombatants drawn by just war theory in its principle of discrimination. Presumably the extermination of a whole nation of fully armed and uniformed combatants would not be genocide; it would, on a larger scale, be tantamount to one battalion wiping out another. In deciding the genocidal character of the United States-caused civilian toll in Vietnam, it is therefore important to ask whether the deaths are those of "noncombatants." Furthermore, since the destruction will be genocide only if it is intentional, it is important to ask whether the United States *intends* to kill people *as noncombatants.* Ramsey answers both questions negatively (most clearly so the second). It is the guerrilla's type of warfare, he claims, which has initially collapsed the distinction between combatants and noncombatants. The guerrillas attempt to live as fish amidst the sea of the population; they try to make the whole population the effective combatants against their enemies; they use the peasants as means to their military ends. Thus many Vietnamese civilians have become "combatants" by their active cooperation with the guerrillas. Furthermore, even if the United States has in fact killed large numbers of civilians who were not so actively cooperating, it has done that without immediately, *intentionally* directing its force against noncombatants; it has intended only to kill active cooperators.

This defense of counter-guerrilla warfare unquestionably goes to the heart of important issues, and it raises in response the following questions (whether it can answer their critical force I will not consider here): if the guerrillas do win the cooperating support of the population, why does that make the population any less a "civilian population"? Why does it not justify the cause of the guerrillas so that we should not be fighting them, whether they are combatants or not? Do the guerrillas "fight the war by *means* of peasants," or is that too "scheming" a description of a natural, indigenous, revolutionary situation? If the insurgents in South Vietnam assassinate civilian Saigon government officials, is their "intentional action" one of "killing civilians" or rather "eliminat-

Moral Argument and the War in Vietnam

ing the leaders and functionaries of a corrupt and oppressive regime"? If the United States forces know that over *a period of time* they are killing "active cooperators" who also lead full civilian and peasant lives, can it continually be said that they do not intentionally kill "civilian peasants"?

If the complex conceptual issues raised about intention should leave one ambivalent about the charge of genocide against the United States, other charges may emerge from the discussion. "Reckless" and "negligent" slaughter of civilians still bears an onus of moral responsibility, even though it is not, of course, fully intentional.[15] Similarly, one may not agree that the facts of destruction mentioned at the beginning of this introduction are sufficient to constitute genocide. Still, other important if somewhat less strident charges against the United States can be made. "Cultural extermination" may be appropriate. (This charge is plausible not only in terms of Mr. Chomsky's claims but on the basis of Mr. McAlister's and Mr. Mus's emphasis in Section IV on the centrality of rural village values in Vietnam before United States intervention.) Or the distant and technological character of our intervention may lead to the following judgments (cast here in the context of a discussion of Cambodia):

> . . . The problem for us Americans, the political and moral problem, is that we are outsiders.
>
> The alien character of our presence in Indochina is symbolized by our use of air power. For it is a means of killing at a distance, without involvement in the society we seek to order. . . .
>
> Without any real political base, without . . . popular support, we . . . use the technology of modern warfare to try to defeat a guerrilla enemy. The result can only be to antagonize the people. . . .
>
> The American government has decided that Cambodians are better off dead than red. For sheer colonial arrogance, that rivals the best that Cecil Rhodes or Cortes could produce.[16]

The three articles in this section cover a wide variety of issues and arguments connected with genocide. Jean-Paul Sartre's essay is the most clear-cut, "radical" and far-reaching statement of the charge. Noam Chomsky presents a slightly different version of the argument and provides many factual details. Mr. Ramsey's vigorous defense of United States policy against any such accusation deals explicitly with some of the more conceptual problems to which I have called attention.

Notes

1 Figures cited by Frank Mankiewicz and Tom Braden in their syndicated column, *The Nashville Tennessean*, July 22, 1970, p. 9.

2 These statistics, from Defense Department sources, were published in the April-May 1969 and May 1970 newsletters of Clergy and Laymen Concerned about Vietnam. In addition they note that International Voluntary Services adds another 1,000,000 uncounted refugees to the 2,000,000 total. The 130,000 ton per month bombing rate in March 1969 is cited by Noam Chomsky, p. 73. The defoliation figures may be ambiguous: the same acre of land defoliated at two different times will show in statistics as two acres.

3 This is impossible to quantify; Noam Chomsky tries to describe some of it in his article, pp.77-78.

4 See here G.E.M. Anscombe, "War and Murder," in Richard A. Wasserstrom (ed.), *War and Morality*, p. 51.

5 Sartre, p. 59.

6 A more detailed outline of this kind of analysis of the war can be found in the selection by Carl Oglesby in Section IV.

7 Anscombe, "War and Murder," p. 46.

8 Ramsey, pp. 110-112.

9 So claims, e.g., Miss Anscombe in "War and Murder," p. 51.

10 Note that criminal law conceives all "homicide" to be "willful," yet has classifications for "justifiable" and "excusable homicide."

11 Little, p. 12; Ramsey, pp. 100-101, 103, 105.

12 Chomsky, p. 78.

13 Ramsey, p. 94; ". . . action in its primary (objective) thrust as well as its subjective purpose. . . ."

14 Anscombe, "War and Murder," p. 51.

15 Wasserstrom, "On the Morality of War," in Wasserstrom (ed.), *War and Morality*, p. 96.

16 Anthony Lewis, column syndicated through the *New York Times* News Service, June 28, 1970.

On Genocide*

by Jean-Paul Sartre

The word "genocide" is relatively new. It was coined by the jurist
Raphael Lemkin between the two world wars. But the fact of genocide
is as old as humanity. To this day there has been no society protected
by its structure from committing that crime. Every case of genocide
is a product of history and bears the stamp of the society which has
given birth to it. The one we have before us for judgment is the act
of the greatest capitalist power in the world today. It is as such that
we must try to analyze it—in other words, as the simultaneous expression
of the economic infrastructure of that power, its political objectives and
the contradictions of its present situation.

In particular, we must try to understand the genocidal intent in the
war which the American government is waging against Vietnam, for
Article 2 of the 1948 Geneva Convention defines genocide on the basis
of intent; the Convention was tacitly referring to memories which were
still fresh. Hitler had proclaimed it his deliberate intent to exterminate
the Jews. He made genocide a political means and did not hide it. A
Jew had to be put to death, whoever he was, not for having been caught
carrying a weapon or for having joined a resistance movement, but
simply *because he was a Jew*. The American government has avoided
making such clear statements. It has even claimed that it was answering
the call of its allies, the South Vietnamese, who had been attacked
by the Communists. It is possible for us, by studying the facts objectively,
to discover implicit in them such a genocidal intention? And after such
an investigation, can we say that the armed forces of the United States
are killing Vietnamese in Vietnam for the simple reason that they are
Vietnamese?

This is something that can only be established after an historical
examination: the structure of war changes right along with the infra-
structures of society. Between 1860 and the present day, the meaning
and the objectives of military conflicts have changed profoundly, the
final stage of this metamorphosis being precisely the "war of example"
which the United States is waging in Vietnam. . . .During the First World
War a genocidal intent appeared only sporadically. As in previous centuries, the essential aim was to crush the military power of the enemy

*Originally printed in *Ramparts,* February, 1968. Copyright Ramparts Magazine, Inc., 1968.
By permission of the editors.

Moral Argument and the War in Vietnam

and only secondarily to ruin his economy. But even though there was no longer any clear distinction between civilians and soldiers, it was still only rarely (except for a few terrorist raids) that the civilian population was expressly made a target. Moreover, the belligerent nations (or at least those who were doing the fighting) were industrial powers. This made for a certain initial balance: against the possibility of any real extermination each side had its own deterrent force—namely the power of applying the law of "an eye for an eye." This explains why, in the midst of the carnage, a kind of prudence was maintained.

However, since 1830, throughout the last century and continuing to this very day, there have been countless acts of genocide whose causes are likewise to be found in the structure of capitalist societies. To export their products and their capital, the great powers, particularly England and France, set up colonial empires. The name "overseas possessions" given by the French to their conquests indicates clearly that they had been able to acquire them only by wars of aggression. The adversary was sought out in his own territory, in Africa and Asia, in the underdeveloped countries, and far from waging "total war" (which would have required an initial balance of forces), the colonial powers, because of their overwhelming superiority of firepower, found it necessary to commit only an expeditionary force. Victory was easy, at least in conventional military terms. But since this blatant aggression kindled the hatred of the civilian population, and since civilians were potentially rebels and soldiers, the colonial troops maintained their authority by terror—by perpetual massacre. These massacres were genocidal in character; they aimed at the destruction of "a part of an ethnic, national, or religious group" in order to terrorize the remainder and to wrench apart the indigenous society.

After the bloodbath of conquest in Algeria during the last century, the French imposed the *Code Civil*, with its middle-class conceptions of property and inheritance, on a tribal society where each community held land in common. Thus they systematically destroyed the economic infrastructure of the country, and tribes of peasants soon saw their lands fall into the hands of French speculators. Indeed, colonization is not a matter of mere conquest as was the German annexation of Alsace-Lorraine; it is by its very nature an act of cultural genocide. Colonization cannot take place without systematically liquidating all the characteristics of the native society—and simultaneously refusing to integrate the natives into the mother country and denying them access to its advantages. Colonialism is, after all, an economic system: the colony sells its raw material and agricultural products at a reduced price to the colonizing power. The latter, in return, sells its manufactured goods to the colony at world market prices. This curious system of trade is only possible if there is a colonial subproletariat which can be forced to work for starvation wages. For the subject people this inevitably means the extinction of their national character, culture, customs, sometimes even language. They live in their underworld of misery like dark phantoms ceaselessly reminded of their subhumanity.

However, their value as an almost unpaid labor force protects them, to a certain extent, against physical genocide. The Nuremberg Tribunal was still fresh in people's minds when the French massacred 45,000 Algerians at Setif, as an "example." But this sort of thing was so commonplace that no one even thought to condemn the French government in the same terms as they did the Nazis.

But this "deliberate destruction of a part of a national group" could not be carried out any more extensively, without harming the interests of the French settlers. By exterminating the subproletariat, they would have exterminated themselves as settlers. This explains the contradictory attitude of these *pieds-noirs* during the Algerian war: they urged the Army to commit massacres, and more than one of them dreamed of total genocide. At the same time they attempted to compel the Algerians to "fraternize" with them. It is because France could neither liquidate the Algerian people nor integrate them with the French that it lost the Algerian war.

These observations enable us to understand how the structure of colonial wars underwent a transformation after the end of the Second World War. For it was at about this time that the colonial peoples, enlightened by that conflict and its impact on the "empires," and later by the victory of Mao Tse-tung, resolved to regain their national independence. The characteristics of the struggle were determined from the beginning: the colonialists had the superiority in weapons, the indigenous population the advantage of numbers. Even in Algeria—a colony where there was settlement as much as there was exploitation—the proportion of *colons* to natives was one to nine. During the two world wars, many of the colonial peoples had been trained as soldiers and had become experienced fighters. However, the short supply and poor quality of their arms—at least in the beginning—kept the number of fighting units low. These objective conditions dictated their strategy, too: terrorism, ambushes, harassing the enemy, extreme mobility of the combat groups which had to strike unexpectedly and disappear at once. This was made possible only by the support of the entire population. Hence the famous symbiosis between the liberation forces and the masses of people: the former everywhere organizing agrarian reforms, political organs and education; the latter supporting, feeding and hiding the soldiers of the army of liberation, and replenishing its ranks with their sons.

It is no accident that people's war, with its principles, its strategy, its tactics and its theoreticians, appeared at the very moment that the industrial powers pushed total war to the ultimate by the industrial production of atomic fission. Nor is it any accident that it brought about the destruction of colonialism. The contradiction which led to the victory of the FLN in Algeria was characteristic of that time; people's war sounded the death-knell of conventional warfare at exactly the same moment as the hydrogen bomb. Against partisans supported by the entire population, the colonial armies were helpless. They had only one way of escaping this demoralizing harassment which threatened to culminate in a Dien Bien Phu, and that was to "empty the sea of its water"—i.e., the civilian population. And, in fact, the colonial soldiers soon learned that their most redoubtable foes were the silent, stubborn peasants who, just one kilometer from the scene of the ambush which had wiped out a regiment, knew nothing, had seen nothing. And since it was the unity of an entire people which held the conventional army at bay, the only anti-guerrilla strategy which could work was the destruction of this people, in other words, of civilians, of women and children. Torture and genocide: that was the answer of the colonial powers to the revolt of the subject peoples. And that answer, as we know, was worthless unless it was thorough and total. The populace—resolute, united by the politicized and fierce partisan army—was no longer to be cowed as in the good old days of colonialism, by an "admonitory" massacre which was supposed to serve "as an example." On the contrary, this only augmented the people's hate. Thus it was no longer a question of intimidating the populace, but rather of physically liquidating it. And since that was not possible without concurrently liquidating the colonial economy and the whole colonial system, the settlers panicked, the colonial powers got tired of pouring men and money into an interminable conflict, the mass of the people in the mother country opposed the continuation of an inhuman war, and the colonies became sovereign states.

There have been cases, however, in which the genocidal response to people's war is not checked by infrastructural contradictions. Then total genocide emerges as the absolute basis of an anti-guerrilla strategy. And under certain conditions it even emerges as the explicit objective—sought either immediately or by degrees. This is precisely what is happening in the Vietnam War. We are dealing here with a new stage in the development of imperialism, a stage usually called neocolonialism because it is characterized by aggression against a former colony which has already gained its independence, with the aim of subjugating it anew to colonial rule. With the beginning of independence, the neocolonialists take care to finance a *putsch or coup d'état* so that the new heads of state do not represent the interests of the masses but those of a narrow privileged strata, and, consequently, of foreign capital.

Ngo Dinh Diem appeared—hand-picked, maintained and armed by the United States. He proclaimed his decision to reject the Geneva Agreements and to constitute the Vietnamese territory to the south of the seventeenth parallel as an independent state. What followed was the necessary consequence of these premises: a police force and an army were created to hunt down people who had fought against the French, and who now felt thwarted of their victory, a sentiment which automatically marked them as enemies of the new regime. In short, it was the reign of terror which provoked a new uprising in the South and rekindled the people's war.

Did the United States ever imagine that Diem could nip the revolt in the bud? In any event, they lost no time in sending in experts and then troops, and then they were involved in the conflict up to their necks. And we find once again almost the same pattern of war as the one that Ho Chi Minh fought against the French, except that at first the American government declared that it was only sending its troops out of generosity, to fulfill its obligations to an ally.

That is the outward appearance. But looking deeper, these two successive wars are essentially different in character: the United States, unlike France, has no economic interests in Vietnam. American firms have made some investments, but not so much that they couldn't be sacrificed, if necessary, without troubling the American nation as a whole or really hurting the monopolies. Moreover, since the U.S. government is not waging the war for reasons of a *directly* economic nature, there is nothing to stop it from ending the war by the ultimate tactic—in other words, by genocide. This is not to say that there is proof that the U.S. does in fact envision genocide, but simply that nothing prevents the U.S. from envisaging it.

In fact, according to the Americans themselves, the conflict has two objectives. Just recently, Dean Rusk stated: "We are defending ourselves." It is no longer Diem, the ally whom the Americans are generously helping out: it is the United States itself which is in danger in Saigon. Obviously, this means that the first objective is a military one: to encircle Communist China. Therefore, the United States will not let Southeast Asia escape. It has put its men in power in Thailand, it controls two-thirds of Laos and threatens to invade Cambodia. But these conquests will be hollow if it finds itself confronted by a free and unified Vietnam with 32 million inhabitants. That is why the military leaders like to talk in terms of "key positions." That is why Dean Rusk says, with unintentional humor, that the armed forces of the United States are fighting in Vietnam "in order to avoid a third world war." Either this phrase is meaningless, or else it must be taken to mean: "in order to *win* this third conflict." In short, the first objective is dictated by the necessity of establishing a Pacific line of defense, something which is necessary only in the context of the general policies of imperialism.

The second objective is an economic one. In October 1966, General Westmoreland defined it as follows: "We are fighting the war in Vietnam to show that guerrilla warfare does not pay." To show whom? The Vietnamese? That would be very surprising. Must so many human lives and so much money be wasted merely to teach a lesson to a nation of poor peasants thousands of miles from San Francisco? And, in particular, what need was there to attack them, provoke them into

Moral Argument and the War in Vietnam

fighting and subsequently to go about crushing them, when the big American companies have only negligible interests in Vietnam? West-moreland's statement, like Rusk's, has to be filled in. The Americans want to show others that guerrilla war does not pay; they want to show all the oppressed and exploited nations that might be tempted to shake off the American yoke by launching a people's war, at first against their own pseudo-governments, the compradors and the army, then against the U.S. "Special Forces," and finally against the GIs. In short, they want to show Latin America first of all, and more generally, all of the Third World. To Che Guevara who said, "We need several Vietnams," the American government answers, "They will all be crushed the way we are crushing the first."

In other words, this war has above all an admonitory value, as an example for three and perhaps four continents. (After all, Greece is a peasant nation too. A dictatorship has just been set up there; it is good to give the Greeks a warning: submit or face extermination.) This genocidal example is addressed to the whole of humanity. By means of this warning, 6 percent of mankind hopes to succeed in controlling the other 94 percent at a reasonably low cost in money and effort. Of course it would be preferable, for propaganda purposes, if the Vietnam-ese would submit before being exterminated. But it is not certain that the situation wouldn't be clearer if Vietnam *were* wiped off the map. Otherwise someone might think that Vietnam's submission had been attributable to some *avoidable* weakness. But if these peasants do not weaken for an instant, and if the price they pay for their heroism is *inevitable* death, the guerrillas of the future will be all the more discour-aged.

At this point in our demonstration, three facts are established: (1) What the U.S. government wants is to have a base against China and to set an example. (2) The first objective *can* be achieved, without any difficulty (except, of course, for the resistance of the Vietnamese), by wiping out a whole people and imposing the Pax Americana on an uninhabited Vietnam. (3) To achieve the second, the U.S. *must* carry out, at least in part, this extermination.

The declarations of American statesmen are not as candid as Hitler's were in his day. But candor is not essential to us here. It is enough that the facts speak; the speeches which come with them are believed only by the American people. The rest of the world understands well enough: governments which are the friends of the United States keep silent; the others denounce this genocide. The Americans try to reply that these unproved accusations only show these governments' partial-ity. "In fact," the American government says, "all we have ever done is to offer the Vietnamese, North and South, the option of ceasing their aggression or being crushed." It is scarcely necessary to mention that this offer is absurd, since it is the Americans who commit the aggression and consequently they are the only ones who can put an end to it.

But this absurdity is not undeliberate: the Americans are ingeniously formulating, without appearing to do so, a demand which the Vietnamese cannot satisfy. They do offer an alternative: Declare you are beaten or we will bomb you back to the stone age. But the fact remains that the second term of this alternative is genocide. They have said: "genocide, yes, but *conditional* genocide." Is this juridically valid? Is it even conceivable?

If the proposition made any juridical sense at all, the U.S. government might narrowly escape the accusation of genocide. But the 1948 Convention leaves no such loopholes: an act of genocide, especially if it is carried out over a period of several years, is no less genocide for being blackmail. The perpetrator may declare he will stop if the victim gives in; this is still—without any juridical doubt whatsoever—a genocide. And this is all the more true when, as is the case here, a good part of the group has been annihilated to force the rest to give in.

But let us look at this more closely and examine the nature of the two terms of the alternative. In the South, the choice is the following: villages burned, the populace subjected to massive bombing, livestock shot, vegetation destroyed by defoliants, crops ruined by toxic aerosols, and everywhere indiscriminate shooting, murder, rape and looting. This is genocide in the strictest sense: massive extermination. The other option: what is *it*? What are the Vietnamese people supposed to do to escape this horrible death? Join the armed forces of Saigon or be enclosed in strategic or today's "New Life" hamlets, two names for the same concentration camps?

We know about these camps from numerous witnesses. They are fenced in by barbed wire. Even the most elementary needs are denied: there is malnutrition and a total lack of hygiene. The prisoners are heaped together in small tents or sheds. The social structure is destroyed. Husbands are separated from their wives, mothers from their children; family life, so important to the Vietnamese, no longer exists. As families are split up, the birth rate falls; any possibility of religious or cultural life is suppressed; even work—the work which might permit people to maintain themselves and their families—is refused them. These unfortunate people are not even slaves (slavery did not prevent the Negroes in the United States from developing a rich culture); they are reduced to a living heap of vegetable existence. When, sometimes, a fragmented family group is freed—children with an elder sister or a young mother—it goes to swell the ranks of the subproletariat in the big cities; the elder sister or the mother, with no job and mouths to feed, reaches the last stage of her degradation in prostituting herself to the GIs.

The camps I describe are but another kind of genocide, equally condemned by the 1948 Convention:

"Causing serious bodily or mental harm to members of the group.

"Deliberately inflicting on the group conditions of life calculated to bring about its physical destruction in whole or in part.

Moral Argument and the War in Vietnam

"Imposing measures intended to prevent births within the group.

"Forcibly transferring children of the group to another group."

In other words, it is not true that the choice is between death or submission. For submission, in those circumstances, is submission to genocide. Let us say that a choice must be made between a violent and immediate death and a slow death from mental and physical degradation. Or, if you prefer, *there is no choice at all.*

Is it any different for the North?

One choice is *extermination*. Not just the daily risk of death, but the systematic destruction of the economic base of the country: from the dikes to the factories, nothing will be left standing. Deliberate attacks against civilians and, in particular, the rural population. Systematic destruction of hospitals, schools and places of worship. An all-out campaign to destroy the achievements of twenty years of socialism. The purpose may be only to intimidate the populace. But this can only be achieved by the daily extermination of an ever larger part of the group. So this intimidation itself in its psychosocial consequence is a genocide. Among the children in particular it must be engendering psychological disorders which will for years, if not permanently, "cause serious . . . mental harm."

The other choice is *capitulation*. This means that the North Vietnamese must declare themselves ready to stand by and watch while their country is divided and the Americans impose a direct or indirect dictatorship on their compatriots, in fact on members of their own families from whom the war has separated them. And would this intolerable humiliation bring an end to the war? This is far from certain. The National Liberation Front and the Democratic Republic of Vietnam, although fraternally united, have different strategies and tactics because their war situations are different. If the NLF continued the struggle, American bombs would go on blasting the DRV whether it capitulated or not.

If the war were to cease, the United States—according to official statements—would feel very generously inclined to help in the reconstruction of the DRV, and we know exactly what this means. It means that the United States would destroy, through private investments and conditional loans, the whole economic base of socialism. And this too is genocide. They would be splitting a sovereign country in half, occupying one of the halves by a reign of terror and keeping the other half under control by economic pressure. The "national group" Vietnam would not be physically eliminated, yet it would no longer exist. Economically, politically and culturally it would be suppressed.

In the North as in the South, the choice is only between two types of liquidation: collective death or dismemberment. The American government has had ample opportunity to test the resistance of the NLF and the DRV: by now it knows that only total destruction will be effective. The Front is stronger than ever; North Vietnam is unshakable. For this very reason, the calculated extermination of the Vietnamese people cannot really be intended to make them capitulate. The Americans offer them a *paix des braves* knowing full well that they will not accept it. And this phony alternative hides the true goal of imperialism, which is to reach, step by step, the highest stage of escalation—total genocide. Of course, the United States government *could have* tried to reach this stage in one jump and wipe out Vietnam in a *Blitzkrieg* against the whole country. But this extermination first required setting up complicated installations—for instance, creating and maintaining air bases in Thailand which would shorten the bombing runs by 3000 miles.

Meanwhile, the major *purpose* of "escalation" was, and still is, to prepare international opinion for genocide. From this point of view, Americans have succeeded only too well. The repeated and systematic bombings of populated areas of Haiphong and Hanoi, which two years ago would have raised violent protests in Europe, occur today in a climate of general indifference resulting perhaps more from catatonia than from apathy. The tactic has borne its fruit; public opinion now sees escalation as a slowly and continuously increasing pressure to bargain, while in reality it is the preparation of minds for the final geno-cide. Is such a genocide possible? No. But that is due to the Vietnamese and the Vietnamese alone; to their courage, and to the remarkable efficiency of their organization. As for the United States government, it cannot be absolved of its crime just because its victim has enough intelligence and enough heroism to limit its effects.

We may conclude that in the face of a people's war (the characteristic product of our times, the answer to imperialism and the demand for sovereignty of a people conscious of its unity) there are two possible responses: either the aggressor withdraws, he acknowledges that a whole nation confronts him, and he makes peace; or else he recognizes the inefficacy of conventional strategy, and, if he can do so without jeopardizing his interests, he resorts to extermination pure and simple. There is no third alternative, but making peace is still at least *possible*.

But as the armed forces of the U.S.A. entrench themselves firmly in Vietnam, as they intensify the bombing and the massacres, as they try to bring Laos under their control, as they plan the invasion of Cambodia, there is less and less doubt that the government of the United States, despite its hypocritical denials, has chosen genocide.

The genocidal intent is implicit in the facts. It is necessarily premeditated. Perhaps in bygone times, in the midst of tribal wars, acts of genocide were perpetrated on the spur of the moment in fits of passion. But the anti-guerrilla genocide which our times have produced requires organization, military bases, a structure of accomplices, budget appropriations. Therefore, its authors must meditate and plan out their act. Does this mean that they are thoroughly conscious of their intentions? It is impossible to decide. We would have to plumb the depths of their consciences—and the Puritan bad faith of Americans works wonders. . . .

Young American men use torture (even including the "field telephone

Moral Argument and the War in Vietnam

treatment"*), they shoot unarmed women for nothing more than target practice, they kick wounded Vietnamese in the genitals, they cut ears off dead men to take home for trophies. Officers are the worst: a general boasted of hunting "VCs" from his helicopter and gunning them down in the rice paddies. Obviously, these were not NLF soldiers who knew how to defend themselves; they were peasants tending their rice. In the confused minds of the American soldiers, "Viet Cong" and "Vietnamese" tend increasingly to blend into one another. They often say themselves, "The only good Vietnamese is a dead Vietnamese," or what amounts to the same thing, "A dead Vietnamese is a Viet Cong."

For example: south of the seventeenth parallel, peasants prepare to harvest their rice. American soldiers arrive on the scene, set fire to their houses and want to transfer them to a strategic hamlet. The peasants protest. What else can they do, bare-handed against these Martians? They say: "The quality of the rice is good; we want to stay to eat our rice." Nothing more. But this is enough to irritate the young Yankees: "It's the Viet Cong who put that into your head; they are the ones who have taught you to resist." These soldiers are so misled that they take the feeble protests which their own violence has aroused for "subversive" resistance. At the outset, they were probably disappointed; they came to save Vietnam from "Communist aggressors." But they soon had to realize that the Vietnamese did not want them. Their attractive role as liberators changed to that of occupation troops. For the soldiers it was the first glimmering of consciousness. "We are unwanted, we have no business here." But they go no further. They simply tell themselves that a Vietnamese is by definition suspect.

And from the neocolonialists' point of view, that is true. They vaguely understand that in a people's war, civilians are the only visible enemies. Their frustration turns to hatred of the Vietnamese; racism takes it from there. The soldiers discover with a savage joy that they are there to kill the Vietnamese they had been pretending to save. All of them are potential Communists, as proved by the fact that they hate Americans.

Now we can recognize in those dark and misled souls the truth of the Vietnamese War: it meets all of Hitler's specifications. Hitler killed the Jews because they were Jews. The armed forces of the United States torture and kill men, women and children in Vietnam merely *because they are Vietnamese*. Whatever lies or euphemisms the government may think up, the spirit of genocide is in the minds of the soldiers. This is their way of living out the genocidal situation into which their government has thrown them. As Peter Martinson, a twenty-three-year-old student who had "interrogated" prisoners for ten months and could scarcely live with his memories, said: "I am a middle-class American.

---

* The portable generator for a field telephone is used as an instrument for interrogation by hitching the two lead wires to the victim's genitals and turning the handle *(Ramparts* editor's note).

I look like any other student, yet somehow I am a war criminal." And he was right when he added: "Anyone in my place would have acted as I did." His only mistake was to attribute his degrading crimes to the influence of war *in general.*

No, it is not war in the abstract: it is the greatest power on earth against a poor peasant people. Those who fight it are *living out* the only possible relationship between an over-industrialized country and an underdeveloped country, that is to say, a genocidal relationship implemented through racism—the only relationship, short of picking up and pulling out.

Total war presupposes a certain balance of forces, a certain reciprocity. Colonial wars were not reciprocal, but the interests of the colonialists limited the scope of genocide. The present genocide, the end result of the unequal development of societies, is total war waged to the limit by one side, without the slightest reciprocity.

The American government is not guilty of inventing modern genocide, or even of having chosen it from other possible and effective measures against guerrilla warfare. It is not guilty, for example, of having preferred genocide for strategic and economic reasons. Indeed, genocide presents itself as the *only possible reaction* to the rising of a whole people against its oppressors. The American government is guilty of having preferred, and of still preferring, a policy of war and aggression aimed at total genocide to a policy of peace, the only policy which can really replace the former. A policy of peace would necessarily have required a reconsideration of the objectives imposed on that government by the large imperialist companies through the intermediary of their pressure groups. America is guilty of continuing and intensifying the war despite the fact that every day its leaders realize more acutely, from the reports of the military commanders, that the only way to win is "to free Vietnam of all the Vietnamese." The government is guilty—despite the lessons it has been taught by this unique, unbearable experience—of proceeding at every moment a little further along a path which leads it to the point of no return. And it is guilty—according to its own admissions—of consciously carrying out this admonitory war in order to use genocide as a challenge and a threat to all peoples of the world.

We have seen that one of the features of total war has been the growing scope and efficiency of communication. As early as 1914, war could not longer be "localized." It had to spread throughout the whole world. In 1967, this process is being intensified. The ties of the "One World," on which the United States wants to impose its hegemony, have grown tighter and tighter. For this reason, as the American government very well knows, the current genocide is conceived as an answer to people's war and perpetrated in Vietnam not against the Vietnamese alone, but against humanity.

When a peasant falls in his rice paddy, mowed down by a machine

Moral Argument and the War in Vietnam

gun, every one of us is hit. The Vietnamese fight for all men and the American forces against all. Neither figuratively nor abstractly. And not only because genocide would be a crime universally condemned by international law, but because little by little the whole human race is being subjected to this genocidal blackmail piled on top of atomic blackmail, that is, to absolute, total war. This crime, carried out every day before the eyes of the world, renders all who do not denounce it accomplices of those who commit it, so that we are being degraded today for our future enslavement.

In this sense imperialist genocide can only become more complete. The group which the United States wants to intimidate and terrorize by way of the Vietnamese nation is the human group in its entirety.

After Pinkville*

Noam Chomsky

On October 15, 1965, an estimated 70,000 people took part in large-scale antiwar demonstrations. The demonstrators heard pleas for an end to the bombing of North Vietnam and for a serious commitment to negotiations, in response to the negotiation offers from North Vietnam and United Nations efforts to settle the war. To be more precise, this is what they heard if they heard anything at all. On the Boston Common, for example, they heard not a word from the speakers, who were drowned out by hecklers and counterdemonstrators.

On the Senate floor, Senator Mansfield denounced the "sense of utter irresponsibility" shown by the demonstrators, while Everett Dirksen said the demonstrations were "enough to make any person loyal to his country weep." Richard Nixon wrote, in a letter to *The New York Times*, October 29, that "victory for the Viet Cong . . . would mean ultimately the destruction of freedom of speech for all men for all time not only in Asia but in the United States as well"—nothing less.

In a sense, Senator Mansfield was right in speaking of the sense of utter irresponsibility shown by demonstrators. They should have been demanding, not an end to the bombing of North Vietnam and negotiations, but a complete and immediate withdrawal of all American troops and matériel—an end to any forceful interference in the internal affairs of Vietnam or any other nation. They should not merely have been demanding that the United States adhere to international law and its own treaty obligations—thus removing itself forthwith from Vietnam; but they should also have exercised their right and duty to resist the violence of the state, which was as vicious in practice as it was illegal in principle.

In October 1967, there were, once again, mass demonstrations against the war, this time in Washington and at the Pentagon. A few months earlier, still larger, though less militant, demonstrations had taken place in New York. The Tet offensive, shortly after, revealed that American military strategy was "foolish to the point of insanity."[1] It also revealed to the public that government propaganda was either an illusion or a fraud. Moreover, an international monetary crisis threatened, attributable in part to Vietnam.

Moral Argument and the War in Vietnam

In retrospect, it seems possible that the war could have been ended if popular pressure had been maintained. But many radicals felt that the war was over, that it had become, in any case, a "liberal issue," and they turned to other concerns. Those who had demanded no more than an end to the bombing of North Vietnam and a commitment to negotiations saw their demands being realized, and lapsed into silence.

These demands, however, had always been beside the point. As to negotiations, there is, in fact, very little to negotiate. As long as an American army of occupation remains in Vietnam, the war will continue. Withdrawal of American troops must be a unilateral act, as the invasion of Vietnam by the American government was a unilateral act in the first place. Those who had been calling for "negotiations now" were deluding themselves and others, just as those who now call for a cease-fire that will leave an American expeditionary force in Vietnam are not facing reality.

As to the bombing of North Vietnam, this had always been a side show, in large measure a propaganda cover for the American invasion of the South. The United States government could not admit that it was invading South Vietnam to protect from its own population a government that we had installed. Therefore it was rescuing the South Vietnamese from "aggression." But then surely it must strike at the "source of aggression." Hence the bombing of North Vietnam. This, at least, seems the most rational explanation for the bombing of North Vietnam in February 1965, at a time when no North Vietnamese troops were in the South, so far as was known, and there was a bare trickle of supplies.

To be sure, those who are "in the know" have different explanations for the bombing of North Vietnam. Consider, for example, the explanation offered by Sir Robert Thompson, the British counterinsurgency expert who has been for many years a close adviser of the American army in South Vietnam—a man who is, incidentally, much admired by American social scientists who like to consider themselves "tough-minded, hard-nosed realists," no doubt because of his utter contempt for democracy and his relatively pure colonialist attitudes. In the British newspaper *The Guardian*, May 19, 1969, his views are explained as follows:

> He also condemns the bombing of the North. The United States Air Force in 1965 was having great budgetary problems, because the army was the only one that had a war on its hands and was thus getting all the money. "So the Air Force had to get in, and you had the bombing of North Vietnam . . . the budgetary problems of the Air Force were then solved."

In his *No Exit from Vietnam* (1969), he explains more graphically the attractiveness of air power:

> One can so easily imagine the Commander of the Strategic Air Command

72

striding up and down his operations room wondering how he could get in on the act. With all that power available and an enormous investment doing nothing, it is not surprising that reasons and means had to be found for their engagement. The war was therefore waged in a manner which enabled this massive air armada to be used round the clock. . . . In this way the war could be fought as an American war without the previous frustrations of cooperating with the Vietnamese. [P. 135.]

Or consider the explanation for the bombing of the North offered by Adam Yarmolinsky, Principal Deputy Assistant Secretary of Defense for International Security Affairs, 1965-66, previous Special Assistant to the Secretary of Defense. According to his analysis, the strategic bombing of North Vietnam "produced no military advantages except for its putative favorable impact on morale in the south. But[this step] was taken, at least in part, because it was one of the things that the United States military forces were best prepared to do."[2]

So North Vietnam was flattened and impelled to send troops to the South, as it did a few months after the bombings began, if the Department of Defense can be believed.

Since the bombing of North Vietnam "produced no military advantages" and was extremely costly, it could be stopped with little difficulty and little effect on the American war in South Vietnam. And so it was, in two steps: on April 1, 1968, when the regular bombing was restricted to the southern part of North Vietnam, and on November 1, when it was halted. At the same time, the total American bombing, now restricted to Laos and South Vietnam, was increased in April and increased again in November. By March 1969 the total level of bombardment had reached 130,000 tons a month—nearly two Hiroshimas a week in South Vietnam and Laos, defenseless countries. And Melvin Laird's projection for the next twelve to eighteen months was the same.[3] The redistribution (and intensification) of bombing and the largely empty negotiations stilled domestic protest for a time and permitted the war to go on as before.

We can now look back over the failure of the "peace movement" to sustain and intensify its protest over the past four years. By now, defoliation has been carried out over an area the size of Massachusetts, with what effect no one has any real idea. The bombardment of Vietnam far exceeds the bombardment of Korea or anything in World War II. The number of Vietnamese killed or driven from their homes cannot be seriously estimated.

It is important to understand that the massacre of the rural population of Vietnam and their forced evacuation is not an accidental by-product of the war. Rather it is of the very essence of American strategy. The theory behind it has been explained with great clarity and explicitness, for example by Professor Samuel Huntington, Chairman of the Government Department of Harvard and at the time (1968) Chairman of the Council on Vietnamese Studies of the Southeast Asia Development

Moral Argument and the War in Vietnam

Advisory Group. Writing in *Foreign Affairs,* he explains that the Viet Cong is "a powerful force which cannot be dislodged from its constituency so long as the constituency continues to exist." The conclusion is obvious, and he does not shrink from it. We can ensure that the constituency ceases to exist by " 'direct application of mechanical and conventional power' . . . on such a massive scale as to produce a massive migration from countryside to city," where the Viet Cong constituency—the rural population—can, it is hoped, be controlled in refugee camps and suburban slums around Saigon.

Technically, the process is known as "urbanization" or "modernization." It is described, with the proper contempt, by Daniel Ellsberg, a Department of Defense consultant on pacification in South Vietnam, who concludes, from his extensive on-the-spot observations, that "we have, of course, demolished the society of Vietnam," that "the bombing of the South has gone on long enough to disrupt the society of South Vietnam enormously and probably permanently"; he speaks of the "people who have been driven to Saigon by what Huntington regards as our 'modernizing instruments' in Vietnam, bombs and artillery."[4] Reporters have long been aware of the nature of these tactics, aware that "by now the sheer weight of years of firepower, massive sweeps, and grand forced population shifts have reduced the population base of the NLF,"[5] so that conceivably, by brute force, we may still hope to "win."

One thing is clear: so long as an organized social life can be maintained in South Vietnam, the NLF will be a powerful, probably dominant force. This is the dilemma which has always plagued American policy, and which has made it impossible for us to permit even the most rudimentary democratic institutions in South Vietnam. For these reasons we have been forced to the solution outlined by Professor Huntington: to crush the people's war, we must eliminate the people.

A second thing is tolerably clear: there has been no modification in this policy. Once again, as two years ago, there is mounting popular protest against the war. Once again, a tactical adjustment is being devised that will permit Washington to pursue its dual goal, to pacify the people of South Vietnam while pacifying the American people also. The first of these tasks has not been accomplished too well. The second, to our shame, has been managed quite successfully, for the most part. Now we hear that the burden of fighting the war is to be shifted away from the American infantry to the B-52s and fighter-bombers and a mercenary force of Vietnamese. Only a token force of between 200,000 and 300,000 men, backed by the Pacific Naval and Air Command, will be retained, indefinitely, to ensure that the Vietnamese have the right of self-determination.

At a recent press conference, Averell Harriman explained that the North Vietnamese cannot believe that we really intend to abandon the huge military bases we have constructed in Vietnam, such as the one

74

at Cam Ranh Bay (*Village Voice*, November 27, 1969). Knowledgeable American observers have found it equally difficult to believe this. For example, as long ago as August 27, 1965, James Reston wrote in *The New York Times*:

> The United States bases and supply areas are being constructed on a scale far larger than is necessary to care for the present level of American forces . . . In fact, the United States base at Cam Ranh . . . is being developed into another Okinawa, not merely for the purposes of this war, but as a major power complex from which American officials hope a wider alliance of Asian nations, with the help of the United States, will eventually be able to contain the expansion of China.

The phrase "contain the expansion of China" must be understood as code for the unpronounceable expression, "repress movements for national independence and social reconstruction in Southeast Asia."

Premier Eisaku Sato, in a speech described by American officials as part of a joint Japanese-American policy statement, announced that we are entering a "new Pacific age" in which "a new order will be created by Japan and the United States" (*New York Times*, November 22, 1969). His words, one must assume, were chosen advisedly. To perpetuate this new order we will need military bases such as that at Cam Ranh Bay, which can play the role of the Canal Zone in the Western Hemisphere. There we can base our own forces and train those of our loyal dependencies.

We will no doubt soon proceed to construct an "Inter-Asian" army that can protect helpless governments from their own populations, much as the Brazilians were called in to legitimize our Dominican intervention. Where popular rebellion is in progress, these forces can gain valuable experience. Thus a senior American officer at Camp Bearcat in South Vietnam, where Thai units are based, explains that "they are infusing their army with experience they could never get in their own homeland . . . They are coordinating their own piece of real estate." And a Thai colonel adds: "If my country ever has the same subversion, I'll have to fight there. I want to practice here." (*New York Times*, December 3, 1969). Surely Reston was right in 1965 in speculating about our long-range plans for the South Vietnamese bases, from which our "token force" of a quarter of a million men will operate in the seventies.[6]

Who can complain about a quarter of a million men, a force that can be compared, let us say, with the Japanese army of 160,000 which invaded north China in 1937, in an act of aggression that scandalized the civilized world and set the stage for the Pacific phase of World War II? In fact, counterinsurgency experts like Sir Robert Thompson have long argued that the American forces were far too large to be effective, and have advocated a "low-cost, long-haul strategy" of a sort which will now very likely be adopted by the Nixon administration, if,

Moral Argument and the War in Vietnam

once again, the American people will trust their leaders and settle into passivity.

As American combat troops are withdrawn, their place, it is hoped, will be taken by a more effective force of Vietnamese—just as Czechoslovakia is controlled, it is reported, by fewer than 100,000 Russian troops. Meanwhile, the war will no doubt be escalated technologically. It will become more "capital intensive." [7] Some of the prospects were revealed in a speech by Chief of Staff William Westmoreland, reported in the *Christian Science Monitor* (October 27, 1969) under the heading: "Technologically the Vietnam War has been a great success." General Westmoreland "sees machines carrying more and more of the burden." He says:

> I see an army built into and around an integrated area control system that exploits the advanced technology of communications, sensors, fire direction, and the required automatic data processing—a system that is sensitive to the dynamics of the ever-changing battlefield—a system that materially assists the tactical commander in making sound and timely decisions.

Further details are presented by Leonard Sullivan, Deputy Director of Research and Development for Southeast Asian Matters:[8]

> These developments open up some very exciting horizons as to what we can do five or ten years from now: When one realizes that we can detect anything that perspires, moves, carries metal, makes a noise, or is hotter or colder than its surroundings, one begins to see the potential. This is the beginning of instrumentation of the entire battlefield. Eventually, we will be able to tell when anybody shoots, what he is shooting at, and where he was shooting from. You begin to get a "Year 2000" vision of an electronic map with little lights that flash for different kinds of activity. This is what we require for this "porous" war, where the friendly and the enemy are all mixed together.

Note the time scale that is projected for Vietnam. News reports reveal some of the early stages of these exciting developments. The *Times* November 22, 1969 (city edition), reports a plan to use remote-controlled unmanned aircraft as supply transports for combat areas. On October 1, the *Times* explains that:

> The landscape of Vietnam and the border regions are studded with electronic sensors that beep information into the banks of computers. Radar, cameras, infrared detectors and a growing array of more exotic devices contribute to the mass of information. Not long ago reconnaissance planes began carrying television cameras.

The data go into the Combined Intelligence Center near Tan Son Nhut

Air Base: "Day and night in its antiseptic interior a family of blinking, whirring computers devours, digests and spews out a Gargantuan diet of information about the enemy," the better to serve the "conglomerate of allied civil and military organizations that work together to destroy the Vietcong's underground government"—freely admitted to have been the most authentic popular social structure in South Vietnam prior to the American effort to demolish the society of Vietnam. One can understand the gloating of Douglas Pike: "The tactics that delivered victory in the Viet Minh war, however impressive once, had been relegated by science to the military history textbook."[9]

What this means is, to put it simply, that we intend to turn the land of Vietnam into an automated murder machine. The techniques of which Westmoreland, Sullivan, and Pike are so proud are, of course, designed for use against a special kind of enemy: one who is too weak to retaliate, whose land can be occupied. These "Year 2000" devices, which Westmoreland describes as a quantum jump in warfare, are fit only for colonial wars. There is surely an element of lunacy in this technocratic nightmare. And if we are still at all capable of honesty, we will, with little difficulty, identify its antecedents.

Our science may yet succeed in bringing to reality the fears of Bernard Fall—no alarmist, and fundamentally in favor of the war during its early years—who wrote in one of his last essays that "Vietnam as a cultural and historic entity . . . is threatened with extinction . . . the countryside literally dies under the blows of the largest military machine ever unleashed on an area of this size." The South Vietnamese minister of information wrote in 1968 that ordinary Vietnamese would continue "to be horrified and embittered at the way the Americans fight their war. . . . Our peasants will remember their cratered rice fields and defoliated forests, devastated by an alien air force that seems at war with the very land of Vietnam."[10]

American reporters have told us the same thing so often that it is almost superfluous to quote. Tom Buckley—to mention only the most recent—describes the delta and the central lowlands:

. . . bomb craters beyond counting, the dead gray and black fields, forests that have been defoliated and scorched by napalm, land that has been plowed flat to destroy Vietcong hiding places. And everywhere can be seen the piles of ashes forming the outlines of huts and houses, to show where hamlets once stood.[11]

The truth about defoliants is only beginning to emerge, with the discovery that one of the two primary agents used is "potentially dangerous, but needing further study" while the other causes cancer and birth defects, and probably mental retardation. Both will continue to be used in Vietnam against enemy "training and regroupment centers"—i.e., anywhere we please, throughout the countryside.[12]

Moral Argument and the War in Vietnam

Of course it may be argued that the American government did not know, in 1961, that these agents were so dangerous. That is true. It was merely an experiment. Virtually nothing was known about what the effects might be. Perhaps there would be no ill effects, or perhaps—at the other extreme—Vietnam would become unfit for human life, or a race of mutants and mental retardates would be created. How could we know, without trying? In such ways "the tactics that delivered victory in the Viet Minh war, however impressive once, had been relegated by science to the military history textbook."

To see what may lie ahead, I'd like to turn away from Vietnam to a less familiar case. It has been claimed that Vietnam is the second most heavily bombarded country in history. The most intensively bombarded, so it seems, is Laos. According to *Le Monde*, "North Vietnam was more heavily bombed than Korea; Laos is now being bombed even more than North Vietnam. And this battering has been going on for over five years. . . . The United States Air Force carries out more than 12,500 raids a month." [13] On the same day, October 1, 1969, *The New York Times* announced its discovery that in Laos, "the rebel economy and social fabric" are now the main target of the American bombardment, which is claimed to be a success:

Refugees from the Plaine des Jarres area say that during recent months most open spaces have been evacuated. Both civilians and soldiers have retreated into the forests or hills and frequently spend most of the daylight hours in caves or tunnels. Refugees said they could only plow their fields at night because they were unsafe during the day. "So long as the United States bombing continues at its new level," a European diplomat said here this week, "so-called Communist territory is little but a shooting range." The bombing, by creating refugees, deprives the Communists of their chief source of food and transport. The population of the Pathet Lao zone has been declining for several years and the Pathet Lao .find it increasingly difficult to fight a "people's war" with fewer and fewer people.

The world's most advanced society has found the answer to people's war: eliminate the people.

It is, incidentally, remarkable that the *Times* can so blandly announce that the rebel economy and social fabric are the main target of the American bombardment. It is remarkable that this claim, which, if correct, sets American policy at the moral level of Nazi Germany, can be merely noted in a casual comment, with—so far as I know—no public reaction of horror and indignation.

Still, it is good that the American press has discovered that the rebel economy, and social fabric are the target of the American bombardment of Laos. Perhaps we will be spared the pretense that our targets are steel and concrete, or that the bombing is "the most restrained in modern warfare" (as McGeorge Bundy so elegantly put it at the time when virtually every structure in North Vietnam, outside of the centers of Hanoi and Haiphong, was being demolished).

The discovery had been mysteriously delayed. For example, in July 1968 the Southeast Asia expert of *Le Monde*, Jacques Decornoy, published detailed reports of his visits to the liberated areas of Laos: ". . . a world without noise, for the surrounding villages have disappeared, the inhabitants themselves living hidden in the mountains . . . it is dangerous to lean out at any time of the night or day" because of the ceaseless bombardment which leads to "the scientific destruction of the areas held by the enemy." "The Americans are trying to 'break' the Laotian Left, both psychologically and, if possible, physically." The nature of their relentless attack "can only be explained if the target is the central administration of the Neo Lao Hak Sat"—the political organization that won handily in 1958 in the only unrigged election in Laos. This electoral victory inspired the American effort at subversion that led to the Laotian crises of the early sixties, which still persists.

Decornoy describes "the motionless ruins and deserted houses" of the central town of Sam Neua district:

> The first real raid against the population center itself was launched on February 19, 1965. Very serious attacks were made on it quite recently on March 17 and 19, 1968. . . . The two ends of the town were razed to the ground. The old ruins of 1965 have disappeared, those of March 1968 were still "smoking" when we visited them. Branches of trees lay all along the length of the river, houses were totally burned out (phosphorus had been used). At the other end of Sam Neua, the sight was even more painful. Everywhere enormous craters; the church and many houses were demolished. In order to reach the people who might be living there, the Americans dropped their all-too-famous fragmentation bombs. Here lay a "mother bomb" disembowelled, by the side of the road. All round, over a dozen meters, the earth was covered with "daughter bombs," little machines that the Vietnamese know well, unexploded and hiding hundreds of steel splinters. . . . One of the officials of Sam Neua district told us that between February 1965 and March 1968, 65 villages had been destroyed. A number impossible to verify in a short report, but it is a fact that between Sam Neua and a place about 30 kilometers away where we stayed, no house in the villages and hamlets had been spared. Bridges had been destroyed, fields up to the rivers were holed with bomb craters.

Decornoy reports that "American raids on 'liberated Laos' began in May 1964, therefore well before the Gulf of Tonkin incident (August 1964) and the policy of escalation to North Vietnam (spring 1965). Under these circumstances, Laos has, in some ways, served as a testing ground or experimental site." He describes the amazing persistence of the Laotians in maintaining and advancing the social revolution in the face

Moral Argument and the War in Vietnam

of this attack, their "virulent nationalism" and refusal to follow foreign models, the schools and factories in caves, the prosperity of the rare villages that have still, for unknown reasons, escaped destruction. Finally he quotes an American diplomat in Vientiane who says: "To make progress in this country, it is necessary to level everything. It is necessary to reduce the inhabitants to zero, to eliminate their traditional culture, for it blocks everything." And Decornoy comments: "The Americans accuse the North Vietnamese of intervening militarily in the country. But it is they who talk of reducing Laos to zero, while the Pathet Lao exalts the national culture and national independence."

No doubt Laos is still serving as a testing ground or experimental site, for the next stage of the Vietnam war, for our new long-haul, low-cost policy. If the American people will only trust their leaders, perhaps there is still a chance to crush the people's war in South Vietnam in ways that will be as well concealed as have been those of the Laotian war.

The secret can be kept. Americans know virtually nothing about the bombing of South Vietnam. To my knowledge, there has been only one pro-Western correspondent who has spent time in the liberated zones of South Vietnam, Katsuichi Honda—and I am sure that his reports in *Asahi Shimbun* in the fall of 1967 are known to very few Americans.[14] He describes, for example, the incessant attacks on undefended villages by gunboats in the Mekong River and by helicopter gunships, "firing away at random at farmhouses":

> They seemed to fire whimsically and in passing even though they were not being shot at from the ground nor could they identify the people as NLF. They did it impulsively for fun, using the farmers for targets as if in a hunting mood. They are hunting Asians. . . . This whimsical firing would explain the reason why the surgical wards in every hospital in the towns of the Mekong delta were full of wounded.

He is speaking, notice, of the Mekong Delta, where few North Vietnamese soldiers were identified until several months after the Tet offensive; where, according to American intelligence, there were 800 North Vietnamese troops before last summer;[15] and, which contained some 40 percent of the population of South Vietnam prior to the American assault.

Occasionally such material finds its way to the American press. Consider again the Mekong Delta. "In March [1969] alone, the United States Ninth Infantry Division reported that it killed 3,504 Vietcong troops and sympathizers in the northern delta [and] senior officers confidently forecast that they will continue to kill at least 100 a day well into the summer." The "conflagration . . . is tearing the social fabric apart." In "free-fire zones, the Americans could bring to bear at any time the enormous firepower available from helicopter gunships, bombers and artillery . . . fighter-bombers and artillery pound the enemy positions into the gray porridge that the green delta land becomes when pulverized by high explosives."[16]

Apparently the performance of the Ninth Division was not entirely satisfactory, however. "[I]n the Mekong Delta, United States military advisers at My Tho told a UPI correspondent, Robert Kaylor, that the government's pacification program was still being hampered by the effects of indiscriminate killing of civilians by United States Ninth Infantry Division troops recently withdrawn from the area. 'You can't exactly expect people who have had parts of their family blown away by the Ninth to be wholeheartedly on our side,' said the United States source, a member of a pacification team."[17]

In the *Christian Science Monitor*, October 14, 1969, there is a front-page story reviewing such efforts. It explains that "the proportion of the country 'pacified' has risen with the flow of peasants to resettlement and refugee areas," although the Viet Cong, "currently are intensifying their campaign to drive peasants back to their home areas where [they] have a better chance of controlling them." The picture is clear. We, in our magnanimity, are using our modernizing instruments, bombs, and artillery, to lead the suffering peasants to the promised land of resettlement and refugee areas, while the ferocious Viet Cong—mere "village thugs," as the MIT political scientist, Ithiel Pool, explains in the journal of the Gandhi Peace Foundation—cruelly drive them back to their homes. The *Monitor* article also notes that "Despite years of thought and effort, officials here are still not agreed on how best to pacify a troubled land. In those years, pacification has advanced from being a theoretical ideal—though inconvenient—to the more important but second-class status of being 'the other war' "—and a proper theoretical exercise for American scientists and scholars.

The New York Times, September 24, 1969, presented an example of how pacification proceeds. Northwest of Saigon, seven hundred soldiers encircled a village, killing twenty-two and arresting fifty-three. It was the fourth such operation in this village in fifteen months. As for the villagers: "The Vietcong are everywhere, they say, and will be back when the Americans leave." An American junior officer, looking at the deserted central market, had this to say: "They say this village is 80 percent VC supporters. By the time we finish this it will be 95 percent." Such reports are hardly more newsworthy than a small item of September 27 which notes "that United States helicopter gunships mistakenly attacked a group of Vietnamese civilians 25 miles west of Tamky Tuesday, killing fourteen civilians. . . . United States helicopter gunships killed seven unarmed civilians and wounded seventeen others in a similar incident Sept. 16 in the Mekong delta." It is not easy to avoid such accidents as we try to ensure that the Viet Cong constituency ceases to exist.

In *Look* magazine, November 18, 1969, Foreign Editor Robert Moskin

81

Moral Argument and the War in Vietnam

describes his visit to a refugee camp, which "tells part of the story of Vietnam's hopelessness." Its 3,125 refugees (240 men) were transferred to this "desolate sand-dune camp" in a military sweep last summer from an island that was regarded as a VC stronghold: "The rest of the men are still hiding with the VC in the tall grass." This is in Quang Nam Province, where even the American officials in charge admit that the battle was lost "to Viet-Cong forces recruited for the most part from within the province."[18] With an honesty that others would do well to emulate, Moskin states that in Vietnam "America's historic westward-driving wave has crested."

With justice, "a staff major [of the Americal Division in Chulai] said: "We are at war with the ten-year-old children. It may not be humanitarian, but that's what it's like.' " [19]

And now there is Song My—"Pinkville." More than two decades of indoctrination and counterrevolutionary interventions have created the possibility of a name like "Pinkville"—and the acts that may be done in a place so named. Orville and Jonathan Schell have pointed out[20] what any literate person should realize, that this was no isolated atrocity but the logical consequence of a virtual war of extermination directed against helpless peasants: "enemies," "reds," "dinks." But there are, perhaps, still deeper roots. Some time ago, I read with a slight shock the statement by Eqbal Ahmad that "America has institutionalized even its genocide," referring to the fact that the extermination of the Indians "has become the object of public entertainment and children's games."[21] Shortly after, I was thumbing through my daughter's fourth-grade social science reader.[22] The protagonist, Robert, is told the story of the extermination of the Pequot tribe by Captain John Mason:

> His little army attacked in the morning before it was light and took the Pequots by surprise. The soldiers broke down the stockade with their axes, rushed inside, and set fire to the wigwams. They killed nearly all the braves, squaws, and children, and burned their corn and other food. There were no Pequots left to make more trouble. When the other Indian tribes saw what good fighters the white men were, they kept the peace for many years.
>
> "I wish I were a man and had been there," thought Robert.

Nowhere does Robert express, or hear, second thoughts about the matter. The text omits some other pertinent remarks: for example, by Cotton Mather, who said that "It was supposed that no less than six hundred Pequot souls were brought down to hell that day."[23] Is it an exaggeration to suggest that our history of extermination and racism is reaching its climax in Vietnam today? It is not a question that Americans can easily put aside.

The revelation of the Song My atrocity to a wide public appears to have been a by-product of the November mobilization. As Richard L. Strout wrote in the *Christian Science Monitor*:[24]

American press self-censorship thwarted Mr. Ridenhour's disclosures for a year. "No one wanted to get into it," his agent said of telegrams sent to *Life, Look,* and *Newsweek* magazines outlining allegations. . . . . Except for the recent antiwar march in Washington the event might not have been publicized. In connection with the march a news offshoot (Dispatch News Service) of the left-wing Institute of Policy Studies of this city aggressively told and marketed the story to approximately thirty United States and Canadian newspapers.

Apart from this, it probably would have disappeared from history, along with who knows what else.

The first investigation by the Pentagon "reported that the carnage was due to artillery fire. Civilian casualties by artillery fire among hostile villages are so common that this explanation ended the inquiry."[25] But the murdered Vietnamese were not the victims of artillery fire. Since the soldiers looked into the faces of their victims, the inquiry must continue, despite the difficulties. Henry Kamm reported in *The New York Times* that:

> The task of the investigators is complicated by the fact that last January, most of the inhabitants of the peninsula were forcibly evacuated by American and South Vietnamese troops in the course of a drive to clear the area of Vietcong. More than 12,000 persons were removed from Bantangan Peninsula by helicopters and taken to a processing camp near this provincial capital. Heavy American bombing and artillery and naval shelling had destroyed many of the houses and forced them to live in caves and bunkers for many months before the evacuation. . . . An elaborate interrogation and screening procedure, in which American Intelligence agents were said to have taken an important part, yielded only a hundred or so active Vietcong suspects. Most of the people were sent to a newly established refugee camp. . . . Despite the extensive movement of the population and the military operation, the Vietcong remain active in the area."[26]

On November 22, Kamm adds the further information that "the number of refugees 'generated'—the term for the people forcibly dislocated in this process—exceeded intelligence estimates four-fold." "The 12,000, instead of being scattered in many hamlets where it would be difficult to keep out the Vietcong, are now concentrated in six guarded, camp-like settlements."

It is perhaps remarkable that none of this appears to occasion much concern. It is only the acts of a company of half-crazed GIs that are regarded as a scandal, a disgrace to America. It will, indeed, be a still greater national scandal—if we assume that to be possible—if they alone are subjected to criminal prosecution, but not those who have created and accepted the long-term atrocity to which they contributed one detail—merely a few hundred more murdered Vietnamese.

Moral Argument and the War in Vietnam

Recently, a study of American public opinion about Vietnam concluded with this speculation: ". . . little reaction to the war is based on humanitarian or moral considerations. Americans are not now rejecting 'war,' they merely wish to see this current conflict ended. To achieve this goal, most Americans would pursue a more militant policy and ignore resultant atrocities." [27] We may soon discover whether this speculation is correct. Of course, there is sure to be a segment of American society that will not "ignore resultant atrocities"—namely, the irresponsible, loudmouth, vocal minority, or those who are described so nicely by Colonel Joseph Bellas, commanding officer of a hospital in Vietnam where soldiers boycotted Thanksgiving dinner in protest against the war: "They're young, they're idealistic and don't like man's inhumanity to man. As they get older they will become wiser and more tolerant." [28] If a majority of the American people will, indeed, ignore resultant atrocities and support Nixon's policy of pursuing a war without discernible end, then this segment of American society may be subjected to domestic repression of a sort that is not without precedent in American history; we seem to be seeing the early signs today with the savage repression of the Panthers, the conspiracy trial in Chicago, and other incidents.

The fact that repression may be attempted does not imply that it must succeed. Surely the possibility exists, today, of creating a broad-based movement of opposition to war and repression that might stave off such an attack. It is now even imaginable, as a few years ago it was not, that a significant American left may emerge that will be a voice in national affairs, and even, perhaps, a potential force for radical social change. There has been a remarkable shift in popular attitudes over the past months, an openness to radical political thinking of a sort that I do not recall for many years. To let these opportunities pass is to condemn many others to the fate of Vietnam.

Is there an "honorable" way out of Vietnam—meaning by that a way that might be tolerable to the present state of American opinion? The question is important, for if the answer is negative, it may well be that the threat of extinction that Fall recognized will in fact be realized. It is important to stress this possibility, in view of the present mood in certain "movement" circles where it is a criterion of one's radicalism to believe that America has been defeated and that the Vietnamese will win. On the contrary, a serious person will follow Gramsci's maxim: pessimism of the intelligence, optimism of the will. There is not much doubt that the United States has the power to deny victory, or even continued existence, to the people of Vietnam. No one knows whether the present strategy of capital-intensive war can reduce the level of organized social life in Vietnam to the point where an American-imposed solution may, in its terms, be successful.

There surely is an "honorable" way of ending the war. The PRG and DRV delegations in Paris have proposed such a way, repeatedly. It is a measure of the government's contempt for the American people that Nixon was willing to publish Ho Chi Minh's conciliatory letter, with the statement that is signified—in Nixon's phrase—"the other side's absolute refusal to show the least willingness to join in seeking peace." It seems that the intermediary in the Ho-Nixon exchange was Jean Sainteny. He was interviewed by Joseph Kraft, who writes:

> I saw Sainteny at the end of September, just after his return from the funeral of Ho Chi Minh in Hanoi. He had had a long talk with Premier Pham Van Dong. He was persuaded that the other side was prepared to accept a settlement that would include an independent and non-Communist South Vietnam set in a neutralist Southeast Asia. The obstacle to agreement in his view was that Hanoi did not have any faith in Mr. Nixon's claim that he wanted an agreement. On the contrary, the North Vietnamese thought the United States was still trying to impose in Saigon, by military means, a pro-American government hostile to Hanoi. M. Sainteny felt—and his feelings were made known to the President—that the United States could dispel Hanoi's doubts in two ways. One would be a formal statement that the United States recognized the principle of total withdrawal of American troops from South Vietnam at some unstipulated date. The other would be by broadening the present regime in Saigon to include some political figures who were not die-hard anti-Communists.[29]

Corroborative evidence appears in an article by Philippe Devillers in *L'Actualité*, October 24, and Averell Harriman has publicly stated that Kraft's report is consistent with his understanding of the situation.[30] Subsequent statements by Xuan Thuy and Mme. Binh in Paris provide further confirmation of the possibilities for a reasonable settlement.

Since 1960, the NLF has demanded that a neutralized South Vietnam be governed by a coalition in which they would have a fair representation. It is this demand that we have consistently opposed—not surprisingly, in view of the judgment of the American mission at the time, and since, on the political power of the NLF relative to that of the succession of puppets we have installed. When the full-scale American invasion began, Bernard Fall cited a remark to George Chaffard of *Le Monde* by a "high-ranking spokesman of the Front"; "We have not fought for all these years simply to end up by installing one set of dictators in place of the old." Fall added: "One does not fight for eight long years, under the crushing weight of American armor, napalm, jet bombers and finally, vomiting gases, for the sheer joy of handing over what one fights for to some bureaucrat in Hanoi, merely on the say-so of a faraway party apparatus."[31] Despite the intensive American effort since 1965 to destroy social life in Vietnam, there is no reason to believe that the situation is fundamentally different today.

Nixon's speech of November 3 must be understood as a rejection of these possibilities for an "honorable" settlement, one that should

Moral Argument and the War in Vietnam

be acceptable to a large, I should think overwhelming, segment of the American public. Nixon denied the existence of the PRG-DRV initiatives, and made it clear that we have no intention of withdrawing our expeditionary force or broadening the Saigon regime. The present Saigon regime, which exists solely by the force of American arms, is not an acceptable partner in a coalition with the PRG and would no doubt collapse were a realistic effort to resolve the conflict seriously contemplated.

Under these conditions, it is important to take note of recent political developments in Saigon. President Thieu has apparently abandoned any effort to construct a significant political base. Elizabeth Pond reports from Saigon that his new party "should be very similar to the Can Lao Party [virtually, a branch of Diem's secret police], as it is being directed by old Diemists, several of whom were Can Lao members." Thieu has been able to find no political base apart from the generals and the Northern Catholics—essentially a reconstruction of the Diem regime.[32]

One of the Hoa Hao factions recently left Thieu's party in protest "against the intensification of military control of the government in recent months—and the president's continuing refusal to deal seriously even with the member groups of his own alliance." Its leader asserted that the President's coalition "cannot do anything good for the country."[33] A report on the non-Communist opposition in South Vietnam quotes Pham Ba Cam, a Hoa Hao leader: "It's not very healthy to be in the opposition in Vietnam. If you want to learn about the status of the non-Communist opposition, go to Con Son [offshore prison island]. That's where you'll find the largest gathering."[34] As Pond reports, "President Thieu's decision to organize an Army/Catholic party—at this time and in this manner—sets the course for increasing isolation of the Saigon regime." It is a decision "to maintain the narrow interests and power of the existing military oligarchy as long as possible."

This narrowing of the base of the Saigon regime reflects the political realities of South Vietnam. It also reflects a rational political judgment on the part of General Thieu:

> As Vietnamese sources analyze President Thieu's thinking, he is calculating that the United States cannot afford to lose the war and is therefore stuck here almost no matter what Saigon does. The United States might dare, it is reasoned, to abandon the Thieu regime within a year or so, but it would never dare to destroy the South Vietnamese Army. If President Thieu links his destiny inextricably to that of the Army, then he may figure that the United States cannot depose him.[35]

Thus current political developments confirm, once again, the failure of the American military to create a workable Quisling regime in the manner of the Russians in Czechoslovakia or the Germans in much of Occupied Europe. The consequences of this situation are summarized adequately by Jacques Decornoy: "Under these conditions, a military solution may be a task for several decades, supposing, that is, that there still remain Vietnamese to fight and Americans to accept a conflict without end and without hope."[36]

Twenty years ago the People's Republic of China was founded. Just a few months earlier, Dean Acheson had formed a committee to reassess American policy in Asia, now that China was "lost." The committee was to operate under this instruction: "You will please take it as your assumption that it is a fundamental decision of American policy that the United States does not intend to permit further extension of Communist domination on the continent of Asia or in the Southeast Asia area...."[37] Acheson made his thoughts more precise, shortly afterward, when writing on the Soviet threat: "It is not only the threat of direct military attack which must be considered, but also that of conquest by default, by pressure, by persuasion, by subversion, by 'neutralism.'..."[38]

In May 1950, Acheson announced that economic aid and military equipment would be sent to the French in Indochina "in order to assist them in restoring stability." Not long after, the State Department explained our support for French imperialism in Indochina in these terms: "... the fall of Indochina ... would be taken by many as a sign that the force of communism is irresistible and would lead to an attitude of defeatism.... Communist forces there must be decisively conquered down to the last pocket of resistance"—in the name of French imperialism.[39] The "much-needed rice, rubber, and tin" were also cited as a justification for our support for the French in their ill-fated effort to reconquer their former colony. Upon their failure, we took over management of the enterprise directly.

In 1955 the Communist threat was defined in *The Political Economy of American Foreign Policy* (see Chapter 1, Section I) as the economic transformation of the Communist powers "in ways which reduce their willingness and ability to complement the industrial economies of the West." Communism, in short, reduces the "willingness and ability" of underdeveloped countries to function in the world capitalist economy in the manner of the Philippines—to take a classic Asian example—where:

> Their economy has for nearly half a century been deliberately geared into that of the United States to an extent which caused Mr. McNutt, in testifying as High Commissioner, to say that "our businessmen and our statesmen in past years allowed the Philippines to become a complete economic dependency of the United States to a greater degree than any single State of the Union is economically dependent on the rest of the United States."[40]

Since then, there has been little substantive change in what United States Ambassador Salvador Lopez called the classic colonial economy

Moral Argument and the War in Vietnam

of the Philippines. To be sure, we have bequeathed them the blessings of democracy. As Tillman Durdin accurately describes this legacy of half a century of colonial domination: "Filipinos view elections as a confirmation of the power of the wealthy business and landed interests who back both parties but usually pick the winners before Election Day and quietly give them the most support. In this case they picked President Marcos."[41] And in gratitude, the Filipinos have helped us in our war in Vietnam, in the manner explained in a recent report of the Symington subcommittee. William Selover summarized this report in a recent *Christian Science Monitor*:

> The hearings showed, for example, that the United States taxpayer has been paying for the Philippine troop commitment in Vietnam. It has also shown that, without this payment, the Philippines would not have sent a single man to help the United States in Vietnam. . . . Administration officials admitted paying the Philippines some $40 million to send the troops to Vietnam.[42]

Still more revealing is the stated purpose of the United States military commitment to the Philippines. Selover reports Lieutenant General Robert H. Warren's admission that the commitment was designed partly "to maintain internal security and stability and, thereby, make our own activities over there more secure." Senator Symington put it succinctly, with General Warren's reluctant assent: "In other words we are paying the Philippine Government to protect us from the Philippine people who do not agree with the policies of the government or do not like Americans." Pentagon officials admitted in the hearings that "the only real threat that the Philippines faces . . . [is] . . . internal subversion." The threat is related, perhaps, to the fact that for most of the population, living standards have not materially changed since the Spanish occupation.

It is this "Communist threat" that we have been combatting in Vietnam, where, as has frequently been noted, Vietnamese communism threatens the new order that we have been trying to construct in Asia with Japan as junior partner, linked to Asia by essentially colonial relationships. As President Eisenhower expressed it:

> One of Japan's greatest opportunities for increased trade lies in a free and developing Southeast Asia. . . . The great need in one country is for raw materials, in the other country for manufactured goods. The two regions complement each other markedly. By strengthening of Vietnam and helping insure the safety of the South Pacific and Southeast Asia, we gradually develop the great trade potential between this region . . . and highly industrialized Japan to the benefit of both. In this way freedom in the Western Pacific will be greatly strengthened.[43]

It remains to be seen how long Japan will be able to fend off economic intervention of a sort that is increasingly turning Western Europe into a dependency of American-based multinational corporations, those "United States enterprises abroad [which] in the aggregate comprise the third largest country . . . in the world—with a gross product greater than that of any country except the United States and the Soviet Union."⁴⁴

It is not likely that the population of the empire—the "integrated world economy" dominated by American capital, to use the technical euphemism—will remain quiescent, willing indefinitely to complement the industrial economies of the West. Seventy-five years ago, shortly before the American invasion of the Philippines in a war that was, apart from scale, rather like our present war in Vietnam, the Philippine nationalist José Rizal castigated his countrymen because they were "like a slave who asked only for a bandage to wrap the chain so that it may rattle less and not ulcerate the skin." Those days are past. Those whom Marx called "the slaves and drudges of [the bourgeois] order" are no longer satisfied with a bandage to wrap their chains, and their discontent will lead to turmoil and violent repression, so long as we consent.

What can we do to affect the events that are to come? First, we must not make the mistake of placing trust in the government. The large upsurge of antiwar sentiment can be an effective device for changing national policy if it is sustained in continuing mass actions across the country. Otherwise the administration can ride out the storm and continue as before to systematically demolish the society of South Vietnam and Laos. It is difficult week after week, month after month, to sustain a high level of protest against the war. As American society becomes more polarized and the true, familiar Nixon emerges in the person of Mitchell or Agnew, as the threat of repression becomes more real, it will be hard to maintain the kinds of resistance and protest that the Vietnam catastrophe demands. As the reports of massacres and automated murder become routine, the impulse to respond by violence may become more difficult to stifle, despite the realization that this can only have the effect of bringing the mass of the population to "ignore resultant atrocities." Continued mass actions, patient explanation, principled resistance can be boring, depressing. But those who program the B-52 attacks and the "pacification" exercises are not bored, and as long as they continue in their work, so must we.

Notes

1 Assistant Secretary of Defense Paul Warnke, as quoted by Townsend Hoopes; see *New York Times*, September 28, 1969.
2 Richard M. Pfeffer, ed., *No More Vietnams?: The War and the Future of American Foreign Policy* (New York, Harper & Row, 1968), p. 107.
3 For detailed analysis based largely on Defense Department sources, see Gabriel Kolko, *London Bulletin*, August 1969.

Moral Argument and the War in Vietnam

4 *No More Vietnams?*, p. 212. For further discussion, see Chapter 1, Section III of *At War with Asia* and my article in *The New York Review*, January 2, 1969.

5 Elizabeth Pond, *Christian Science Monitor*, November 8, 1969.

6 On December 10, 1969, Reston returned to the question of Cam Ranh Bay, stating that it was now "an air and naval base which is the best in Asia," and that it has been a "fundamental question throughout the Paris negotiations" whether the United States is willing to abandon it "and many other modern military bases." He raises the question whether the United States would withdraw all troops or only all "combat forces," a plan which "could leave a couple of hundred thousand Americans in Vietnam to maintain and fly the planes and helicopter gunships and continue to train and supply and help direct the Vietnamese."

There is no indication of any serious intention to withdraw all forces or to abandon the bases. As Joseph Kraft has reported (see page 107, below) the American refusal to commit itself to the principle of complete withdrawal is one of the factors blocking progress in Paris.

7 In the apt phrase of E. Herman and R. Duboff, "How to Coo Like a Dove While Fighting To Win," pamphlet of Philadelphia SANE, 20 South 12th Street, Philadelphia, 19107.

8 *Congressional Record*, August 8, 1969, F 9589. Cited in the *Bulletin of Concerned Asian Scholars*, Vol. 2, No. 1 (October 1969), 1737 Cambridge Street, Cambridge, Mass.—an important journal for those concerned with Asian affairs.

9 *War, Peace, and the Viet Cong* (Cambridge, Mass., the M.I.T. Press, 1969). He estimates that in 1963 "perhaps half the population of South Vietnam at least tacitly supported the NLF." The same estimate was given by the United States Mission in 1962. Elsewhere, he has explained that in late 1964 it was impossible to consider an apparently genuine offer of a coalition government, because there was no force that could compete politically, with the Viet Cong, with the possible exception of the Buddhists, who were, not long after, suppressed as a political force by Marshal Ky's American-backed storm troopers. The same difficulty has been noted, repeatedly, by spokesmen for the American and Saigon governments and reporters. For some examples, see Herman and Duboff, *op. cit.*, or my "The Logic of Withdrawal," *American Power and the New Mandarins* (New York, Pantheon Books, 1969), pp. 221-94.

10 *New York Times*, June 11, 1968.

11 *New York Times Magazine*, November 23, 1969.

12 See *Washington Post*, October 31, 1969; *Los Angeles Times*, October 31; *New York Post*, November 4; *Science*, November 7. A Vietnamese student in the United States, Ngo Vinh Long, has summarized much of what is known, including his personal experience from 1959 to 1963 when he visited "virtually every hamlet and village in the country" as a military-map maker, in *Thòi-Báo Gà*, November 1969, 76a Pleasant Street, Cambridge, Mass., a monthly publication of Vietnamese students in the United States. He describes how defoliation has been used since 1961 to drive peasants into government-controlled camps, and from his own experience and published records in Vietnam, he records some of the effects: starvation, death, hideously deformed babies. He quotes the head of the Agronomy Section of the Japan Science Council who claims that by 1967 about half the arable land had been seriously affected. For American estimates, see the report of the Daddario subcommittee of the House Committee on Science and Astronautics, August 8, 1969. They estimate the total area sprayed through 1968 as 6,600 square miles (extrapolating through 1969 the figure would reach 8,600 square miles, about 60 percent of this respraying—over 10 percent of it crop destruction).

13 *Le Monde Weekly Selection*, October 1, 1969.

14 They have appeared in English, and can be obtained from the Committee for the English Publication of "Vietnam—A Voice from the Villages," c/o Mrs. Reiko Ishida, 2-13-7, Nishikata, Bunyo-ku, Tokyo.

15 "Before this summer, the enemy in the delta consisted mostly of indigenous Vietcong units and guerrillas, many of whom worked during the day in the rice fields and fought at night. The only North Vietnamese were troops and officers who led some of the guerrilla units. They numbered about 800 as against an estimated total of 49,000 Vietcong soldiers and support troops." *New York Times*, September 15, 1969. On September 16, the *Times* reports that "for the first time in the war, a regular North Vietnamese army unit, the 18B Regiment, had attacked in the delta."

16 *New York Times*, Peter Arnett, April 15, 1969. Arnett claims that only 90 percent of the enemy forces of 40,000 are recruited locally, giving a far higher estimate of North Vietnamese than the intelligence reports cited above, or others: e.g., *Christian Science Monitor*, September 16, which reports that in the early fall of 1969 "North Vietnamese troops

in the delta doubled in number, to between 2,000 and 3,000 men."

17 *Boston Globe,* December 1, 1969.
18 William Nighswonger, *Rural Pacification in Vietnam* (Praeger Special Studies; New York, Frederick A. Praeger, 1967), p. 116.
19 Henry Kamm, *New York Times,* December 1, 1969.
20 *New York Times,* September 26, 1969.
21 In Pfeffer, ed., *No More Vietnams?,* p. 18. On the widely noted analogy between Vietnam and the Indian wars see my *American Power and the New Mandarins,* pp. 279-80, n. 42.
22 Harold B. Clifford, *Exploring New England* (New Unified Social Studies; Chicago, Follett Publishing Co., 1961).
23 See Howard Zinn, "Violence and Social Change," Boston University *Graduate Journal,* Fall, 1968. When disease decimated the Indians, Mather said: "The woods were almost cleared of those pernicious creatures, to make room for a better growth."
24 On November 24, 1969. Attention, Mr. Agnew.
25 *Christian Science Monitor,* November 29, 1969.
26 Henry Kamm, *New York Times,* November 15, 1969.
27 J. Robinson and S. G. Jacobson, in Walter Isard, ed., *Vietnam: Some Basic Issues and Alternatives* (Cambridge, Mass., Schenkman Publishing Company, 1968), a symposium of the Peace Research Society (International). This organization, following a script by Orwell, is concerned with a special kind of peace research: the question of "how pacification can be achieved in turbulent village societies," along lines that we have been pioneering in Vietnam, for example. But even the Peace Research Society (International) is not monolithic. It would be unfair to assume that the conclusion of the cited study is mere wishful thinking. It has to be taken seriously.
28 Reuters, *Boston Globe,* November 27, 1969.
29 *Boston Globe,* November 10, 1969.
30 In a panel at Johns Hopkins University, November 14, 1969.
31 *New Society,* April 22, 1965, reprinted in Bernard B. Fall and Marcus G. Raskin, eds., *The Viet-Nam Reader* (New York, Vintage Books, 1965). Those who speak so glibly of "bloodbaths" might note the casualty figures that Fall cites; for example, 89,000 Viet Cong killed between 1961 and April 1965 (United States sources); 66,000 Viet Cong killed between 1957 and 1961 (AFP), 160,000 South Vietnamese (presumably NLF) killed thus far in the war (NLF sources).
32 *Christian Science Monitor,* November 6, November 8, November 14, 1969. Miss Pond has been one of the few correspondents, over the years, to give any serious attention to Vietnamese political and social life. In the past, her analyses have proved quite accurate. For additional corroboratory information, see D. Gareth Porter, "The Diemist Restoration," *Commonweal,* July 11, 1969.
33 John Woodruff, *Baltimore Sun,* October 25, 1969.
34 Terence Smith, *New York Times,* dateline October 24, 1969. The scale and character of forceful repression of dissent in South Vietnam have been amply reported. See, for example, Herman and Duboff, *op. cit.,* and references therein.
35 Pond, *Christian Science Monitor,* November 6, 1969.
36 *Le Monde diplomatique,* November 1969.
37 Memorandum from Acheson to Philip Jessup, cited by Gabriel Kolko, *The Roots of American Foreign Policy* (Boston, Beacon Press, 1969), p. 95.
38 Cited by Walter LaFeber, *America, Russia and the Cold War 1945-1966* (Ithaca, N.Y., Cornell University Press, 1967), p. 102.
39 *Ibid.,* p. 116.
40 Rupert Emerson, in J. C. Vincent, ed., *America's Future in the Pacific* (New Brunswick, N.J., Rutgers University Press, 1947), p. 87.
41 Commenting on the recent elections, *New York Times,* November 16, 1969. For some discussion of Philippine politics, see Onofre D. Corpuz, *The Philippines* (Englewood Cliffs, N.J., Prentice-Hall, 1965).
42 November 28, 1969: "From the hearings it is learned that the United States paid South Korea and Thailand as well to send their troops to Vietnam in a show of solidarity." This was somewhat more expensive. According to the *Times,* December 1, the bribe to Thailand amounted to a billion dollars.
43 April 4, 1959, quoted in Harry Magdoff, *The Age of Imperialism* (New York: Monthly Review Press, 1969). See Chapter 1, pages 33–35.
44 Leo Model, *Foreign Affairs,* July 1967, quoted in Magdoff, *op. cit.*

How Shall Counter-Insurgency War Be Conducted Justly?*

by Paul Ramsey

"Modern war" is not nuclear war. Instead, the possibility of nuclear war has made the world safe for wars of insurgency. The balance of terror, which some foolishly thought would compel peace, produces instead a multiplication of wars. The military strength of the nation-state, which we thought made it impossible ever again to have a successful revolution, has led instead to an era of revolutionary wars. The possibility that any war may escalate into all-out nuclear war makes insurgency wars, in many areas of the world, an increasingly feasible choice. The fact that it would be nonsense for nations ever to fight the "central" war, or all the war they are today technically capable of fighting, produces "peripheral" wars. When the security and order of the world depends on arsenals of *militarily* useless weapons (nuclears whose use is their deterrent nonuse), you can be sure that insurgency, subversion, and disorder can win victories with meager weapons that have at least this virtue, namely, that they can be used in support of somebody's purpose or policies. Thus at the heart of the great strength of the modern state there is weakness (as Mao Tse-Tung, Ho Chi Minh, General Nguyen Giap, and Che Guevara discerned). And in the weakness of the present guerrilla there is strength: better to strike and run away, and live to fight another day; and if there are enough of him who endure long enough they may bring down a whole nation without ever winning a conventional battle. This will remain the military situation for decades to come.

Therefore the type of warfare that deserves to be called truly "modern" is "insurgency" warfare, "subversive" war, "sublimited" or "subconventional" war, "revolutionary" war or "wars of national liberation," "guerrilla" war or the "war of the flea"'—or whatever you want to call it. There can be no doubt that the most urgent, practical, military and political question during our lifetime is, how is it possible, if indeed it is possible, to mount an *effective* counter-insurgency war, and to deliver such retribution upon it that future insurgency will be deterred, and thus the precarious, politically-embodied justice in the world be given some protection?

*This is the title of Chapter 18 of The Just War: Force and Political Responsibility by Paul Ramsey. The excerpts reprinted here are from Chapters 17, 18, and 22 of the book: pp. 427-433, 507, 434-438, 444-446, 397-403, 414-416. Reprinted by permission of Charles Scribner's sons from The Just War, copyright © 1968 Paul Ramsey.

Moral Argument and the War in Vietnam

That, however, is not my question. Mine is rather to ask, how is it possible, if indeed it is possible, to mount a *morally acceptable* counter-insurgency operation? Among the many considerations that are relevant to a decision that it is politically wise and necessary to resort to arms, and among the several considerations that determine the justice of a war, I shall restrict my remarks to the justice of war's *conduct*. This is to prescind from questioning the justice of the cause, the end for which the war is fought, and from making any judgment about the comparative rectitude of the social systems, the regimes, and nations that may resort to war. I shall ask (in words that were the subtitle of a book I published in 1961), How shall modern war be conducted justly? The contemporary meaning of that question can only be grasped if we formulate it to read, How shall counter-insurgency war be conducted justly?

In determining the justice of war's conduct there are two criteria or tests that are applicable. These are the principles of discrimination and the principle of proportion.

First, a word about the meaning of and the relation between these tests—before we get down to insurgency cases. The principle of discrimination is shorthand for "the moral immunity of noncombatants from direct attack." This does not require that civilians never be knowingly killed. It means rather that military action should, in its primary (objective) thrust as well as in its subjective purpose, discriminate between directly attacking combatants or military objectives and directly attacking noncombatants or destroying the structures of civil society as a means of victory. When this distinction is made, it becomes clear that the latter is the meaning of murder, which is never just, even in war; while the former is the meaning of the killing in war which can be justified, including the collateral and foreseeable but unavoidable destruction of noncombatants in the course of attacking military objectives.

An exact analogue to discrimination in the conduct of war (and one which shows that this principle means to refer *both* to subjective intention and to the objective direction of the act) is to be found in the ruling of the United States Supreme Court that state action unavoidably affecting religious practices in some of its consequences may nevertheless be constitutional provided the legislation had a "secular legislative *purpose* and *primary* effect."[3]

The second test of justice in the conduct of war is the principle of proportionality. All that Reinhold Niebuhr ever said about politics and war falls under this heading, since the principle of proportion says simply that nations, statesmen, and citizens are acting responsibly when they choose and vigorously support policies and decisions which are likely to secure the lesser evil (or the greater good) among their mixed consequences.

In summary of the two criteria governing the justice of war's conduct, an act of war may be gravely wrong, for one thing, because its primary

94

thrust and purpose is to kill the innocent: that is murder, which no good end can justify. The same act, or another act, may be gravely wrong, for another thing, because of a serious disproportion between its good and evil effects in comparison with the mixed consequences of another deed that might have been actualized instead.

The meaning of these two "rules of practice" in warfare can perhaps be made somewhat clearer by considering the different meanings the expression "doing evil" has in connection with the one and the other criterion. Under the first test, "doing evil" means doing evil directly, having in view some good end or consequence to come from it; and that is inherently wrong. It is inherently wrong because of the nature and structure of the action itself, without yet counting all the costs. That is, the agent's primary purpose (if not his ultimate prediction or expectation) was the doing of an evil (for the sake of a subsequent good, of course) and the primary, direct, immediate effect was this evil. Under the second test, however, "doing evil" means doing the *lesser* evil among manifold consequences of a *not indiscriminate* act. In this sense and when one comes to count the costs "doing evil" is not always wrong. It is not immoral to do the lesser evil from among consequences that are more evil. In fact, not to do so and to allow a greater evil to prevail would be gravely wrong. Anyone who identifies every sort of "doing evil" with wickedness simply has not faced the fact that most actions—whether they are in the personal or the political or the military realms—have many consequences and not one effect only. Some of the effects of not indiscriminate actions are good, some are evil; some, a greater or a lesser evil; some, a greater or a lesser good. To choose the least evil that can be done is to choose the good that alone is possible. So there should be a proportion among the good and evil effects of an action; the good accomplished or the evil prevented must be sufficient to justify (in a comparison of effects) the evil that is unavoidably also done. This is the principle of proportion, or the requirement of prudence, in any course of conduct that can finally be justified and termed right. There must be a calculation of the costs and the benefits that flow from any action that itself is not wrong, before one knows whether to do it or not.

In summary, actions, such as acts of war, having manifold effects may be disordered from justice because the primary thrust of the act was deliberately directed toward the evil effect or toward some enlargement of it, or such actions may be disordered from justice because the primary good consequence was not worth paying and exacting the price of the evil effects. These criteria are always valid, always distinct, yet always inseparably related in judging actions having a number of effects some of which are evil. Like any two persons of the Trinity or the two natures of Christ, the principle of discrimination and the principle of proportion ought never to be either confused or separated.

The relation between the tests seems to be as follows: the ends justify

Moral Argument and the War in Vietnam

the means, šince nothing else can; but they do not justify *any* means. The means which no ends can justify have to be determined by the principle of discrimination. The statement that only the ends justify the means is a statement falling under the principle of proportion; so understood, it is unquestionably correct. The statement that the ends do not justify the means (or are not capable of justifying any and all means) is a statement falling under the principle of discrimination; so understood, it too is unquestionably correct. The principle of proportion is regulative of all actions that are finally *to be done;* prudence governs in determining the effects or consequences that ought ever to be let loose in the world. Especially in politics, only the ends justify the means.

(Yet) proportion or prudence or judgments concerning the lesser evil among the ends of action have nothing to do with whether something is the direct object of the action's impact and something else the collateral or side-effect unavoidably also produced by the action. That depends on the verdict under the first test, the principle of discrimination. This test can and should be independently applied, and an assessment of any proposed action should first be made in terms of discrimination, in order to determine the actions that are permissible. Then one has to choose, from among actions that are morally tolerable because they are not indiscriminate, those actions that should actually be done because of an apt proportion between their good and evil consequences.

Thus, one does not calculate a prudent number of babies to be murdered (directly killed) for the sake of any good consequences (such as getting at the government); but one tragically may and must calculate the prudent number that will and may be killed as an unavoidable side or collateral effect of military operations targeted upon the force to be repelled and whose goal and other consequence is expected to be the saving of many more from slaughter or from an oppressive tyranny, or in order to preserve in the international system accepted patterns in the actions of states on which grave consequences depend. Murder is never ordinate; but unfortunately a good deal of killing may be. Direct attacks upon a civil population can never be justified; but unfortunately—in this world to date—a good many incidental deaths and extensive collateral damage to civil society may still be knowingly done lest worse befall. So prudence rules, but it does not initiate or obliterate the discriminations that should first be made as to who is and who is not a legitimate military target.

So there are two ingredients in the moral economy governing the use of force: discrimination and proportion. Noncombatant immunity assesses the action itself with no prudential reference yet to the totality of the consequences, while the principle of proportion takes all the effects for the first time into account. An action having multiple consequences, some of which are evil, must pass both tests before it should ever be actually done. Since prudence is a virtue, to do deliberately an imprudent or a disproportionate evil is vicious. It is seriously wrong, and not only "inexpedient," to act contrary to the requirement that the use of force, which also invariably produces evil, can be justified only if it is likely to achieve greater good effects (or greater evil prevented). Still, whether the conduct is murderous must be taken up first, because one doesn't justify a proportionate number of murders. This of course is a question that is not settled by reference to subjective intention alone; we must also take into account the objective nature of what was done, the structure and outward nature and direction of the action as such. One must ask not only whether one *wanted* but also whether one *did* kill the innocent *directly*.

We must now apply the principle of discrimination and the principle of proportion in order to reach an assessment of the morality of insurgency warfare and the morality of counter-insurgency.

When today insurgency resorts to arms, it avoids striking the government's military forces with military means. Instead, it deliberately strikes the civil population, or a selected number of the civil population, in order to subvert a whole country's traditions and institutions and to bring down the government. The moral quality of such action, though perhaps not the extent of the damage, is like making fire-storms or city-busting an integral part of military strategy at the conventional or the nuclear level.

Of course, modern revolutionary wars are the most political kind of warfare that can be imagined. Of course, the insurgents win the allegiance of people by many other appeals; and when they gain control they often "out-administer" the government. It is not impossible for their cause to be the more just one. So did the Allies have greater justice on their side against the Hitler regime. Still what we did to Dresden was wrong, and not only because of the body-count or the extent of the damage. No matter how much a person who passionately believes and perhaps correctly believes in a revolutionary "just cause" may squirm on the point of the argument, he can avoid being impaled on it only by asserting that "just conduct" need not be taken into account in any resorts to violence.

In order to analyze the morality of the conduct of insurgency warfare, it is not necessary to examine the program of "national liberation." Instead, we must focus attention upon what happens when insurgency resorts to arms. The fact that insurgency wins by many other appeals; and resorts to terror, when it does, only in the form of *selective* terror, may be sufficient to qualify it under the requirement that cost-effects be wisely proportioned to what are believed to be good-effects. But consequences are not the only test. There is also the principle of discrimination, and this cannot justify selecting only a comparatively few among the noncombatant population to be made the direct object of attack. There are not a prudent number of babies to be murdered in order to dissuade their fathers from their evil deeds. Neither are there a prudent number of villagers, or petty officials and their families, to

Moral Argument and the War in Vietnam

be disembowelled in the village square in order to dissuade others from allegiance to the existing social processes and institutions. If it is not incorrect to say that the strategy of contemporary insurgency in its (even in its minimal) use of violence is to strike selectively the civil population in order to subvert the country and to gain control of what's left of the government, then it is *correct* to say that this is an inherently immoral plan of war, no matter how many benefits are supposed to accrue from it. . . .

One does not justify adultery by saying that it is *selective*. Not even with the additional finding that with one's various mistresses one mainly enjoys the finer things of life and has achieved an orderly domestic economy. Neither does one justify deliberate terror in the conduct of war or revolution by saying that it is selective. Not even with the additional finding that the insurgents win the allegiance of people by many other appeals or also by a program of national liberation. The fact that insurgency resorts to terror, when it does, only minimally or only upon selected people does not qualify it as a discriminating resort to force. That is simply not the meaning of the principle of discrimination in the use of means of violence. It is in fact, morally, the meaning of total war. Decision as to the inherent evil of an act of war or revolution cannot be settled by the body count. There is not a prudent number of villagers, school teachers, or petty local officials and their families that it would be right to disembowel in the village square to dissuade others from allegiance to the existing social processes and institutions, all to the good end of destroying the social fabric of a traditional society and taking over and reforming the country.

Guerrilla war by its main design strikes the civil population (albeit selectively and as rarely as need be) in order to subvert, while striking as few legitimate military targets as possible. This terrible terror, while "selective" is not therefore limited or a rarity. In 1960-61 alone, the Vietcong murdered 6,130 and abducted 6,213 persons, or a total of over 12,000. Proportionately, this is as if the U.S. were under subversive assault in which 72,000 prominent persons, crucial in the life of the nation and its community services, were murdered or abducted annually! This is an inherently immoral plan of war or of revolution and one that cannot be rendered morally tolerable by reference to the social reforms by which insurgency mainly proposes to succeed. . . .

The chief question, then, concerning any *counter*-insurgency operation is whether it can be effective without adopting a military strategy that is, like that of insurgency, morally intolerable. Can insurgency be countered only by strikes deliberately directed upon the civil population, or select portions of it, as a means of getting at the insurgency forces? Is it possible successfully to oppose these revolutionary wars without joining them in direct attacks upon the very people we are undertaking to protect? Are insurgency and counter-insurgency *both* bound to be warfare over people as a means of getting at the other forces?

There is evidence for believing that during the Japanese occupation of the Philippines, the Huk guerrillas pinned down in the islands a large number of Japanese forces only by terrorizing their own people more than the Japanese did. This may have contributed significantly to final victory in a war prosecuted at another level primarily against forces, even while plans were in the making for direct and indiscriminate attacks against civilians in the fire bombs over Tokyo and the A-bomb over Hiroshima that brought the war to an end. Still it is true to say that selective and not so selective terror were peripheral to the main war that was going on. What has happened in "modern" war—both at the highest nuclear level and at the subconventional level—is that the injustice that was peripheral even if widespread in wars of the past has now become the central war.

In particular, the problem posed by insurgency warfare is whether modern warfare, by becoming more and more political in nature and correspondingly more and more selective and coldly calculating in its attacks upon the lives of noncombatants, has at the same time become irremediably indiscriminate (in the moral if not in the merely quantitative meaning of that term) by an entire rejection of the moral immunity of noncombatants from direct attack. Can counter-insurgency abide by the distinction between legitimate and illegitimate military objectives while insurgency deliberately does not?

Perhaps the term "counter-*insurgency*" contains the suggestion that the insurgency forces are the direct object of counterattack. If so, this term entails a plan of war that is significantly different from that of contemporary insurgency itself. (According to another possible and widely accepted interpretation of the expression, however, "*counter*-insurgency" entails the belief that only "defense" against "aggression" is ever justified, with the implication that if this is the reason for resorting to arms there is nothing more to be said about it. Such a view not only makes too much of the test of who first crossed the legal boundaries or who struck first. It also contains the suggestion that the manner in which a defensive war or a *counter*-insurgency operation is conducted can find its warrant in proving that someone else did something dastardly *first.*) If an act of war is *malum in se,* if selective terror is intrinsically wrong conduct, then the doing of such an evil by one side can never justify the doing of the same evil by the other side in return. "Retaliation in kind" is justified as "protective retribution" only when the kind of retaliation is not intrinsically wrong. If only proportion governed the justice of retaliation, then only wanton or excessive punishment could be ruled out, i.e., retaliation disproportionate to the protection in view or to deterring such acts in the future; and all or any kind of actions needed to do this would be justifiable. If, however, the principle of discrimination is among the laws of war, if this also governs the practice, then not all retaliation in kind can be justified. This depends on the kind. There are some forms of retaliation that ought never to be done,

Moral Argument and the War in Vietnam

not even for the sake of deterring barbaric acts of war in the future and enforcing the rules of civilized warfare itself. Just so, domestically, we say that there are "cruel (and unusual) punishments" that are not to be justified simply because they "punish," deter future violation, and thus sustain the legal order.

I believe that there can be and should be a counter-insurgency that meets the tests of just conduct in war, while insurgency does not. (Insurgency does not, if I have not incorrectly described the facts concerning how contemporary revolutionary warriors who are politically weak, idealistic, and impatient proceed to leave the field of community-building where their energies might be constructive and attempt to gain power more quickly and to bend a whole society to their will by the use of armed force upon selected civilians.) The meaning of a morally acceptable "counter-*insurgency*" operation is suggested by where I place the italics in that expression. This entails, of course, that counter-insurgency should primarily be directed to defeating insurgencv by political and economic means, since that is the challenge thrown down by insurgency and the only way finally to come to grips with it. But we are prescinding from that in order to concentrate attention on the use of armed force that is needed in extension and in defense of even the best political purposes. Counter-insurgency as a military operation can and should make the insurgent forces the primary object of attack. That it *should* do so is clear, if there is the principle of discrimination, and not only the principle of proportion morally regulating every political use of violence. That it *can* do so becomes clear if only we have in mind a correct understanding of the meaning of the principle of discrimination as we seek to apply it to the admittedly difficult situation and turmoil (the "quagmires") created by insurgency.

In order to understand the principle of discrimination and correctly to appeal to this in ethical analysis, one must understand that (1) this requires not the avoidance of all death and damage to civilians (which, of course, is impossible), but the withholding of *direct attacks* upon them and thereafter understand that the amount of collateral destruction that is morally acceptable is governed entirely by the principle of proportion); and (2) a "combatant" means anyone who is an actual bearer of the force one seeks to repress by resorting to arms. While in conventional warfare this seems easily determined by whether or not a man is in military uniform, it is still the case that (a) persons in command positions are "combatants" even though they wear tweed suits; (b) closeness of material cooperation may define a civilian as a "combatant"; (c) a man still in uniform after he surrenders is not one of the "combatants" it is just to repress; yet (d) it can be questioned whether a soldier who has surrendered may not remain a "combatant" in some fluid, jungle warfare situations in which it is impossible to insure that he will stay "surrendered." Guilt or innocence in the sense of malice or good will (even if it were possible in war to weigh hearts) would scarcely assist us to apply the principle of discrimination in the conduct of war.

In contemporary insurgency, the fact is that a peasant is often a civilian by day and a combatant by night. Others are close cooperators all or some of the time, and therefore technically combatants also. In short, the decision of the insurgents to conduct war by selective terror results in a situation in which a whole area is inhabited mainly by "combatants" in the ethically and politically relevant sense that a great number of the people *are* from consent or from constraint the bearers of the force to be repressed. "There is no profound difference between the farmer and the soldier," wrote Mao Tse-tung,[4] and so saying made it so. *The insurgents themselves* have enlarged the target it is legitimate for counter-insurgents to attack, so far as the principle of discrimination is concerned; and it is therefore mainly the principle of proportion that limits what should be done to oppose them. Since in the nature of insurgency the line between combatant and noncombatant runs right through a great number of the able-bodied people in a given area, male or female, above, say ten years of age, and since anyone may cross over this line in either direction by the hour, it is not the business of any moralist to tell the soldiers and military commanders who are attempting to mount an effective counter-insurgency operation that this cannot be done in a morally acceptable way because under these circumstances they have no legitimate military target. In devising a military riposte, it will not be those who are directing the counter-insurgency who illicitly enlarged the target and chose to fight the war indiscriminately. Instead the tragedy is that they *have* an enlarged legitimate target because of the decision of the insurgency to fight the war by means of peasants. Whether because he is idealistically persuaded or terrorized, many a South Vietnamese lad qualifies as a combatant without malice. It is a terrible human tragedy when American soldiers discover among the casualties after a Vietcong attack the body of a twelve-year-old-boy, his maps on him, who an hour before had shined their shoes near the compound; but I do not see how it is possible to accuse them and not the Vietcong of the wickedness.

Also it is the insurgency and not counter-insurgency that has enlarged the area of civilian death and damage that is legitimately collateral. When war is planned and carried out by an opponent on the principle that the guerrilla lives among the people like a fish in water, we may be justified in accepting the destruction of an entire school of fish (and the unavoidable and foreknown destruction of a great many people intermingled with them) incidental to the elimination of the guerrillas, provided only that the elimination of the school of fish is important enough to the whole course of the war, the winning of which is judged to be the lesser evil (or greater good). In other words, again it is proportion and not discrimination which counter-insurgency is in peril of violating. The principle of discrimination has already been violated by the

Moral Argument and the War in Vietnam

practice of Mao Tse-tung's maxim,[5] with the result that not only is the category of combatancy enlarged but also the extent of permissible collateral damage. Of course modern revolutionary wars should be opposed, if at all, primarily by political means. We should attempt to withdraw the water and see what then happens to the fish. Still when contemporary insurgents resort to arms in support of their policies, this is the way it is done. It is therefore the shape of insurgency warfare that defines the contours of the legitimate combatant destruction with its associated civil damage that it may be just to exact in order to oppose it, subject to the limits of proportionately lesser evil. The only way to avoid this conclusion is to suppose that the just-war theory is a device for abolishing war by a (false) definition of discrimination and insuring perpetual peace by a shibboleth. Instead, the just-war theory establishes the limits and tests that should surround justified resorts to arms in a world where there is yet no peace and many new wars, in order to insure that the precarious justice politically embodied in this world can be preserved and not left defenseless in the face of selective or non-selective terror.

It is true that Mao Tse-tung stressed political warfare as the primary meaning of his fish-water maxim. "It is only undisciplined troops," he wrote, "who make the people their enemies and who, like the fish out of its native element, cannot live."[6] And in his "Three Rules and Eight Remarks," the rules are: "All actions are subject to command, Do not steal from the people, Be neither selfish nor unjust"; and the eight remarks read: "Replace the door when you leave the house, Roll up the bedding on which you have slept, Be courteous, Be honest in your transactions, Return what you borrow, Replace what you break, Do not bathe in the presence of women, Do not without authority search the pocketbooks of those you arrest."[7] Still I think it cannot be denied that the guerrilla immerses himself in the medium in which he swims when he *fights* no less than when he is making friends and influencing people. Selective terror is definitely also one of the actions that are "subject to command." The injunctions that the guerrilla avoid offending people may not unfairly be compared, in the crucial point, to the standards of personal conduct sought to be imposed upon the élite Nazi troops. Although the former is a social ethic and the more apt means of political, revolutionary war, while the latter was a rather arbitrary personal ethic, *neither* supplants nor basically changes the nature of the selective and the not so selective terror used in the conduct of insurgency by violent means. Both as a political movement and in its resort to arms, contemporary revolutionary warfare proposes to "mobilize the common people of the whole country" and to "create a vast sea of humanity and drown the enemy in it." Such is the new shape of an otherwise shapeless sort of warfare. This defines who and where are the targets that are legitimate in the conduct of counter-insurgency, and it also tragically defines how extensive is the collateral civil damage morally acceptable.

To draw any other conclusions would be like, at the nuclear level, granting an enemy immunity from attack because he had the shrewdness to locate his missile bases in the heart of his cities. Instead of saying that we have no legitimate targets because of the extensive civil damage unavoidably associated with knocking out such missile bases, the case is rather that the enemy deliberately enlarged the extent of foreknown but collateral civil destruction in his attempt to gain a privileged sanctuary by adopting a military posture which aims at success by making hostages of more of his own population. If in U.S. policy it were possible to mount an effective deterrence by Morgenstern's "oceanic system" of Polaris submarines *alone,* and if it is possible to secure graduated and flexible military responses below and at the nuclear-missile level by locating *none* of these military bases on territory where people live, then we would have to say that it was grossly immoral for us to have made Omaha, Nebraska, and Colorado Springs, Colorado, legitimate objects of enemy attack. The onus of the wickedness cannot then be shifted to acts of war which in the future may destroy these cities in the course of destroying the bases and command posts. No more can the onus for having placed multitudes of peasants within range be shifted from insurgency to counter-insurgency.

Still it is the case that the principle of discrimination with its distinction between combatant and noncombatant can be shown to be intrinsic to proper counter-insurgency operations. This is still the regulative norm, as can be seen from a brief examination of the "strategic hamlet" program. This counters insurgency by attempting to withdraw the water to see what then happens to the fish. This program of "civilizing" was a success against the insurgents in Malaya, because the terrain was not so lush as in South Vietnam, because the source of guerrilla recruitment, supplies, and intelligence was an identifiable part of the population (the Chinese), and because the program was not financially corrupt or used to impose a dictatorial control over the country (as in the Diem regime). Yet as a strategy it is clear that the strategic village is an attempt to impose controls on a situation created by the Vietcong, in which all or almost all of the people are "fighters" and many, many more have been placed in peril collaterally, by enabling the combatant and the noncombatant in every man to come out and to settle down into a way of distinguishing one man from another and telling who and where he is. Thus, the principle of discrimination governing just conduct in war is the regulative norm of a central part of the counter-insurgency effort in South Vietnam. Just so, the moral immunity of a surrendering soldier from execution is still valid, even in jungle situations in which it may not be possible to guarantee that he will not promptly become a fighter again if he is not killed; the requirement is still relevant in that every effort must be made, compounds should be constructed if at all possible, etc., to enable the noncombatant to be securely distin-

Moral Argument and the War in Vietnam

guishable from the combatant. Suppose, however, that the "strategic hamlet" program does not succeed in enticing the noncombatant to become separated from the combatant. Suppose it has not succeeded in a given area of the country. Suppose there are entire areas controlled and "militarized" by the Vietcong. At this point political and military decisions are to be limited and determined by the principle of proportionately lesser evil.

The U.S. bombing of the central highlands and other areas of South Vietnam that are in the control of the Vietcong seems on the face of it more indiscriminate than the bombing of selected military targets in the North. The use of our advanced technology as a way of avoiding a decade of counter-guerrilla warfare on the ground is bound to occasion the greatest qualms of conscience in anyone who knows that the conduct of war should be both discriminating and proportionate if it is to be a barely human and a politically purposive enterprise. What should be said concerning bombing raids, launched from Guam, upon target areas (Vietcong "strongholds") in South Vietnam? These raids, like any other actions in war, may be (a) indiscriminating (in which case one need not ask whether more good or less evil consequences are expected from them), (b) indiscriminating and also disproportionate (if one incriminates them also in terms of their mixed effects), (c) discriminating yet excessive acts of war in that they result in greater evil than the good to be gained, or (d) neither indiscriminate nor disproportionate.

While one's first impulse is to say that (a) or (b) must be the correct verdict, I believe that a correct assessment of the bombing in South Vietnam in terms of a *correct understanding* of what discrimination does and does not require will reveal that the debate should be between (c) and (d). In the foregoing, it was argued not only that the conduct of contemporary insurgency warfare is wrong in itself (in that it selectively attacks noncombatants directly); but also that it vastly enlarges the number of people in the territories controlled by the insurgents who should be regarded as combatants, and that, by the guerrilla practice of moving and fighting in the midst of the people like fish swimming in water, insurgency is responsible for extending the scope of possibly legitimate collateral death and damage in an entire area. This is the original wickedness that can only be compared to protecting one's forces by locating missile bases in the middle of a metropolis. In reply it may of course be contended that, even if this is the manner by which contemporary revolutionaries propose to seize power, the situation is no longer the same in territories over which they have established control. There, it might be said, one has a "government," not a revolutionary war. This is doubtful, in view of the fact that this year so far the Vietcong have disembowelled, decapitated, or shot four hundred village officials and grenaded scores of buses and taxis.[8] Granting that there is considerable difference between contemporary revolutionary war and the revolutionary shadow "government" of a "stabilized" area, the *moral* issue that should be pondered is whether the situation is then so radically different that we can no longer say that the guerrilla attempts to make a virtue of fighting behind and between the people among whom he lives, and thus presents the counter-guerrilla with an enlargement of the target, with its associated areas of secondary damage, which then it is quite legitimate for him to strike. Moreover, in the notably civilian area controlled by the Vietcong, namely, the Mekong Delta, the war has proceeded more gingerly, ambush by ambush; our very effective "air cavalry" is a discriminating weapon; and it can be contended that the strongholds in the highlands that have been bombed are as a matter of fact base areas.[9] Then the question is whether there are not military objectives in South Vietnam that measure many miles in diameter. When the Sixth World Order Study Conference meeting in St. Louis recommended that the U.S. "alleviate the desperate plight of noncombatants in South Vietnam by immediately restricting aerial bombardments within the country to military targets," its resolution was based on an entirely too restrictive notion of a military target or else on an erroneous assumption as to the facts. There is good reason to believe it recommended that our present policy be carried out.

The weighing of all these considerations in reaching a conclusion justifying or not justifying bombing guerrilla-held territories is quite difficult. One can "admire" in a certain sense those who do not have any doubt about their judgments; but, to say the least, no one should emulate or be swayed by public pronouncements that confuse and mislead public opinion by using an entirely false notion of the principle of discrimination. Thus, *The Call to the March on Washington for Peace in Vietnam* affirmed (under the heading of "atrocities") that "all of the brutality practiced by Vietnamese on Vietnamese of both sides is of *small scale* besides the enormity of the suffering, crippling, and destruction visited on combatants and noncombatants alike by the U.S. forces in the indiscriminate use of weapons far too powerful to be confined to the supposed foe."[10] This may be an "enormity": that it is has to be proved in terms of cost/benefits, taking into account all that is at stake and weighing this against the cost/benefits of genuine alternatives. But the assertion that weapons are being indiscriminately used because they are "far too powerful to be confined to the supposed foe" is *ab initio* mistaken. The principle of discrimination never required that the use of weapons be "confined" to the foe. To "prove" that the stepped-up action in South Vietnam is an atrocity because it necessarily causes a large number of civilian casualties, and *therefore* is *indiscriminate,* must simply be set down as an effort to stop a war by using an erroneous notion of what would be a discriminating one. The fact that The Call was signed by a number of leading intellectuals and ministers shows a breakdown of the tradition of justice in warfare that is almost without cultural parallel. When the leaders of public opinion show themselves not even to be within hailing distance of a discrim-

Moral Argument and the War in Vietnam

inating understanding of the principle of discrimination, by using a notion of just conduct in war to which no war was ever supposed to conform in order to try to stop this one, then it is not surprising that in the present age some military leaders and analysts would use no notion of discrimination at all in the regulation of military action.

Still the least that can be said, and I think the most, is that the question whether the bombing of "stabilized" Vietcong "strongholds" is discriminating enough raises initially grave doubts about the morality of this action. The resolution of this question depends on one's answer to this more basic question, Has the insurgency itself presented us with an enlargement of the target with an associated area of vastly increased secondary damage? And the least that can be said concerning the question whether, even so, the destruction entailed is incommensurate with a realistic estimate of the political benefits that there is hope of gaining is that no one should surrender to certitude concerning his own prudential judgments or impune the motives or the wisdom of men who disagree. . . .

The objective of combat is the incapacitation of a combatant from doing what he is doing because he is this particular combatant in this particular war; it is *not* the killing of a man because he is a man or because he is this particular man. The latter and only the latter would be "murder." This is the indestructible difference between murder and killing in war; and the difference is to be found in the intention and direction of the action that kills. From the requirement that just acts of war be directed upon the combatant and not upon the man flows the prohibition of the killing of soldiers who by surrender have taken themselves out of the war and incapacitated themselves from continuing it. The men are not to be killed when effective combatancy is no longer in them, since all along it was the combatant and not the man who had to be stopped.

From this also flows the cardinal principle governing just conduct in war, namely the moral immunity of noncombatants from deliberate, direct attack. This is the principle of *discrimination*, and in it there are two ingredients. One is the prohibition of "deliberate, direct attack." This is the immutable, unchanging ingredient in the definition of justice in war. In order to get to know the meaning of "aiming discriminately" *vs.* "aiming *in*discriminately," one has only to pay attention to the nature of an action and analyze action in a proper fashion. The second ingredient is the meaning of "combatancy-noncombatancy." This is relativistic and varying in meaning and application. . . . "Combatancy-noncombatancy" is a function of how the nations and their forces are organized for war, and it is in some measure a function of military technology.

There are at least three constituent elements in the moral life and in any ethical analysis of morality. There are first the *motives* of the agent and any other ingredients that may, so to speak, be in his head or in his subjective consciousness. There is secondly the *intention* of the action. And there is thirdly the ultimate ends or consequences of the action. Each of these has to be reckoned in a complete appraisal of morality. While the terms moralists use vary, ordinarily *goodness* or its opposite are said to characterize the motives of agents; *right or wrong,* the intended shape of the action; and *good* or *evil,* the ultimate effects.

Since the moral immunity of noncombatants from direct attack is a doctrine that rests upon an analysis of the intentionality of actions of a military sort, the *pons asinorum* for understanding the meaning of this requires that the intention of the action be always distinguished from the motives of men (and from anything else that may be in their heads besides intentional aims) and from the final, expected consequences of the course of events set going by those actions. Any collapse of these elements into one another will be a mistake. This is what accounts for most of the gross misunderstandings of what is even proposed by proponents of the principle of discrimination in the political use of violence. This also accounts for Tucker's* evident misreading of the meaning of right conduct in *bellum justum.*

Tucker seems to agree that the subjective motives of men should be largely set aside in trying to penetrate the meaning of *just conduct* in war. He says that subjective consciousness is too "indeterminate," by which I judge he means that motives and the subjective states of agents are too various and variable to be of much help in determining the meaning of just conduct or of prudent conduct in politics and in military strategy. This is correct, however important the motives of men are in character analysis and even if moral motives and character are not without significance in the conduct of affairs.

Presumably the death of combatants ideally should not be *wanted. Wanting* the death that is done to combatants and *not wanting* the death done to noncombatants cannot, then, be the meaning of the principle of discrimination surrounding the latter with moral immunity from direct attack in war. Still Tucker fails to maintain this distinction between whatever else may be in the heads of human agents and the intention of their actions, or between the intention of an action and its ultimate consequences.

He collapses *foreknowledge* of unavoidable death and damage to civilians collateral to the destruction of legitimate military targets into the meaning of *intending* or meaning to kill them. Anything I *knew* would happen must be an undifferentiated part of the meaning of what I meant or intended to do. This is simply a flaw in ethical analysis that cannot withstand examination. If motives such as hatred or subjectively wanting or not wanting the killing are not decisive in determining the intention

---

*Mr. Ramsey's reference here is to Robert W. Tucker's *Just War and Vatican Council II: A Critique* (New York: Council on Religion and International Affairs, 1966). *"Bellum justum"* in the succeeding part of the sentence refers to "just war."

Moral Argument and the War in Vietnam

of the action, neither is knowledge of the attendant results along with the intended results sufficient to obliterate a significant moral and political distinction between these two sorts of immediate effects of all acts of war. Indeed, in one important respect Professor Tucker's language is not apt or technical enough to lead him to a right understanding of this teaching in the theory of *bellum justum*. He correctly speaks of *direct* and *indirect action*. But then he speaks in parallel fashion of *directly* or *indirectly intending* something, where the doctrine speaks instead of intending or *not* intending something. The deaths of noncombatants are to be only *indirectly done* and they should be *un*intended in the just conduct of war whose actions may and should be, and are intended to be, directed upon combatants and legitimate military objectives. This aiming of intention and of action is entirely compatible with *certain* knowledge that a great number of civilian lives will unintendedly be indirectly destroyed. (Both are quite different from *wanting* either from malicious motives.)

Thus, Professor Tucker deduces the intention of an act of war from the consequences that are foreseen. In fact, he is inclined to deduce intention from the nature and objective amount of the destruction done. When this latter step has been taken, the excellent start that was made by distinguishing between wanting and intending something remains in the words only, and is of little usefulness in the analysis of military plans and actions. Because Professor Tucker finally believes that intention is as indeterminate and variable as motive, he rightly locates motives in the hearts of men where they have no immediate significance in analyzing statecraft or acts of war, and he wrongly deduces or determines the intentions of political agents and of military actions by reference to events in the objective order alone. Between the motives of men and the total consequences of their actions, the meaning of intention is squeezed out.

This simply makes it impossible for Tucker to grasp the meaning of "aiming indiscriminately," or the meaning of the intention. Thus the actual aiming and the actual or the foreseen destruction are telescoped together, or at least the meaning of the intention is given by the destruction foreseen. But since he wishes to retain the word "intention," and wishes to use it in political analysis at least to refute *bellum justum,* he gives it a meaning it never had in that theory.

In only extreme cases will it appear to be proper to move from events in the objective order to the attribution of intentions to agents or to their actions. If I use a sledge hammer to kill a fly on my neighbor's bald head it may be not unreasonably supposed that I had a grudge against my neighbor in my motives and also that by my action I *meant* (intended, "aimed") to do him harm. This might be called getting bonus-neighbor-damage while prosecuting man's war against the insects, if indeed killing the fly was not itself incidental to the aiming of my destructive act upon his head. Similarly, from the extensive de-

108

struction of Dresden, from the cruciality of the vast fire-storm to the plan of attack (to light the way for successive waves of bombers), it is not unreasonable to conclude that the destruction of the railway complex was incidental, even if we had no other evidence for the fact the railway complex was not even aimed at.

In general, it simply has to be said that these days we are better able to analyze play-acting than moral action. We speak of the "intention" of a drama as something in the play, in the action itself, not to be identified with everything the author thought he was writing. Similarly, the intention of a human action cannot be identified with everything the author thought or knew, or thought he knew, about the total consequences. Beginning in the *aiming* of the action, the intention of an act then includes the main *thrust* of it upon its immediate objective. There is, thus, a distinction between what is directly done by the thrust of action and what is incidentally, indirectly done attendant upon this thrust. Only the immediate objective is subjectively intended; the other foreseeable effects are *un*intended.

This brings us to the need to distinguish the intention of the act and its immediate effects from the ultimate consequences. The intention or thrust of the action is by no means directed immediately toward ultimate consequences, but toward the production of an immediate event that is reasonably believed itself to be productive of those future good consequences. Professor Tucker magnifies the doing of evil that good may come, first, by falsely implying that everything foreseeably done in the event was in some sense intended and then, secondly, by lumping everything done in the event (including collateral civilian deaths) without differentiation into the "means" by which politically good consequences are obtained. This too is a mistake in the analysis of action.

Perhaps an illustration will demonstrate more clearly what is at stake in distinguishing between the immediate effects of action (some intended and direct, others unintended and indirect) from the ultimate good consequences an action seeks to serve. The intention or present thrust of action concerns immediate effects, not the ulterior purposes or objectives. The latter may be *good* and yet the intention (the direct immediate *thrust* of the action) may be *wrong*. Indeed in some respects it would be more correct to say that the motives of men rather than their intentions are oriented upon ultimate objectives. While granting that this may only be a verbal convention, it has at least to be said that the "intention" of which *bellum justum* speaks is not fixed on ultimate ends. Perhaps we need to change the convention and speak of intention in two different senses. There would be intention (1) to indicate the usage of this word in *bellum justum*. Then there is intention (2) to indicate the meaning Tucker gives to this word.[11] But this is certain: Tucker's meaning cannot be used to interpret the meaning this word has in *bellum justum*, or to refute that theory by proving it ambiguous. It can only be used to

109

Moral Argument and the War in Vietnam

displace it, and thus to instate another understanding of morality or of statecraft, or both. Before coming fully to grips with Tucker's displacing definition, I will stick with the convention, and ask:

What is at stake in not collapsing the intention of human actions into orientation upon the ends produced?

Take the case of moral conflict between the life of a mother and her unborn child. It is well known that Roman Catholic teaching prohibits, in this conflict between equals, *direct* abortion as a means of saving the mother's life. Suppose someone wants to contend against this verdict and so justify *direct* abortion in such cases. Unless he denies the premise that the unborn child is a human being, it will not be sufficient for him simply to *assert* arbitrarily that direct abortion is the right action because this will save the life of the mother. The goodness of this ultimate result was never in question. No one doubts that the proposed medical action will respect the sanctity of the mother's life. The question that was raised is whether direct abortion is not in every way incompatible with any remaining regard for the sanctity of the nascent life.

In order for anyone to wrestle with his Catholic brother over the verdict forbidding direct abortion, he will have to propose another penetration of the intention and main thrust of this action and its immediate effects. He will have to say something significantly different from the Catholic view about direct abortion *as an action brought upon the child.* If instead he prattles endlessly about saving the mother's life he shows only that he does not know where the argument is, since that ultimate good was never in question. It helps not at all to say that we should do what a charitable reason requires in the final consequence, since the question is whether every shred of respect for the sanctity of nascent life must not be abandoned ever to do such a thing (direct killing of the innocent) for the sake of those consequences. No one ever doubted that the proposed action has effects that are ultimately charitable to the mother. It is therefore no argument to say that it is. The issue to be faced is whether the present action demonstrates (in its intention and in the shape of its primary thrust in the world and its immediate effects) any remaining recognition of the fact that the littlest and least important human life has a sanctity that is not wholly to be denied in anything we now do.

This is precisely the issue raised by proponents of the moral immunity of noncombatants from direct attack (or, more briefly, the principle of discrimination) as a principle that should govern the political use of violence. It is no answer to affirm that there are ultimate ends which statecraft must have in view, even the preservation of a just or humane political order as a safe dwelling place for the human beings remaining alive and for future generations of men all of whom have a dignity and sanctity which should be respected. It is not enough simply to reiterate that this is a good and proper end of politics, with the implication, without argument, that to this all else is properly menial. The question that was raised was how the ends of the state can be served by plans and acts of war that evidence some remaining respect for the sanctity of persons now alive and with whom we are presently engaged. The proposal was that, if one focuses attention upon the intention and thrust of present action, it will be evident that acts of war *aimed indiscriminately* at the destruction of entire cities and extensive areas along with their populations cannot possibly be compatible with any remaining regard for the sanctity of human life as such. The contention is that if one is going to justify killing in war this must be intentionally limited (in the sense explained) to combatants and to the destruction of legitimate military objectives, and that one's just regard for the dignity of manhood and one's resolve not to reduce this to a mere instrument of statecraft will manifest itself in noncombatant immunity as a regulative principle. It is no answer to this argument to proceed to collapse the intention of present action into the ultimate ends of statecraft, the goodness of which no proponent of *bellum justum* ever meant to question. What would be required, in order to refute the traditional understanding of just conduct in war, would be another penetration of the present intention and thrusts of acts of war and their immediate effects that seeks to show that noncombatant immunity or the principle of discrimination does not adequately express the justice governing present action and intention. What is required would be a reforming and not a displacing definition of intention. I venture to believe that such a properly targeted rebuttal cannot succeed. . . .

Perhaps it would be helpful to introduce here a few illustrations in which the "scope of the death and injury" remains the same whatever be the intention. From these cases it may be seen that the meaning of the intention can be reasonably and "objectively" discriminated from the "incidentality" of other effects falling unavoidably *within* the scope of the destruction. From these cases we can also see the *importance* of making this distinction even in cases in which the objective damage remains the same. This will prove that, so far as the theory under discussion is concerned, it is incorrect to define what is intended or what is the means leading to the manifold effects of action simply in terms of the objective consequences.

An obstetrician has two women as patients. Both have cancer of the uterus requiring prompt surgical action to remove it. One is pregnant, the other is not.

In both cases it is possible to know the intention of the surgical action. Whether the death of the fetus is directly intended or is beside the intention is clearly *not* determined by the scope of the injury. It is not a matter of quantity. The death of the fetus is *not* a means to saving the mother's life simply because this end cannot be secured without that effect. Nor should it be said that the fetal death is *as much a means* as the destruction of the cancerous uterus, which is the legitimate

Moral Argument and the War in Vietnam

surgical objective. The doctor does not intend that consequence simply because he *knows* that it will result from his surgery and nevertheless performs the operation. To have in mind the death of the fetus that will be brought about is not his intention. He does *not* intend the one effect as much as he intends the other effect. Unless of course he was going about getting bonus-fetal-damage. However, we could not determine whether he was or was not meaning to kill the fetus without first knowing the meaning of the direct intention and thrust of proper surgery in this instance. The other case, of the nonpregnant cancerous uterus, shows that this discrimination can be made rationally even in the case of the pregnant woman. In both cases the means of "victory" was the destruction of the diseased uterus, and not also, in the one case, the foreseeable collateral, "incidental" death of the fetus.

The intention of combat and the result of action is the incapacitation of a combatant, not the killing of a man. *Objection:* He is killed in any case. The "scope" of the injury is the same. The consequence is the same. *Reply:* Yes, but the importance of distinguishing the main thrust of an act of combat from the unavoidable, foreseeable attendant killing of a man even when these produce the same objective event becomes manifestly clear when one asks about the treatment to be justly accorded soldiers who incapacitate themselves as combatants and take themselves out of the war by surrendering. The rule of practice that captured soldiers are not to be killed, and which protects them from gross mistreatment, is a dictate of the justice *inherent* in the conduct of war as a barely human enterprise. This is a regulative principle, a rule of civilized warfare itself. Its bearing upon the conduct of war may not be that captured soldiers ought never to be killed (in fluid, jungle situations in which the "noncombatant" is liable to return quickly to the status of combatant, there being no stockades in which to insure that he will remain a nonwarrior.) The bearing of this rule of practice in war may be instead the requirement that every effort be made to implement this limit upon the killing in the entire shape, manner, and "institutions" mounted in the conduct of war. This illustration should also serve to indicate something that is too often forgotten when one hears ethicists discussing the moral dimensions of the political use of violence. The upshot is never mainly the definition of culpable individual acts or agents—defining "sin" and making "sinners"—but rather the criticism of institutions and practices. Thus is *bellum justum* a theory of statecraft.

The "incidentality" of killing the man to stopping the combatant is not determined by objective consequences, or by the scope of the death. The incapacitation of a combatant is the means, not the other effect without which this cannot be secured. One need *not* intend this other consequence he knows will result beside the intention and beside the prime objective of combat, if, knowing killing to be unavoidable, he nevertheless engages in combat. The case of the surrendered soldier shows this clearly to be the case, whatever may be the vagaries and furies of men. Justice in the treatment of the man after surrender helps us to see the discrimination to be made in analyzing the difference between "killing in war" and "murder." This shows that the distinction between objectives is *there*, and can be drawn.

During World War II, some of the prominent leaders of world Judaism tried to persuade the Allies to bomb all of Hitler's concentration camps and extermination ovens, even though this would certainly kill all of the inmates at the time of the action. They reasoned that more innocent victims would be saved in the time that would elapse before the camps could be reconstructed and their genocidal work be going again, than lives would be lost "incidental" to destroying the target-camps and personnel that should justly have been repressed. Would this have been to do evil that good may come? Prescinding from whether the proposed action would, or would likely enough, have achieved the proportion of effectiveness and value expected (which would be sufficient reason for declaring that this should not be done), we need to ask, would such strikes against the concentration camps have been deliberate, direct attacks upon the innocent no less than upon the furnaces?

The answer to this is clearly, No. This shows that one does not deduce intention from the consequences. In this case, also, whether the deaths are directly intended or beside the intention cannot be determined by the scope of the death and destruction. Incidentality is not a matter of quantity, even where the quantity remains the same and cannot be altered by any difference in the intention

Notes

1 The title of a book by Robert Taber (New York: Lyle Stuart, 1965) "The guerrilla fights the war of the flea, and his military enemy suffers the dog's disadvantage; too much to defend, too small, ubiquitous, and too agile an enemy to come to grips with."

2 *War and the Christian Conscience* (Durham, N.C.: Duke University Press, 1961).

3 McGowan v. Maryland, 336 U.S. 420 at 422 (1961) (italics added). For other illustrations of the meaning of the distinction between "primary" and "secondary" effects and intentions, see p. 315, n. 2 of my *The Just War: Force and Political Responsibility*. I have elsewhere shown that at its heart this distinction originated historically, and logically always must arise, from charity seeking to deal with difficult cases in which the good alone cannot be done. This "justification" does not fall within the purposes of this paper. We must rather proceed to the "doing" of political ethics.

4 *Mao Tse-tung On Guerrilla Warfare*, translated by Brigadier General Samuel B. Griffith USMC (Ret.) (New York: Frederick A. Praeger, Publishers, 1961/65), p. 73.

5 "The [people] may be likened to water and the [army] to the fish who inhabit it." "With the common people of the whole country mobilized, we shall create a vast sea of humanity and drown the enemy in it . . ." (Q. by E. L. Katzenbach, Jr.: "Time, Space, and Will: The Politico-Military Views of Mao Tse-tung," in *The Guerrilla—and How to Fight Him*, ed., by Lt. Col. T. N. Greene (New York: Frederick A. Praeger, 1962), p. 14.

6 *Mao Tse-tung on Guerrilla Warfare*, p. 93.

7 *Ibid.*, p. 92 and Greene, *op. cit*, p. 6.

8 See William Tuohy's "A Big 'Dirty Little War' " in *The New York Times Magazine*, Sunday, Nov. 28, 1965.

9 See the report by Charles Mohr on "Rising War Worries Vietnamese in South but They Stay Loyal," *The New York Times*, Nov. 28, 1965.

10 *The New York Times*, Nov. 25, 1965, p. 29.

11 This distinction between two sorts of intention is related to the distinction Ralph Potter made—in his comment upon Tucker's essay—between two sorts of "evils." My "intention (1)" may be linked with Potter's "evil" (the evil *consequences* of action that may not be "morally reprehensive" ("evil ²")). See p. 58 of *Just War and Vatican Council II*, cited at the beginning of this present chapter.

Part III

Solutions?

Solutions?

Introduction

Mary McCarthy remarks that the question, What is the United States to do now that it *has* so heavily intervened in Vietnam? is bound to strike the critic of American policy as "a real crusher."[1] I suspect that observation is not unrelated to another which we might make: the question, What are the moral principles relevant to finding a solution to the war? is equally "a crusher." The main thrust of the previous two sections' moral discussion has been directed at the morality of the war itself, not simply at how to conduct it. And yet when those conclusions about the war itself—suppose they turn out negative—are applied to the task of getting out, they may seem to yield little. It is always at least conceivable that the results of withdrawal could outweigh in their evil the results of staying in. The goods and evils of getting out must be weighed against the goods and evils of *staying* in, not the values of having gotten in, for moral *decision*, rather than moral judgment, is necessarily a decision for the present and future. Historical judgments and the "backward-looking" character of much moral evaluation are relevant to decision *only* as they can be shown to affect evaluation of present and future events. Of the five just war criteria previously discussed, for instance, only the last, the weighing of goods and evils, seems at first clearly to fit the business of making a moral decision about what to do now. Yet that is probably the one criterion of those five which is hardest to apply. For one thing, looking to the future is attempting to evaluate contingent events which we cannot be sure will happen. This, of course, cuts both ways: it is no easier, in light of the contingency of the future, morally to commit ourselves to staying in (or withdrawing as gradually as in the present administration's policy) than it is to commit ourselves to any of the plans for promptly getting out. So here, just where we yearn for moral criteria to help us the most, they lend us the weakest hand.

This skepticism about moral criteria for solutions is founded on some correct observations, but it is also, I think, a skepticism which can be modified substantially by clear moral reflection. These introductory remarks will focus on two concepts in the solutions debate which leave much room for discussion of important moral principles: "honor" and "reciprocity." Hopefully, the ensuing selections will then seem a little more relevant than they would otherwise.

Moral Argument and the War in Vietnam

Much is made of the need for an "honorable exit" from Vietnam. First, it should not be automatically assumed that a fully honorable solution is possible, and if it is not possible we need not, of course, make it a working goal of our efforts. There are tragic and shameful situations from which an exit can be honorable only in the extremely relative sense of being better than others which are much worse. It is possible that, no matter what terms of honor we agree on, United States involvement in Vietnam might be such a situation.

I will not belabor that point. More important to notice is that the terms of honor open a field for widely diverse moral judgments. "Honorable" can mean simply "ultimately successful militarily," a strategic retreat from a tough corner. Such a retreat from Vietnam could also be termed "strategically successful" in terms of the same larger policy goals we had in getting into Vietnam—supposedly the containment of aggressive communism, the enhancement of formal democratic ideals, and the preservation of an international stability in which traditional United States interests, could be pursued. That should make us notice that honor is defined by certain underlying goals. If agreement cannot be reached on what goals the United States ought to pursue in the larger foreign policy context of its Vietnam action, then agreement on what constitutes honor will not be attainable. Suppose a critic of the war disagrees that any sovereignty of the Saigon government needed to be preserved by United States intervention against the allegedly externally sponsored aggression by the NLF; then he will hardly define an honorable exit from Vietnam as one which preserves some control by the present Saigon government and denies dominance to the NLF.

It may seem that honor is a much narrower concept, founded not on ultimate goals but on commitments and decisions which have already been made. Thus President Nixon speaks of "prestige" in its "not empty" sense—a concept closely linked to "honor"—as the integrity of a nation "in defending its principles and meeting its obligations."[2] "Its principles" and "its obligations" here imply that a nation already *has* them; it is irrelevant whether we should have made these our principles or whether we should have made the commitments which created our obligations. The fact is that we *have* decided on these principles, and we *have* made these commitments, and *therefore* we have such-and-such obligations to uphold them.

Now it is certainly true that making commitments and decisions does create obligations. But the obligations so created are not necessarily our *final* obligations to actually do a certain thing. We can, of course, change our decisions or principles—not, certainly, on whim, yet nevertheless on reflection. And even commitments can be changed. One's having made a promise to someone, e.g., does not close the question of his obligation to fulfill it. It may have been a promise he should not have made, or keeping the promise may conflict with certain other moral obligations. Then, to be sure, he is faced with a *dilemma* and not just a completely one-sided case against keeping the promise. Yet it is quite possible that he should finally break it. Promise-keeping is not the only morally relevant consideration in such a case. Likewise, the moral obligations of nations will not be determined solely by keeping commitments and persevering in the principles on which the nation has decided. Saying this does not in itself decide any concrete matter about the morality of United States withdrawal from Vietnam. That requires some further moral imputs—the value we give to the "stability" arising from our nation's commitment fulfillment, the morality of those commitments themselves, etc. It does reveal that "honorable solution" is a claim that may consistently be made for many different proposals, each from its own moral perspective.

This puts the focus of argument over honorable exit from Vietnam back onto certain fundamental policies and goals. In proposing any solution to the war it is crucial to recognize this. Mr. Kissinger, for instance, notes that an "imprudent risk" for peace is likely to lead not to peace but to escalation.[3] He is quite correct for the situation he has in mind: if our military effort is sharply curtailed in hopes of a negotiated compromise and the other side does not respond as the public would hope, then the American government would no doubt be pressed to remove all last restraints on our military effort. What needs to be noticed, however, is that risks for peace are only "imprudent" when they rest on the same minimal willingness to compromise that emerged from the basic policies and attitudes which led to the military involvement in the first place. But *if those* are changed, if as Mr. Schoenbrun says the "plan is a change of attitudes and objectives,"[4] then risks for peace cease to be imprudent, or even "risks" at all.

The same analysis may be applied to the risks which Mr. Hassler describes the "Third Force" in Vietnam to be willing to take for peace.[5] Their solution may seem risky to proponents of American policy (can they really be so idealistic as to predict that the NLF will not override even their own groups in the political struggle ensuing after United States withdrawal?), but it may not appropriately be called a risk at all if it is not so much a prediction—shaky as predictions always are—as a different value, attitude, and objective.[6]

A second major concept in need of clarification is "reciprocity." The process of "negotiation" is usually expected to be a reciprocal process: both sides give up something, and both sides gain (or stand an equal chance to gain) something else. Such a reciprocal process is thought to result in a *fair* compromise. Thus Mr. Little in an earlier section accuses the NLF of unfairness in its attitude toward negotiations: it negotiates only for solutions vastly in its favor.[7] That is morally condemnable, for one moral obligation men have is to be *fair*. Mr. Kissinger explains that the premise of the political settlement which he advocates as the central aim of negotiations is that "both sides think they have a chance to win, or at least to avoid losing."[8] Mr. Huntington speaks

119

Moral Argument and the War in Vietnam

of both sides "accommodating" themselves to the "realities" of the population the other "controls."[9]

In many situations this is precisely the relevant model for compromise, negotiation, and fair settlement, but it depends on two assumptions, and it can be argued that either or both is missing in Vietnam: no one side is clearly right in its initial moral claims about the situation, and the situation at the time of negotiations is presumed to be one of "equality." Both moral and historical factors may enter into criticism of these assumptions, and therefore also into criticism of Messrs. Little's, Kissinger's, and Huntington's (and presumably the United States government's) views of a fair settlement. Mr. Kolko defends North Vietnam's and the NLF's argument that mutual withdrawal of North Vietnamese and American forces from South Vietnam unfairly places the aggressor on the same plane as the victim. He relates historical judgments about aggression to subsequent achievement of a genuinely fair settlement. Mr. Draper asks what reciprocity can mean between the technological might of the United States and the relatively peasant economy of North Vietnam. And he claims that reciprocity means nothing (or its conception has to be very different from the usual one) once the United States has thrown its massive weight into a civil war.[10] If Mr. Huntington is correct in contending that United States intervention has drastically reduced the social basis of the NLF, then the alleged fairness of any settlement based on the present realities of power in South Vietnam begs the question of the morality of United States intervention in the first place. Likewise, a model based on the portion of the populace each side "controls" through sheer power may beg the morally important factor of the "support" which each side has.[11] If, as Mr. Draper claims, the United States has previously sabotaged negotiations at times when Allied control in South Vietnam was much less than it is now, then it may not be fair in present negotiations to grant to the United States the increased Allied power that has been created in the meantime. If the United States and Diem were mainly to blame for the collapse of the scheduled 1956 elections which the other side would handily have won, holding elections in the now different situation may not be a fair way of presently proceeding. Mr. Hassler claims that a new Third Force government in Saigon cannot itself be elected, for that would beg the question of who would organize fair and free elections.[12] That point, too, is the rub between the NLF and United States negotiating positions: the United States will accept a "coalition government" after elections; the NLF demands it before the elections are held.

The articles and organization of this section will probably seem to the reader to be less clearly focused on moral issues than those of the previous sections. I hope that does not decrease their value. The selections by Mr. Schoenbrun and Miss McCarthy explicitly relate historical and moral judgments to the question of present action. Messrs. Ackland and Porter's article attempts to clear one argument out of the way—that the United States must not withdraw, because it is obligated to the thousands who would be massacred by a victorious enemy. Mr. Kissinger's selection, the official statements of the United States government, and the NLF's Ten Points present the basic negotiating positions of two of the parties at the Paris conference. Mr. Draper's article critically reflects on some past United States negotiating. The paper by Mr. Huntington and the selection by Mr. Hassler present proposals rather different from any official position at the talks.[13]

Notes

1 McCarthy, p. 129.

2 Nixon, p. 157-158.

3 Kissinger, p. 151.

4 Schoenbrun, p. 128.

5 Hassler, pp. 207-208, 211.

6 That, too, may be part of the reason the Third Force thinks they, as the majority of the South Vietnamese populace, should have the right to decide to take that risk, while to United States policy-makers it seems quite in order for Americans (in conjunction with the Saigon government) to decide not to take it. It seems less elitist and colonialist for us to base our policy on *predictions* different from theirs than on values, attitudes, and objectives different from theirs. One claim of knowledge may be rather definitively *justified* over and against another, but one value, attitude, or objective seems less justified and more simply chosen. (This last explanation may seem to rest on a philosophical objectivism in epistemology and relativism in value theory. It *can* rest on that, but it need not. It may rest only on the observation that knowledge claims are potentially less relative or more objective than valuation. I merely note here this connection with some major subjects of philosophical inquiry, and do not pursue it in its own right.)

7 Little, p. 24.

8 Kissinger, p. 155. Note that Mr. Kissinger assumes this to be possible. But that may be in question. If the differences between opposing sides in Vietnam are so great; if the situation is fully revolutionary in the sense that the two sides have fundamentally different, pervasive ideas on the structure of the society; if one side or the other rests on such a narrow base that any serious compromise would jeopardize its very existence, then that kind of solution may not be feasible.

9 Huntington, pp. 193-194.

10 Draper, pp. 186-190.

11 Huntington explicitly wants to talk in terms of control, not support, p. 194.

12 Hassler, p. 206.

13 I have not included any material assessing the Nixon administration's Vietnamization program. My excuse, for the very little it may be worth, is a lack (to my knowledge) of outstanding writing on this subject at this time. Another factor may be more a reason and less an excuse: the basic moral questions about United States intervention in Vietnam and support of the Saigon government apply to the continuing air, tactical, and financial support that is still a necessary part of any "Vietnamization" program.

Vietnam: The Case for Extrication*

David Schoenbrun

Most of the men who rule Saigon have, like the Bourbons, learned nothing and forgotten nothing. They seek to retain those privileges they have and to regain those they have lost. In Vietnam only the Communists represent revolution and social change. The Communist party is the one truly national organization that permeates both North and South Vietnam. It is the only group not dependent on foreign bayonets for survival. For its own strategic and political ends the United States is thus protecting a non-Communist Vietnamese social structure that cannot defend itself and that perhaps does not deserve to be defended.

Our responsibility for prolonging what is essentially a civil conflict may be one of the major reasons for the considerable amount of confusion, guilt and soul-searching among Americans over the Vietnam War. I simply cannot help worrying that, in the process of waging this war, we are corrupting ourselves. I wonder when I look at the bombed-out peasant hamlets, the orphans begging and stealing in the streets of Saigon, and the women and children with napalm burns lying on the hospital cots, whether the US or any nation has the right to inflict this suffering and degradation on another people for its own ends.

I agree with the paragraphs above although I did not write them. They are composed of sentences excerpted from a much remarked-upon article in *The New York Times Magazine* (Oct. 9, 1966) "Not a Dove, But No Longer a Hawk" by Neil Sheehan, who has been covering the Pentagon since returning from Vietnam last August.

Neil Sheehan is not a Nervous Nelly, not a Peacenik, not a Vietnik, not even anything so supposedly un-American as an intellectual. He is a professional reporter who once "believed in what my country was doing in Vietnam," but who, as of October 9, 1966, no longer believes. Along with many of his fellow citizens, he goes so far as to "wonder" whether his country "has the right to inflict this suffering and degradation on another people for its own ends." His is the cry of anguish of an honest man who has gone far toward the realization that his country is doing something very wrong. He has not yet gone that one vital step further to the only attitude that has both practical and moral importance: the willingness to right the wrong. His cry of anguish ends

Moral Argument and the War in Vietnam

with a whimper: "Despite these misgivings I do not see how we can do anything but continue to prosecute the war"—and with a pious prayer: "I hope that we will not, in the name of some anti-Communist crusade, do this again."

A professional reporter myself, with long experience in Vietnam, particularly the larger region—Vietnam, Cambodia and Laos—once known as French Indochina, I read Sheehan's article with strong emotion: admiration for the sweep and depth of his reporting: respect for his distress and soul-searching, bemusement as to why he did not include more of these facts in his daily reports from Vietnam: finally, a hot flash of anger at his grotesque conclusion that we must continue to prosecute an evil war that cannot be won. How many readers, like myself, clutched at their sanity as an otherwise lucid writer concluded that there is no way out of a frightful mess other than to dig deeper into it?

A Personal and National Dilemma

If this were Neil Sheehan's personal dilemma it could easily be dismissed in light of his valuable documentation. But the greater value of Sheehan's article is that it so fully reflects a national dilemma, broad and deep across the country and indeed, within the government itself. . . .

This attitude is most frequently expressed in the statement: Maybe we shouldn't have gotten into this, but since we have, we must see it through.

Perhaps the most prominent spokesman for this view is General Eisenhower, whose recent reversal of attitude reflects this widely held position. In October, 1966, Eisenhower said we must do everything necessary to wage the war successfully, and he refused to rule out even the possibility of using atomic weapons. Yet I heard General Eisenhower talk very differently two years ago.

I visited Eisenhower at his farm in Gettysburg, on August 25, 1964, on the occasion of the twentieth anniversary of the liberation of Paris. In the course of a talk lasting several hours the General reminisced about the French Indochinese War and the pressures he had put upon the French to conduct it differently. They could not rally the people to their side, he recalled, adding that no white, Western nation could win colonial war in Asia. He then talked about our own dilemma in Vietnam and his decision to give economic aid to Ngo Dinh Diem to help him resist communism. "That's the only way it can be done," Eisenhower told me. "We can only help them to help themselves." He thought then that we could not and should not try to do their fighting for them. Today he thinks differently and the reason is surely evident: our massive commitment to defeat communism in Vietnam has in Eisenhower's view created a new situation.

Eisenhower has not contradicted himself. He now believes that the context has so changed that we need no longer concern ourselves with what changed it; perhaps we should never have gotten involved, but there is no point in dwelling upon past history. Historian Arthur Schlesinger, Jr., apparently agrees. He began his article "A Middle Way Out of Vietnam" in *The New York Times Magazine* (Sept. 18, 1966) by stating: "Why we are in Vietnam today is a question of only historical interest. We *are* there, for better or for worse, and we must deal with the situation that exists. . . . Our stake in South Vietnam may have been self-created, but it has nonetheless become real."

The Value of Looking Backward

Nothing could be more dangerous than this kind of thinking. The point in examining the past is not to cry over spilled milk or to indulge in useless blame-finding, but to find out what went wrong and why so that we might see more clearly, first, how to put it right and, second, how best to answer Sheehan's prayer that we don't do it again.

To illustrate the value of looking backward in the dispute, let us examine the question of the nature of the war, particularly the issue of aggression. The Johnson administration talks constantly of North Vietnamese "aggression," sometimes simplifying it to "Communist aggression." Over and over at the Manila Conference, and in its final communique, aggression was the word used to describe the war. If we simply accept this charge without checking it against the historical record—that is, if we persuade ourselves that "now" is unrelated to "then"—it will be almost impossible, I believe, to find the way to peace. Hanoi will certainly not enter negotiations as the "aggressor."

Examination of the record would show a situation very different from today. (Is that why we are so often urged to forget it?) Certainly Hanoi is taking aggressive action now in sending regular soldiers to fight in South Vietnam. But Hanoi's view, which is accepted by most observers outside the US, is that the original provocation was committed by South Vietnamese and by the US in jointly refusing to carry out the provisions of the Geneva Accords. North Vietnam did not send troops south until after the American build-up.

Hanoi has been reacting to both the American intervention and the refusal of South Vietnam to hold free elections. It is also reacting to the usurpation of power by a military clique that is not representative of the Vietnamese people, and not even of the South Vietnamese, since Premier Ky and his principal aides are refugees from the North.

It does not invalidate these facts to argue that Ho Chi Minh does not represent the people either, or that what we are facing is some new kind of internal aggression. That is precisely what all the turmoil has been about. From the very start there has been a civil war among the Vietnamese, not a Korean-like aggression by the North against the South. And if this fundamental truth cannot be accepted, then any kind of an honorable settlement is beyond hope. You can't settle a fight

Moral Argument and the War in Vietnam

if you do not know what it is all about. I do not speak of history only from hindsight. I watched all of this happen. I was at the Battle of Dienbienphu; when I saw the Chinese mortars going into position on the crest of the hills above the valley, I knew I was watching the end of the era of Western dominance in Asia. I flew from Hanoi to Saigon to Geneva with Prince Buu Loc, then Prime Minister of South Vietnam. I covered the conference and interviewed the principal actors. They came to the conclusion that Western powers could no longer determine the flow of history in Asia; that the best that could be expected for the West was an independent, neutralist Vietnam, Communist but not a satellite of China.

I have come to believe that period deserves the closest study by American citizens, not because errors were made or evil done intentionally, but because the leaders of our country, Eisenhower and Kennedy in turn, either were not aware of the dynamics that would follow from their decisions or discounted the dangers too readily. If we turn our backs on the dynamic process that led us, without intent, into a war we know we should not be fighting, how will we avoid making the same mistakes in the future?

Our predicament began with the judgment of John Foster Dulles—a correct judgment—that Ho Chi Minh had become so popular a national hero that he would win free elections by a big margin (80 percent, President Eisenhower estimated in his memoirs). Every informed observer concurred. It was not the judgment that was wrong, but the conclusion Dulles drew from it. Dulles decided that we must organize an Asian equivalent to NATO, support an anti-Communist leader in South Vietnam and stall off the free elections provided by the Geneva Accords. This led to Eisenhower's letter to Ngo Dinh Diem, our selection as anti-Communist champion, offering economic aid.

Eisenhower then believed that the South Vietnamese needed only our friendly help and guidance. This policy was based on America's brilliant success in Europe, where the Marshall Plan, the Truman Doctrine and NATO combined to provide the fruitful use of economic aid under a military shield against external aggression. The error, of course, was the assumption that a policy that had worked in industrialized, technologically advanced, white, Christian Europe could also work in rural, backward, yellow, non-Christian Asia.

We also failed to understand how the mechanism of our program of aid leads inexorably from butter to guns. We start with the simple proposition that communism is evil and should be stopped from spreading. Therefore anti-Communists must be helped. When we give economic aid, we soon discover we must also provide technological help.

To persuade Congress and the people to give tax dollars the anti-Communists are described as fighters for freedom. When they fail to carry out our proposals for reforms, the fact is hidden because more aid must now be given to prevent their collapse. The investment in aid and technical advisors becomes so great that soldiers are sent to protect it. The soldiers are shot at, so they are authorized to shoot back. The Communists strike harder to prevent the American program from shoring up the adversary. More soldiers are sent and bases are built. Once our honor and power are committed, it becomes our war. And once it becomes our war, then we devise new rules. Thus an Eisenhower who once believed that only Asians should fight an Asian war can two years later approve an American commitment greater than the commitment of the South Vietnamese themselves. . . .

Situations inevitably become polarized into the fatal alternatives: victory or defeat. This false dichotomy is what leads a Neil Sheehan from lucidity to absurdity. He and many other Americans see only a continuation of the war or a "precipitate retreat, degenerating into a rout." Or, as I have heard it said again and again across the nation, "we can't turn tail and run." Of course that isn't the answer; the trouble is, it isn't even the question. The real question is how to find a middle ground between victory and defeat. Is there, as Sheehan suggested, really nothing to do but make a bigger mess?

Is It Too Late to Reverse Our Error?

It is at this point that someone inevitably asks: what can be done about it? I would suggest first of all that we stop using such loaded words as withdraw or retreat. Our problem is rather to *extricate* ourselves from a difficult position, not to fight our way out or to turn tail and run. To extricate ourselves would require a lot of truth-telling. Yet very few Americans even try to examine what others think is the truth.

We charge China with being aggressive and expansionist, but most of the world believes that *we* are the expansionist power. American soldiers, businessmen, and technicians are seen almost everywhere in the world. Hardly a single Chinese soldier is seen outside China, and few Chinese diplomats or technicians are seen anywhere. We believe we are not expansionist because we clearly do not covet territory, but we fail to see that others regard the extension of influence on a global scale as a new form of expansionism. They do not believe that we are in Vietnam only to prevent a South Vietnamese Communist victory of a South Vietnamese military clique. They have long believed—and feel their suspicions confirmed by President Johnson's Asian tour—that the US, a Pacific power, now has a new objective: to extend its power from the Pacific to the continent of Asia.

I have never believed that America's vital interests were at stake in the Vietnamese civil war. I have never accepted the correlation between Munich and a settlement in Vietnam. Mao Tse-tung is not a Hitler, nor is Ho Chi Minh his servant. North Vietnam is not a powerful imperialist nation like Germany. If Ho is comparable to any European, he is the

127

Moral Argument and the War in Vietnam

Tito of Asia. That is, a national Communist, at the head of a small state, trying to keep independent of an enormous Communist neighbor—in the case of Tito, Russia, in the case of Ho, China. If we can live with Tito to the tune of one billion dollars of aid, why is it so unthinkable to live in a world with Ho? Why do we fight for the South Vietnamese when we did not go to war for the Freedom Fighters of Hungary or for the East Germans? By what logic do we now offer more trade and closer relations with Russia and all of Eastern Europe but feel we must make war in Vietnam?

The crux of the matter is this: should not the Vietnamese have been permitted to determine their own fate in the first place? And is it now too late to reverse that error? Can we not return to the basic principle of the Geneva Accords: the creation of a military cease-fire and the beginnings of a negotiation among the Vietnamese themselves by themselves, between the NLF and Saigon in the South and also between South and North?. . . .

No detailed plan would be of any real value today in any case. What is more immediately important than a plan is a change of attitudes and of objectives. If it becomes more important to Americans to end the anguish of this war than to continue it, there will be no problem finding a plan. Plans are, after all, only ways of carrying out what one wants to do. If we want to end the war, to keep Southeast Asia from becoming a world battleground, to neutralize it for everyone's safety, then the detailed plan will easily be found.

Neither a plan nor a prayer would be meaningful except in the service of a new policy.

Solutions*

by Mary McCarthy

"Well, what would you do?" Sooner or later, the critic of U.S. policy in Vietnam is faced with that question—a real crusher. Up to that point, he may have been winning the argument. His opponent may have conceded that it was a mistake to send American troops here in the first place, that there was no commitment under SEATO or any other "instrument" requiring it, that the war is horribly destructive, that pacification is not working, that Hanoi is not responding cooperatively to the bombing—in short, that everything that has been done up to the present instant has been wrong. But now resting comfortably on this mountain of errors, he looks down magnanimously on the critic and invites him to offer a solution. He is confident that the critic will be unable to come up with one. And in a sense he is right. If you say "Get Out"—the only sane answer—he pounces. "How?" And he sits back smiling. He has won. The tables are turned, and the critic is on the defensive. If he tries to outline a plan for rapid withdrawal, conscious that 464,000 troops, plus their civilian supporting services, cannot be pulled out overnight (and what about the "loyal" Vietnamese—should they be left behind or do we owe them an airlift to Taiwan?), the plan inevitably appears feeble and amateurish in comparison with the massed power and professionalism of the war actually being waged.

The fatal weakness in the thinking of most of Johnson's critics is not to perceive that that question is a booby trap. In general, the more eminent they are, the more alacrity they show in popping up with "positive recommendations for policy," "solutions," proposals for gradual and prudent disengagement, lest anybody think they are just carping and have no better alternatives of their own. Take the painful example of Arthur Schlesinger's *The Bitter Heritage*: "cogent, lucid, penetrating—tells us what really ought to be done about Vietnam" (John Gunther). It is cogent, lucid, penetrating *until* Schlesinger tells us what ought to be done in a wishful chapter entitled "The Middle Course," urging a political solution while insisting on the need to keep applying force (in moderation) to get it, the pursuit of negotiations while "tapering off" the bombing (no cease-fire on the ground, he warns—too dangerous), a promise to the Viet Cong of a "say" in the future of Vietnam

*Chapter 4 in *Vietnam*, copyright 1967 by Mary McCarthy. Reprinted by permission of the author and Harcourt Brace Jovanovich, Inc.

Moral Argument and the War in Vietnam

but not, it is implied, too much of a say, reliance on Oriental "consensual procedures" or the precedent of Laos to solve any little difficulties in the way of a coalition government—a chapter that anyone who agrees with Schlesinger's negative arguments would like to snip out of the volume, working carefully with a razor blade so as to leave no traces before lending it to a less convinced friend. Presented with Schlesinger's formula for meeting the Communist "threat," the reader is likely to think that Johnson's formula is better.

The same sinking feeling was produced by Richard Goodwin in *The New Yorker,* by J. K. Galbraith's "moderate solution" (hailed by James Reston), by Senator Fulbright's eight-point program, and, sad to say, by the Fulbright hearings taken as a whole. What emerges, when all the talk is over, is that none of these people really opposes the war. Or not enough to stop thinking in terms of "solutions," all of which imply continuing the war by slightly different means until the Viet Cong or Hanoi (Schlesinger holds out the exciting possibility of an "exploitable split" between the Viet Cong and Hanoi) is ready to make peace.

Even a man like George Kennan, who evidently believes the war to be wrong and testified impressively against our policy before the Fulbright Committee, did not have an inner attorney to warn him to rest his case there. Instead, pressed by bullish senators to say what he would do in the president's place (never mind what he would have *done*), Kennan fell back on the enclave strategy, making an easy target for the military, who can demonstrate without trouble how enclaves failed the French in *their* war, how Tito's Partisans knew they had won when they finally maneuvered the Nazis into coastal enclaves, how in fact the last place you want to be when faced with guerrillas is holed up in an enclave. And Kennan himself must have known that he had lost a round in the fight for peace when he allowed himself to be cornered into offering inconsequent armchair recommendations, in the midst of the hostile terrain, bristling with alert TV aerials, of U.S. popular feeling.

These are the errors of an opposition that wants to be statesmanlike and responsible, in contrast to the "irresponsible" opposition that is burning its draft card or refusing to pay taxes. To make sure that it can be told apart from these undesirables, it behaves on occasion like a troop of Eagle Scouts. Think of the ludicrous message sent to North Vietnam by sixteen Congressional doves—an appeal to Ho to understand that they are a) an unrepresentative minority and b) loyal Americans whose speeches were not meant to be overheard and "misinterpreted" by Hanoi.

Or it can assume the voice of Johnson. A recent New York *Post* editorial sternly criticized the Ky government's suspension of free speech (guaranteed by the new Constitution) and then continued: "We cannot heed the counsel of timid or misguided persons and withdraw. We dare not shrink from the duty democracy demands." The truth is, the *Post* is too cowardly to call for withdrawal. For the respectable opposition, unilateral withdrawal has become steadily more unthinkable as United States intervention has widened. It was perfectly thinkable before 1961. It was even thinkable for Bobby Kennedy as late as September 1963, at a meeting of the National Security Council, when he asked whether *now* might be the time to get out. It is still thinkable, though not by the Kennedy men, who, out of power, dare not reason as they might have in the privacy of a president's councils.

We could still, if we wished, take "French leave" of Vietnam, and *how* this should be done ought not to be the concern of those who oppose our presence there. When the French schoolteachers and intellectuals of the Committee of 121 insisted that France get out of Algeria, they did not supply De Gaulle with a ten-point program telling him how to do it. That was De Gaulle's business. He was responsible, not they. As intellectuals, they confronted their government with an unequivocal moral demand, and far from identifying themselves with that government and thinking helpfully on its behalf, they disassociated themselves from it totally so long as it continued to make war in Algeria. The administrative problems of winding up the war were left to those who had been waging it, just as the political problems of reconciling the French electorate to a defeat was left in the hands of De Gaulle, a politician by profession.

Our pamphleteers and polemicists, if they were resolute, would behave in the same way. Not: "We see your dilemma, Mr. President. It won't be easy to stop this war, but here are a few ideas." The country needs to understand that the war is wrong, and the sole job of the opposition should be to enforce that understanding and to turn it, whenever possible, into the language of action. It is clear that U.S. senators and former ambassadors are not going to sit at the Pentagon or hurl themselves at troop trains; nobody expects that of them and nobody seriously expects elected or appointed officials to practice tax refusal. But one *could* expect practical support for the young people who are resisting the draft from a few courageous officeholders and from private figures with a genuine sense of public responsibility.

Instead of hoping to avoid identification with unruly picketers and other actionists, Americans who are serious in opposing the war should be refusing to identify themselves with the U.S. government, even a putative government that would change to a defensive "posture" and prepare, as they say, to sit the war out. The question is simple: Do I disapprove *more* of the sign that picket is carrying—and the beard he is wearing—or of the Vietnamese war? To judge by introspection, the answer is not pretty. For the middle-class, middle-aged "protester," the war in Vietnam is easier to take than a sign that says "JOHNSON MURDERER."

The war does not threaten our immediate well-being. It does not touch us in the consumer-habits that have given us literally our shape. Casualty figures, still low, seldom strike home outside rural and low-income

Moral Argument and the War in Vietnam

groups—the silent part of society. The absence of sacrifices has had its effect on the opposition, which feels no need, on the whole, to turn away from its habitual standards and practices—what for? We have not withdrawn our sympathy from American power and from the way of life that is tied to it—a connection that is more evident to a low-grade G.I. in Vietnam than to most American intellectuals.

A sympathy, sneaking or otherwise, for American power is weakening the opposition's case against Johnson. He acts as if he had a mournful obligation to go on with the war unless and until somebody finds him an honorable exit from it. There is no honorable exit from a shameful course of action, though there may be a lucky escape. But the mirage of an honorable exit—a "middle road"—remains the deceptive premise of the liberal opposition, which urges the mistrustful president to attempt it on a pure trial-and-error basis; you never know, it may work.

For example, "Stop the bombing to get negotiations"—meaning the bombing of the North; strangely, nothing is said about the much worse bombing of the South. But in reality no one knows, unless it is Ho Chi Minh, whether a cessation of bombing would bring negotiations or not and, if it did, what the terms of Ho would be. Stop it for six months and see, suggests Bobby Kennedy. "Don't pin it down. Be vague," others say. But how does this differ, except in duration, from one of Johnson's famous bombing pauses, which failed, so he claimed, to produce any response? Moreover, if stopping the bombing is only a trick or maneuver to get negotiations (that is, to see the enemy's cards), then Rusk and Joseph Alsop have equal rights to argue that talk of negotiations, put about by the friends of Hanoi, is only a trick to stop the bombing and give the North a chance to rebuild. And what if the bombing stops and Hanoi does come to the conference table or comes with intransigent terms? Then the opposition, it would seem, is bound to agree to more and perhaps bigger bombing. Advocates of a failed hypothesis in wartime can only fall silent and listen to Big Brother.

To demand a halt to the bombing unconditionally, without qualifications, is quite another matter. The citizen who makes that demand cannot be "proved" wrong by subsequent developments, e.g., the obduracy of Hanoi or an increase in infiltration. Either it is *morally* wrong for the United States to bomb a small and virtually defenseless country or it is not, and a student picketing the Pentagon is just as great an expert in that realm, to say the least, as Dean Rusk or Joseph Alsop. Surely, in fact, the student who *demands* that the bombing stop speaks with a greater authority than the professor who *urges* it.

Not being a military specialist, I cannot plot the logistics of withdrawing 464,000 American boys from Vietnam, but I know that it can be done, if necessary, and Johnson knows it too. *Everybody* knows it. A defeat in battle on the order of Dien Bien Phu, if it happened, could provide Johnson's generals with the opportunity to plan and execute a retreat. That is their job, and Johnson might even snatch honor from it. Look-at Churchill and the heroic exploit of Dunkirk, which did not depend on prior negotiations with Hitler. But we cannot wait for a major defeat in battle to cover Johnson's withdrawal with honor or even to save his face for him. Nor can we wait for a Soviet or a Chinese intervention, which might have the same effect (if not a quite different one) by precipitating a Cuban-style confrontation; the war then could terminate in a withdrawal of the big powers, leaving a wrecked Vietnam to the Vietnamese. That, no doubt, would be a "solution" acceptable to the men in power.

In politics, it seems, retreat is honorable if dictated by military considerations and shameful if even *suggested* for ethical reasons—as though, by some law of inertia, force could only yield to superior force or to some natural obstacle, such as unsuitable terrain or "General Winter," whom Napoleon met in Russia. Thus the American superiority of arms *in itself* becomes an argument for staying in Vietnam; Indeed, at this point, the only argument. The more troops and matériel committed to Vietnam, the more retreat appears to be cut off—not by an enemy, but by our own numbers. To call for withdrawal in the face of that commitment (the only real one we have made in Vietnam) is to seem to argue not against a policy, but against *facts*, which by their very nature are unanswerable. In private, a U.S. spokesman may agree that the Americans cannot win in Vietnam. "But they can't lose either," he adds with a satisfied nod. Critics of U.S. policy, when they go to Vietnam, are expected to be convinced by the fact of 464,000 troops, once it sinks in; and indeed what can you say to it? Johnson's retort to his opponents has been to tersely add *more* facts, in the shape of men and arms. Their utility is not just to overwhelm the Viet Cong by sheer force of numbers, but to overwhelm domestic disbelief; if they cannot stop the VC, they can stop any talk of unilateral withdrawal. Under these circumstances, the idea that he subtract a few facts—deescalation—is rejected by Johnson as illogical. The logic of numbers is the only one that convinces him of the rightness of the course he is bent on.

Meanwhile, the generals are sure they could win the war if they could only bomb the port of Haiphong and the Ho Chi Minh trail in Laos. They blame politics for their failure to win it, and by politics is meant the existence of counter-forces in the theater: China, Russia, the Pathet Lao, and simply people, civilians, a weak counterforce, but still an obstacle to total warfare under present conditions. It used to be said that the balance of terror would give rise to a series of limited wars. Up to now, this has been true, so far as geographical scale goes, but the abstention from the use of atomic arms, in Vietnam, has not exactly worked to moderate the war.

On the contrary, the military establishment, deprived for the time being of tactical atomic weapons (toys being kept in the closet) and held back from bombing the port of Haiphong and the Ho Chi Minh trail, has compensated for these limitations by developing other weapons and

Moral Argument and the War in Vietnam

devices to the limit: antipersonnel bombs; a new, more adhesive napalm; a twenty-pound gadget, the E-63 manpack personnel detector, made by General Electric, replacing British-trained bloodhounds, to sniff out Viet Cong; a battery-powered blower that raises the temperature in a VC tunnel network to 1000 degrees Fahrenheit (loudspeakers, naturally, exhort the Viet Cong in the tunnels to surrender); improved tear gases; improved defoliants. The classic resistance offered by climate and terrain to armies of men, one of the ancient limitations on warfare, will doubtless be all but eliminated as new applications for patents pour into the U.S. Patent Office. The jungle will be leafless and creeperless, and the mangrove swamps dried out; the weather will be controlled, making bombing possible on a 365-day-a-year basis, exclusive of Buddha's birthday, Christmas, and Têt. The diseases of the jungle and tropical climates are already pretty well confined to the native population, thanks to pills and immunization. In other words, for an advanced nation, practically no obstacles remain to the exercise of force except "politics."

U.S. technology is bent on leaving nothing to chance in the Vietnamese struggle, on taking the risk out of war (for ourselves, of course, while increasing the risk for the enemy). Whatever cannot be controlled scientifically—shifts of wind, rain—is bypassed by radar and electronics. Troop performance is fairly well guaranteed by the Selective Service system and by rotation; the "human element," represented by the Arvin, prone to desert or panic, is despised and feared. And if chance can be reduced to a minimum by the "miracle" of American technology, there is only one reality-check on American *hubris*: the danger of Chinese or Russian intervention, which computers in the Pentagon are steadily calculating, to take the risk out of *that*.

Yet the peculiar fact is that this has been a war of incredible blunders, on the American side; you never hear of blunders, though there must be some, on the part of the Viet Cong. Leaving aside the succession of political blunders, starting with the great Diem gamble and going right up to the Ky gamble (the current embarrassment of U.S. officials), there has been a startling number of military blunders: government villages bombed, Cambodian villages bombed, a Strategic Hamlet gunned by a U.S. helicopter on the day before the ambassador's scheduled visit, U.S. troops bombed and shelled by their own aircraft and artillery, "Friendlies" bombed and shelled, a Russian ship bombed in Haiphong harbor, overflights into China.

In the case of North Vietnam, blunder must be a misnomer for what has been done with regularity to villages, churches, hospitals, a model leper colony, schools. American opinion refuses to hear of a "deliberate bombing pattern" in North Vietnam, though there is plenty of testimony and photographic evidence of the destruction of populated centers. The administration insists that we are bombing military targets only, though it has finally conceded, after too many had been found, that we were using antipersonnel bombs in the North, without specifying how these inventions, designed to fragment a soft human body, were effective against bridges, power plants, and railway yards. Yet even those who are unconvinced by the administration's regularly issued denials prefer to think that what is happening is the result of human or mechanical error—a possibility categorically excluded by the U.S. Navy.

On the nuclear carrier *Enterprise*, a squadron of Intruder pilots in their air-conditioned ready room assured journalists, myself included, that under no circumstances did they hit anything in the North but military targets. How did they know? Because they only bombed targets assigned to them, which had been carefully selected with the aid of computers working on aerial photographs. Besides, post-raid reconnaissance recorded on the film the "impact" of every delivery; there was no chance of error. Did it ever happen that, returning from a mission and having failed for some reason—flak or whatever—to reach their assigned targets, they jettisoned their bomb load on the countryside? Never. Always into the sea. What about those accounts of devastated villages and hamlets? Impossible. "Our aerial photographs would show it." You could not shake their placid, stolid, almost uninterested conviction. Yet somebody's cameras were lying. Those of the journalists and other witnesses who bring back ordinary photographs they have snapped in the North or the unmanned cameras of the U.S. Navy?

Their faith in technology had put these men, in their own eyes, above suspicion. They would as soon have suspected the totals of an adding machine. Was it conceivable that in flying they kept their attention glued to their instrument panels and their radar screen, watching out for MIGs and SAMs, no more interested in what was *below* them, in both senses, than they were in our questions?

The same faith in technology commands the administration to go on with the war, in defiance of any evidence of failure, bringing to bear American inventiveness, not only in the field of weaponry, but also in the field of propaganda—loudspeakers, broadcasts from the air, cunning messages inserted literally between the lines of ornamented New Year's calendars distributed free to the people—"We don't make it too obvious." The next step in this field would be subliminal suggestion, psychedelic bombardments in light and color to be pioneered by General Electric, free "trips" offered to the population by the Special Forces, with CIA backing—the regular Army would disapprove.

"Politics" gets in the way of technology. If the world could be cleansed of politics, including South Vietnamese politicians, victory might be in sight. Politics, domestic and international, is evidently the only deterrent recognized by the Americans to an all-out onslaught on the Vietnamese nation; it is the replacement of the inner voice of conscience, which nobody but a few draft-resisters can hear. Johnson, who keeps acting as if he were bowing to necessity, looks to "politics"—*i.e.*, Hanoi—to release him, the prisoner of circumstance. He invites his enemy and

Moral Argument and the War in Vietnam

his critics to "show him the way out." At the same time he insists that "the door is always open," which means, if anything, that the portals of peace will swing wide at the bidding of Ho Chi Minh but remain locked to *him*, beating and signaling from the inside. What he appears to be saying is that Ho Chi Minh is free whereas he and his advisers are not.

This hypocritical performance may, like most play-acting, have a certain psychological truth. Johnson and his advisers, like all Americans, are the conditioned subjects of the free-enterprise system, which despite some controls and government manipulation, appears to function automatically, requiring no consent on the part of those involved in it. A sense of compulsion, dictated by the laws of the market, permeates every nerve of the national life. Industry, for example, has been "compelled" to automate by the law of cost-cutting, which works in "free" capitalism with the same force as a theorem in geometry. And the necessity to automate is accepted throughout society without any question. The human damage involved, if seen close up, may elicit a sigh, as when a co-operative apartment building fires its old Negro elevator operators ("Been with us twenty years") to put in self-service: "We had to, you see. It was cheaper." Or ask a successful author why he has changed from his old publisher, who was virtually his parent, to a new mass-market one. "I had to," he explains, simply. "They offered me more money."

A feeling of having no choice is becoming more and more widespread in American life, and particularly among successful people, who supposedly are free beings. On a concrete plane, the lack of choice is often a depressing reality. In national election years, you are free to choose between Johnson and Goldwater or Johnson and Romney or Reagan, which is the same as choosing between a Chevrolet and a Ford—there is a marginal difference in styling. Just as in American hotel rooms you can decide whether or not to turn on the air conditioners (that is your business), but you cannot open the window.

It is natural that in such a system the idea of freedom is associated with escape, whether through trips or "trips," rather than with the exercise of one's ordinary faculties. And at the same time one's feeling of imprisonment is joined to a conviction of innocence. Johnson, perhaps genuinely, would like to get out of his "commitment" to the war in Vietnam, and the more deeply he involves himself in it, the more abused and innocent he feels, and the less he is inclined to take any steps to release *himself*, for to do so would be to confess that he is culpable or—the same thing—that he has been free at any time to do what he would now be doing.

Those of Johnson's critics who, like Senator Fulbright, repudiate the thought of a "disorderly" retreat by implication favor an orderly retreat, with the panoply of negotiations, guarantees, and so on, *i.e.,* a retreat assisted and facilitated by Hanoi. But that choice, very likely, is no longer open, thanks to Johnson himself. He would be very lucky, at this point, to get negotiations at the mere cost to him of ending the bombing of the North—a cost that to Ho or any rational person seems derisory, since, as our military spokesmen have complained, there are no targets in North Vietnam left to destroy, except the port of Haiphong, which Johnson, for his own reasons and not to please Ho, has spared up to now. Indeed, to have something of value to offer short of troop withdrawal, Johnson's peculiar logic would lead him to *start* bombing the port of Haiphong in order to *stop* bombing it—exactly the chain of reasoning that sent our planes north back in February 1965, and has kept them pounding ever since.

The opposition's best hopes for an orderly retreat rest on the South Vietnamese, just as, probably, the administration's fears do. The notion that the elections this September *might* put in a government that could negotiate a separate peace with the NLF is once again reviving; some people are daring to bank on the return of General Minh as a coalition candidate. *If* he is permitted to return and if *he* is elected, with the support of the radical Buddhists and liberal groups in the Constitutional Assembly, that would allow the Americans to leave by invitation—a very attractive prospect. And were they to decline the invitation and try to depose him (as in effect they did once before, considering him too "leftish"), they might have a double civil war on their hands, a more serious repetition of what happened in the spring of 1966. In either case, the Vietnamese elections could be a turning point. Or, failing that, the American elections of 1968. The opposition prays for the nomination of a Romney or a Percy, who *might* beat Johnson and *might* end the war, as Eisenhower did in Korea. And it dreads the nomination of a Nixon or a Reagan, which could "compel" it to vote again for Johnson—a perfect illustration of American consumer choice.

These are all hopes for a Redeemer who will come from the *outside* to save us from our own actions: an Asian general, a Republican who does not fit into the party program or picture. In the same way, Johnson may be hoping for a Redeemer in the form of Kosygin to get him to the peace table. Or he may have a more far-reaching design: the eventual occupation of the North and the establishment of U.S. bases next to the Chinese border. Yet if such a design exists, it must be in the *back* of the administration's mind and be, itself, more a cunning hope than a businesslike calculation, a thought held in the pending file and marked "Cosmic."

Actually, so far as is known, Johnson has no program for ending the war in the South. Asked what *he* would do, he, too, no doubt would be reduced to head-scratching. He has given a promise to withdraw American troops as soon as hostilities are over—a promise that evidently cannot be kept. The consequences of bilateral withdrawal would be nearly as "disastrous" as the consequences of unilateral withdrawal: the return of the Viet Cong. The Vietnamese know this, which makes

Moral Argument and the War in Vietnam

them uncertain what to fear most. A new man in the White House who might decide to keep it? Or permanent colonial status?

"The Vietnamese must choose for themselves," the Americans repeat, having done their best to deprive them of the power of choice during thirteen years of American military assistance that slowly turned into a full-scale American invasion—there is no other word for it. The Americans pretend that this was somehow forced on them; in reality, it was forced on the Vietnamese, as is clear from the low morale of their troops. "They just don't want to fight,' American officers say with an air of puzzlement. If the Vietnamese want to be rid of the Americans, they must turn toward the NLF—a hard decision for some French-educated idealists, who, despite their experience with the American brand as an export product, still have hopes of democracy. Yet the brutality of the war is reconciling certain middle-class Saigon groups to making discreet overtures toward their class enemy; meanwhile, in the field, the Viet Cong forces have been increasing—which our spokesmen ascribe to "better recruiting methods." In their turn, Americans concerned for the future of the Republic, rather than for the future of American power, are reduced to hoping that the Viet Cong can hold out in the face of the overwhelming *facts* marshaled against it—as though its often primitive and homemade weapons possessed a moral force of resistance denied to members of the Great Society.

The uselessness of our free institutions, pleasurable in themselves, to interpose any check on a war of this character, opposed, though not enough, by most so-called thinking persons, suggests that freedom in the United States is no longer a political value and is seen simply as the right to self-expression, as in the dance, psychodrama, be-ins, kinky sex, or baking ceramics. The truth is, only a minority is *interested* in the war in Vietnam, and debate about the subject is treated as a minority pastime, looked on by the majority with more or less tolerance. "The country can afford it," is the attitude. Or: "It's a free country," which has come to mean "I've got mine, Jack. Everybody to his taste." A little less tolerance might harden the opposition. If the opposition wants to make itself felt politically, it ought to be acting so as to provoke intolerance. It is hurt because the administration ignores it. There are various ways of obliging the administration—and more importantly the country—to take notice: some extremely radical, like the bonze's way of self-immolation; some less so, ranging from tax refusal through the operation of underground railroads for protesting draftees, down to simple boycotts of key war industries; nobody who is against the war should be receiving dividends from the manufacture of napalm, for instance, which is calling to be outlawed.

Since the Revolution, this country has had no experience of foreign occupation and consequently of resistance movements; in that field, it lacks inspiration and inventiveness and is readily discouraged. But the professors and students who lost heart when the teach-ins failed to change U.S. policy might study the example of the Abolitionists—the nearest thing to a resistance movement the Republic has had. Obviously no single plan of action can stop the war in Vietnam, and maybe a hundred plans concerted could not stop it. But if it can be stopped, it will be through initiatives taken by persons or groups of persons (whether they be Johnson or Ho or a Republican president or Big Minh or the readers of this pamphlet) and not through cooked-up "solutions" handed to somebody else to act on, like interoffice memoranda. The "hard thinking" about this war needs to begin at home, with the critic asking himself what *he* can do against it, modestly or grandly, with friends or alone. From each according to his abilities, but to be in the town jail, as Thoreau knew, can relieve any sense of imaginary imprisonment.

Vietnam: The Bloodbath Argument*

D. Gareth Porter and Len E. Ackland

As pressure builds on the Nixon administration to withdraw American troops rapidly from Vietnam, proponents of the war are beginning to emphasize the argument that if the Communists were allowed to gain control, there would be a massive bloodbath of Vietnamese.

This argument is not new. Joseph Alsop invoked the bloodbath specter last May when he wrote that "at least a million South Vietnamese . . . would be doomed to prompt execution, in the event of a nationwide Communist takeover." About the same time an aide to Nixon's adviser Henry Kissinger told a group of visitors to the White House that there would certainly be a "bloodbath" if American forces pulled out of Vietnam too soon. Six weeks later Alsop raised his estimate to 1.5 million, a figure he claimed was officially accepted. And in September he warned that "too many troop withdrawals" would expose Vietnamese to massacres that would make Hué look like a "Sunday school picnic."

Like all political propaganda, these predictions are intended to inspire support for official policy rather than to increase understanding. Those of us Americans who are genuinely concerned about the Vietnamese people want sober information on the facts, not appeals to emotion. Let us therefore look at the relevant historical evidence.

Political murder is no new thing in Vietnam. The French used it consistently to destroy nationalist political movements. The Viet Minh and their successors employed it whenever they thought it would be useful in their struggles against the French, the Americans and their internal foes. In 1945 and 1946 they systematically assassinated many potential rivals for power, and since 1956 they have killed thousands of local officials and other pro-government figures in South Vietnam.

Similarly, the Vietnam Nationalist party (V.N.Q.D.D.) had a reputation in earlier years for kidnaping and assassinating Viet Minh agents, while members of the Hoa Hao religious sect tied groups of Viet Minh together and threw them alive into canals. More recently assassination squads hired by the U.S. have sought out members of the National Liberation Front's political and administrative organization. As we said, political murder is no new thing in Vietnam.

But to predict the mass murder of former foes once the conflict has

Moral Argument and the War in Vietnam

ended is quite another matter. Alsop asserts—apparently with 'official encouragement—that both the history of North Vietnam after the Geneva Conference of 1954 and the Communist occupation of Hué during the 1968 Tet offensive portend a policy of mass liquidation if the Communists come to power in the South. The historical record, however, does not support any such conclusion.

The 1954 Geneva agreement called for what was intended to be twofold protection from reprisals by either the Viet Minh or the French administration. First, it provided for free movement of the population, between the two "temporary zones" north and south of the seventeenth parallel, to be effective for a year following the cease-fire. Second, it prohibited reprisals against those who collaborated with either army during the war. While there is evidence that the Hanoi government, stunned by the massive movement of population out of the northern zone, violated the accords in attempting to impede that flow, it also seems clear that there was no campaign of reprisals against pro-French elements.

I

International Control Commission reports, while not definitive, give us a reasonable account of the situation in North Vietnam after the 1954 accords. During the period from 1955 to 1961, a total of forty-three complaints alleging reprisals in the North were submitted to the I.C.C. by the French and the Diem regime. Of the first twelve complaints lodged by the French High Command, the I.C.C. investigated three and dismissed all of them as unfounded. Of 41 personal petitions alleging such D.R.V. reprisals that were presented to the commission, half of them were dismissed as not falling under the reprisal provision of the accords. Although most of the I.C.C. reports do not specify the nature of the uninvestigated complaints, it appears that very few of them involved charges of murder. For example, of the eighteen incidents of reprisal alleged by the French to have taken place between December 1955 and July 1956, only one involved murder.

Thus the sum total of the allegations lodged against the D.R.V. hardly supports the "bloodbath" predictions made by Alsop *et al*. True, the movement of 750,000 to 1 million anti-Communists, Catholics and other collaborators with the French to South Vietnam before July 1955 undoubtedly reduced the number who might have been punished. Nevertheless, despite the alarms often sounded about the fate of Vietnamese Catholics at the hands of the Communists, 600,000 Catholics remained in the North, and there is no evidence that they were punished for their lack of pro-Viet Minh sentiment. In fact, Catholics in North Vietnam continue to exercise their religion freely, although there are limitations on their seminaries and high taxes on church lands.

Moreover, the small number of complaints against the D.R.V. must be compared with the wholesale reprisals by the Diem regime in South Vietnam against former collaborators with the Viet Minh. In 1955—violating the Geneva agreements, which were binding on his government—Diem launched an "anti-Communist denunciation campaign" which soon acquired a frenzied momentum of its own and spiraled out of his control. No one knows how many "Viet Minh" were killed during the campaign, which lasted until 1958. It is known, however, that tens of thousands, many of them innocent of any connection with the Communists, were rounded up in concentration camps. The High Command of the North Vietnamese army submitted to the I.C.C. 869 complaints, many of which alleged that Viet Minh sympathizers had been murdered.

When proponents of the bloodbath argument mention massacres in the North, they are referring not to political reprisals against former enemies of the Viet Minh but to the harshly implemented land reform program of 1955-56. The purpose of that program was to mobilize political support among the poor peasants, who were encouraged to denounce "rich landlords." As in the South, denunciations went out of control, as zealous cadres and local grudge-bearers combined to bring about massive executions and imprisonments which went far beyond what the regime had intended. Historian Joseph Buttinger, whose sympathies lay with Diem, has estimated that perhaps 10,000 or 15,000 were killed during the period, but here again no reliable estimate is available.

By mid-1956 Ho Chi Minh, aware that the program had been a disaster, admitted "errors" and promised to correct them. In October he dismissed Truong Chinh, the primary advocate of an extreme left-wing "Chinese" policy in agriculture, from both his positions as director of land reform and party secretary. In a display of public repentance, the government launched a "campaign for rectification of errors" and did what it could to repair the damage. But the sharp reversal of policy did not come in time to stave off an open rebellion in Nghe An province, where hundreds of peasants were reportedly killed in the fighting. It seems doubtful that, having experienced the disaster of 1955-56, Hanoi's leadership would make the mistake of applying the same extremist policy in the South.

II

Both Alsop and the administration have exploited American horror at the executions in Hué during the 1968 Communist Tet offensive to stir fears of a nationwide massacre in Vietnam following American withdrawal. But closer examination of the circumstances surrounding the executions in Hué is necessary before conclusions can be reached concerning the probability of such a grim outcome.

One of the authors of this paper lived and worked in Hué during 1967 and returned after the Tet offensive of 1968 to interview Vietnamese

Moral Argument and the War in Vietnam

and reconstruct the events surrounding the N.L.F. occupation there. The focus of this research was Gia Hoi, a precinct with 25,000 residents, one-fourth of Hué's population. Gia Hoi was under uncontested N.L.F. control for twenty-six days—longer than any other area of the city. There the Front established a revolutionary government, provided administrative services, held public meetings and distributed weapons. The story of Gia Hoi's occupation reveals that the mass executions perpetrated there were not the result of a policy on the part of a victorious government but rather the revenge of an army in retreat.

When, on the first day of the attack, about twenty Vietcong entered Gia Hoi in order to secure the area, they carried with them a list of those who were to be killed immediately as "enemies of the people." According to Le Ngan, director of Hué's special police, the list consisted of five names, all those of officers of the special force. Four were captured and summarily killed; the fifth, Le Ngan himself, spent twenty-one days dodging the Communists before escaping to safety.

After establishing control the Vietcong drew up a second list naming all soldiers, policemen and government functionaries and all employees of the Americans. A third list, compiled in Gia Hoi by the N.L.F. guerrillas, included high school and university students, workers and servants who would probably serve the revolution once they were contacted.

III

The administration of the Gia Hoi was in the hands of local N.L.F. cadres, most of them poor peasants from the countryside surrounding Hué, who obviously found the city an alien environment. The North Vietnamese troops who had a command post in Gia Hoi kept out of political matters and were, by all accounts, well mannered and highly disciplined throughout their stay. Meanwhile, physicians in Gia Hoi began staffing public dispensaries and a social service committee distributed rice from a government storehouse to needy families. But the primary business of the local administration was to create political support for the new regime. Small meetings were held continuously during the following three weeks, with separate study sessions for teachers, workers and students to enable the cadres to use the most persuasive arguments on each group.

During the first week and a half of the occupation few people were killed in Gia Hoi. Some did not report to the committees and were punished as examples; others, such as special police agent Le Van Rut, were executed because they had been particularly unpopular with Hué's population. After February 9, as the fighting across the canal became more vicious and the U.S. counterattack against the Citadel began, the attitude of the N.L.F. toward those on the "re-education" list began to change. For it became increasingly apparent that the Front would not be able to stay in Hué indefinitely. Every night for the next

Solutions?

two weeks their cadres knocked on doors and ordered certain people to attend sessions, and almost every night new executions were carried out in the yard of the Gia Hoi high school.

On February 22 all remaining soldiers, police, functionaries and employees of the Americans were ordered to report a second time, and those who reported or were located never returned. By then the Front knew that it would have to evacuate shortly, and it was in the final three days of the occupation that most of the killing in Gia Hoi took place. On the last day those who had collaborated with the Front during its twenty-six days were asked if they wanted to return to the mountains with the N.L.F. troops. According to an A.R.V.N. intelligence officer, over 100 did go with the troops, but many persons who chose to remain behind were shot.

According to Ranger Captain Phan Van Phuoc, the government chief of the precinct, 60 percent of the 350 bodies found in Gia Hoi were those of policemen and soldiers. The remainder were civil servants, employees of the Americans, members of the old right-wing Nationalist party (which had long provided cadres for the government's pacification and counterterror programs in central Vietnam), and some innocent civilians.

The Catholics were not singled out for retribution even after February 22. The Catholic priest in Gia Hoi told one of us that none of his clergy or parishioners were harmed by the N.L.F. In other parts of the city as well, priests reported that the Vietcong who approached them were "correct" though not friendly. One Benedictine priest was killed apparently because he was chaplain to the Americans. But the murder of two French priests on February 25 was probably not carried out on orders from local leaders, since both had been known to be friendly to the N.L.F.

Some of the killing in the final three days was apparently the result of individual acts by the Front's cadres, long suspicious and resentful toward the city's people whom they had associated with the enemy and now further embittered by defeat and by the loss of many of their comrades in the battle. A later defector from the Front, who was with the retreating Front forces in the mountains west of Hué when they held a self-criticism session, reported that they were severely criticized by their superiors for excesses which had "hurt the revolution."

Elsewhere in Hué a similar pattern was followed: the vast majority of policemen, civil servants and soldiers were initially on "re-education" rather than on "liquidation" lists, but the number of killings mounted as the military pressure on the N.L.F. and North Vietnamese increased.

The notion that the Communists will mount massive killings after taking power in the South is further weakened by the testimony of Tran Van Dac, one of the highest-ranking defectors from the N.L.F. In an interview published last year by the Joint U.S. Public Affairs Office in Saigon, he explained that, if they took over, the Communists would send military

Moral Argument and the War in Vietnam

officers and former civil servants to "concentration camps to be re-educated" and in some cases to do hard labor, until they became "submissive." And of course, all those whose social class or former position makes them objects of suspicion would be "carefully watched" by the authorities.

Neither the earlier consolidation of power in North Vietnam, nor the occupation of Hué in 1968, nor the testimony of a high-ranking defector, supports the conclusion that Hanoi intends to bring about a "bloodbath" after achieving control in the South. Whatever the utility of eliminating government personnel during the war, the Communist leadership has no interest in liquidating Saigon's military officers or civil servants. If there are political executions, the victims are most likely to be those who are highly unpopular with the citizens, such as the secret police officers on the highly selective list of "enemies of the people" in Gia Hoi.

The past offers ample evidence that long-standing hatreds can result in individual vendettas, and the highly political central Vietnamese are especially prone to such settling of old scores. If the U.S. really wishes to fulfill its moral obligation to those who fear for their safety in the absence of the American presence, it can do so easily by pledging to provide transportation to new homes for all who desire it.

The Nixon administration and its supporters appear more interested, however, in the exploitation of the bloodbath theme than in taking the practical steps to provide safety. And while they appeal to the American abhorrence of an imagined massacre, the real killing of thousands of Vietnamese and Americans goes on month after month.

The Viet Nam Negotiations*

By Henry A. Kissinger

The peace negotiations in Paris have been marked by the classic Vietnamese syndrome: optimism alternating with bewilderment; euphoria giving way to frustration. The halt to the bombing produced another wave of high hope. Yet it was followed almost immediately by the dispute with Saigon over its participation in the talks. The merits of this issue aside, we must realize that a civil war which has torn a society for twenty years and which has involved the great powers is unlikely to be settled in a single dramatic stroke. Even if there were mutual trust—a commodity not in excessive supply—the complexity of the issues and the difficulty of grasping their interrelationship would make for complicated negotiations. Throughout the war, criteria by which to measure progress have been hard to come by; this problem has continued during the negotiations. The dilemma is that almost any statement about Viet Nam is likely to be true; unfortunately, truth does not guarantee relevance.

The basic problem has been conceptual: the tendency to apply traditional maxims of both strategy and "nation-building" to a situation which they did not fit.

American military strategy followed the classic doctrine that victory depended on a combination of control of territory and attrition of the opponent. Therefore, the majority of the American forces was deployed along the frontiers of South Viet Nam to prevent enemy infiltration and in the Central Highlands where most of the North Vietnamese main-force units—those units organized along traditional military lines—were concentrated. The theory was that defeat of the main forces would cause the guerrillas to wither on the vine. Victory would depend on inflicting casualties substantially greater than those we suffered until Hanoi's losses became "unacceptable."

This strategy suffered from two disabilities: (a) the nature of guerrilla warfare; (b) the asymmetry in the definition of what constituted unacceptable losses. A guerrilla war differs from traditional military operation because its key prize is not control of territory but control of the population. This depends, in part, on psychological criteria, especially a sense of security. No positive program can succeed unless the population feels safe from terror or reprisal. Guerrillas rarely seek to hold real estate;

*Excerpted by permission from *Foreign Affairs*, Volume 47, no. 2 (January, 1969), pp. 211-234. Copyright Council on Foreign Relations, Inc., New York, 1969.

Moral Argument and the War in Vietnam

their tactic is to use terror and intimidation to discourage cooperation with constituted authority.

The distribution of the population in Viet Nam makes this problem particularly acute. Over 90 percent of the population live in the coastal plain and the Mekong Delta; the Central Highlands and the frontiers, on the other hand, are essentially unpopulated. Eighty percent of American forces came to be concentrated in areas containing less than 4 percent of the population; the locale of military operations was geographically removed from that of the guerrilla conflict. As North Vietnamese theoretical writings never tired of pointing out, the United States could not hold territory and protect the population simultaneously. . . .

The North Vietnamese and Viet Cong had another advantage which they used skillfully. American "victories" were empty unless they laid the basis for an eventual withdrawal. The North Vietnamese and Viet Cong, fighting in their own country, needed merely to keep in being forces sufficiently strong to dominate the population after the United States tired of the war. We fought a military war; our opponents fought a political one. We sought physical attrition; our opponents aimed for our psychological exhaustion. In the process, we lost sight of one of the cardinal maxims of guerrilla war: the guerrilla wins if he does not lose. The conventional army loses if it does not win. The North Vietnamese used their main forces the way a bullfighter uses his cape—to keep us lunging in areas of marginal political importance.

The strategy of attrition failed to reduce the guerrillas and was in difficulty even with respect to the North Vietnamese main forces. Since Hanoi made no attempt to hold any territory, and since the terrain of the Central Highlands cloaked North Vietnamese movements, it proved difficult to make the opposing forces fight except at places which they chose. Indeed, a considerable majority of engagements came to be initiated by the other side; this enabled Hanoi to regulate its casualties (and ours) at least within certain limits. The so-called "kill-ratios" of United States to North Vietnamese casualties became highly unreliable indicators. Even when the figures were accurate they were irrelevant, because the level of what was "unacceptable" to Americans fighting thousands of miles from home turned out to be much lower than that of Hanoi fighting on Vietnamese soil.

All this caused our military operations to have little relationship to our declared political objectives. . . .

The Tet offensive brought to a head the compounded weaknesses—or, as the North Vietnamese say, the internal contradictions—of the American position. . . . Two claims had been pressed on the villages. The United States and Saigon had promised that they would be able to protect an ever larger number of villages. The Viet Cong had never made such a claim; they merely asserted that they were the real power and presence in the villages and they threatened retribution upon those who collaborated with Saigon or the United States.

As happened so often in the past, the Viet Cong made their claim stick. Some twenty provincial capitals were occupied. Though the Viet Cong held none (except Hué) for more than a few days, they were there long enough to execute hundreds of Vietnamese on the basis of previously prepared lists. The words "secure area" never had the same significance for Vietnamese civilians as for Americans, but, if the term had any meaning, it applied to the provincial and district capitals. This was precisely where the Tet offensive took its most severe toll. The Viet Cong had made a point which far transcended military considerations in importance; there are no secure areas for Vietnamese civilians. . . .

For all these reasons, the Tet offensive marked the watershed of the American effort. Henceforth, no matter how effective our actions, the prevalent strategy could no longer achieve its objectives within a period or with force levels politically acceptable to the American people. . . . Thus the stage was set for President Johnson's speech of March 31, which ushered in the current negotiations.

II. The Environment of Negotiations

. . . Between 1965 and 1968, the various parties publicly stated their positions in a variety of forums: Hanoi announced Four Points, the NLF put forth Five Points, Saigon advanced Seven Points and the United States—perhaps due to its larger bureaucracy—promulgated Fourteen.

These public pronouncements produced a fairly wide area of apparent agreement on some general principles: that the Geneva Accords could form the basis of settlement, that American forces would be withdrawn ultimately, that the reunification of Viet Nam should come about through direct negotiation between the Vietnamese, that (after a settlement) Viet Nam would not contain foreign bases. The United States has indicated that three of Hanoi's Four Points are acceptable.[1]

There is disagreement about the status of Hanoi's forces in the South; indeed, Hanoi has yet to admit that it has forces in the South—though it has prepared a "fall-back position" to the effect that North Vietnamese forces in the South cannot be considered "external." The role of the NLF is equally in dispute. Saigon rejects a separate political role for the NLF; the NLF considers Saigon a puppet régime. There is no agreement about the meaning of those propositions which sound alike or on how they are to be enforced. . . .

Both the Hanoi government and the United States are limited in their freedom of action by the state of mind of the population of South Viet Nam which will ultimately determine the outcome of the conflict. The Vietnamese people have lived under foreign rule for approximately half of their history. They have maintained a remarkable cultural and social cohesion by being finely attuned to the realities of power. To survive, the Vietnamese have had to learn to calculate—almost instinctively—the

Moral Argument and the War in Vietnam

real balance of forces. If negotiations give the impression of being a camouflaged surrender, there will be nothing left to negotiate. Support for the side which seems to be losing will collapse. . . . Within twenty-four hours after announcement of the halt, both Hanoi and Saigon made statements of extraordinary bellicosity, which, taken literally, would have doomed the substantive talks about to begin. But their real purpose was to reassure each side's supporters in the South. Saigon especially has had a difficult problem. It has been pictured by many as perversely stubborn because of its haggling over the status of the NLF. However, to Saigon, the status of the NLF cannot be a procedural matter. For South Viet Nam it has been very nearly the central issue of the war. Washington must bear at least part of the responsibility for underestimating the depth and seriousness of this concern.

The situation confronted by Washington and Hanoi internationally is scarcely less complex. Much of the bitter debate in the United States about the war has been conducted in terms of 1961 and 1962. Unquestionably, the failure at that time to analyze adequately the geopolitical importance of Viet Nam contributed to the current dilemma. But the commitment of 500,000 Americans has settled the issue of the importance of Viet Nam. For what is involved now is confidence in American promises. However fashionable it is to ridicule the terms "credibility" or "prestige," they are not empty phrases; other nations can gear their actions to ours only if they can count on our steadiness. The collapse of the American effort in Viet Nam would not mollify many critics; most of them would simply add the charge of unreliability to the accusation of bad judgment. Those whose safety or national goals depend on American commitments could only be dismayed. In many parts of the world—the Middle East, Europe, Latin America, even Japan—stability depends on confidence in American promises. Unilateral withdrawal, or a settlement which unintentionally amounts to the same thing, could therefore lead to the erosion of restraints and to an even more dangerous international situation. No American policymaker can simply dismiss these dangers. . . .

III. Lessons of the Bombing Halt

The bombing halt occupied the first six months of the Paris talks. The formal positions were relatively straightforward. The American view was contained in the so-called San Antonio formula which was put forth by President Johnson in September 1967: "The United States is willing to stop all aerial and naval bombardment of North Viet Nam when this will lead promptly to productive discussions. We, of course, assume that while discussions proceed, North Viet Nam would not take advantage of the bombing cessation or limitation." In its main outlines, the American position remained unchanged throughout the negotiations.

Hanoi's reaction was equally simple and stark. It scored the obvious debating point that it could guarantee useful but not "productive" talks since that depended also on the United States.[2] But in the main, Hanoi adamantly insisted that the bombing halt had to be "unconditional." It rejected all American proposals for reciprocity as put forward, for example, by Secretary Rusk: respect for the DMZ, no attack on South Vietnamese cities, reduction in the level of military operations.

Though this deadlock had many causes, surely a central problem was the difficulty each side had in articulating its real concern. Washington feared "trickery;" it believed that once stopped, the bombing would be politically difficult, if not impossible, to start again even in the face of considerable provocation. Too, it needed some assurance as to how the negotiations would proceed *after* a bombing halt. Washington was aware that a bombing halt which did not lead rapidly to substantive talks could not be sustained domestically.

The legalistic phrasing of these concerns obscured their real merit. If bombing were resumed under conditions of great public indignation, it would be much harder to exercise restraint in the choice of targets and much more difficult to stop again in order to test Hanoi's intentions. The frequently heard advice to "take risks for peace" is valid only if one is aware that the consequences of an imprudent risk are likely to be escalation rather than peace.

Hanoi, in turn, had a special reason for insisting on an unconditional end to the bombing. A government as subtle as Hanoi must have known that there are no "unconditional" acts in the relation of sovereign states, if only because sovereignty implies the right to reassess changing conditions unilaterally. But Hanoi has always placed great reliance on the pressures of world opinion; the "illegality" of U.S. bombing was therefore a potent political weapon. Reciprocity would jeopardize this claim; it would suggest that bombing might be justified in some circumstances. Hanoi did not want a formula under which the United States could resume bombing "legally" by charging violations of an understanding. Finally, Hanoi was eager to give the impression to its supporters in the South that it had induced us to stop "unconditionally" as a symbol of imminent victory. For the same reason, it was important to us that *both* sides in South Viet Nam believe there had been reciprocity.

As a result, six months were devoted to defining a quid pro quo which could be represented as unconditional. The issue of the bombing halt thus raised the question of the nature of an international commitment. What is the sanction for violation of an understanding? The United States, for a long time, conducted itself as if its principal safeguard was a formal, binding commitment by Hanoi to certain restraints. In fact, since no court exists to which the United States could take Hanoi, the American sanction was what the United States could do unilaterally should Hanoi "take advantage" of the bombing pause. Hanoi's fear of the consequences is a more certain protection against trickery than

Moral Argument and the War in Vietnam

a formal commitment. Communicating what we meant by taking advantage turned out to be more important than eliciting a formal North Vietnamese response.

The final settlement of the problem seems to have been arrived at by this procedure. In his address announcing the bombing halt, President Johnson stressed that Hanoi is clear about our definition of "take advantage." Hanoi has not formally acknowledged these terms; it has, in fact, insisted that the bombing halt was unconditional. But Hanoi can have little doubt that the bombing halt would not survive if it disregarded the points publicly stated by Secretary Rusk and President Johnson. . . .

It has become axiomatic that a bombing halt would lead—almost automatically—to a cease-fire. However, negotiating a cease-fire may well be tantamount to establishing the preconditions of a political settlement. If there existed a front line with unchallenged control behind it, as in Korea, the solution would be traditional and relatively simple: the two sides could stop shooting at each other and the cease-fire line could follow the front line. But there are no front lines in Viet Nam; control is not territorial, it depends on who has forces in a given area and on the time of day. If a cease-fire permits the government to move without challenge, day or night, it will amount to a Saigon victory. If Saigon is prevented from entering certain areas, it means in effect partition which, as in Laos, tends toward permanency. Unlike Laos, however, the pattern would be a crazy quilt, with enclaves of conflicting loyalties all over the country.

This would involve the following additional problems: (1) It would lead to an intense scramble to establish predominant control before the cease-fire went into effect. (2) It would make next to impossible the verification of any withdrawal of North Vietnamese forces that might be negotiated; the local authorities in areas of preponderant Communist control would doubtless certify that no external forces were present and impede any effort at international inspection. (3) It would raise the problem of the applicability of a cease-fire to guerrilla activity in the non-Communist part of the country; in other words, how to deal with the asymmetry between the actions of regular and of guerrilla forces. Regular forces operate on a scale which makes possible a relatively precise definition of what is permitted and what is proscribed; guerrilla forces, by contrast, can be effective through isolated acts of terror difficult to distinguish from normal criminal activity.

There would be many other problems: who collects taxes and how, who enforces the cease-fire and by what means. In other words, a tacit de facto cease-fire may prove more attainable than a negotiated one. By the same token, a formal cease-fire is likely to predetermine the ultimate settlement and tend toward partition. Cease-fire is thus not so much a step toward a final settlement as a form of it.

This is even more true of another staple of the Viet Nam debate:

Solutions?

the notion of a coalition government. Of course, there are two meanings of the term: as a means of legitimizing partition, indeed as a disguise for continuing the civil war; or as a "true" coalition government attempting to govern the whole country. In the first case, a coalition government would be a façade with non-Communist and Communist ministries in effect governing their own parts of the country. This is what happened in Laos, where each party in the "coalition government" wound up with its own armed forces and its own territorial administration. The central government did not exercise any truly national functions. Each side carried on its own business—including civil war. But in Laos, each side controlled contiguous territory, not a series of enclaves as in South Viet Nam. Too, of all the ways to bring about partition, negotiations about a coalition government are the most dangerous because the mere participation of the United States in talking about it could change the political landscape of South Viet Nam. . . .

The notion that a coalition government represents a "compromise" which will permit a new political evolution hardly does justice to Vietnamese conditions. Even the non-Communist groups have demonstrated the difficulty Vietnamese have in compromising differences. It is beyond imagination that parties that have been murdering and betraying each other for twenty-five years could work together as a team giving joint instructions to the entire country. The image of a line of command extending from Saigon into the countryside is hardly true of the non-Communist government in Saigon. It would be absurd in the case of a coalition government. Such a government would possess no authority other than that of each minister over the forces he controlled either through personal or party loyalty. . . .

In short, negotiations seeking to impose a coalition from the outside are likely to change markedly and irreversibly the political process in South Viet Nam—as Vietnamese who believe that a coalition government cannot work quickly choose sides. We would, in effect, be settling the war on an issue least amenable to outside influence, with respect to which we have the least grasp of conditions and the long-term implications of which are most problematical.

That is not to say that the United States should resist an outcome freely negotiated among the Vietnamese. It does suggest that any negotiation on this point by the United States is likely to lead either to an impasse or to the collapse of Saigon.

V. Where Do We Go From Here?

Paradoxical as it may seem, the best way to make progress where distrust is so deep and the issues so interrelated may be to seek agreement on ultimate goals first and to work back to the details to implement them.

This requires an analysis of the strengths and weaknesses of both

Moral Argument and the War in Vietnam

sides. Hanoi's strength is that it is fighting among its own people in familiar territory, while the United States is fighting far away. As long as Hanoi can preserve some political assets in the South, it retains the prospect of an ultimately favorable political outcome. Not surprisingly, Hanoi has shown a superior grasp of the local situation and a greater capacity to design military operations for political ends. Hanoi relies on world opinion and American domestic pressures; it believes that the unpopularity of the war in Viet Nam will ultimately force an American withdrawal.

Hanoi's weaknesses are that superior planning can substitute for material resources only up to a point. Beyond it, differences of scale are bound to become significant and a continuation of the war will require a degree of foreign assistance which may threaten North Viet Nam's autonomy. This Hanoi has jealously safeguarded until now. A prolonged, even if ultimately victorious war might leave Viet Nam so exhausted as to jeopardize the purpose of decades of struggle. . . .

American assets and liabilities are the reverse of these. No matter how irrelevant some of our political conceptions or how insensitive our strategy, we are so powerful that Hanoi is simply unable to defeat us militarily. By its own efforts, Hanoi cannot force the withdrawal of American forces from South Viet Nam. Indeed, a substantial improvement in the American military position seems to have taken place. As a result, we have achieved our minimum objective: Hanoi is unable to gain a military victory. Since it cannot force our withdrawal, it must negotiate about it. Unfortunately, our military strength has no political corollary; we have been unable so far to create a political structure that could survive military opposition from Hanoi after we withdraw.

The structure of the negotiation is thus quite different from Korea. There are no front lines with secure areas behind them. In Viet Nam, negotiations do not ratify a military status quo but create a new political reality. There are no unambiguous tests of relative political and military strength. The political situation for both sides is precarious—within Viet Nam for the United States, internationally for Hanoi. Thus it is probable that neither side can risk a negotiation so prolonged as that of Panmunjom a decade and a half ago. In such a situation, a favorable outcome depends on a clear definition of objectives. The limits of the American commitment can be expressed in two propositions: first, the United States cannot accept a military defeat, or a change in the political structure of South Viet Nam brought about by external military force; second, once North Vietnamese forces and pressures are removed, the United States has no obligation to maintain a government in Saigon by force.

American objectives should therefore be (1) to bring about a staged withdrawal of external forces, North Vietnamese and American, (2) thereby to create a maximum incentive for the contending forces in South Viet Nam to work out a political agreement. The structure and content of such an agreement must be left to the South Vietnamese. It could take place formally on the national level. Or, it could occur locally on the provincial level where even now tacit accommodations are not unusual in many areas such as the Mekong Delta.

The details of a phased, mutual withdrawal are not decisive for our present purposes and, in any case, would have to be left to negotiations. It is possible, however, to list some principles: the withdrawal should be over a sufficiently long period so that a genuine indigenous political process has a chance to become established; the contending sides in South Viet Nam should commit themselves not to pursue their objectives by force while the withdrawal of external forces is going on; in so far as possible, the definition of what constitutes a suitable political process or structure should be left to the South Vietnamese, with the schedule for mutual withdrawal creating the time frame for an agreement.

The United States, then, should concentrate on the subject of mutual withdrawal of external forces and avoid negotiating about the internal structure of South Viet Nam for as long as possible. The primary responsibility for negotiating the internal structure of South Viet Nam should be left for direct negotiations among the South Vietnamese. If we involve ourselves deeply in the issue of South Viet Nam's internal arrangements, we shall find ourselves in a morass of complexities subject to two major disadvantages. First, we will be the party in the negotiation least attuned to the subtleties of Vietnamese politics. Second, we are likely to wind up applying the greater part of our pressure against Saigon as the seeming obstacle to an accommodation. The result may be the complete demoralization of Saigon, profound domestic tensions with the United States and a prolonged stalemate or a resumption of the war.

Whatever the approach, the negotiating procedure becomes vital; indeed, it may well determine the outcome and the speed with which it is achieved. . . .

But why should Hanoi accept such an approach? The answer is that partly it has no choice; it cannot bring about a withdrawal of American forces by its own efforts, particularly if the United States adopts a less impatient strategy—one better geared to the protection of the population and sustainable with substantially reduced casualties. Hanoi may also believe that the NLF, being better organized and more determined, can win a political contest. (Of course, the prerequisite of a settlement is that both sides think they have a chance to win or at least to avoid losing.) Above all, Hanoi may not wish to give the United States a permanent voice in internal South Vietnamese affairs, as it will if the two-sided approach is followed. It may be reinforced in this attitude by the belief that a prolonged negotiation about coalition government may end no more satisfactorily from Hanoi's point of view than did the Geneva negotiations over Viet Nam in 1954 and Laos in 1962. As for the United States, if it brings about a removal of external forces and

Moral Argument and the War in Vietnam

pressures, and if it gains a reasonable time for political consolidation, it will have done the maximum possible for an ally—short of permanent occupation. . . .

A negotiating procedure and a definition of objectives cannot guarantee a settlement, of course. If Hanoi proves intransigent and the war goes on, we should seek to achieve as many of our objectives as possible unilaterally. We should adopt a strategy which reduces casualties and concentrates on protecting the population. We should continue to strengthen the Vietnamese army to permit a gradual withdrawal of some American forces, and we should encourage Saigon to broaden its base so that it is stronger for the political contest with the Communists which sooner or later it must undertake.

No war in a century has aroused the passions of the conflict in Viet Nam. By turning Viet Nam into a symbol of deeper resentments, many groups have defeated the objective they profess to seek. However we got into Viet Nam, whatever the judgment of our actions, ending the war honorably is essential for the peace of the world. Any other solution may unloose forces that would complicate prospects of international order. A new administration must be given the benefit of the doubt and a chance to move toward a peace which grants the people of Viet Nam what they have so long struggled to achieve: an opportunity to work out their own destiny in their own way.

Notes

1 These are: withdrawal of U.S. forces, the provision of the Geneva agreements calling for neutrality for North and South Viet Nam, and reunification on the basis of popular wishes. The United States has rejected the third point which implies that the internal arrangements for South Viet Nam should be settled on the basis of the NLF program—though the United States has agreed to consider the NLF program among others.
2 Article by Wilfred Burchett, *The New York Times*, October 21, 1967.

The Official U. S. Positi
In Negotiations

*Address by President Nixon**

. . . .In weighing alternative courses, we have had to recognize that the situation as it exists today is far different from what it was two years ago or four years ago or ten years ago.

One difference is that we no longer have the choice of not intervening. We have crossed that bridge. There are now more than half a million American troops in Viet-Nam, and 35,000 Americans have lost their lives there.

We can have honest debate about whether we should have entered the war. We can have honest debate about the past conduct of the war. But the urgent question today is what to do now that we are there, not whether we should have entered on this course, but what is required of us today.

Against that background, let me discuss, first, what we have rejected, and second, what we are prepared to accept.

Essential Principles

We have ruled out attempting to impose a purely military solution on the battlefield.

We have also ruled out either a one-sided withdrawal from Viet-Nam or the acceptance in Paris of terms that would amount to a disguised defeat.

When we assumed the burden of helping defend South Viet-Nam, millions of South Vietnamese men, women, and children placed their trust in us. To abandon them now would risk a massacre that would shock and dismay everyone in the world who values human life.

Abandoning the South Vietnamese people, however, would jeopardize more than lives in South Viet-Nam. It would threaten our longer term hopes for peace in the world. A great nation cannot renege on its pledges. A great nation must be worthy of trust.

When it comes to maintaining peace, "prestige" is not an empty word. I am not speaking of false pride or bravado—they should have no place in our policies. I speak rather of the respect that one nation has for

*Nationwide broadcast address by United States President Richard Nixon on May 14, 1969. The excerpts reprinted here originally appeared in print in *The Department of State Bulletin*, Volume 60, June 2, 1969.

another's integrity in defending its principles and meeting its obligations.

If we simply abandoned our effort in Viet-Nam, the cause of peace might not survive the damage that would be done to other nations' confidence in our reliability.

Another reason stems from debates within the Communist world between those who argue for a policy of confrontation with the United States and those who argue against it. If Hanoi were to succeed in taking over South Viet-Nam, by force—even after the power of the United States had been engaged—it would greatly strengthen those leaders who scorn negotiation, who advocate aggression, who minimize the risks of confrontation. It would bring peace now, but it would enormously increase the danger of a bigger war later.

If we are to move successfully from an era of confrontation to an era of negotiation, then we have to demonstrate—at the point at which confrontation is being tested—that confrontation with the United States is costly and unrewarding.

Almost without exception, the leaders of non-Communist Asia have told me that they would consider a one-sided American withdrawal from Viet-Nam to be a threat to the security of their own nations.

In determining what choices would be acceptable, we have to understand our essential objective: We seek the opportunity for the South Vietnamese people to determine their own political future without outside interference.

Let me put it plainly: What the United States wants for South Viet-Nam is not the important thing. What North Viet-Nam wants for South Viet-Nam is not the important thing. What is important is what the people of South Viet-Nam want for themselves.

The United States has suffered over 1 million casualties in four wars in this century. Whatever faults we may have as a nation, we have asked nothing for ourselves in return for these sacrifices. We have been generous toward those whom we have fought, helping former foes as well as friends in the task of reconstruction. We are proud of this record, and we bring the same attitude to our search for a settlement in Viet-Nam.

In this spirit, let me be explicit about several points:

—We seek no bases in Viet-Nam.

—We insist on no military ties.

—We are willing to agree to neutrality if that is what the South Vietnamese people freely choose.

—We believe there should be an opportunity for full participation in the political life of South Viet-Nam by all political elements that are prepared to do so without the use of force or intimidation.

—We are prepared to accept any government in South Viet-Nam that results from the free choice of the South Vietnamese people themselves.

—We have no intention of imposing any form of government upon the people of South Viet-Nam, nor will we be a party to such coercion.

—We have no objection to reunification, if that turns out to be what the people of South Viet-Nam and the people of North Viet-Nam want; we ask only that the decision reflect the free choice of the people concerned.

At this point, I would like to add a personal word based on many visits to South Viet-Nam over the past five years. This is the most difficult war in America's history, fought against a ruthless enemy. I am proud of our men who have carried the terrible burden of this war with dignity and courage despite the division and opposition to the war in the United States. History will record that never have America's fighting men fought more bravely for more unselfish goals than our men in Viet-Nam. It is our responsibility to see that they will not have fought in vain.

In pursuing our limited objective, we insist on no rigid diplomatic formula. Peace could be achieved by a formal negotiated settlement. Peace could be achieved by an informal understanding, provided that the understanding is clear and that there were adequate assurances that it would be observed. Peace on paper is not as important as peace in fact.

The Negotiations

This brings us, then, to the matter of negotiations.

We must recognize that peace in Viet-Nam cannot be achieved overnight. A war which has raged for so many years will require detailed negotiations and cannot be settled at a single stroke.

What kind of settlement will permit the South Vietnamese people to determine freely their own political future? Such a settlement will require the withdrawal of all non-South Vietnamese forces from South Viet-Nam and procedures for political choice that give each significant group in South Viet-Nam a real opportunity to participate in the political life of the nation.

To implement these principles, I reaffirm now our willingness to withdraw our forces on a specified timetable. We ask only that North Viet-Nam withdraw its forces from South Viet-Nam, Cambodia, and Laos into North Viet-Nam, also in accordance with a timetable.

We include Cambodia and Laos to ensure that these countries would not be used as bases for a renewed war. The Cambodian border is only 35 miles from Saigon; the Laotian border is only 25 miles from Hué.

Our offer provides for a simultaneous start on withdrawal by both sides; agreement on a mutually acceptable timetable; and for the withdrawal to be accomplished quickly.

If North Viet-Nam wants to insist that it has no forces in South Viet Nam, we will no longer debate the point—provided that its forces cease to be there and that we have reliable assurances that they will not return.

Moral Argument and the War in Vietnam

The North Vietnamese delegates have been saying in Paris that political issues should be discussed along with military issues and that there must be a political settlement in the South. We do not dispute this, but the military withdrawal involves outside forces and can therefore be properly negotiated by North Viet-Nam and the United States, with the concurrence of its allies. The political settlement is an internal matter which ought to be decided among the South Vietnamese themselves and not imposed by outside powers. However, if our presence at these political negotiations would be helpful, and if the South Vietnamese concerned agreed, we would be willing to participate, along with the representatives of Hanoi if that were also desired.

Recent statements by President Thieu have gone far toward opening the way to a political settlement. He has publicly declared his government's willingness to discuss a political solution with the National Liberation Front and has offered free elections. This was a dramatic step forward, a reasonable offer that could lead to a settlement. The South Vietnamese Government has offered to talk without preconditions. I believe that the other side should also be willing to talk without preconditions.

The South Vietnamese Government recognizes, as we do, that a settlement must permit all persons and groups that are prepared to renounce the use of force to participate freely in the political life of South Viet-Nam. To be effective, such a settlement would require two things: first, a process that would allow the South Vietnamese people to express their choice; and second, a guarantee that this process would be a fair one.

We do not insist on a particular form of guarantee. The important thing is that the guarantees should have the confidence of the South Vietnamese people and that they should be broad enough and strong enough to protect the interests of all major South Vietnamese groups.

This, then, is the outline of the settlement that we seek to negotiate in Paris. Its basic terms are very simple: mutual withdrawal of non-South Vietnamese forces from South Viet-Nam and free choice for the people of South Viet-Nam. I believe that the long-term interests of peace require that we insist on no less and that the realities of the situation require that we seek no more.

Programs and Alternatives

To make very concrete what I have said, I propose the following measures, which seem to me consistent with the principles of all parties. These proposals are made on the basis of full consultation with President Thieu.

—As soon as agreement can be reached, all non-South Vietnamese forces would begin withdrawals from South Viet-Nam.

—Over a period of twelve months, by agreed-upon stages, the major portions of all U.S., Allied, and other non-South Vietnamese forces would be withdrawn. At the end of this 12-month period, the remaining U.S., Allied, and other non-South Vietnamese forces would move into designated base areas and would not engage in combat operations.

—The remaining U.S. and Allied forces would move to complete their withdrawals as the remaining North Vietnamese forces were withdrawn and returned to North Viet-Nam.

—An international supervisory body, acceptable to both sides, would be created for the purpose of verifying withdrawals and for any other purposes agreed upon between the two sides.

—This international body would begin operating in accordance with an agreed timetable and would participate in arranging supervised cease-fires.

—As soon as possible after the international body was functioning, elections would be held under agreed procedures and under the supervision of the international body.

—Arrangements would be made for the earliest possible release of prisoners of war on both sides.

—All parties would agree to observe the Geneva accords of 1954 regarding Viet-Nam and Cambodia, and the Laos accords of 1962.

I believe this proposal for peace is realistic and takes account of the legitimate interests of all concerned. It is consistent with President Thieu's six points. It can accommodate the various programs put forth by the other side. We and the Government of South Viet-Nam are prepared to discuss its details with the other side. Secretary Rogers is now in Saigon and will be discussing with President Thieu how, together, we may put forward these proposed measures most usefully in Paris. He will, as well, be consulting with our other Asian allies on these measures while on his Asian trip. However, I would stress that these proposals are not offered on a take-it-or-leave-it basis. We are quite willing to consider other approaches consistent with our principles.

We are willing to talk about anybody's program—Hanoi's four points, the NLF's ten points—provided it can be made consistent with the few basic principles I have set forth here.

Press Conference With Secretary Rogers*

Q. Mr. Secretary, in order to give the people, all the people of South Viet-Nam, a fair shake, the NLF [National Liberation Front] apparently feel that they have to be part of the government machinery in some form. Would we be prepared to encourage them to play a substantial role on a supervisory commission to supervise free elections in the South?

*Official Press Conference of June 5, 1969 with U.S. Secretary of State William P. Rogers. The excerpts reprinted here were first printed in The Department of State Bulletin, Volume 60, June 23, 1969.

Moral Argument and the War in Vietnam

A. Well, I think we have to be prepared, and I think the President indicated in his speech that we are prepared, to set up an international supervisory body to make certain that the elections are fair and free elections. What that body will consist of should be decided in the negotiations. I think that we have to recognize that the other side would have to have some guarantee that there would be no coercion and that their votes could be cast without coercion and counted properly. And whether that would be supervised by an international group made up of outside nations or whether it would include the NLF or not, I don't know. I certainly would not be opposed to that. But I want to make it clear that that is not a coalition government. . . . *Do you regard the idea of a mixed commission possibly as a means of bridging the gap between Saigon's insistence that there be no coalition government and the NLF's demands for some kind of participation?*

A. Well, as we have said on several occasions, we think this question should be answered by the South Vietnamese. I don't want to say anything here that differs from that position. But I would think that as long as it is clearly understood that we are not talking about a change of the government and we are talking merely about some supervisory commission that would guarantee the fairness of the election, that would be a possibility. . . . I am talking about the speech that the president made on May 14, where he said the future of South Viet-Nam should be decided by elections and that the particular kind of elections, their timing, and what they would consist of should be determined by the people of South Viet-Nam. And that should be done by negotiations. Unfortunately, the very, I thought, constructive proposal of President Thieu that he negotiate directly with the NLF has so far received no response. If the NLF would sit down with the government of South Viet-Nam, which is something they previously said they wanted to do, they could negotiate these matters. It is not too difficult to provide a method of giving the people of a country of that size the right to select their own leadership and their own form of government if the other side is willing to do it. So far the other side is talking about imposing a government on the South. And we suspect that what they are interested in is to attack the present government, cause confusion and chaos, and thereby impose a governmental structure on South Viet-Nam that will not represent the will of the people. Now, that the president has made clear he will not accept.

Q. *Mr. Secretary, there have been reports from Asia while you were there on your trip that you had indicated such questions as amending the South Vietnamese Constitution, holding special elections under that Constitution, the question of an interim coalition government in South Viet-Nam are open to negotiation at Paris. Is that a correct reflection of your position?*

A. Well, you have asked quite a few questions in one. Let me talk about coalition government first. I had a background conference—I think it was in Saigon—and if there is any question about what I said, we have a transcript. I made it clear at that time that we think that the political questions about the future of South Viet-Nam should be decided by the South Vietnamese. And I said that I thought that the phrase "coalition government," as used by the Communists, would be unacceptable because it is used to convey the thought that they will impose certain of their leaders on the people of South Viet-Nam. So that from that standpoint, if that is what the phrase means, it would not be acceptable to anybody on our side.

Now, on the other hand, the president, President Nixon has stated, and President Thieu has stated, that as a result of an election if the people want to vote for the Communists or any other system of government and their vote is freely cast and counted, then all parties will abide by their choice.

Now, if that is what you mean by a government that represents both leaders now in South Viet-Nam and some Communists, obviously that would be acceptable to us. And, obviously, that would be acceptable to the South Vietnamese.

. . . President Thieu has indicated he is willing to discuss the elective process with the other side in order to set up a system which will permit the people of the South to express their views, and their views will be controlling.

Q Mr. Secretary, you speak of free elections and of letting the people of South Viet-Nam decide, and yet you have just been to Saigon, you know there is no freedom of press, that the jails are full of oppositionists, many of them non-Communist. What have you done about the absence of civil liberty and the absence of any atmosphere that would promise free elections in South Viet-Nam? . . . Have you taken this up with the government or done anything about it?

A. I don't agree with your premise. It is true I was in South Viet-Nam. [Laughter.] I don't think that the jails are full. In any war situation, the government in the war has some problems.

Now, in terms of free press, there are plenty of newspapers there. I think any nation at war has some difficulty with the press. As a matter of fact, even nations at peace have a little difficulty with the press. If you remember our situation during World War II, we had some press problems. We also—if you will remember—on the west coast, we took some action that we are not particularly proud of now.

Now, I think President Thieu is making every effort to provide a free society in South Viet-Nam consistent with the war. . . .

Statement at Paris by Negotiator Walsh*

. . . . Let us look at the positions your side has taken on the principal questions involved in a settlement.

Moral Argument and the War in Vietnam

On the question of withdrawal of forces, you say U.S. and Allied forces must withdraw from South Viet-Nam unconditionally. You refer to the problem of Vietnamese forces in South Viet-Nam as one to be resolved by the Vietnamese parties among themselves.

That position gets us nowhere. Why do you avoid stating whether North Vietnamese forces in South Viet-Nam are going to go back to North Viet-Nam? Vague reference that the Vietnamese parties will resolve that problem is not enough.

That position of the United States government on the question of withdrawals must be clearly understood. We will not accept a one-sided withdrawal from South Viet-Nam. There must be a withdrawal of all non-South Vietnamese forces.

You reject the idea of mutual withdrawal because you say it places the aggressor on the same level as the victim of aggression.

We could, with more justification, argue that in reality it is your side which seeks to confuse the aggressor—North Viet-Nam—with the victim of aggression—South Viet-Nam. This kind of argument, however, does not help to advance the negotiations. The practical fact is that North Viet-Nam, as well as the United States and its allies, has forces in South Viet-Nam. A negotiated settlement requires that all non-South Vietnamese forces be withdrawn from South Viet-Nam. . . .

Let me now turn to the question of political settlement. You call for the overthrow of the government of the Republic of Viet-Nam. You demand the formation of a coalition government. And you state that until these demands are met, progress cannot be made in the Paris meetings. This amounts to saying that you will not enter into meaningful negotiations with our side unless we accept in advance the outcome which you seek. That is a position which seems designed to block progress at these negotiations.

Your side came to these Paris meetings which were convened for the purpose of trying to bring the war in Viet-Nam to an end through negotiations in which the government of the Republic of Viet-Nam would participate. Yet you now say that you will not negotiate unless that government is first eliminated.

The government of the Republic of Viet-Nam has indicated that it is prepared to discuss all aspects of a political settlement. It has not demanded that your side accept any preconditions before negotiations can begin. Rather, the government of the Republic of Viet-Nam has made clear that it is prepared to discuss a political settlement without preconditions. That offer still stands.

The government of the Republic of Viet-Nam is prepared to accept free elections under international supervision. It has offered guarantees

*The opening statement made by Lawrence Walsh, deputy head of the U.S. delegation, at the 22nd plenary session of the meetings on Viet-Nam at Paris on June 19, 1969. The excerpts reprinted here first appeared in print in *The Department of State Bulletin*, Volume 61, July 7, 1969.

and safeguards for free elections. Therefore, if you truly believe you have the support of the people of South Viet-Nam, you should be prepared to test your claims in genuinely free elections rather than trying to impose your views at these negotiations. . . .

Last week, your side accused us of not responding seriously to your ten-point proposal. The truth is that we have at every plenary meeting since your side presented these proposals examined your points, asking for clarification of them, comparing them with our own proposals, and seeking common ground between your proposals and ours.

At the twentieth plenary session, Ambassador Lodge explained our proposals and asked a number of questions about your ten points. He did this in the hope that clarification of your proposals would help to define the issues and would assist us in seeking common ground and eventual agreement between us.

We still await your response to our questions. Let me recall those questions:

a. Does the first point of your side's ten-point program mean that in order to achieve the fundamental national rights of the Vietnamese people, North Viet-Nam is prepared to carry out the principles of the 1954 Geneva Accords, namely, withdrawal of forces, noninterference, and reunification through free choice?

b. Are North Vietnamese forces prepared to withdraw from South Viet-Nam?

c. Does your ten-point program mean that North Viet-Nam is prepared to withdraw its forces from Cambodia and Laos?

d. What are your views on international supervision of other aspects of a settlement beyond that mentioned in your tenth point?

e. Why does your side hesitate to enter into productive negotiations of a political settlement with the government of the Republic of Viet-Nam?. . . .

The Ten Points of the National Liberation Front

Introduction*
by Gabriel Kolko

. . . .It is remarkable that the N.L.F. and P.R.G. [National Liberation Front of South Vietnam, and the Provisional Revolutionary Government of South Vietnam] alternatives, so much more definite and comprehensive than any Washington or Saigon have ever issued, have not been easily obtainable and used as a basis of discussion within prowar or antiwar groups in the United States. That the Nixon administration has been able to avoid justifying its immediate rejection of the N.L.F. Ten-Point statement, much less the even more detailed Fundamental Reso lutions and Declaration of the P.R.G., has unquestionably permitted Washington to obfuscate its real strategy in the Paris talks and to win time and a somewhat greater degree of public toleration for its essentially military response to the tragic Vietnam imbroglio. (The State Department immediately designated objectionable the demands for the unconditional withdrawal of all United States and foreign troops and the inclusion of the N.L.F. in any government. These clauses are critical to an overall settlement, but the administration instead asked the N.L.F. in Paris to negotiate those sections of the Ten Points, which, taken in isolation, would scarcely comprise a peace settlement. The United States, referred the N.L.F. to the Thieu regime for direct talks on political matters. The U.S. persists in its rejection of the Ten Points. . . .)

The simple lack of public knowledge of what must be judged as an eminently sensible program to end the war and for the reconstruction of a war-wracked nation deprived administration critics of one of their most powerful tools for dissecting and exposing Washington's intransigence at the Paris Conference. For in Paris America's representatives have condemned as obdurate and impractical the most critical parts of the N.L.F. Ten Point plan, the only detailed proposal ever submitted to the Conference, the only arrangement that took into account the existing political-military realities of South Vietnam and the principle of national self-determination. . . .

The Nixon administration's present basic Vietnam policy ignores the critical premises of the N.L.F.'s position and is attempting to settle the

*Excerpts from Mr. Kolko's Introduction to *Three Documents of the National Liberation Front* (Boston: Beacon Press, 1970). Reprinted by permission of the Beacon Press. Introduction copyright 1970 by Gabriel Kolko.

Moral Argument and the War in Vietnam

fate of Vietnam on the battlefields rather than at the negotiating table. This proposition merits brief examination because, if it is valid, then the price Americans may expect to continue to pay in blood, money, and the increasing alienation of their youth will be very great indeed over an indefinite number of future years.

The keystone of the N.L.F. program is that the Vietnamese can attain national self-determination only after all American and foreign troops withdraw and the Vietnamese people then are able to settle their own affairs. But the American response, from the beginning of the intervention, has been that there are two main bodies of foreign troops in South Vietnam—their own and those from North Vietnam. Since Washington's abandonment of this assumption is a precondition of diplomatic progress, examining its validity in the light of some historical facts is in order here.

The Geneva Agreements of 1954 at no place refers to "South Vietnam" or to the "Republic of Vietnam," and it designated the seventeenth parallel as a "provisional" border until July, 1956, when all Vietnam was to hold internationally supervised elections to reunify the country under a common government. The Democratic Republic of Vietnam (D.R.V.) in Hanoi repeatedly asked the U.S.-backed Diem regime and the French, before and after the 1956 deadline, to fulfill the Geneva election proviso, but they consistently refused. But at no time was there any doubt that Vietnam was one nation, culturally and historically, and the fiction that Vietnamese from the north of an arbitrary line are as alien in their own land as Americans has proved an insurmountable obstacle in Paris.

Had the U.S. supported the implementation of the Geneva Agreements there would not have been a continuation of the anticolonial war which began against the Japanese and French, but the internationally recognized premises of the Agreements were in total conflict with America's objectives in Southeast Asia. Not unreasonably, the N.L.F. insists that Vietnamese cannot be foreigners in their own country, that they have no distant land to which to withdraw, and that what they now seek is the implementation of the spirit and purpose of the 1954 Geneva Agreements. Additional proof of the indivisibility of all Vietnam is the fact that Ky, Thieu, and many of the leaders of the Saigon regime were born north of the seventeenth parallel and also regard the Geneva partition as temporary. Both the Johnson and Nixon administrations have rejected this quite traditional notion of nationality, though during the American Civil War, ironically, Washington articulated a doctrine of national unity and integrity nearly identical to that the N.L.F. and D.R.V. apply to Vietnam today.

Nixon's May 14, 1969 speech, and the statements of all American officials, have alleged that the N.L.F. is an "alien," "subversive" force, "controlled from Hanoi" to quote Secretary of Defense Laird, and that it is unnecessary to negotiate with it as a distinct party. Indeed, the

United States at Paris has consistently demanded that N.L.F. armed units withdraw from the south along with D.R.V. forces. Both Nixon and the Thieu regime have made it plain that the N.L.F.'s disarmament and reunification of force in the future is the precondition of its later promised entry into Saigon's political system. And this has only further deepened the impasse at Paris, for the N.L.F. insists that the future of South Vietnam's politics is for the Vietnamese themselves to determine, without foreign interference. The exact formulation of the N.L.F.'s proposals for establishing a peace coalition consistent with national autonomy may be found in the Ten Points and Declaration. But the reader can also ask himself whether true independence can occur in Vietnam with American troops present.

Nixon and Thieu, in presenting their various election plans, consistently argue that Saigon's 1967 election was "free" despite Thieu's jailing and outlawing of all opposition, from independent Buddhist to N.L.F. and that the existing constitution, which bans "Communism" and the N.L.F., is a viable framework for Thieu's promised "democracy." Such reasoning also assumes that the Thieu-Ky regime, with its numerous predecessors, represents something more than a minute handful of Vietnamese. But even the U.S. projects for erstwhile "international supervision," which would produce the same undemocratic and unstable results as in Greece in 1946 and South Korea in 1948, did not stand very long before Thieu and his foreign minister in July, 1969, admitted that they would not permit "Communists" to run in any election, which, Thieu later observed, would require at least two years to organize. And Ky's mid-September threat of a coup against any coalition including the N.L.F. made it clearer yet that so long as the U.S. keeps the entirely dependent Thieu-Ky regime in power there can be no political settlement nor reconciliation among the Vietnamese themselves.

Today it is extremely unlikely that the American public, important sectors of business, and many GI's will agree to sustain the war, at any level, into the indefinite future. For a nation already traumatized by the event, the continued internal social and economic costs alone would prove prohibitive. If and when Nixon confronts and finally accepts this inhibiting reality and comprehends the limits of American power against an indigenous peasant-based movement that has fought successfully for nearly twenty-five years and stands prepared to persevere indefinitely, diplomatic negotiations will, for the first time, assume prime importance. And their successful fruition will come only when Nixon accedes to the entirely just and sensible principle, which not only the N.L.F. but a large and ever-growing portion of the American population demands, of total and immediate U.S. and foreign troop withdrawals. At that time—hopefully very soon—the relevance of the N.L.F. solution, in all its dimensions, will be paramount. It should now be fully clear, after many years of resistance, that the N.L.F. will not bargain away the principle of national self-determination free from foreign interference

Moral Argument and the War in Vietnam

in any shape. The Vietnamese people are no less patriotic and patient than those American revolutionists were nearly two centuries ago in their successful struggle against a minority of privileged pro-British colonists in their midst and the military power of the world's mightiest empire. The N.L.F. position on the right of Vietnamese to determine their own political future, a deep commitment they refuse to compromise at the Paris Conference, should evoke wide sympathy from Americans who recognize it as being consistent with the spirit of the American Revolution. . . .

Principles and Main Content of an Overall Solution to the South Viet Nam Problem—The Ten Points of the National Liberation Front of South Viet Nam*

The United States policy of intensifying the war and negotiating from a position of strength has kept the Paris Conference on Viet Nam at a standstill, against the desire of the people in Viet Nam, in the U.S. and in the world. That policy has brought the U.S. heavy failure. Ardently cherishing independence and freedom, the South Viet Nam people have been resolutely pushing ahead their sacred resistance; they have won new glorious victories in their Spring offensive. The U.S. aggressive war is being further driven into an impasse. The military, political and diplomatic difficulties of the U.S. are piling up. No sooner have more than one hundred days elapsed since it came into office, than the Nixon administration has been condemned everywhere in the world and in the United States itself. As for the Saigon administration, it has exposed all its traitorous features, and becomes more isolated and weaker than ever before.

Broad sectors of the public opinion in the U.S. and in the world are demanding that the Nixon administration put an immediate end to the aggressive war in Viet Nam, withdraw unconditionally all U.S. and satellite troops from South Viet Nam, and promptly restore peace in Viet Nam.

In order to open the way to the progress of the Paris Conference on Viet Nam, as desired by the people in Viet Nam, in the U.S. and in the world, the Delegation of the South Viet Nam National Front for Liberation, by order of the Central Committee of the South Viet Nam National Front for Liberation, presented to the sixteenth Plenary Session, May 8, 1969, the following document of the South Viet Nam National Front for Liberation:

Principles and Main Content of an Overall Solution to the South Viet Nam Problem to Help Restore Peace in Viet Nam

Proceeding from a desire to reach a political solution with a view to ending the U.S. imperialists' war of aggression in South Viet Nam and helping restore peace in Viet Nam;

On the basis of the guarantee of the fundamental national rights of

---

*The version reprinted here is Mr. Kolko's excerpts from the statement by Mr. Tran Buu Kiem at the 16th Plenary Session of the Paris Conference on Viet Nam, May 8, 1969.

Moral Argument and the War in Vietnam

the Vietnamese people;

Proceeding from the fundamental principles of the 1954 Geneva Agreements on Viet Nam and the actual situation in Viet Nam;

On the basis of the Political Programme and the 5-point position of the South Viet Nam National Front for Liberation, which are in keeping with the 4-point stand of the government of the Democratic Republic of Viet Nam;

The South Viet Nam National Front for Liberation sets forth the principles and main content of an overall solution to the South Viet Nam problem to help restore peace in Viet Nam as follows:

1—To respect the Vietnamese people's fundamental national rights, i.e., independence, sovereignty, unity and territorial integrity, as recognized by the 1954 Geneva Agreements on Viet Nam.

2—The U.S. Government must withdraw from South Viet Nam all U.S. troops, military personnel, arms and war materiel, and all troops, military personnel, arms and war materiel of the other foreign countries of the U.S. camp without posing any condition whatsoever; liquidate all U.S. military bases in South Viet Nam; renounce all encroachments on the sovereignty, territory and security of South Viet Nam and the Democratic Republic of Viet Nam.

3—The Vietnamese people's right to fight for the defense of their Fatherland is the sacred, inalienable right to self-defense of all peoples. The question of the Vietnamese armed forces in South Viet Nam shall be resolved by the Vietnamese parties among themselves.

4—The people of South Viet Nam settle themselves their own affairs without foreign interference. They decide themselves the political regime of South Viet Nam through free and democratic general elections. Through free and democratic general elections, a Constituent Assembly will be set up, a Constitution worked out, and a coalition Government of South Viet Nam installed, reflecting national concord and the broad union of all social strata.

5—During the period intervening between the restoration of peace and the holding of general elections, neither party shall impose its political regime on the people of South Viet Nam.

The political forces representing the various social strata and political tendencies in South Viet Nam, that stand for peace, independence and neutrality, including those persons who, for political reasons, have to live abroad, will enter into talks to set up a provisional coalition government based on the principle of equality, democracy and mutual respect with a view to achieving a peaceful, independent, democratic and neutral South Viet Nam.

The provisional coalition government is to have the following tasks:

a) To implement the agreements to be concluded on the withdrawal of the troops of the U.S. and the other foreign countries of the American camp, etc.

b) To achieve national concord, and a broad union of all social strata, political forces, nationalities, religious communities, and all persons, no matter what their political beliefs and their past may be, provided they stand for peace, independence and neutrality.

c) To achieve broad democratic freedoms—freedom of speech, freedom of the press, freedom of assembly, freedom of belief, freedom to form political parties and organizations, freedom to demonstrate, etc.; to free those persons jailed on political grounds; to prohibit all acts of terror, reprisal and discrimination against people having collaborated with either side, and who are now in the country or abroad—as provided for in the 1954 Geneva Agreements on Viet Nam.

d) To heal the war wounds, to restore and develop the economy, to restore the normal life of the people, and to improve the living conditions of the labouring people.

e) To hold free and democratic general elections in the whole of South Viet Nam with a view to achieving the South Viet Nam people's right to self-determination, in accordance with the content of point 4 mentioned above.

6—South Viet Nam will carry out a foreign policy of peace and neutrality:

To carry out a policy of good neighbourly relations with the Kingdom of Cambodia on the basis of respect for her independence, sovereignty, neutrality and territorial integrity within her present borders; to carry out a policy of good neighbourly relations with the Kingdom of Laos on the basis of respect for the 1962 Geneva Agreements on Laos.

To establish diplomatic, economic and cultural relations with all countries, irrespective of political and social regime, including the U.S., in accordance with the five principles of peaceful coexistence: mutual respect for the independence, sovereignty and territorial integrity, nonaggression, noninterference in the internal affairs, equality and mutual benefit, peaceful coexistence; to accept economic and technical aid with no political conditions attached from any country.

7—The reunification of Viet Nam will be achieved step by step, by peaceful means, through discussions and agreement between the two zones, without foreign interference.

Pending the peaceful reunification of Viet Nam, the two zones shall reestablish normal relations in all fields on the basis of mutual respect.

The military demarcation line between the two zones at the seventeenth parallel, as provided for by the 1954 Geneva Agreements, is only of a provisional character and does not constitute in any way a political or territorial boundary. The two zones shall reach agreement on the statute of the Demilitarized Zone, and work out modalities for movements across the provisional military demarcation line.

8—As provided for in the 1954 Geneva Agreements on Viet Nam, pending the peaceful reunification of Viet Nam, the two zones, North and South of Vietnam, undertake to refrain from joining any military alliance with foreign countries, not to allow any foreign country to maintain military bases, troops and military personnel on their respective soil, and not to recognize the protection of any country or military alliance or bloc.

9—To resolve the aftermath of the war:

a) The parties will negotiate the release of the armymen captured in war.

b) The U.S. Government must bear full responsibility for the losses and devastations it has caused to the Vietnamese people in both zones.

10—The parties shall reach agreement on an international supervision of the withdrawal from South Viet Nam of the troops, military personnel, arms and war materiel of the U.S. and the other foreign countries of the American camp.

The principles and content of the overall solution expounded above form an integrated whole. On the basis of these principles and content, the parties shall reach understanding to the effect of concluding agreements on the above-mentioned questions with a view to ending the war in South Viet Nam, and contributing to the restoration of peace in Viet Nam.

The overall solution put forward by the South Viet Nam National Front for Liberation fully meets the national rights of the Vietnamese people and the interests of world peace.

The South Viet Nam National Front for Liberation, which has organized and led the South Vietnamese people in their struggle against U.S. aggression, is the authentic representative of the South Viet Nam people, fully competent to settle all problems relating to South Viet Nam. The aforesaid overall solution to the South Viet Nam problem once again demonstrates our correct position, and the consistent goodwill and serious intent of the South Viet Nam National Front for Liberation.

This overall solution ensures the fundamental national rights of the Vietnamese people and the right to self-determination of the South Viet Nam people. It ensures a lasting peace in Viet Nam. It embodies the spirit of broad national concord of the South Viet Nam people and the National Front for Liberation. It contributes to preserve peace and security in IndoChina and Southeast Asia, responds to the aspirations for peace of the American people as well as the world's people. This solution creates conditions for the U.S. to put an honourable end to its war, a war which is costly in human life and property, unpopular and prejudicial to the U.S. prestige.

The South Viet Nam National Front for Liberation is firmly confident that the people of both South and North Viet Nam, standing shoulder to shoulder in their common struggle for independence, freedom and peace, will no doubt wholeheartedly support this overall solution.

The South Viet Nam National Front for Liberation, which is closely united with the Viet Nam Alliance of National, Democratic and Peace

Forces, believes that because of its policy of broad national union and concord, all religious, political, social and cultural organizations in South Viet Nam, all political forces and Vietnamese residents abroad will warmly hail this solution; and the national-minded members of the Saigon army and administration who desire peace will sympathize with it.

The people and governments of the socialist countries and of the peace and justice-loving countries, the peace and democratic organizations in the world, which have always given vigorous support to the South Viet Nam people's resistance war against U.S. aggression and for national salvation, will surely support the overall solution to the South Viet Nam problem put forward by the National Front for Liberation. Together with the progressive people in the U.S., those American personalities, intellectuals and clergymen who have voiced their opposition to the U.S. unjust war in Viet Nam, and those American servicemen who are fed up with the war of aggression and who desire to be rapidly brought home, will no doubt sympathize with this solution too.

The overall solution to the South Viet Nam problem of the South Viet Nam National Front for Liberation is very logical and reasonable. The U.S. Government must adopt a serious attitude. It must put an end to its war of aggression, abandon its manoeuvre of maintaining neocolonialism in South Viet Nam, and respect the right of the Vietnamese people to settle themselves their internal affairs, without foreign interference. Therefore, it must withdraw from South Viet Nam all its troops and the troops of the other foreign countries of the American camp, without posing any condition whatsoever.

The U.S. must cease maintaining the present warlike, corrupt puppet administration in South Viet Nam. The South Viet Nam National Front for Liberation supports the struggle of the urban population in South Viet Nam for the replacement of Thieu-Ky-Huong, for the establishment of a peace cabinet so as to promptly end the war and restore peace. It is ready to enter into talks with persons of goodwill who stand for peace, independence and neutrality.

If the U.S. government is bent on intensifying its war of aggression, cherishing the illusion of gaining a position of strength on the battlefield as well as at the conference table, the people of South Viet Nam, under the glorious banner of the National Front for Liberation, overcoming all sacrifices and hardship, will continue to step up their fight and will certainly win final victory.

Vietnam: How Not to Negotiate*

Theodore Draper

The Vietnam War again seems bound to become dirtier, larger, and costlier on both sides. It may even have passed the point of no return and may settle down as a grim, pestilential "protracted war," the Chinese Communist equivalent of the old-fashioned "war of attrition." If so, the fatal turning point came in February 1967, preceded and followed by weeks of fancy diplomatic footwork, false hopes, and phony peace formulas.

As each move and maneuver comes into the news, it tends to live a life of its own, undefiled by previous moves and maneuvers. Yet, as every historian knows, history is not made that way, and it is necessary to put the pieces together to understand any one of them. The fate of the Johnson-Ho Chi Minh correspondence in February or of Secretary-General U. Thant's new three-point peace plan in March cannot be understood by itself, divorced from the events which led up to it or the consequences that flowed from it. Both these episodes and others in the recent past need to be seen in a somewhat larger historical perspective if they are to be rescued from providing more pretexts for waging an ever more brutalizing and destructive war.

The most striking and peculiar aspect of the latest turn of the war is that both sides seemed to be coming closer to a basis for negotiation just before the United States made the decision in February to intensify and broaden the scale of the attack on North Vietnam. The form of the complex, deceptive, and promising diplomatic maneuvers resulted in large part from the "negotiating positions" which both sides had previously taken. To see these positions clearly, it is necessary to go back about two years.

The basic North Vietnamese position went back to the four-point program enunciated by President Pham Van Dong on April 8, 1965. This had called, in substance, for (1) withdrawal of all United States military forces from South Vietnam, (2) neutralization of both South and North Vietnam, (3) settlement of South Vietnam's internal affairs "in accordance with the program" of the National Liberation Front, and (4) peaceful reunification. Pham Van Dong had offered it as "the basis for the soundest political settlement of the Vietnamese problem." If this

*Reprinted (excerpts) by permission of the author from the New York Review of Books, Volume VIII, May 4, 1967.

Moral Argument and the War in Vietnam

basis were "recognized," he said, "favorable conditions" for the peaceful settlement of the problem would be created and an international conference "along the pattern of" the Geneva conference of 1954 could be reconvened.[1]

On the surface, none of these four points appeared to be an insuperable obstacle to some form of peaceful negotiations. In his testimony before the Senate Foreign Relations Committee on February 18, 1966, Secretary of State Rusk said that the United States could accept three of the four points, the first, second, and fourth. The only exception he took was to the third, which he called "the core of the Communist position." In order to make it totally unacceptable, however, Secretary Rusk had to engage in one of his most tortuous intellectual exercises.

Instead of being content, for diplomatic purposes, to view the disputed third point as meaning no more and no less than what it said, he chose to reinterpret it according to the original NLF program of December 1960, issued in the heyday of Ngo Dinh Diem's regime. By this means Secretary Rusk sought to convince the committee that Pham Van Dong's third point implied prior recognition of the National Liberation Front as "the sole spokesman for the people of South Vietnam," which "hence should control them." Yet the earlier document had merely called for the overthrow of Diem's regime and its replacement by a broad "coalition government." Mr. Rusk leaped from the 1965 point to the 1960 program to arrive at the utterly gratuitous conclusion that Hanoi had really demanded the acceptance in advance of the NLF "as the sole bargaining representative of the South Vietnamese people."[2] In reality, the December 1960 program was such a lengthy, diffuse, and essentially moderate political mosaic, carefully contrived to appeal to the greatest number and variety of anti-Diem elements, that it could have been used as a basis of negotiations without committing anyone to anything very much in advance.[3] Unfortunately, no one on the committee seemed to know the documents intimately enough to challenge the Secretary's fanciful exegesis.

In its own propaganda, the NLF had styled itself "the only genuine representative of the fourteen million South Vietnamese people," a type of claim even democratic politicians have been known to make. But Pham Van Dong had made the issue the NLF's nebulous "program," designed to be all things to all men, rather than its organizational status. Only after the bombing of North Vietnam had gone on for almost a year did Ho Chi Minh demand that the United States "must recognize the NLFSV as the sole genuine representative of the people of South Vietnam and engage in negotiations with it."[4] Whatever significance this hardening of the North Vietnamese position may have had in 1966, it was not at issue in 1965 except to the extent that American diplomacy chose to give the most extreme interpretation to Pham Van Dong's third point, the only one that ostensibly stood in the way of accepting all four as a basis of negotiations. And even for that purpose, it would have been necessary for Secretary Rusk to reinterpret the third point in terms of later rather than earlier Communist statements.

It may be suspected that the real reason for straining at this point was less semantic than military. In April 1965, the United States feared the total collapse of the South Vietnamese military front. Experience has shown that diplomatic negotiations, whatever their "basis" may be, tend to reflect the relative positions of power. This is, in my view, reason enough to explain American reluctance to engage in negotiations at that time. The American ability to bring its own overwhelming military power quickly into the balance, however, may easily have given the Communist side pause and forced it to settle for much less than the existing balance of forces within South Vietnam seemed to indicate. In any case, negotiations in the first half of 1965—the last time they might have taken place in a relatively restrained atmosphere—would have demanded that both sides be content with something short of "victory." Instead, the impression was created of irreconcilable positions that were virtually mirror images of each other—of a National Liberation Front that claimed "to represent" all the people of South Vietnam, and of a National Liberation Front that represented virtually no one in South Vietnam.

II

The American negotiating position can be traced back to April 1965. Until that time, the United States did not really have a negotiating position because it did not believe in negotiations as a means of ending the war. As late as April 2, Secretary of State Rusk spoke disparagingly: "What is there to be negotiated? Who is going to negotiate, and to what end?" He complained that what was missing was "some private contact that indicates that a satisfactory basis of settlement can be found." A British correspondent asked: "You've had silence, completely?" To which Mr. Rusk seemed to give an affirmative, if somewhat ambiguous, answer: "No indication that —despite a number of contacts of various sorts—no indication that Hanoi is prepared to leave Laos and South Vietnam alone." In this period, the United States position, as expressed by Mr. Rusk, was to look for an "indication," or what he had previously called a "crucial element," from Hanoi "to stop doing what it is doing and what it knows it is doing against its neighbors." This attitude was a corollary of the State Department thesis, adopted publicly in February 1965, that North Vietnam was and had always been the cause of the trouble in South Vietnam. Instead of negotiating, Mr. Rusk merely advised North Vietnam to stop "what it is doing." It was this approach which had doomed Secretary General Thant's efforts at the end of 1964 and the beginning of 1965.

On April 7, only five days after Secretary Rusk's brush-off of possible negotiations, President Johnson abruptly inserted in his speech at Johns Hopkins University, a passage which put him on record in favor of

Moral Argument and the War in Vietnam

"unconditional discussions."[5] The same words were used in the US reply the following day to an appeal from seventeen nations for negotiations without preconditions. It was not clear whether "discussions" were the same as "negotiations," but the important word seemed to be "unconditional."

At this point, a French initiative gave Secretary Rusk an opportunity to reveal just how unconditional this unconditional offer was. In May 1965, Foreign Minister Couve de Murville confidentially told a group of correspondents in Paris that North Vietnam had signified a willingness to talk without conditions, but that he had found Washington unreceptive to the news. At a press conference on August 27, Secretary Rusk was asked about reports that President de Gaulle was waiting for the right moment "to personally negotiate an end to the Vietnam war." The question was raised: "Would we welcome any such efforts by de Gaulle?" After remarking, somewhat acidly, that neither side had "nominated attorneys in this field," as if that were the issue, Mr. Rusk went on to give some insight into what he considered to be "unconditional discussions." He said that he was waiting for a "key signal" to turn up, and that his "antennae" had not yet picked it up. Thus, it appeared, the "unconditional discussions" were dependent on a prior condition that Mr. Rusk's antennae should pick up a "key signal," the nature of which he coyly refused to reveal. At least something new had been added to the language of diplomacy—the conditional unconditional.

From this and other statements and incidents later that year—including Eric Sevareid's disclosure of the late Adlai Stevenson's troubled conscience over the State Department's handling of U Thant's peace efforts—the US negotiating position in 1965 was made unmistakably clear. First, the impression was created early that year that there was nothing, and no one with whom, to negotiate. Second, the other side was outbid with what seemed like a most magnanimous commitment to engage in "unconditional discussions." Third, the unconditional was gradually conditioned to mean that the United States had to be previously convinced of the other side's intention to be "serious" and "meaningful." Fourth, this in turn depended on Secretary Rusk's "antennae" receiving a "key signal" in advance. Fifth, the "key signal" was nothing less than the other side's precedent undertaking "to stop trying to impose their will by force on South Vietnam," that is, to agree to unilateral renunciation of the armed struggle. No doubt mere words would not have carried conviction with Mr. Rusk and the enemy would have had to satisfy some test of deeds to get the "key signal" through to his antennae.

As long as this was the United States negotiating position, all efforts to arrange for negotiations were bound to fail because the missing "crucial element" and "key signal" were designed to give the United States what it wanted in advance as the price of so-called negotiations. Whether a different policy might have led to meaningful negotiations in 1965 is another question. But at least the United States would not have stood in the way. And, as a fringe benefit, we would at least have been spared some peculiarly irritating double talk.

III

In 1966, the key issue increasingly became the cessation of American bombing of North Vietnam. The more destructive the bombing, the more determined the North Vietnamese were to stop it before entering into anything resembling negotiations.

But the United States again demanded a price, this time for stopping the bombing, and henceforth the American negotiating position hinged on the concept of "reciprocity." Throughout 1966, American spokesmen tried to define this accordion-like term. Secretary Rusk tended to stretch it the most. He usually demanded that the "other side" had to give up its "aggression" or "abandon [its] attempt to take South Vietnam over by force" in return for a cessation of the bombing. In the summer of 1966, President Johnson seemed to put forward a more concrete condition. He said that the United States had offered to stop the bombing immediately "if they will stop sending troops into South Vietnam." This seemed to imply that North Vietnam did not have to withdraw troops, but the president went on to observe that the South Vietnamese could not decide the kind of government and country they wanted "while armed troops from North Vietnam are waging war against their people and against their villages," which suggested that he expected far more than a cessation of North Vietnamese reinforcements in exchange for a cessation of the bombing.

The various formulas employed in this period were sufficiently vague to give North Vietnam considerable leeway in making known its decision to satisfy the American demand, but the essence of that demand was never left in doubt—the abandonment by North Vietnam of the struggle for power in the South. If, as the United States claimed, the North was responsible for that struggle, the withdrawal of the North was equivalent to its total abandonment. While much ink and breath were wasted over such questions as which side had to make the first move, whether the North demanded permanent as well as unconditional cessation of the bombing, and how the North could convince the United States of its "serious" intentions, the "key signal" had not changed and was well understood by both sides—Communist abdication in the struggle for power in South Vietnam. The United States was deliberately vague because it was less interested in the form than in the substance, and because it preferred to treat the struggle for political power as if it were merely a foreign military aggression.

Toward the end of 1966, another effort was made to break through the diplomatic impasse. According to the most circumstantial report, United States Ambassador Henry Cabot Lodge met on December 2 and 3 with the Polish representative on the International Control Commission,

Moral Argument and the War in Vietnam

Ambassador Janusz Lewandowski, at the home of the Italian ambassador in Saigon. As reported by Robert H. Estabrook in the *Washington Post*, Lodge asked Lewandowski to set up "contacts" with Hanoi. On or about December 4, Estabrook wrote, Polish Foreign Minister Adam Rapacki sent back word that Hanoi had agreed to unconditional talks on the ambassadorial level in Warsaw, and Washington was asked to send a special representative for this purpose. Before the talks could be held, however, the American bombing offensive was suddenly stepped up. On December 13 and 14, a railway yard only six miles from the heart of Hanoi and a trucking depot only five were heavily attacked—the first time President Johnson had permitted the bombing of targets so close to the city limits of the North Vietnamese capital. For the next two weeks, a debate raged whether these attacks had caused widespread damage to civilian areas.[6] Far more significant perhaps, but still unknown to the general public, was the fact that the bombings had abruptly cut short a seemingly promising peace approach. . . .

The December 1966 incident was handled in a most peculiar way. At a news conference on February 2, 1967, President Johnson gave the impression that the "other side" had shown little or no interest in any steps toward peace. At one point he said that he was not "aware of any serious effort"; at another that there were no "serious indications"; and at still another that they had "not taken any [step] yet." On February 4, the day after the president's interview was published, interested sources enabled Estabrook to divulge the story of the December overtures in the Washington *Post*. That same day, confirmation that something unusual had been going on came from Walt W. Rostow, the president's special assistant. Professor Rostow refused to comment directly on the Washington *Post's* version on the ground that "this is an extremely interesting and delicate phase in what is or might turn out to be a negotiating process." But then he, too, made "serious" the key word in the American attitude to such situations: "Nothing has yet happened that would justify us as saying we have a serious offer to negotiate." One would be justified in interpreting these words to mean that some kind of "pre-negotiating" moves had been going on, and that some sort of "offer," serious or not, had been made.

Finally, on February 7, Prime Minister Harold Wilson told the House of Commons that he knew all about "events in December" relating to what he referred to as "Polish discussions," whose failure he attributed to "a very considerable two-way misunderstanding," the nature of which he did not specify. The Australian Communist journalist Wilfred G. Burchett later disclosed that "first contacts for talks" had been "foiled" by the bombings of December 13-14.[7] If, as Prime Minister Wilson claimed, the breakdown had been caused by a "misunderstanding," the question still remained why, with so much at stake, it could not have been rectified and the "Polish discussions" somehow reinstated.

For a time, indeed, it seemed that such an effort was being made. Until the end of 1966, the main obstacle seemed to be Hanoi's four points, despite the incongruity that three of them were acceptable to the United States and the only objectionable one had to be given the most extreme and arbitrary interpretation to make it acceptable. Early in January 1967, however, the Hanoi leaders apparently made an attempt to remove the four points as the main source of confusion and disagreement. In an interview with Harrison E. Salisbury on January 3, Premier Pham Van Dong referred to them as matters for "discussion" rather than as "conditions" prior to negotiations. At the same time, Secretary General U Thant made known his view, after two weeks of behind-the-scenes probing, that the only thing which stood in the way of peace talks was the question of unconditional cessation of the United States bombing of North Vietnam. The reduction of the problem to this one point seemed to bring both sides closer than ever before to some kind of accommodation. In his press conference on February 2, President Johnson was asked, "Are you prepared at all to tell us what kind of other steps the other side should take for this suspension of bombing?" The President replied, "Just almost any step." Though he had previously stressed the word "serious" rather than "any"—another accordion-like use of terms—the latter received much publicity and seemed to narrow the gap to a merely formal gesture. In any event, a reply soon came from North Vietnamese Foreign Minister Nguyen Duy Trinh. Through Burchett, who had not anticipated such a concession,[8] the North Vietnamese made known that "if the bombings cease completely, good and favorable conditions will be created for the talks." That this was intended by Trinh as a response to the president was shown by the following remark: "President Johnson said he was only awaiting a sign. Well, he's had the sign."[9] . . . .

IV

Most important, a letter from President Johnson to President Ho Chi Minh, dated February 2, was delivered to a North Vietnamese representative in Moscow on February 8. . . .

By that date, it had become perfectly clear that the North Vietnamese negotiating position had been reduced to its irreducible minimum. There was no doubt in President Johnson's mind what it was, because he explicitly stated it in his letter—"direct bilateral talks with representatives of the United States government provided that we ceased 'unconditionally' and permanently our bombing operations against your country and all military actions against it." He noted that this position had been confirmed in the last day by "serious and responsible parties"—one of them, no doubt, Premier Kosygin.

The next point of particular interest in President Johnson's letter is why this proposal could not be accepted. It gave two reasons: a halt

Moral Argument and the War in Vietnam

in the bombing would tell the world that discussions were going on and impair their "privacy and secrecy"; and North Vietnam would use the halt to "improve its military position." The American counterproposal was then put forward to get around these seemingly dire eventualities.

I am prepared to order a cessation of bombing against your country and the stopping of further augmentation of US forces in South Vietnam as soon as I am assured that infiltration into South Vietnam by land and by sea has stopped. These acts of restraint on both sides would, I believe, make it possible for us to conduct serious and private discussions leading toward an early peace.

The question which will be long debated is whether this counterproposal was justified by the two reasons given for making it necessary. If an unconditional cessation of the bombing would have given away the projected discussions and impaired their privacy and secrecy, would not a cessation of the bombing plus demonstrated North Vietnamese cessation of infiltration have resulted in exactly the same thing? Would anyone have been deceived any more by North Vietnamese acceptance of the United States terms than United States acceptance of North Vietnam's terms? The first "difficulty" then, could hardly be taken seriously.

The second objection raised by President Johnson was more troublesome—but only if one side used it exclusively against the other. Both sides were capable of improving their military positions in South Vietnam, if they so desired, with or without bombing of North Vietnam. Moreover, the transport facilities of the United States forces were vastly greater than those of North Vietnam. Indeed, the Têt truce was actually used by both sides to bring in new equipment and troops. United States officials charged that North Vietnam made an unprecedented effort to move arms and supplies into the South.[10] But US Air Force officials in Saigon reported that US cargo planes had carried a one-day record of 2,762 tons of equipment to US troops on February 8, the first day of the truce and the very day President Johnson's letter was handed to Moscow. The total for February 8-10 was 7,042 tons of equipment and more than 17,000 troops delivered by the Air Force alone.[11] One wonders what the United States would have done and how its citizens would have felt if the positions had been reversed and they had read the following report from the official French news agency in Le Monde of February 12-13, 1967:

Saigon, February 11 (A.P.F.,)—While American agencies call attention to a considerable intensification of road, railroad, river and sea traffic in North Vietnam, press correspondents could affirm on Friday [February 10] on the Saigon-Tay Ninh road that the American commissariat also took advantage of the Têt truce to increase troop resupply in combat rations as well as arms.

Long rows of trucks belonging to military transport companies were lined up on the North-West road. They were protected by tanks and helicopters flying at tree level. In the area of Tay Ninh, enormous trucks or towing tractors brought shells for 105 mm. and 155 mm. guns to the American units stationed on the periphery of the Vietcong's Zone C.

Thus, at worst, the United States was quite capable of holding its own in the improvement of the relative military position. It might have made more sense for North Vietnam to worry about what the United States could do to improve its military strength in the South, in the event of negotiations based wholly on a halt of bombing in the North. Only the United States, in fact, was by this time capable of mounting large-scale offensives on the ground in the South. . . .

President Johnson's letter of February 8 did not reach Ho Chi Minh in Hanoi until February 10. . . . February 12 was apparently the day of decision. For on February 13, President Johnson announced the resumption of "full-scale hostilities," including the renewed bombing of North Vietnam. He blamed the decision on the Hanoi government which, he said, had used the truce for "major resupply efforts of their troops in South Vietnam."

Thus, it appears, only three days elapsed between the time Ho Chi Minh received President Johnson's letter in Hanoi and the President's decision to resume the fighting and bombing. Ho Chi Minh's reply to the letter had nothing to do with the decision because it was not sent until two days later, February 15. Indeed, Ho Chi Minh's reply may have been influenced by the president's decision, not vice versa. . . .

V

Suddenly, after all the meetings and letters and go-betweens, the war broke loose again, and more destructively than ever before.

The resumption of hostilities was on not only a full but also a new scale. On February 22, United States artillery for the first time fired across the demilitarized zone into North Vietnamese territory. On February 26, United States warships for the first time shelled supply routes in North Vietnam on a continuing basis without restrictions. On February 27, United States planes for the first time began to mine North Vietnam's rivers. On March 10, United States bombers for the first time attacked a major industrial plant in North Vietnam, the iron and steel combine at Thainguyen, 38 miles north of Hanoi. The military decisions for this raid were made in mid-February, but unfavorable weather conditions and technical preparations had delayed the operation itself for about three weeks. Subsequent attacks on this and other industrial installations made clear that the now US bombing policy was intended to destroy the economic foundation or "infrastructure" of North Vietnam's military capability.

185

Moral Argument and the War in Vietnam

The thinking behind this "escalation"—a forbidden word for a familiar fact—began to emerge in statements that were probably less guarded because they were made before the Johnson-Ho Chi Minh correspondence came out publicly. On February 27, President Johnson described, with uncharacteristic understatement, the three new military actions of the preceding five days as a "step up" and "more far-reaching." He restated the logic of every turning point in these terms: "Our principal objective is to provide the maximum deterrent to people who believe aggression pays with a minimum cost to us and to them." As always, the "maximum deterrent" and "minimum cost" had been forced up to higher and higher levels. . . .

VI

Meanwhile, however, the United States uncompromising rejection of prior cessation of the bombing of North Vietnam unexpectedly paid off in an unexpected quarter. On March 14, 1967, Secretary-General U Thant submitted a new three-point plan which clearly reflected concessions to the American position. For more than two years, he had steadfastly maintained that only unconditional cessation of the bombing could lead the way to a settlement; now he was merely content to mention it in passing as a "vital need," but to leave it out entirely as a practical consideration. His old Point One—cessation of the bombing of North Vietnam—was replaced by a new Point One: "a general stand-still truce" without supervision. Old Point Two—substantial reduction of all military activities in South Vietnam—was replaced by new Point Two: "preliminary talks" between the United States and North Vietnam. Old Point Three—participation of the National Liberation Front or Viet Cong in any peaceful settlement—was replaced by new Point Three: "reconvening of the Geneva Conference." A favorable reply was received from the United States on March 18, though it deviated from the Secretary-General's proposal in two ways which might have, in any case, proved troublesome. . . .A North Vietnamese spokesman unequivocally rejected the new plan on March 27. . . .

In any event, Thant's new plan was doomed because it was based on seemingly formal equality between unequal forces, resulting in unequal consequences. Without a prior cessation of the bombing, North Vietnam was still placed in the position of agreeing to terms with a gun at the temple. The relatively compact, traditionally organized American military forces could easily be regrouped and supplied during a cease-fire; their morale was likely to rise in the absence of combat. The Viet Cong guerrillas were by their very nature difficult to coordinate especially if North Vietnam did not control them as much as the United States wanted to believe; their morale was bound to fall in the absence of combat. The North's regular troops in the South ran the risk of becoming hostages, cut off hundreds of miles from their home bases, scattered in jungles or forests. The only conceivable *modus vivendi* for an effective cease-fire in the peculiar South Vietnamese circumstances would have required a physical separation of the two sides, amounting to *de facto* division of South Vietnam into regrouping zones—a form of provisional partition which the United States had many times ruled out. The very nature of guerrilla warfare made an old fashioned cease-fire, based on some fixed line, incongruous. The Viet Cong guerrillas and even the North Vietnamese regulars cooperating closely with the guerrillas could not be made to "stand still," suddenly and indefinitely, without risking their disintegration as a fighting force, a danger not faced by the US troops. Since Thant's new plan was introduced at a very late date, after the diplomatic breakdown of the preceding two months and the exacerbation of the bombing against key North Vietnamese economic centers, already largely or partially destroyed, the time was not propitious for another effort which on its face posed almost insuperable practical problems and represented a sharp political shift in favor of the United States position. In the end, this initiative did no good and merely compromised the Secretary-General. . . .

At the core of the American case, making meaningful negotiations difficult, if not impossible, was the concept of "reciprocity." It became the leitmotif of official American policy in 1966-67, though it was another word that lent itself to different interpretations. When President Johnson asked almost plaintively on March 9, 1967 for "just almost any reciprocal action on their part," it seemed to mean any kind of North Vietnamese response, even of a purely symbolic character. Yet when he went on, almost in the same breath, to demand that North Vietnam should stop its "aggression and infiltration," he implied that he expected something that he considered to be a more or less equivalent or analogous response. On March 15, he made reciprocity "the fundamental principle of any reduction in hostilities," and again seemed to be using the concept in the second, more inclusive and far-reaching sense. When his February 8 letter to Ho Chi Minh was made public on March 21, the latter interpretation could no longer be questioned. The letter concretely defined reciprocity as: the United States to halt the bombing of North Vietnam and stop further augmentation of its forces in South Vietnam; and North Vietnam to provide assurance that its infiltration forces in South Vietnam by land and sea had ceased. Clearly, when President Johnson called on February 2 for "just almost any [step]," and on March 9 for "just almost any reciprocal action," he had not intended these words to be taken literally.

But—and this was the critical question—what could "reciprocity" mean between a strong, rich power like the United States and a weak, poor power like North Vietnam?

In February 1967, for example, the United States and allied foreign forces in South Vietnam numbered: United States, more than 400,000;

Moral Argument and the War in Vietnam

South Korea, 45,000; Australia, 4,500; New Zealand, 360—a total of more than 450,000. The North Vietnamese forces in the South were estimated at about 50,000. President Johnson's proposal of February 8 amounted, in effect, to freezing the forces on both sides in the South in return for a cessation of United States bombing in the North but not in the South. By stopping all movement to the South, which was undoubtedly what would have been required, North Vietnam could not even have maintained the forces which it already had in the South because it could not provision them by plane and ship, as the United States was able to do. Just as the United States felt that it could not accept any offer which might discourage or demoralize its South Vietnamese wards, so the North Vietnamese leaders doubtless felt the same way about their own troops and protégés in the South.

President Johnson, it should be noted, did not offer a military truce or cease-fire in the South in exchange for halting the bombing of the North. In the event of a total cessation of the fighting in both North and South, the freezing of the numbers in the South would not have mattered so much. But if the war in the South went on unabated, with the North Vietnamese troops cut off from their sources at home and the United States committed only to a limitation of men but not materiel, the latter factor would have become increasingly decisive in the further conduct of the war. On the American side particularly, firepower rather than manpower counts. Thus, morally, numerically, and materially, the proposal of February 8 was palpably unequal because the sides were so unequal.

The United States was, in effect, doing what General James M. Gavin (Ret.) warned against in his testimony before the Senate Foreign Relations Committee on February 21—using the bombing of the North as a bargaining instrument. The bombing had been initiated in February 1965, primarily to bolster the South Vietnamese government's faltering morale. At that time, according to Secretary of Defense McNamara, North Vietnam's regular troops in the South had numbered only about 400, and the bombing could not have been justified on the ground that it was necessary to interdict their lines of communication with the North.[12] First came the bombing, and then came an escalation of the war on both sides, which provided the major justification for the bombing. In February 1965, the bombing of the North represented a desperate United States effort to save the South Vietnamese forces from defeat; in February 1967, it represented an offensive effort to bring about North Vietnam's defeat. After two years of bombing which had unilaterally changed the pre-1965 rules of war, the North Vietnamese and United States conceptions of "reciprocity" were understandably different. North Vietnam could not stop bombing the United States in exchange for a similar courtesy on the part of the United States in North Vietnam. The price the United States demanded was in South Vietnam, where the advantages and disadvantages on both sides were so different that the concept of "reciprocity" was far from the simple numerical arrangement that President Johnson proposed on February 8.

A cessation of the bombing of North Vietnam was vital to the latter precisely because it had nothing to exchange for it in the North or in the United States and could pay for it only by reciprocating unequally in the South. The bombing was so important to the bargaining position of the US that President Johnson had, perhaps, excessively, referred to it on March 9 as if it were the United State's entire "half the war," or as if its half depended on it. For the United States, the bombing was an infinitely extensible threat. In January 1967, Secretary McNamara told a Senate committee: "I don't believe that bombing up to the present has significantly reduced, nor any bombing that I could contemplate in the future would significantly reduce, the actual flow of men and materiel to the south." When this was established, the United States stepped up its bombing the following month to reduce North Vietnam's industrial base to a mass of rubble. At best North Vietnam could retaliate only against South Vietnam, which it considered part of its own country, not against the United States, which it considered its main enemy. Germany's indiscriminate bombing of Britain in late 1940 was answered with equally indiscriminate and even more punishing bombing of Germany later in the war. But the positions of the United States and North Vietnam were so different that nothing comparable could take place.

VII

. . . In a peculiar way, the United States seems to be faced with a variety of frustrations in South Vietnam at the same time that it is able to do almost as it pleases to North Vietnam. So long as the American leaders consider the bombing to be one of their few assets and bargaining levers, they are bound to try to extort as high a price as possible for it in the guise of "reciprocity." Senator Jackson was quite right to suggest that the bombing of North Vietnam is the United States trump card—and that is why the game has become so dangerous. The bombing is the one thing that can be most easily and destructively intensified and enlarged to increase the pressure on North Vietnam and enhance the embarrassment of its allies. The power at the disposal of the United States is so great and so unprecedented that the only questions are how much power it is willing to use and how much punishment North Vietnam is willing to take. Inescapably, the more punishment North Vietnam is willing to take, the more power the United States is willing to use. The more power the United States uses, the less difference it makes how much more power it will use, for beyond a certain point, degrees of destructiveness begin to lose their meaning.

This is the vicious circle which was set in motion by transferring the main arena of the war from South to North Vietnam and by deciding to use bombing to impose the will of the United States on North Vietnam.

Moral Argument and the War in Vietnam

The only way to break the circle is to halt the bombing and reconsider the problem of South Vietnam on the basis of genuine reciprocity—among the Vietnamese. Once the United States threw its weight into the balance, there could be no meaningful reciprocity, unless a great Communist power reciprocated on behalf of North Vietnam. Instead of bringing peace nearer, this concept is more likely to bring about a Vietnamese edition of the 1962 missiles crisis in circumstances far less favorable to the United States. In 1962, the United States could claim to be directly threatened by offensive missiles only 90 miles from its shores; in 1967, the United States is not directly threatened, and cannot appeal to world opinion on that ground; and it is inviting two or more to play at its own game. The escalation of the war *in* Vietnam is bound to bring about an escalation of the war *over* Vietnam. Those who wish to taunt or goad the Soviets, if not the Chinese, to put up or shut up are living in a fantasy world if they think that the Cuban precedent will necessarily be followed in Vietnam. On the contrary, there has been and continues to be a stubborn underestimation of how far the Communists can go to escalate their side of the war. And if the war *over* Vietnam in some form materializes, will it be another instance of the "politics of inadvertence"?

When one gets away from each individual move and maneuver, and views them as a whole over the past two years, the guidelines of American policy emerge quite clearly—to separate North Vietnam from the Soviet Union, and to separate North Vietnam from the Viet Cong in the South. Even if the United States were successful in either or both of these objectives, the war in the South would admittedly still go on, though certainly not on the vast scale as at present. But neither of these objectives has been achieved; on the contrary, North Vietnam is likely to get more Soviet aid, and the North is likely to gird itself for an even more determined effort in the South, escalating whatever it can escalate. Ironically, the United States itself made it more difficult for North Vietnam to abandon the South by attributing such preponderance to the Northern role in the South. The American propaganda line first maintained that the war in the South could not go on without the North's "aggression," and then insisted that the North should get out of the South. This line was conceived to justify US bombing of the North, but it does not help to facilitate the North's withdrawal from the South. The main thing that has been achieved by the recent diplomatic maneuvers is what Washington considers to be a more favorable public-relations ambience for making the war bigger, bloodier, and beastlier. This is the transcendent triumph of Johnsonian diplomacy which the American press has recently been celebrating. Recent events have demonstrated that outsiders are not capable of ending the war in South Vietnam. Their own interests and need to save face have infinitely complicated the indigenous difficulties. The best chances for peace probably lie with the Vietnamese themselves. The more patriotic or nationalistic among them, on both sides, will not forever tolerate this orgy of destruction which was started to save them and which will end by leaving little or nothing to save. The decisive impulse for peace, in some way not yet perceptible, may have to come from the Vietnamese themselves.

Notes

1 The full text of the four points first appeared in *The New York Times*, April 14, 1965, and this version may be found in *The Viet-Nam Reader*, edited by Marcus Raskin and Bernard B. Fall, pp. 42-43. The problem of correctly interpreting or even translating the third point is discussed in George McTurnan Kahin and John W Lewis, *The United States in Vietnam* (Dial, 1967, p. 210). They report that the Chinese version would have made the third point completely innocuous. A literal English translation of the text used by the *Jenmin Jih-pao* (People's Daily), the official Peking organ, of April 14, 1965, reads: "According to the program of the Southern National Liberation Front, the affairs of the South must be settled by the Southern people themselves without foreign interference." Of such stuff are diplomatic imbroglios sometimes made, when there is no will to get together

2 *The Vietnam Hearings* (Vintage Books, 1966), pp. 246-247.

3 The December 20, 1960, "action program" of the NLF called for a "broad, national, and democratic coalition government composed of representatives of every sector of the population, various nationalities, political parties, religious communities, and patriotic personalities." It wanted to "abolish the present constitution of the Ngo Dinh Diem dictatorial government and with universal suffrage elect a new National Assembly. Freedom of expression, press, assembly, association, travel, religion, and other democratic liberties will be promulgated. Religious, political, and patriotic organizations will be permitted freedom of activity regardless of beliefs and tendencies," etc. The entire document may be found in Douglas Pike, *The Viet Cong*, pp. 344-47, who devotes an entire chapter to tracing the various changes in the NLF's programmatic efforts (pp. 344-71). There is a somewhat different but similar translation in Bernard Fall, *The Two Viet-Nams*, pp. 449-53. It may be argued that the NLF program was democratic window-dressing to lure the greatest number of anti-Diem opponents; it cannot be argued that it was an outright bid for sole Communist control. Secretary Rusk refers to the NLF program as announced from Hanoi on January 29, 1961, instead of using the more usual date, December 20, 1960, when it was first issued.

4 Ho Chi Minh, Letter to World Communist leaders, dated Hanoi, January 24, 1966.

5 The circumstances tend to support the assertion of Rowland Evans and Robert Novak that the reference to "unconditional discussions" was "a last-minute concession to the Peace Bloc that amazed those who had seen the earlier version of the speech" (*Lyndon B. Johnson: The Exercise of Power*, New American Library, 1966, p. 544).

6 It took almost two weeks for American officials to admit officially that the bombings had caused civilian casualties as well as widespread damage to civilian areas, and then only after *The New York Times* of December 27, 1966, had published Harrison Salisbury's eyewitness report of such damage. At this time, American officials still stressed that the bombs were aimed at "military targets" only but that civilian casualties were accidental, unavoidable, and, above all, not "deliberate." On December 30, 1966, the military correspondent of *The New York Times*, Hanson W. Baldwin, disclosed that "United States ordnance is being expended in North and South Vietnam at an annual rate of about 500,000 tons, somewhat more than the Army Air Forces expended against Japan in the Pacific during World War II." At this rate, which soon rose sharply, the problem arises whether the inevitability of the consequences are not more important than the deliberateness of the motivation. One who fires a machine gun into a crowd in order to kill a single person can hardly protest that he did not mean to injure anyone else "deliberately"—especially if he misses his intended victim, as sometimes happens in the bombing of military targets. The indirect but unavoidable by-products of a course of action cannot be exempted morally. The same problem is raised by Viet Cong terrorists, but the moral equation here is, to my mind, complicated by two questions: (1) whether the terror and counterterror of Vietnamese against Vietnamese should

Moral Argument and the War in Vietnam

be put on the same level as the violence and counterviolence of a foreign power against Vietnamese, and (2) whether the scale of destructiveness of a few mortar shells balances that of a sustained downpour of 1000-pound bombs. The *scale* of destructiveness cannot, in my view, be disregarded in this consideration of "moral double bookkeeping." If the Nazis had exterminated 600 or even 6000 Jews, it would have been an unmitigated moral crime but it would not have been a moral enormity on the scale of 6,000,000. Hiroshima has shaken the conscience of the world not because a bomb was used but a bomb of unprecedented destructiveness. If there is no moral distinction between a terrorist and an atomic or nuclear bomb, we have already prepared the ground, psychologically and morally, for using weapons of unimaginable destructiveness.

7 *Washington Post*, February 8.

8 In a letter dated October 29, 1966, Burchett had expressed extreme pessimism with respect to a possible basis for negotiations. Previously, he said, the North Vietnamese leaders had not demanded prior withdrawal of any American forces as a condition of negotiations, but the continued build-up had convinced them that some "concrete acts" of withdrawal would be necessary (*War/Peace Report*, November 1966, p. 5).

9 Washington *Post*, February 8. Curiously, the otherwise similar version of Burchett's article published in *The New York Times*, February 8, 1967, does not contain the second sentence. Trinh had first broached this line to Burchett in an interview on January 28, 1967.

10 This may have been one of the greatest hoaxes of the war, and one of the greatest derelictions of the American press. With the exception of *I. F. Stone's Weekly*, I have seen no serious questioning of the propaganda handed out by the Department of Defense to justify the resumption of the bombing. As reported in *U.S. News & World Report* of March 27, 1967, a lavish briefing at the Pentagon on March 17, 1967, was said to demonstrate: "While US bombers were grounded from February 8 through February 11, the Communists made hay in the North, moving a staggering volume of arms, equipment, food and supplies toward infiltration routes into South Vietnam for use against American and Allied forces." The tonnage moved from North to South was first given as 35,000 tons and then reduced to 23,000 tons, all based on "photographic and visual sightings" from the air. As I. F. Stone pointed out (March 27, 1967), the reporting was incredibly sloppy: the Pentagon spokesman did not go farther than to claim a knowledge of "Resupply Activities Within North Vietnam," and there was no evidence that any of the trucks sighted had moved out of the North; there was no way of identifying whether the trucks carried military supplies or not; and it was even admitted that some of the supplies were nonmilitary and "not all bound for South Vietnam." Since the scare stories about the North Vietnamese "resupply efforts" were crucial to the resumption of the bombing, which was crucial to all the subsequent events, a thorough examination of this dubious justification for breaking the truce is by now long overdue.

11 *The New York Times*, February 6, 1967; *Newsweek*, February 13, 1967; *The New York Times*, March 13, 1967; *Time*, March 17, 1967.

12 On April 16, 1965, Secretary McNamara stated that "evidence accumulated within the last month," that is, since late March, had confirmed the presence in the northwest sector of South Vietnam "of the 2nd Battalion of the 325th Division of the regular North Vietnamese Army," and he estimated the size of the battalion "on the order of 400 to 500 men" (*Department of State Bulletin*, May 17, 1965, pp. 750 and 753). On June 16, 1966, in an address at Yeshiva University, Senator Mike Mansfield declared: "When the sharp increase in the American military effort began in early 1965, it was estimated that only about 400 North Vietnamese soldiers were among the enemy force in the South which totaled 140,000 at that time." The Pentagon soon confirmed that it was the source of Senator Mansfield's figure (Ted Knap, Washington *Daily News*, June 28, 1966). The strange and persistent efforts by Secretary of State Rusk to blow up the North Vietnamese "invasion" to at least the proportion of an entire division by January 1965 in the face of both Secretary McNamara's and Senator Mansfield's testimony are dealt with at length in my forthcoming book, *Abuse of Power*.

The Bases Of Accommodation*

By Samuel P. Huntington

A viable political settlement in South Vietnam will reflect and give some legitimacy to the balance of political, military and social forces produced by a decade of internal conflict and five years of large-scale warfare. A successful settlement can also inaugurate a process of political accommodation through which the various elements of Vietnamese society may eventually be brought together into a functioning polity. American objectives and American expectations of what can be achieved at the conference table and on the battlefield should, correspondingly, be based on the realities of power and the opportunities for accommodation.

Much of the discussion of Viet Nam in the United States, however, has been couched in terms of stereotypes and slogans which have little relation to the political forces and social trends in Vietnamese society. Critics of the administration often tend to glorify the Viet Cong and the National Liberation Front and to magnify the extent of their support.

Spokesmen for the administration, on the other hand, have in the past underrated the strength of the Viet Cong and have ascribed to the Saigon government a popularity which had as little basis in fact as that which the critics attributed to the NLF. . . .

The realities of the situation in Viet Nam will not please the extremists on either side. If properly perceived and accepted, however, they may provide some basis for accommodation and an eventual compromise settlement. The military strengths and weaknesses of each side are manifest in each day's news reports, and will no doubt shape the outcome of the negotiations. The success of that outcome, however, may well depend on the extent to which it reflects the political and social strengths and weaknesses of both sides. These are less obvious but more fundamental, than the military factors.

II

The overall proportion of the population that is more under government than Viet Cong control has risen rather strikingly in three years from a little over 40 porcent of the total to 60 percent or more. This change, however, has been largely, if not exclusively, the result of the

*Excerpted by permission from *Foreign Affairs*, Volume 46, no. 4 (July, 1968), pp. 642-656. Copyright Council on Foreign Relations, Inc., New York, 1968.

193

Moral Argument and the War in Vietnam

movement of the population into the cities rather than the extension of the government's control into the countryside. The two most important facts which an accommodation will have to reflect are, first, the continuing role of the Viet Cong in the countryside and, second, the declining role of the countryside in South Viet Nam as a whole. . . .

Discussion of Viet Nam often revolves about the question: "Whom do the majority of the people really support?" This is a reasonable and practical question to ask in a stable Western constitutional democracy. For Viet Nam, however, it is unanswerable and, in large part, irrelevant simply because it is quite clear that no government or political grouping has been able to win widespread popular support—or seems likely to do so. The most one can realistically speak of is the relative ability of the government and the VC-NLF to exercise authority and to control population. And even here, as the allied sweeps through hard-core Viet Cong areas and the Tet offensive amply demonstrate, each side's authority is nowhere beyond at least temporary challenge by the other side. In addition, an underground Viet Cong organization presumably exists in many areas where government authority is normally exercised.

The crucial characteristic of the heavily contested rural areas is the absence of effective social and political organizations above the village level, if even there. The strength of the Viet Cong is its ability to fill this vacuum of authority; the weakness of the government has been the failure of its pacification programs to generate self-sustaining local organizations.

It is often said that the war in Viet Nam is a "political" war, and that consequently winning the war requires the government to appeal to "the hearts and minds of the people" by promoting rural development, land reform, education, official honesty and other specific and usually material benefits. In fact, however, there is little evidence to suggest that the appeal of the Viet Cong derives from material poverty or that it can be countered by material benefits. The one systematic study of this question, focusing on land tenure, indeed came to precisely the opposite conclusion. Government control was found to be greatest in those provinces in which "few peasants farm their own land, the distribution of landholdings is unequal, no land redistribution has taken place, large French landholdings existed in the past, population density is high, and the terrain is such that accessibility is poor."[1] This seemingly perverse product of statistical analysis is bolstered by other substantial if less systematic evidence for Viet Nam as well as by much experience elsewhere. The appeal of revolutionaries depends not on economic deprivation but on political deprivation, that is, on the absence of an effective structure of authority. Where the latter exists, even though it be quite hierarchical and undemocratic, the Viet Cong make little progress. . . .

The acid test of pacification is whether a locality develops the will and the means to defend itself against Viet Cong attack or infiltration.

With a few exceptions, mostly among the communal groups, the current pacification effort has not as yet met this test. In some cases, the intrusion of national governmental authority from the outside may undermine the authority of the local village leaders; when the agents of the national government move on, they may leave the situation worse than it was before they arrived. In those instances, the government prepares the way for the Viet Cong.

It thus seems unlikely that the current pacification program will significantly change the pattern of political control—or lack of control—in the contested areas in the immediate future. If a cease-fire led to reductions in either the government's military-administrative presence or U.S. forces in these areas, the way would be opened for the Viet Cong to move in and extend its control through political means. The only practical alternative, available in some instances, would be for the authority vacuum to be filled by some other social-political group with roots in the locality.

The security of that one-third of the rural population which is under a relatively high degree of government control is in large part the product of communal—ethnic or religious—organizations. It is commonly assumed that rural security is the product of identification with and loyalty to the government, which, in turn, is the product of the extension of governmental presence into the villages. In much of South Viet Nam, however, the sequence has not been: governmental control, national loyalty, internal security. It has been, instead: communal organization, internal security, governmental control. The exercise of governmental authority has resulted from internal security produced by other factors. Governmental authority is, in fact, most effectively exercised in those rural areas where the government has come to terms with the local power structure and with ethnic or religious groups. . . .

The ethnic and religious communities have thus played a crucial role in extending government control into rural areas. They have done this despite the suspicion and hostility of at least some elements in the government. After a cease-fire, these are the principal groups which will be able to compete with the Viet Cong in the political organization of the peasantry.

The remaining third of the rural population lives in "hardcore" Viet Cong areas, some of which have been almost continuously under Viet Minh and Viet Cong control since the 1940s. . . .

To eliminate Viet Cong control in these areas would be an expensive, time-consuming and frustrating task. It would require a much larger and more intense military and pacification effort than is currently contemplated by Saigon and Washington. Consequently, effective Viet Cong control of these areas is a political fact which does not seem likely to change for some while, if indeed it ever does. In a politically reintegrated South Viet Nam, there would probably be a fairly steady population drain from them into more prosperous rural and urban localities.

Moral Argument and the War in Vietnam

The achievement of such political reintegration clearly will depend, however, upon the recognition and acceptance of Viet Cong control of local government in these areas. It is here that accommodation in the most specific sense of the word is a political necessity.

The most striking feature of these varied patterns of rural political control—contested, communal and Viet Cong—has been their resistance to change. The French, Diem, the post-Diem régimes, the Viet Minh and Viet Cong have all tried, without significant success, to produce permanent changes in them. The huge current pacification program has been another effort to bring about a *political* revolution, in the relations between the government and the countryside. It may succeed where the others have failed, but as yet there is no conclusive evidence of this. On the other hand, the massive American effort is producing a *social* revolution in the Vietnamese way of life which will be of far greater consequence to the future of the country.

III

The most dramatic and far-reaching impact of the war in South Viet Nam has been the tremendous shift in population from the countryside to the cities. In the early 1960s it was still accurate to speak of South Viet Nam as 80 to 85 percent rural. Today, no one knows for certain the size of the urban population, but it is undoubtedly more than double and perhaps triple what it was a few years ago. A reasonable current estimate of people in cities of 20,000 or more would be about 40 percent of the total, or 6,800,000 of a total of 17,200,000. By this standard South Viet Nam is now more urban than Sweden, Canada, the Soviet Union, Poland, Austria, Switzerland and Italy (according to early 1960s data). Apart from Singapore, it is easily the most urban country in Southeast Asia. The image of South Viet Nam as a country composed largely of landlords and peasants—an image still prevalent among many Vietnamese intellectuals who continue to quote the 85 percent rural figure—has little relationship to reality. . . .

The principal reason for this massive influx of population into the urban area is, of course, the intensification of the war following the commitment of American combat troops in 1965. About 1,500,000 of the total increase in urban population is accounted for by refugees, half still in refugee camps and others settled in new areas. At least an equal number of people have moved into the cities without passing through refugee camps. The social costs of this change have been dramatic and often heart-rending. The conditions in the refugee camps, particularly in I Corps, have at times been horrendous, although some significant improvements are now taking place. Urban welfare and developmental programs require increasing priority from the United States and Vietnamese governments.

The immediate economic effects of urbanization are somewhat more mixed. Those who were well-off in the countryside often suffer serious losses in the move to the city. The rural poor, on the other hand, may well find life in the city more attractive and comfortable than their previous existence in the countryside. The urban slum, which seems so horrible to middle-class Americans, often becomes for the poor peasant a gateway to a new and better way of life. For some poor migrants, the wartime urban boom has made possible incomes five times those which they had in the countryside. In one Saigon slum, Xom Chua, in early 1965 before the American build-up, the people lived at a depressed level, with 33 percent of the adult males unemployed. Eighteen months later, as a result of the military escalation, the total population of the slum had increased by 30 percent, but the unemployment rate had dropped to 5 percent and average incomes had doubled.[2] In several cases urban refugees from the war refused to return to their villages once security was restored because of the higher level of economic well-being which they could attain in the city. The pull of urban prosperity has been a secondary but not insignificant factor in attracting people into the city.

In the long run urbanization will create major political problems. Typically, the second generation—the children of the slums, not the migrants to the slums—provides participants for urban riots and insurrections. After the war, massive government programs will be required either to resettle migrants in rural areas or to rebuild the cities and promote peacetime urban employment. In the meantime, while the war continues, urbanization is significantly altering the balance of power between the Saigon government and the Viet Cong.

More than anything else urbanization has been responsible for the striking increase in the proportion of the population living under government control between 1964 and 1968. The depopulation of the countryside struck directly at the strength and potential appeal of the Viet Cong. For ten years the Viet Cong had waged a rural revolution against the central government, with the good Maoist expectation that by winning the support of the rural population it could eventually isolate and overwhelm the cities. The "first outstanding feature . . . of People's Revolutionary War, as developed by Mao Tse-tung and refined by the North Vietnamese in the two Indochina wars," Sir Robert Thompson argued in a recent issue of this journal, "is its immunity to the direct application of mechanical and conventional power."[3] In the light of recent events, this statement needs to be seriously qualified. For if the "direct application of mechanical and conventional power" takes place on such a massive scale as to produce a massive migration from countryside to city, the basic assumptions underlying the Maoist doctrine of revolutionary war no longer operate. The Maoist-inspired rural revolution is undercut by the American-sponsored urban revolution. . . .

In the past the Viet Cong could expect to win the war simply by preventing Saigon from extending its control in the rural areas. This

Moral Argument and the War in Vietnam

the Viet Cong can still do but it is no longer sufficient to achieve victory. Increasingly the Viet Cong must also demonstrate their ability to win support and to exercise authority in the cities. So far, they have been even less successful in these efforts than the government has been in winning support in the countryside. In this sense, history—drastically and brutally speeded up by the American impact—may pass the Viet Cong by. Societies are susceptible to revolution only at particular stages in their development. At the moment the rates of urbanization and of modernization in the secure rural areas exceed the rate of increase in Viet Cong strength. At a time when the South Vietnamese Army is beginning to show signs of being able to operate on its own, the Viet Cong are becoming increasingly dependent on North Viet Nam for manpower as well as supplies. A movement which once had the potential for developing into a truly comprehensive revolutionary force with an appeal to both rural and urban groups could now degenerate into the protest of a declining rural minority increasingly dependent upon outside support.

In an absent-minded way the United States in Viet Nam may well have stumbled upon the answer to "wars of national liberation." The effective response lies neither in the quest for conventional military victory nor in the esoteric doctrines and gimmicks of counterinsurgency warfare. It is instead forced-draft urbanization and modernization which rapidly brings the country in question out of the phase in which a rural revolutionary movement can hope to generate sufficient strength to come to power.

Time in South Viet Nam is increasingly on the side of the government. But in the short run, with half the population still in the countryside, the Viet Cong will remain a powerful force which cannot be dislodged from its constituency so long as the constituency continues to exist. Peace in the immediate future must hence be based on accommodation.

IV

During the past three years the pattern of the military conflict has been largely determined in Hanoi and Washington, which are also playing the dominant role in negotiations. The stability of the political settlement which eventually results in South Viet Nam, however, will depend primarily upon the extent to which it reflects the social and political forces within that country rather than on external influences, either military or diplomatic. Hence, there is good reason to encourage the early inauguration of a political process within South Viet Nam in which all significant political groups can participate and to allow that process rather than a diplomatic conference to have the lion's share in determining the future of the country.

It is often argued that this process should begin with the creation

198

of a coalition government. There are, however, many disadvantages to such an approach. . . .

The rural-urban division of the country and the mixed pattern of political control in rural areas suggests that the process of political accommodation should start at the bottom and work up rather than the reverse. Some forms of local accommodation have, of course, existed for some time in parts of the country, particularly in the Delta. Most frequently they have involved "live-and-let-live" arrangements among local military commanders. To some extent they have also involved mutual tolerance of each other's revenue-raising activities. On the government side, the weakness of its forces and the natural desire to remain in the towns and avoid the efforts and dangers of combat have provided incentives to accept these arrangements, while for the Viet Cong it has been a general war-weariness among local cadres, especially in the Delta. To expand these local accommodations substantively and geographically will entail many difficulties. None the less, this is the way to start a political process which will reflect the actual balance of forces within the society

If accommodation worked in a majority of provinces, the way would be opened for its extension to the national government. The next step would be the election of a new constituent assembly, perhaps in part by universal suffrage and in part by the provincial councils, to devise new basic laws and choose a new central government. If as a result of this process the VC-NLF secured control of the central government, the United States would obviously regret the outcome but could also accept it and feel under little compulsion to reintervene.

In the interests of promoting widespread access to the government and accommodation among groups, it would be wise for the constituent assembly to shift some authority from the central government to provincial and local governments. Centralization of authority in the national government simply complicates the problem of accommodating Viet Cong and non-Communist forces. If all power resides in the central government, the struggle for control is all the more intense; coöperation becomes nearly impossible. Political integration from the bottom up will facilitate the loosening up of the political structure, and the loosening of the political structure will at the same time promote political accommodation, particularly at the national level. . . .

In the recent past, the French, Bao Dai, Diem, each in different ways, attempted to perpetuate centralized authority, and in every case they weakened it. To strengthen political authority, it is instead necessary to decentralize it, to extend the scope of the political system and to incorporate more effectively into it the large number of groups which have become politically organized and politically conscious in recent years. Such a system might be labeled federal, confederal, pluralistic, decentralized—but, whatever the label, it would reflect the varied sources of political power. In the recognition of and acceptance of that diversity lies the hope for political stability in Viet Nam.

Moral Argument and the War in Vietnam

Notes

1 Edward J. Mitchell, "Inequality and Insurgency: A Statistical Study of South Vietnam," *World Politics*, April 1968, p. 438.

2 Marilyn W. Hoskins and Eleanor M. Shepherd, "Life in a Vietnamese Urban Quarter," Carbondale, Ill.; The Graduate School, Southern Illinois University, 1965, (updated in 1966 as a U.S. AID memorandum).

They Call It A 'Third Solution'*

by Alfred Hassler

Is there a Third Force in Vietnam?. . . .

There is obviously a "first force": the Saigon government. . . .Politically the Thieu-Ky government is constructed on a very narrow base. Rumors throughout the spring and summer of 1969 that it was to be broadened in order to seek a more moderate policy were effectively squashed in August with the forced resignation of Premier Tran Van Huong. Huong, a respected civilian who had come in third in the 1967 presidential race, had accomplished relatively little during his tenure as Premier, but he *had* ordered the release of some six thousand political prisoners during Thieu's absence from the country and had tried to reduce some of the pervasive corruption in the government.[1] He was replaced by Khiem, top-ranking army general, already Deputy Premier and head of the National Police. Khiem was also President Thieu's closest personal friend and devoted to an equally hard line on the war.

A new cabinet, announced immediately after Khiem's elevation, consisted of four generals, two lesser military officers, and a miscellaneous collection of civil servants and technicians who were political unknowns. Even a constricted new "party" created by Thieu a few months earlier in a transparent attempt to create the appearance of a political opposition was not represented, let alone the genuine opposition centered in the Buddhists of the An Quang Pagoda and their allies. The key posts—the Premiership and the Ministries of Interior, Defense, and Rural Development—are all occupied by military men, while four ministers and one deputy minister, according to *The New York Times* of September 2, 1969, are former supporters of the late President Diem.

Chosen by less than 20 percent of South Vietnam's electorate in an election it organized and corrupted, openly detested by its own people, governing from a narrow political base while carrying on an unpopular and losing war, the Thieu-Ky Khiem government has one powerful supporter—the United States of America. Without it, Saigon would collapse; with it, it retains a precarious hold on power by the device of terrorizing its own population into a sullen silence.

Openly arrayed against the Saigon-Washington alliance is the "second

Moral Argument and the War in Vietnam

force,'' the National Liberation Front of South Vietnam (Vietcong), its ally, the Democratic Republic of (North) Vietnam, and its supporters, the People's Republic of China and the Soviet Union. . . .

From the start the National Liberation Front was much more than a tool of the Communists, North or South. In a real, if ironic sense, it was the creation of Diem and his American supporters. . . . Diem was overthrown not by the NLF but by his own people, from whom he had demanded absolute fidelity while crushing their own aspirations for independence, and in the period 1963-65 the strength of the NLF in what was still a civil war was only the other side of the Saigon government's weakness and its inability to win the support of its own people. . . . It was clear they were about to win, which is why Americanization of the war began.

After that the character of the war changed. Vietcong guerrillas were reinforced by trained North Vietnamese regulars; captured and outmoded rifles were replaced by Chinese-made AK-47 automatic rifles superior to the Americans' own M-16. Hanoi and other heavily bombed areas of North Vietnam were ringed with the most sophisticated Soviet-made air defenses the world has ever seen; and similarly sophisticated weapons began to appear in the fighting in South Vietnam, bringing a new vulnerability to American bases and South Vietnamese cities alike.

So the two principal contending forces are known and identified. . . . Millions of Vietnamese . . . are unwilling to accept either of these groups as the sole architects of their national future. It is they, and their spokesmen, who constitute the Third Force. Their existence and their actions have both been visible for the last six years and can be recognized at once by observers who bear in mind four attributes that characterize the Third Force:

1. It has operated in the cities, where it is most vulnerable to police and other government reprisals.

2. It has been heavily committed to nonviolent tactics not only because rejection of violence is basic to Buddhism but because to use violence would inexorably force alignment with one of the two warring forces.

3. It is not a force in search of power for itself, but of a solution that would end the war and make possible a Vietnamese society that would permit the full participation of all Vietnamese.

4. It is pitted against not only the Vietnamese who rule the country, but also the military, political and economic strength of the most powerful nation on earth, the United States.

In such circumstances, given the conditions of Vietnamese society described earlier, the search for the Third Force and its strength and meaning must be conducted with imagination and understanding, reading statements with regard to the context in which they were written, rather than as they would appear in a Western democracy, seeing actions as they are measured against the potential punitive measures they incur. . . . Is there a Third Force? In the summer of 1963 the American civil rights movement mobilized 300,000 people for a demonstration in Washington. Four years later, the American peace movement produced 400,000 people for a demonstration in New York. . . .

In January, 1969, the peace movement in South Vietnam produced a demonstration in Saigon that involved an estimated total of half-million participants. No chartered trains or buses or planes came in. The railroad in South Vietnam has not run for years, bus trips are few and dangerous, and although there are an immense number of planes in South Vietnam's skies. they are not under the operation of people sympathetic to peace demonstrations.

So that the Saigon demonstration was made up almost entirely of Saigonese—500,000 demonstrators out of a population of three million, one out of every six, in the capital city of a country where even speaking for peace is a crime! Granted that no police can arrest or gun down a half-million people; still fear is an individual matter, and each Vietnamese who joined that mass outcry for peace must have been aware of the risk.

Like Washington and New York, the Saigon manifestation. along with all the others that had preceded it, was visible evidence of the political reality of what has been called the Third Force. If one were to extrapolate from the size of the respective demonstrations relative to the populations from which they were drawn, to the size of the constituency represented, it obviously bespoke an immense supporting public.

So the Third Force goes about demonstrating its existence and potency

It has a leadership, most of it in prison, exile, or hiding, but always with a handful of bold souls to speak out in the center of enemy territory.

It has a political program—a procedure for ending the war and arranging for the withdrawal of foreign troops; a foreign policy based on neutralism vis-à-vis the power blocs and an insistence that no political strings be attached to economic help in rebuilding the country; a domestic policy that foresees a structure based on democratic socialism, with immediate reopening of trade and travel with North Vietnam; and a method of arranging with the NLF the genuinely free elections, with all citizens and factions participating, to create a coalition government to implement such a program.

And it has a constituency, obviously very large, that has manifested its presence in every conceivable way open to it, under conditions of great hazard. . . .

So there is a Third Force in South Vietnam, making its presence and extent known in every way open to it, in the face of brutal, legalized intimidation and suppression. Yet even the people whose actions demonstrate its existence are uneasy with the description. It is not a three-

Moral Argument and the War in Vietnam

sided war, they insist. The Third Force is a convenient but misleading description of the millions of Vietnamese who would support a "third solution" to this apparently endless conflict. It must not be seen as a new alignment contesting for power against the others, but as a reasonable program that expresses the genuine aspirations of the people for peace.

Inevitably, such a "solution," of course, has important political implications, which is why neither side has grasped at it as a means of bringing the war to a conclusion.

For one thing, it would insist on the complete withdrawal of American military forces, although it would have the new government welcome continued friendly relations and economic aid from the United States and other Western countries as well as from those of the East.

It would resist any attempt to force a South Vietnamese alignment with either side in the contest between the Communist world and the West. Instead it would seek the neutralization, not only of Vietnam, itself but also of all of Southeast Asia. (Though its advocates make no demands that North Vietnam become neutralized along with the rest of Indochina, they obviously think that the North Vietnamese would be wise to join them in such a status.)

It would require the Vietnamese Communists, who are in complete control of the National Liberation Front, to share that control in a coalition government constructed by two political groupings rather than by one.

The response of the NLF to such proposals has been equivocal. Communists, like other men, do not gracefully relinquish power they have once acquired. Many of them are deeply and sincerely committed to the belief that only the imposition of a Marxist-Leninist system can solve Vietnam's political and economic problems; they have fought long and vigorously and so are even less disposed to meaningful sharing of power. Consequently, the NLF's inclusion of Buddhists, Catholics, Cao Daiists, and others in a governing committee has been on an individual basis, and its public assurances that all elements in South Vietnam would be welcomed in a coalition government have been carefully phrased not only to exclude supporters of the Thieu-Ky government but also to refer to such elements in individual, rather than corporate terms. . . .

But the NLF is also aware of the realities of the situation, and so, while its representatives reiterate their own preeminent claim to represent the people of South Vietnam and carefully emphasize the "divisions" within the Buddhist church—divisions that have been more the propaganda creation of the Thieu government than reality—they have also indicated repeatedly their interest in the emergence of a non-NLF, "interim" government with which peace and long-term arrangements could be negotiated. NLF spokesmen have described the "turmoil" in the cities of South Vietnam as an indication of the popular demand for the replacement of the "Saigon regime," without claiming credit for having initiated it. And references made repeatedly to the desirability of a "peace cabinet" recall that the same suggestion, in the same words, has been made by Vo Van Ai, the Buddhist representative-in-exile, since 1965.

Indeed, some Westerners, anxious to end the war and noting the similarity between the proposals of the NLF and the Third Force, and the "willingness" of the National Liberation Front to accept non-NLF "patriotic elements" into a new government, have wondered impatiently why the Buddhists do not simply join the NLF. The answer to that question, in several sections, defines the nature and importance of the forces supporting the Third Solution.

The answer is first a practical one. Neither side, say its proponents, can win a military victory in the war with their present investment of forces. The United States of 1969 is not the France of 1954. . . . On the other hand, neither can the United States and its South Vietnamese, South Korean, and Thai allies win the war. . . . From this perspective the Neutralists foresee the continuation of war, whether in set battles or by guerrillas, as far into the future as it has gone on in the past. And, since the ultimate decision must be made in Washington rather than in Saigon or Hanoi, for the Third Force elements openly to join the NLF would be more likely to harden the polarization of both sides than to contribute to an end of the war.

Along with this consideration, paradoxically is their recognition that either side *could* win the war if it were determined to do so, that the war, however horrifying, has been fought under a type of restraint that is always dangerously strained and that at any time may become untenable. By this reasoning, while the Vietnamese on both sides have been fighting total war, their supporters have not. . . .

Such restraints, Vietnamese neutralists reason, are a new element in international war, and undependable. Vietnam, already entangled in the competitions of the Great Powers, stands in imminent danger of becoming the battleground on which they not only test out their new techniques, but also lock in the final death grip of their insane enmity.

"We are torn," declared Vo Van Ai, of the Overseas Vietnamese Buddhist Association, at a conference of the International Peace Bureau, "between choices which have no solution. We can choose to combat aggression, in which case we must ally ourselves with one power bloc for support. We thence fall immediately into the vicious circle of conflict, and are drawn into the orbit of conflict between the two major power blocs. Thus our survival depends on the play of chance in the hands of the power bloc. We will have lost our identity. We are no longer ourselves."

In such circumstances, argue the Third Force adherents, to insist on an elusive and unattainable victory is the ultimate absurdity; only peace can give their people and country the chance to survive. And

Moral Argument and the War in Vietnam

even if a victory were possible, they add, it would plummet Vietnam inexorably into the grip of one power bloc or the other, dependent "on the play of chance" between them. Since peace is their only hope of survival, neutralism is their only hope not to "lose their identity."

But there are other considerations that reach further and plumb more deeply. These are Vietnamese permeated by a Buddhist tradition of tolerance and compassion, accustomed to accepting and absorbing what seems good in new or alien ideologies, finding fanatic commitment to any political or ideological view completely uncongenial. They know the claims and conflicts that are being fought over them and they are not prepared to accept either set uncritically. They are drawn to and repelled by aspects of both Eastern and Western societal organizations and see important things lacking in both.

They recognize that capitalism as it is practiced in the United States is unadaptable to the Vietnamese situation whatever its relevance at home. . . .

Yet those constituting the Buddhist-influenced element are not prepared to accept the imposition of socialism as implemented by a Communist party, either. . . .

So the ideologies of communism and capitalism alike seem to the Buddhist-influenced Vietnamese to be unacceptable examples of fanaticism, certain to lead to an inhuman, depersonalized, mechanistic society even if they manage to escape the ultimate horror of nuclear war. . . .

So the Vietnamese in the Third Force, seeing peace as essential to the survival of their people and nation and despairing of peace through the military efforts of either side in the war, offer their Third Solution to both. As a means of ending the war, it has five simple elements:

1. Replacement of the Thieu-Ky-Khiem regime by an "interim" government representative of the actual popular forces in South Vietnam and committed to ending the war. Obviously such a government could not be elected. A major part of the struggle in Paris is over the question of who would organize "free" elections, since the organizer could so easily manipulate and control the results. But the "interim" government could come to power without elections, as Duong Van Minh came to power in 1963, the Third Solution people believe, if one thing only happens: that is if the United States withdraws its unqualified support from the Thieu regime.

2. The interim government would immediately order the South Vietnamese army to cease firing, and ask both its allies and adversaries to join in the suspension of hostilities.

3. Simultaneously, the new government would ask the United States for the complete withdrawal of its troops and dismantling of its military bases, and initiate negotiations with the North Vietnamese government for withdrawal of its troops and on procedures looking toward eventual reunification.

4. Proposals would be made to North Vietnam for the lifting of bans

on travel and trade between the two zones to take effect immediately regardless of any ultimate decisions on reunification.

5. Negotiations would begin at once with the National Liberation Front for the holding of genuinely free elections, overseen by whatever form of international supervision was mutually acceptable to choose a government representing all factions and tendencies in the country.

The proposals have been greeted with skepticism by "practical" Westerners, whether they oppose or back the NLF.

If a cease-fire were declared by such a government, say Washington's supporters, who would prevent the Vietcong and the North Vietnamese from sweeping over the new government and seizing complete control? Or, since the American troops would be there until their withdrawal had been effected, why would not the Vietcong *then* overrun the country? And would there not then be a blood bath? The South Vietnamese army cannot cope with the Vietcong now; how could it hope to do so without American help, or would it even want to?

On the other side, among those whom suspicions of American intentions are without limit, the danger seems to be of a different nature. If such a new and admittedly more representative government were to come to power, even under the designation of "interim," they say, it would simply supply the United States with a new excuse for continuing the war by legitimizing the Saigon government. "Look," they hear Washington saying, "the bad guys are out and the good guys are in. Surely no one can now doubt the sincerity of our efforts to defend freedom!" And even if the new Vietnamese officials sincerely wanted to follow the program they had outlined, say these critics, would not the temptation to reinforce their position by relying on United States power be irresistible?

There are both simple and complicated answers to such questions, and the Vietnamese are often exasperatedly prone to supply the simple ones first.

"Do not believe," wrote the university students to their American counterparts early in 1967, "that the danger of a Communist takeover justifies continuation of the war. We believe we are strong enough to form an independent government. *The decision, however, should be ours, not yours, when it is our lives and our country that are being destroyed!*"

And Thich Nhat Hanh, replying to a questioner who had raised the possibility of a "blood bath," said gently:

"We are not savages, we are a people with an ancient culture, and we are sick in our very bones of war. I do not believe there would be a blood bath, but I wonder when you ask such a question how you would describe what your military forces are doing to my people now." . . . .

The war remains basically a guerrilla campaign despite the presence of many North Vietnamese regulars, and guerrillas, as Mao Tse-tung

Moral Argument and the War in Vietnam

has said, move among the population as the fish swim in a friendly sea. The peasant, though often unenthusiastic about the Vietcong who tax him and conscript his sons, still identifies the Vietcong as his own people fighting the white foreigner, and the sea, while not completely friendly, is tolerant enough to hide the fish. But let the sea become unfriendly, and the fish find their task more difficult. And, the Third Force people say, the sea would become definitely hostile if the Vietcong tried to overthrow a Vietnamese government that had achieved an end to the war and was negotiating the removal of the Western imperialists.

"But it's more than that, even," another young Vietnamese faculty member explained, "The VC is full of our friends! You must not think in terms of two irreconcilable hostile forces. Of course the Front is directed by Communists, but most of its members and soldiers are like us, Vietnamese, non-Communist nationalists, longing for peace, Buddhists in their upbringing. I do not believe for a moment that the VC would try to continue the war, or take over militarily, if such a government came into power and declared a cease-fire. He mused a moment, then smiled, "Why should they take the risk of alienating the whole population by continuing the killing when they expect to win the political struggle later on anyway. But they won't, you know, if we can produce a government that will really serve the people. And I think we can. I think we can." . . . .

Whether such blueprints and plans exist in systematic form, whether there have been discussions and agreements among the religious and political leadership of the Third Force, is impossible to demonstrate. The mere revelation that such discussions had taken place would make life impossible for their participants, who would have to disappear from sight, as did the identified members of the abortive Alliance of National Democratic and Peace Forces announced by the NLF after the launching of the Tet offensive early in 1968.

But it is beyond doubt that such discussions have taken place and that plans have been prepared. The evidence of them can be seen in such statements as the program of the Buddhists Socialist Bloc, publicized by exiled Vietnamese in Paris, and in such acts as Thich Tri Quang's call for a "government of national reconciliation," the organization by Tran Ngoc Lieng, vice-presidential candidate on the aborted ticket of Duong Van Minh, of the Progressive National Force (Luc Luong Quog Gia Tieu Bo) committed to the creation of such a government, and the news released by the Overseas Vietnamese Buddhist Association that unnamed parties had formed a "shadow cabinet" in South Vietnam.[2] That individuals identified with such moves, or even suspected of being identified, promptly deny or minimize the reports when they are questioned, reveals only the continuing mortal danger of expressing any sentiments that the Thieu-Ky-Khiem regime considers unfriendly.

But the difficulties of disclosing anything but the vaguest outlines of a political program or organization are not the only reason for an absence of "hard information." The Vietnamese do not want attention distracted from the essential point, which is ending the war, nor do they want to encourage non-Vietnamese to believe that they have any right to debate or decide the political and economic future of Vietnam.

So the Buddhists and their allies tread a narrow, difficult path, allying themselves with neither side, seeking no one's defeat for its own sake, but rather showing their ability to mobilize the people behind a genuine program for peace. Their pleas have gone to both sides. To Vietnamese fighting one another they have sent messages asking for a cease-fire and discussions among them as Vietnamese, recognizing the common ties that bind them against the ideological disagreements that divide.

Their most urgent and insistent plea, however, continues to be to the United States. The Americans have the initiative; they are the foreigners who have invaded Vietnam, and until they leave it is inconceivable that Vietnamese resistance to their presence will cease. They are much the stronger, too, able to take the steps that will lead to peace without fearing the reality of defeat or any suffering for their own people. So for the American insistence on "peace with honor," the Vietnamese respond as did Thich Nhat Hanh in the United States.

"How can the United States withdraw with honor? What is honor? The honor of the American devotion to democracy is widely known, but if that honor cannot be shown in Vietnam, then honor is not served. Stopping the bombing and shooting of Vietnamese will not harm honor." And they remind the Americans of France's experience in ending the Algerian war by its own withdrawal, "thereby recovering the honor it had lost in fighting it."

How can the United States withdraw? Millions of Americans have come to share the Vietnamese poet's view. It is in the continuation of the war that dishonor lies; honor is not in the form of the withdrawal, or in conditions attached to it, but in the withdrawal itself.

"They ask me how to withdraw," said a speaker. "The answer is simple: in ships." A highly vocal segment of the antiwar movement echoes the statement. Withdraw, unilaterally, unconditionally, immediately. Let the Vietnamese settle their affairs themselves; we have already interfered too much. "There is nothing to negotiate," said another speaker, "except the timetable of withdrawal."

But of course it is not really that simple, and even negotiation on the "timetable of withdrawal" would necessitate a formidable agenda. Is the timetable to be agreed upon by all four parties in the Paris talks, including the Thieu-Ky government? To ask the question is to answer it. Saigon will approve only token withdrawal, since the Thieu-Ky regime cannot survive if withdrawal is complete. So far, the United States has deferred to Saigon, and if some judicious arm-twisting has been applied to President Thieu, still the White House has not protested his assertion that it will be "years and years" before all American troops can be brought home.

Moral Argument and the War in Vietnam

Or will withdrawal occur in spite of Saigon, as a result of agreements between the United States on the one hand and Hanoi and the NLF on the other? In that case, one of two things could be expected to happen in South Vietnam. One would be a desperate attempt by the Saigon government to retain control of the army and continue the war. That would mean battles fought through and around American troops, who are stationed all over the country, frequently in the same camps and bases as the South Vietnamese, over the months that would be required to move out half a million men and their impedimenta. It would be manifestly impossible, even with maximum cooperation from the NLF, for United States forces to avoid involvement in such actions, even perhaps to the point of finding themselves fighting their erstwhile allies!. . . .

Would the United States then set up its own interim government to avert total chaos until it had managed to get all of its people out?'

Or would the "timetable negotiations" make arrangements for NLF cadres to move into the Saigon government offices as the Thieu government moved out? It may be that the NLF could mobilize the necessary talent, and such an arrangement would at least furnish history with another novelty. After having fought the NLF to save South Vietnam from its rule, the United States would now, with no more consultation than before, impose the same organization on the people!

But these are idle speculations because it is inconceivable that any government, let alone the present American one, would venture anything of the sort. "Withdrawal" is a great slogan—short and crisp and explicit enough to fit on signs and bumper strips—but, when qualified only by such words as "unconditional," "immediate," and "unilateral," it is still only a slogan, the assertion of an objective, not a program for achieving it. For such a program, only the Third Solution provides the answer.

That answer hinges on the replacement of the Thieu-Ky government as the first move in the equation of withdrawal, not the last. A new government, representative of the people, committed to ending the war and then arranging for honest, countrywide elections for a coalition government, would have as one of its earliest tasks the supervision of United States military withdrawal, while assuming simultaneously the responsibility for running the machinery of civilian government, distributing food and supplies, and carrying on the multitude of other tasks that go with the intricate business of ending a war.

It will not be easy to open the way for such a government without hopelessly prejudicing it in the process. To "arrange" it through a convenient coup engineered by the CIA in its inimitable way would be to give it the kiss of death. Any suspicion that a new Third Force government was in fact a creature of Washington, the result of a "deal," would sentence that government to the same hatred and distrust now directed at the Thieu-Ky-Khiem regime. Fundamentally, the United States is called upon to do one thing: *make clear to the Saigon government and to the people of South Vietnam its unwillingness any longer to prevent the replacement of that government with one genuinely representative of the popular will. . . .*

The degree to which this direction is being opened up to discussion is further suggested by the resolution—S.R.268—introduced by Senator Thomas F. Eagleton of Missouri and Harold E. Hughes of Iowa, and co-sponsored by several other senators. The resolution would have the Senate urge that the government of South Vietnam be required to take four actions "within the next sixty days" or suffer the termination of all American military, political, and economic assistance. These actions are:

1. Grant liberty and amnesty to all of those held in custody as political prisoners;

2. Lift the censorship of all communications media, foreign and domestic, including especially those newspapers which have been closed down;

3. Permit political parties the freedom to organize and operate without governmental controls; and

4. Present a plan for a provisional government, broadly representative of the main political ethnic and religious groups of South Vietnam, whose principal function will be to maintain government effectively during the transition from war to peace.

There is no assurance that such a procedure would "work." The fabric of Vietnamese life has been shredded, and it may be that the battered and persecuted nationalists could not, when the chips are down, summon enough political and personal cohesion to create and sustain a government of the sort they seek against the skillful organization the NLF would bring to the contest. In that case the war might go on, though at a decelerating tempo and between Vietnamese, or it might be that South Vietnam would come quickly under a Communist form of government, albeit a highly nationalistic form of communism. Either would be an improvement over the present endless bloodletting, for both the Vietnamese and us.

But the Third Force spokesmen do not think the outlook is so gloomy. Let the United States declare unequivocally its intention to withdraw all its military forces; let it call for a cease-fire or even announce its intention of declaring one unilaterally, and let it make known that it no longer insists on imposing on the South Vietnamese a government they detest.

"Then," said a young university student, "we will soon have the government we want and be on the way to peace."

Notes

1 Huong was himself a political prisoner at one point during his career, a fact of which he was reminded by a representative of the International Red Cross who was pleading for

Moral Argument and the War in Vietnam

permission to provide clothing and other necessities for political prisoners as well as prisoners of war. He recalls that Huong, who is a poet and former teacher, became lost in memories. "I will never forget the dawns," the Premier said, "and the listening for the sound of the guard's footsteps in the corridor, and then the door of the cell opening, and the guard beckoning me out, to the interrogation room—where you know what happened to me." Then he gave the asked-for permission.

2 Michael Morrow, "The Neutralists Speak Out," *Dissent*, September-October 1969.

Part IV

Can Ethics, Ideology, and History Meet?

Can Ethics, Ideology, and History Meet?

Introduction

The tenor of our discussion up to this point has reflected the assumption that the most basic evaluations of United States policy in Vietnam are *moral* ones. We really mean to ask, as *ethical* questions, whether we *should* have intervened and what we *should* do now. Policy questions, even perhaps the same questions that policy-makers ask, have been explicitly kept in mind all along, but it is *moral* principles and *moral* argument which has batted them around. In the previous section a serious initial breach between moral judgment and policy making was faced, but two policy concepts—"honor" and "reciprocity"— were explained to have ethical foundations. This section will deal with two other kinds of approaches to policy in Vietnam which are often thought to bypass many ethical questions. One is "ideological" criticism or defense of policy. In particular I have in mind the ideologies of democratic-capitalist anticommunism, and communism itself, which might argue on the basis of what policy serves their ideological goals and ask few further moral questions. The second is a certain kind of historical judgment difficult to describe in its many forms but paradigmatically represented by arguing from the "natural, historically inevitable" development of the nation of Vietnam.

Ideological considerations displace ethical ones at both subtle and explicit points in arguments. Two very explicit ones would admit that United States policy was destroying the nation of Vietnam yet justify that policy because it deters communism; or would ignore all questions about the internal character of the NLF-led revolution, remain unruffled even if shown that Hanoi had initiated and led that "revolution" with a full-scale invasion of a sovereign South Vietnam, and simply justify Hanoi's action because theirs was a "Marxist" cause. In practice, ideological arguments usually operate much more subtly. The American policy supporter may recognize the ambiguity of many traditional moral questions about the internal character of the Vietnamese situation and grudgingly admit that continuing our intervention is not quite to the overall good of Vietnam; yet, he will say, upholding the United States pledge to turn back insurgent Communist guerrilla warfare is so important for the credibility of forces working to contain communism that it far outweighs any doubts about the morality of our intervention. It is, after all, the diplomacy of nations within their huge blocs of allies

215

Moral Argument and the War in Vietnam

which gives major significance to this war. *Credibility* and *stability* are larger diplomatic values which are ignored by "local" analyses of the Vietnam situation and subsequent proposals for prompt withdrawal.

Yet just why are diplomatic credibility and stability so crucial? Mr. Oglesby explains them to have emerged from the cold war experience of *détente:* in order to make the cold war manageable, it is necessary to build up clear truce lines which each opposing bloc clearly understands shall mark the domain of the other. Stability is thus crucial: if internal upheavals keep occurring within a bloc's domain and are supported psychologically by the opposing bloc's ideology, then the truce line is no longer clear, military confrontation and intervention will likely occur in particular areas, and the chances of the cold war becoming a hot and global one will increase immensely. Instability is bound to arise if each bloc's credibility in preventing cracks on its side of the truce line is doubted. There you have it: Vietnam is the big testing ground for Western-versus-Communist maneuver.

Since our Vietnam policy thus grows so logically out of our position in the cold war, Mr. Oglesby contends that the only way to challenge the necessity of the war is to question the necessity of the cold war itself and the value of the position within it that the United States upholds. He moves to a lengthy analysis of the cold war. He observes that America has functionally defined the "Free World" as areas open to United States corporate-capitalist investment and operation, strongly disputes the benefit of that capitalist economics for the Third World, and concludes that the whole ideological, larger diplomatic backdrop to our position in Vietnam is indefensible. He is then free to adopt an opposing "ideological" position of his own. He need not define it positively, as essentially Communist; he need only define it negatively, as opposed to United States capitalist imperialism. And it has an important international dimension: given the extent and record of the American empire which Mr. Oglesby describes, there is bound to arise against it an admirable "international conspiracy" of sorts. Solidarity and coordination between those groups trying to throw off the yoke of the American empire is inevitable. This accumulates its own credibility: it must not let the American empire turn it back in Vietnam, for that will affect its movement around the world. Its survival is at stake in Vietnam, though it is also a survival of the Vietnamese revolting against American domination. Ethics and ideology still have some strong connection here, besides the ethical basis of the ideology itself. But the United States survival at stake in Vietnam is not the survival of our people, only the survival of our empire; the link between ideology and the basic ethical premise that violence is more justified when committed by people whose lives are directly at issue is broken. In our policy, as Mr. Oglesby lays it out, ethics gets lost in the shuffle—or the steamroller—of power-bloc diplomacy and ideology.

It is interesting to note the different areas of agreement and disagreement between Mr. Scalapino's and Mr. Oglesby's analyses of our policy. Mr. Scalapino speaks often of the "equilibrium" and "balance of power" necessary "if peace is to be underwritten." Instabilities in "divided states" such as Germany, Korea, or Vietnam are much more than civil wars; they are direct challenges to the "political equilibrium of the entire region, and hence to world peace." Extreme escalation as well as withdrawal is ruled out because of threatened involvement of China or the Soviet Union. "The Vietnam struggle must always be kept in its larger context."[1] But Mr. Scalapino also emphasizes the internal character of the Vietnam war as an upset of equilibrium aggressively and externally led by Communists (of course Oglesby's analysis would regard that as only a surface deception hiding the real "ideological substrata" of United States policy).

A question raised by Mr. Scalapino's last point is the relation of nationalist upheavals to the international equilibrium of the cold war. If one were to show that the Marxist-oriented and NFL-led revolution in Vietnam was nationalist in character and not externally developed, would *that* prove that the revolution was not an upset of the diplomatic-ideological equilibrium necessary for cold war peace? It would not, *if* one could show that the nationalism of Marxists could never be genuine nationalism but was always subordinate to internationalist tendencies. Messrs. McAlister and Mus deny any necessary incompatibility between the genuine nationalism of a revolutionary party and the international, globally ideological features of Marxism.[2] But the question threatens to go further: in the present state of the cold war, *can* such a compatibility of nationalism and Marxist ideology be accepted *as such* by the anti-Communist bloc? The cold war and the political realities of the ideological struggles may relegate even the most genuine nationalist foundation of Marxist revolutions to comparative insignificance. If that is the case, then one has to shove the discussion up to the level of which side of the ideological struggle to take. Is Marxism good or bad for the Third World? Messrs. McAlister and Mus may be taken to give one kind of answer to that question: they explain the value of a Marxist revolution for the modernization of a village-oriented Vietnamese culture and nation.

Historical explanation is another type of argument which may bypass ethical issues. One can explain, for instance, the westward expansion of the early United States as a "natural" and "expected" development from certain economic and cultural characteristics of the country, without necessarily thereby morally condoning it. The Indians, after all, were colonized and nearly extinguished in the process. Similarly one may historically and culturally explain how a Marxist-oriented revolution has developed in Vietnam in the twentieth century without thereby affirmatively evaluating that movement. A "manifest destiny" for Marxism in Vietnam may be no more morally acceptable than America's "manifest destiny" at the turn of this century. More narrowly, it is conceivable

Moral Argument and the War in Vietnam

that one could explain (as in Mr. Lacouture's previous selection) how the politics of the NLF were bound historically to become more and more radical and Marxist without lauding, admiring, or even condoning that development. In fact, some historians would jealously guard their work from anything but morally neutral use.

Yet that combination of historical explanation without moral affirmation may be more conceivable than likely. History is used in moral arguments, not simply because we need to dig up facts to plug into moral premises to yield concrete judgments, but because "natural, historical" development is itself closely related to moral questions. An element of traditionalism and respect for the roots of the past is present in all of us, not simply as a reactionary idolization of the past but as a disgust at seeing cultures, societies, and peoples destroyed by those who would have no such respect. It may be moral that cultures be altered and that they be pushed to evolve. Or it may be moral that they even be nearly destroyed if they are hopeless and corrupt enough. But who would say that Vietnamese society was so corrupt and hopeless that we need have no regard for its roots and social values in assessing how it should grow into a modern era? The result of answering that rhetorical question is a guarantee that historical explanation of various factors behind the Vietnam War will carry considerable, if not absolutely determinant, moral weight. Thus, for instance, the claim by Messrs. McAlister and Mus that the basic communal and "universe-view" values of Marxism have deep roots in the traditional society of Vietnamese villages must be seriously considered in any moral evaluation of the place of Marxism in Vietnam.

All three selections in this section relate to the place of ideology in argument about the war. In addition, the item by John McAlister and Paul Mus exemplifies the kind of cultural-historical explanation relevant to moral judgment.

Notes

1 Scalapino, pp. 245, 249, 255, 257.
2 McAlister and Mus, pp. 269-272.

The Cold Warrior's Story
of Vietnam*

by Carl Oglesby

Secretary Rusk is no dope; why does he keep on saying this?
—Senator Clifford Case[1]

One might ponder the official reasons Washington gives for our fighting in Vietnam, and think: These reasons are so bad that we must have fallen into the hands of fools. But one might also think: These reasons are so bad that there must be *other* reasons. The second thought is better.

Other reasons exist. There seem, in fact, to be several grades and varieties of *raisons de guerrilla* that overlie one another like so many geologic strata, the softer reasons lying at the surface, and the harder, the stronger ones, below it. So we must do some strip-mining, peel away the top propaganda layer to expose the firmer underlying layers of ideology that give the propaganda its ground-base and purpose. That is the objective of this chapter: to move the analytic focal point past the white line of warfare politics into the ideological substrata where the less pious, more honest war reasons are embedded. With Senator Case, I am unwilling to conclude that Dean Rusk is a dope. If Rusk pretends to be convinced by arguments that should convince no one as intelligent as he, then he must have been convinced by other arguments which for some reason he prefers not to develop. I think the more convincing arguments can be reconstructed; the Cold Warrior's story can be pieced together. But first his propaganda has to be cleared away.

We are legally obligated to fight. It is obvious that there are no unambiguously binding agreements, the SEATO pact having even more escape clauses in it than has NATO's. It is still more obvious that no strong state will hesitate for a moment to violate a treaty which it judges to be harmful to its national interests. If we fight, it must be because we think we *must* fight, not because we have been trapped by a legal instrument.

*From Oglesby and Richard Shaull, *Containment and Change: Two Dissenting Views of American Foreign Policy* (New York: The Macmillan Co., 1967). The excerpts reprinted here are from Chapters II and V of the section by Mr. Oglesby, pp. 7-15, 18-31, 106-130, 132-134. Copyright 1967 by Carl Oglesby. By permission of The Macmillan Co. and the authors.

Moral Argument and the War in Vietnam

We are responding to an emergency plea from the Vietnamese people. We have never heard from the Vietnamese people. We have heard only from those elite Vietnamese sympathetic enough with our own politics to have been allowed their hour in the Saigon Presidential Palace.

Our global reputation is at stake. Maybe it is, and maybe that is important. But this argument cuts both ways. No less than President Johnson, the dissenters consider themselves to be the partisans of America's prestige, which they define differently. The only question is, What kind of reputation do we want our country to have?

We are resisting an invasion: (a) The National Liberation Front of South Vietnam is the political creature of North Vietnam. The best development of this argument can be found in a lengthy, highly detailed essay in the April 1968 issue of *Foreign Affairs*, "The Faceless Viet Cong." The author, George A. Carver, Jr., is identified as a former AID official in Saigon. In view of AID's notorious intimacy with the CIA in Vietnam and the wealth of what appears to be privileged intelligence to which Carver has had access, one has to wonder if his piece is not, more or less, a CIA document. Since it might be just that, it is only prudent to be skeptical about Carver's "facts."* But where exactly does skepticism leave us in a case where the "facts" are so inaccessible? For all we can ever know for sure, Carver's elaborate description of the genesis of the National Liberation Front (NLF) might be little more than a Borgesian fantasy; it might also be complete and perfect truth. What tests can we make? We could compare Carver's version with Wilfred Burchett's,[2] but Burchett is no less a partisan than Carver. French scholars Bernard B. Fall, Philippe Devillers, and Jean Lacouture are more trustworthy by any ordinary academic standard, and all three describe the NLF in ways that differ much more from Carver than from Burchett; but they might be wrong. What does one do with a "proof" which cannot be checked?

Accept it. Concede that Hanoi, with that vicious skill by which we know our Enemy, intrigued to create and retain control over the NLF. This concession allows us to ask Carver what he knows about that *other* intriguer, Ngo Dinh Nhu, and that *other* "creature" organization, Nhu's Committee for the Liberation of North Vietnam. . . . No scholarship in the world will tell us which of these two "liberation creatures" was

---

* Several samples of CIA historiography might be cited. For one, the Bay of Pigs; Murray Zeitlin and Robert Scheer (Cuba: *Tragedy in Our Hemisphere*, 1964) have established that the CIA badly tampered with the texts of Castro speeches that it presented to State Department and White House analysts; that is, the CIA appears to have consciously falsified the supposedly objective information on which our policy-makers were basing their plans. And the CIA's contention just before the invasion that the Cuban people were prepared to join in revolt against Castro is bizarre if we do not assume that the CIA's purpose was to involve the United States is a situation from which few administrations could have decided to withdraw. In January 1964, for another example, the CIA leaked the "information" that the U.S.S.R.'s 6 to 10 percent annual growth rate had fallen in 1962-63 to 2.5 percent, a decline that most Western experts found unbelievable. Paul Blackstock (*The Strategy of Subversion*, 1964) writes that this report "was widely interpreted as an attempt to influence U.S. allies not to extend large export credits to the U.S.S.R." (p. 187).

invented first, which was the first blow and which the counterblow.

But much more important than questions about the bureaucratic origins of the NLF is the question, Why did it grow? Suppose that the North Vietnamese regime promulgated certain decrees through an underground in South Vietnam: Why did so many South Vietnamese people respond? How could it be that this illegitimate invasion from without was experienced by so many South Vietnamese as an entirely legitimate revolution from within? Because there was terror? There was terror on both sides; why did only one work? Because there was a tightly disciplined secret organization? There were tightly disciplined secret organizations on both sides; why did only one work?. . . .

George Carver, the CIA, the State Department, and the White House probably know as well as anyone else (we shall return to this) what it is that creates popular wars, just as they quite probably know that the issuing of orders in Hanoi has precious little to do with the way those orders will bite in South Vietnam. If revolt is needed, it will come, orders or no; and if it is not needed, no orders in the world can instigate it. In view of the mountainous fact that South Vietnam revolted, Carver's fine-spun arguments about "puppet" and "creature" organizations lose all their body.

We are resisting an invasion: (b) North Vietnamese troops are fighting in the south. Compelling enough if one knows nothing else, this line of argument finally seems the most dishonest of all. Americans are shown a number and handed a gun. That is not enough. There are other numbers, other facts. One is that our militarization of South Vietnam was solidly under way by the end of 1954, well before the period of French control was to have ended, and long before there was any substance to the infiltration-from-the-north charge.[3] What comes before cannot have been caused and cannot be excused by what comes after.

But much more surprising than this omission is the inconclusiveness of the infiltration statistics themselves. With all the official furor, one is prepared to hear that our enemy consists mostly of northern troops, just as in the Korean War. But the case turns out to be different. In midsummer 1966, total NLF strength was officially estimated at 282,000 men, an increase of 52,000 since the beginning of the year.[4] This figure, incidentally, is politically menacing. In this same period, we claim 31,571 "kills," the largest total yet for any six-month period. The old pattern repeats itself: The more there are who die, the more come to fight. Of these 282,000, about 50,000 are supposed to be northern infiltrators—and the great majority of these 50,000 are said to have entered the south since the systematic American bombing of North Vietnam commenced in February 1965. Thus, North Vietnamese, who may think they have a good reason to fight, still account for no more than 18 percent of the total NLF force. The administration's performance on other statistical matters (these same "kills" for example) give us no right to believe that this estimate is not inflated for maximum political

Moral Argument and the War in Vietnam

effect. But even if it is not, we are still left with no "outside-aggressor" explanation for fully four out of five active military partisans of the revolution. The invasion argument seems undermined by its own best evidence. Certainly that evidence does not seem to justify our own force level, which now surpasses North Vietnam's "invader" force by better than six to one.

We might dwell for a moment on the political strategy of this preoccupation with "foreign" troops. It conceals two crucial assumptions.

The first is that an army's claim to nationalist revolutionary status is bogus if a substantial number of its troops are foreign. But this is clearly incorrect; and of all people, we Americans should know that. Recall the extent to which our own revolution was directly and indirectly supported by France, Spain and Holland. Recall our national feeling for Lafayette. . . .

This of course is not to say that the American and Vietnamese revolutions are alike. It is only to say that the presence of outside troops or the making of alliances or the interferences on either side of third-party states proves nothing whatsoever about the internal political nature of the conflict. Some Czechs supported Hitler's Wehrmacht; that does not make Hitler a Czech revolutionary. Some third parties support Nguyen Huu Tho's NLF; that does not make Tho an aggressor's agent.

The second concealed assumption of the invasion argument is that between North and South Vietnam a politically ordinary invasion is possible. That is, the argument assumes that there are two separate and sovereign Vietnams, one of which could aggress against the other's territory. Thus, the administration has depicted the seventeenth parallel—the 1954 Geneva Conference's "temporary military demarcation line"—as a permanent national frontier, permanent at least for the duration of the cold war. . . . Vietnam is divided now, rightly or wrongly, strictly at the insistence of the United States, and strictly because there was a revolution in China which the United States finds appalling.

If we fail to contain Them here,we shall have to contain Them someplace else. . . .

Every master of a global empire since [1779] has found occasion to dust off what we now call the domino theory. The theory's implicit description of the way in which the demand for change emerges and is shaped by international events is primitive, paranoid, and mechanistic. But its most fundamental assumption still seems sound: Nationalism is a threat to imperialism. . . . Its popular version begs or circles all the really important social questions on which Westerners generally and Americans in particular are in such need of enlightenment. Is stability more important than social justice? Can change be managed within the status quo? Can Western acquisition of global economic hegemony coexist with the just aspirations of small states? Can the progress of that acquisition be reversed without violence? The domino theory has nothing to say about the very conditions and problems that give it the

222

lame life it has. It pretends that there are no questions at all to ask about our extremely advanced international positions, with infuriating arrogance it depicts Vietnam and all the other dominoes as possessions of the Free World (read, the United States) which, being possessed by us, are ours to lose; and implicitly denying that men revolt for human cause, it implicitly outlaws rebellion as a criminal if not diabolic act. Generally, it evokes the images of a very legendary threat, wants us to believe that there is a Gate and that the Enemy is at it—or about to be. There *is* a struggle in the world. That struggle very much *does* involve America. And that struggle needs to be understood. But the domino theorists beat the drums of anticommunism, and the war is on. A good people have been given no chance to wonder who their enemy is and why their enemy fights; have been given no time to think through the astounding implications of a foreign policy which has crept upon them without being explained or debated, a foreign policy which Gary Porter, borrowing from Walter Lippmann and George Ball, has aptly termed "globalism—the ideology of total world involvement."[5]

From fighting for freedom to stopping Them now, these reasons for war are little more than the slogans of a hard-sell sales campaign, an unchecked federal executive hawking his wares on the public money. By these slogans, the nation's heart is warmed for the sacrifice, the young men are summoned, the heroes are decorated, the dead are buried, a diffuse and sometimes easy-going nationalism is given point and passion.

The slogans also do something more subtle: they rivet our attention on Vietnam itself. Even when we grow critical, these slogans manipulate our thought, invite us to reenact in our solitude the birth of rebellion and its spread, to master the sense of Hoa Hao and keep the Cao Dai straight, to labor over the fine meanings of treaties and their clauses, to probe statistics for their secrets and their prophecies, to lampoon certain brown-robed figures and commiserate with others. We Americans debate and debate, always sucked again into that Southeast Asian vortex. What does the Ho Chi Minh want exactly? Is Le Duan stronger than Vo Nguyen Giap or Pham Van Dong? What factions struggle within the NLF? Is Mao alive or dying or dead? What new shapes will this confetti of statistics, names, and dates take on in the future? What will *Asia* do? Meanwhile, in stunning contrast to this problem for an undiscovered calculus, America stands all but aloof in the serene simplicity of her purpose, as if the only hard part of her Vietnam policy were the purely technical chore of applying, in Asia's turbulence, her elemental desire for justice. Even the critics do not tamper much with the idea that justice is what America wants. Instead, good, learned men bend themselves over and again to one more perusal of the Vietnamese puzzle, the better to prove to someone that we have or have not been mistaken in our choice of Vietnamese beneficiaries.

This is wrong. The subject matter of a serious political analysis of

Moral Argument and the War in Vietnam

Vietnam is America. What is it that the good Cold Warrior must see behind his propaganda? What persuades him to deceive other Americans? Why does Secretary Rusk, who is no dope, "keep on saying this"?

This can be answered. We need only review the past two decades, guided in that review by the most commonplace assumptions of cold war anticommunism, America's leading political ideology. . . .

With the Soviet Union, we have gone from confrontation to *détente*. The relationship is no longer defined by its anger and uncertainties. Its bitterness has lost the old edge, become blunted by the mundane securities of daily usage. Direct military collision is feared and avoided equally by both sides, crises are referred to hot lines instead of war rooms, and one sometimes wonders if there is not something still springier in the air: a slow convergence of political aims. . . .

A substitute for war has evidently been found. Most often, to be sure, with a devious motion, power nevertheless moved to understand itself in distinctively new ways, moved to accept in new ways the existence of other power. This was not a mere renovation of nineteenth-century sphere-of-influence politics whose aim was dominance. The aim now was thought of as "conflict management." The demands of power slowly lost their nearly metaphysical status. Positions became negotiable, attitudes mutable, antagonisms conditional instead of absolute. Politics is detheologized in our time; it becomes secular and pragmatic.

The fact that the seemingly predestined war did not take place is perhaps what now beguiles us. How did we manage to come through? By what luck or wisdom was the inevitable reduced to the problematic? The problematic to the improbable? Above all, can we capture the secrets of this alchemy that changed graves into bombshelters and bombshelters into houses?

The political intuitions produced in our statesmen by twenty years of European cold war can no doubt be made explicit in a number of different ways; it is not as if there is one definite exposition. But we can proceed from the broadly held assumption that the mutually qualifying aims of American policy are the avoidance of war and the creation of a stable global society in which liberal values will predominate. To the extent that pursuit of these aims is steadily less obstructed in the present European *détente*, one can generalize our experience there in terms of a conflict-management theory which consists of four very basic propositions:

First, each side must commit itself to the view that global war is an unsatisfactory means of securing global objectives, since what such a war might win is under all conditions drastically less than what it will most certainly lose.* This commitment *must* be established. But

---

* For example, Secretary McNamara's words: "Now people realize what hardly anybody realized five years ago—*that it's impossible to win an all-out nuclear exchange.* Once you realize this, you arrive at certain rational conclusions." (Quoted in Stewart Alsop, "His Business is War," *Saturday Evening Post*, May 21, 1966, p. 30.)

unwise nations may not understand that. So it sometimes becomes essential for the wise nations to produce that commitment among the unwise. The wise do this by producing military power, and by so exhibiting that power before the eyes of the unwise that they cannot possibly misconstrue the message. You will pay badly for any foolishness. Power plus the credibility of its use equals deterrence, which makes all nations pacifists and creates time and room for diplomatic maneuver. The Strategic Air Command was not trying to be ironical when it made its motto "Peace is our profession."

Second, a global truce line must be unambiguously drawn. The establishing and maintenance of this line are top-priority matters. Under most conditions, in fact, no objective is more important that its protection. One must be prepared even to go to war to keep it intact. The other side must understand that. (The two Cuban crises may mean that in some geopolitical settings, a position on one's own side of the line can be allowed to decay, but it will still remain forbidden territory to the major opposition power.)

Third, it is through the process of defining and securing the truce line that the *rival powers build up a store of information about each other, develop and habituate themselves to a modus vivendi, and begin to create a communication system*—initially, of course, irregular, informal, and unreliable—which with time grows more trustworthy, broader, and more secure. Most important perhaps during this phase is what passes unspoken between the two sides, the quiet unadvertised awareness that this experience of adversity is shared, that what frightens one diplomat's nation frightens another's. This experience gradually builds up a fulcrum for a new balance of trust. We begin to know this enemy of ours. We begin to learn how to dance with him. We begin to trust him not to expect too much. In his actions, we recognize our motives. We grow sensitive to his special internal problems and even begin to have favorites within his house. We see him return occasionally to the temple of his nation's myths and enact there for the benefit of the unsuspecting masses—and those narrow-eyed ascetics, the generals—the eternal drama of his patriotism, heroism, tribal loyalty. We hear harsh words; our names are implicated; certain threats and accusations begin to have a seasonal fashion; but we understand: He is protecting his budget, vying for power, neutralizing an opponent. We are all men of the same world.

Finally, the dividend of this patience is that the common interests so necessary to a more productive relationship will have had time to incubate. This is the crux of the distinctively *liberal* understanding of power politics. There is an underlying faith that men will be able to work together usefully in the world if they can only escape the shibboleths of man's past. There has to be a time, then, when history stops insistently repeating them. There must be a stillness among us. If history

Moral Argument and the War in Vietnam

is the interruption of war by truces, or if it is the continual reconfiguration of boundaries and the power clusters they stand for, then the cold war is a time in which history does not take place, a dictated twilight in which movement is restrained, a cease-fire and stand-fast, a suspension of those forces that kept the wheel in its sorry motion. Over and over again these twenty years, opportunities appeared which tempted both sides to break the unnatural charm. On both sides, of course, there are those who live in a state of perpetual, wanton surrender to this temptation; there are still others who weaken when the strains are great; but on balance the anchor men on both sides resisted and restrained them. And because of that, there begins to be a bit of hope.

This is not a bad vision, this bit of hope. Maybe it is even a bit more of hope than we deserve. But, one way or another, the drift of Soviet-American relations since World War II—at least, one may so imagine—suggests a way in which the vision might be realized everywhere: Make up your minds to have no big war; draw clearly in the world's good honest dirt a line which you will neither violate nor see violated; in the joint superintending of that line, learn a few things about one another, stop dreaming apocalyptic dreams, stop evangelizing the millennium, face the fact that the future is no nation's private property—and so make peace.

Look now at Asia in this wisdom's light.

Red China and America glower at one another across the Pacific—rather, across the Formosa Strait, the Yellow Sea, the Sea of Japan. We are enemies, no question about it. There even seems to be something familiar in the situation. As we had cooperated with the other Western democracies in attempting to reverse the Russian Revolution, so we had tried (but even harder) to reverse the Chinese Revolution. As we had interrupted our quarantine of Russia to make common cause against Nazi Germany, so we had tried to combine the Chinese Communist and Nationalist armies for common cause against Fascist Japan. As our chief European enemy became in defeat our chief friend, and our chief wartime friend became in victory our major foe, so with Japan and China in the Pacific. Frustrated again in our second attempt at a major counterrevolution and nursing an ugly shame for having failed, we confronted in the Korean War years a question quite like the European question of 1946: Shall we annihilate Red China? Or shall we have an Asian cold war too?. . . .

The first principle of the European wisdom was applied: We shall seek no war with China, the primary reason being (as with Russia?) that her army was too big, her land too vast. To prove that we meant what we said, General MacArthur was retired, and the Korean War was cautiously made to disappear. The second principle now had to be established: The truce line had to be fixed. We hold here, they there. No violence must be done to this line; it is the only hope we have that Chinese people decades from now can at last clasp hands with American people. Nor does this line represent an unfairly one-sided division. Korea remains only divided. Chiang Kai-shek remains present but pent up. We wring our hands for the rich ruling clergy of Tibet, but make no move to intervene: Tibet becomes the Asian Hungary. Peking can trust us to make no sudden moves against the northern half of Vietnam. Let the Socialist government there make what it can of its opportunities. But let there be no incursions on this border. Let Cambodia "lean to one side" in her neutralism; but let there be no disturbance in Thailand. This line must hold. Accept this line, Red China, and we can begin to talk of other matters—of doctors and reporters exchanged, of your participation in disarmament talks, of a somewhat freer economic arrangement with our industrial protégés in Japan, even of your membership in the United Nations. Of course, there will be difficulties. But with a little patience and skill, there might easily be an Asian *détente* too. The unnegotiable condition of every prospect, however, is that the line of truce in the Asian cold war must not be broken. Until that fact is accepted, there is little use in talking about the future.

The Cold Warrior who sees Asian affairs in this way might be forgiven his exasperation with both China and the American peace movement. He does not need to be reminded of the carnage in Vietnam. Many of his kind have seen it much closer up than the unblooded peaceniks ever will. He is, after all, a man, this cold war dialectician; he has sons and daughters and he prefers life to death; no one has any right to assume that he is less anguished than the next man by the sight of scorched earth, burnt flesh, and torture. From our observation post outside the Establishment, where we suppose for some reason that the visibility is better, we critics inform him that his war is not helping the Vietnamese. If he were not gagged by the official pretense that it is, maybe he would reply to us: "Of course. I know that. Do you take me for an idiot?" We inform him that his bombing raids in the countryside and whorehouse abandon in the cities are laying that nation waste, and that this physical and cultural slaughter, by a familiar psychology, is only making more Vietnamese turn Communist. Maybe he wants to say: "What could be more obvious? I struggle with this problem day and night. But why can't you see," he might say to us critics, "that Red China has to yield to the partitioning of Vietnam? Of course, that's hard for many Vietnamese to take. But is it really more than history demanded of the Germans, whose society was, after all, mature and a million times more integrated than Vietnam's? And don't we have a perfect precedent in Korea? This tiny sliver of a country that has been partitioned for most of its life—at one time into three parts by the French and before that into hundreds of parts by its own warlords—is its present temporary partition really so high a price to pay, if in return for what we purchase stability in Asia? And if the price of refusing partition is the undermining of that truce line upon which we build all our hopes for an Oriental reconciliation? Be realistic," he says to us idealists; "This

Moral Argument and the War in Vietnam

is not a perfect world by any measure, and it just so happens that history is all against us. We are doing everything we know how to do to change man's fate by making peace *practical*. We do this not only in the teeth of Red China and these scandalous persistent Vietnamese guerrillas, but here at home we must also fend off you softheads who want an impossible peace and those hardheads yonder who want an unthinkable war."

The point has been made by Zbigniew Brzezinski, director of the Research Institute on Communist Affairs at Columbia University, consultant to the State Department on policy planning, and one of the foremost of our cold war scholars.

> The long road to international morality leads through the creation of international order, and international order necessitates, first of all, the creation of international stability. We can only create international stability if all the major powers in the world accept the principle that in the nuclear age no side can change the political *status quo* through the use of force and through direct challenge to another side. We restrained ourselves from doing that in Hungary, in spite of our policy of liberation. The Soviets learned that lesson more painfully in Cuba. That lesson is still to be learned in many parts of the world, but I believe that the cause of peace, the cause of global reconciliation, the cause of international adjustment, requires, first, the creation of stability, and stability in Asia will not be achieved by American disengagement or Chinese expansion.[6]

Some of us object: You have not proved that this Vietnam war is China's fault. Far from it. Even now, your gravest charge concerns a few aircraft flying from Hanoi and a few thousand technicians who only repair American-bombed roads and railroads at the Yunnan border. This war in Vietnam is at bottom a revolution, we say, and it came not from China's export commisariat, but from the torpid colonial feudalism of that society. No one at all sensitive to the history of Vietnam could ever question this.

But for such an argument, there may now be a quite intriguing answer.

It is important to be clear first about what the answer would *not* be. It would *not* be that China is directly at fault for this war; *not* that Hanoi is acting on Peking's orders; *not* that Hanoi commanded and is directing the performance of a puppet in the south; *not* that the NLF, instead of being revolutionary, is only a new-fashioned invasion force. . . .

It grows clear that the War Room may very well know what the picket line knows: We face revolution, not invasion. . . . We may at least have found a different picture of Washington's beliefs about the war. It may not really be the inside view, then, that Comrade Mao made a secret decision years ago and passed it through the mountain gates of Yunnan Province into the hands of Ho Chi Minh, who sent it on south to a hidden headquarters deep in Nam-Bo, where the old Vietminh guns were hanging fire for the high sign.

228

Can Ethics, Ideology, and History Meet?

The answer might simply be: So what?

Or it might be that *this does not matter!* American policies cannot be asked to react to speculations about chain-of-command structures, they must react to *events.* And the very plain fact of the matter is this: If the Chinese *did* control Hanoi, and through Hanoi, the National Liberation Front, *then the situation in Vietnam would look exactly as it does.* Whether we confront in Vietnam a replica or an extension of the Chinese will, whether this revolution is an intentional or accidental copy of China's policy or the thing in itself, makes absolutely no difference at all. China is the threat. The appearance of her spirit within the forbidden zone, on the wrong side of the global line of truce, or whatever time and through whatever agency, must be denied. Thus, to speak of the historical "origins" of the war is politically frivolous. In substance, in aspiration, and in effect, Chinese-like or plain, straight Chinese, this war remains indistinguishable from the war the Chinese want. The consequence is that it must be treated as though it *were* a Chinese war.

This leads us to the quite unexpected but nevertheless entirely reasonable complaint that even if China does *not* control Hanoi and the NLF, *it nevertheless remains true that she should be controlling them.* The politics of cold war peacekeeping makes it essential for major powers to control the events within their sphere of influence. For a major state not to have control over minor confederate states is inexcusable. Without that control, the means through which conflict can be managed no longer exist, and statesmen are faced with an unpredictable environment. Less control means less stability and hence greater danger for everyone; less certainty about the perceptions and inclinations of the other side forces diplomacy to be more guarded and restrictive and edgy. For all its old bitterness about West Germany, for example, the Soviet Union would no doubt be horrified to discover an East German plot to spring an invasion over the Wall, or even a few good blows of sabotage beneath it. And the same would hold for us: Park will very well stay put in South Korea; Chian will grumble his bellyful in Taipeh but he shall go no further. We guarantee this. China must learn to make similar guarantees. It thus becomes essential, *in the name of peace*, for China to commit the expansionist crime of which she stands accused. And the American refusal to accept the NLF as the responsible agent in this war begins to seem not so obtuse at all; it appears instead to be an almost exquisite diplomatic brilliancy, for this refusal is perhaps a concealed attempt to extend a *responsible Chinese authority* into Vietnam and over the Communist parties to the south.

Surely this sounds too Machiavellian. But on January 30, 1966, in what was described as a "major" foreign policy speech, George Ball, then Under Secretary of State, said:

A main force of the [East-West] struggle has shifted recently from Europe

229

Moral Argument and the War in Vietnam

to Asia because the Soviet Union, having grown powerful, has begun to have a stake in the *status quo*. The purpose of the forcible containment of Communist China is to induce a similar change in its outlook. . . . This is the issue in Viet-Nam. This is what we are fighting for. This is why we are there.[7]

One would not fight Vietnamese rebels in order to "induce a change" in China's outlook unless one believed either (*a*) that China controlled those rebels, or (*b*) that China, whether she controls them or not, bears the ultimate responsibility for their behavior. We have already noted that Washington probably rules out the first premise. That leaves us with the second. To inform China that she is responsible for these Vietnamese events is quite openly to demand of China that she take control over those who make them. That is, our Vietnam policy warns China that she must expand her influence, accept the discipline of the cold war, and impose that discipline on her Vietnamese friends. . . .

We explore one level of the Cold Warrior's Vietnam story and discover a stronger box within the propaganda box. Uncritically, we accept the most elemental Western assumptions about the origin and progress of the cold war. Manipulating by means of this ideology the main political features of the war for South Vietnam, we find ourselves in the possession of a conflict which no longer seems so senselessly holy. The war may now seem to be merely practical.

If the cold war is really what most Americans consider it to be, then the cold war is necessary. If it is necessary, then it may very well be necessary for America to maintain her hold over South Vietnam.

So we have to reach inside our cold war truths to see if they do not conceal some other truths. We have to be very naive and ask: What is this cold war all about? And is it really necessary?. . . .

[For the next 80 pages Mr. Oglesby lays out his analysis of the cold war. The excerpts here now pick up at the end of that discussion, and then move back to the case of Vietnam.]

The United States has shown in Europe that it knows how to reconstruct bombed-out capitalist economies. But it has not shown in the Third World that it can develop Western-style political economies: in preindustrial countries where there is no capitalist class structure, no entrepreneurial tradition, no skilled urbanized work force, and no internalized commitment to capitalist life-styles, the arrival of the American corporatist is in fact a disaster. Preoccupied with the extraction of resources for export and the immediate exploitation of all opportunities without regard to the damage this does to others, our business statesmanship may justly claim to have excited the underdeveloped world's growing revolutionary demands. But it is nothing but double talk for this same statesmanship to pretend that it assents to those demands—the demands for unobstructed opportunity to develop the natural wealth of the nation, for time and freedom to cultivate a national economic style, for exemption from the cold war, for political independence.

America is not baby-simple, and her imperialism has other moods. There is, for example, the apparently genuine effort of some AID (and even some CIA) people to foster social reform under frustrating and often dangerous conditions; there is the Peace Corps, which, as badly as it has been abused, no doubt embodies a popular American willingness to be of help to other people; there is the Asian Rice Institute in the Philippines, a joint effort of the Rockefeller and Ford foundations which may prove very valuable to the people of Asia. If these represented the behavioral core, the main driving force of American foreign policy, a political humanist could throw his efforts behind that policy without much hesitation. But all imperialisms have produced their mercy angels, and one has to conclude that the good people of AID, the Peace Corps, the Rice Institute, are performing only marginal and auxiliary roles. The America which the rising world most deeply experiences is the America of United Fruit and the U.S. Marines, cool plunder, and the napalm fist. One may wish that the Peace Corps were the State Department. It is not even a match for the CIA's third string. America is not the friend but the enemy of that deformed, uneven, frustrated, and frightening revolution whose fundamental motives seem so compelling and whose fundamental claims seem so just.

It is hard to see how it could be otherwise with the corporate state. Adolf Berle, Jr., who has been a sympathetically insightful analyst of American corporatism, has himself recognized that "preachments about the value of private enterprise and investment and the usefulness of foreign capital [in the underdeveloped countries] were . . . a little silly. . . . Foreign and/or private investment may industrialize, may even increase production, and still leave the masses in as bad a shape as ever."[8] It may seem strange to hear as much from Berle. But worried corporate capitalists are not at all hard to find. It is often from them, in fact, that we get the most perceptive and realistic descriptions of Free World imperialism's effects on the backward. Gerassi quotes the 1958 statement by J. P. Grace, Jr., President of Grace & Co., whose Latin American profits are immense: "Chile, Peru, Mexico and Bolivia," said Grace, "have seen the export prices of their metals drop from 40 percent to 50 percent during the last several years. At the same time, since 1951, the average price that Latin America pays for its imports from the United States has risen about 11 percent."[9]

The editors of *Fortune* have pointed out that the long-term debt of the underdeveloped countries, some $40 billion in 1966, costs $4.5 billion annually in interest charges and consumes one eighth of all their foreign-trade earnings. "To get enough foreign exchange for what they import [underdeveloped countries] have to borrow more, which in turn means they will have to meet greater servicing costs."[10] Sanz de Santamaria, chairman of the Inter-American Committee of the Alliance for Progress, has made the same point: [Latin American] debt amortization alone will require $1.7 billion this year [1966], thus preempting 16 percent of all export earnings."[11] Josué de Castro, one of Brazil's foremost economists and a former president of the United States Food and Agriculture Organization, has written of the Alliance for Progress that it "is nothing but pure colonialism. . . . Colonialism is the only cause of hunger in Latin America."[12]

That might seem a bitter exaggeration. But there is only a difference of tone, not of substance, between that statement and the following passages from the editorial page of the *Wall Street Journal*:

> The industrial nations have added nearly $2 billion to their reserves, which now total $52 billion. At the same time, the reserves of the less-developed group not only have stopped rising, but have declined some $200 million. To analysts such as Britain's [Barbara] Ward, the significance of such statistics is clear: the economic gap is rapidly widening "between a white, complacent highly bourgeois, very wealthy, very small North Atlantic elite and everybody else, and this is not a very comfortable heritage to leave one's children." "Everybody else" includes approximately two thirds of the population of the earth, spread through about 100 nations. . . . Many diplomats and economists view the implications as overwhelmingly—and dangerously—political. Unless the present decline can be reversed, these analysts fear, the United States and other wealthy industrial powers of the West face the distinct possibility, in the words of Miss Ward, "of a sort of international class war."[13]

But there is rarely any indication that this problem is *caused* by someone, that it is in preponderant part caused by American corporations, that this problem (instead of communism) is what lies behind Third-World revolution. Indeed, there is always an implicit suggestion that the man who can solve this problem best is none other than the Free World capitalist himself. It seems to be certainly true that many aspects of the development problem could be solved by that figure—if he would just remove himself from the picture. But how will he be persuaded to do that? To surrender in someone else's name the immense profits which he considers it his main business to make? Further, how is his disengagement to be achieved by a government which has always considered his foreign successes to be America's domestic successes, and which is unalterably committed to the political ideology of free enterprise?

Consider that the capitalist's commitment to capitalism does not entail a commitment to other capitalists. The ideology obliges him only to *compete*, and the interwoven morality obliges him to win *as much as he can*. If his dominance is to be restricted, his victories contained, that will only happen through the independent competitive action of other capitalists. In theory, this is indeed how the system is supposed to operate. New entrepreneurs, new capitalists, steadily emerge to create and wield new power, and thus continuously reconstitute the dynamics of the open, free market. But we have noticed a problem: Even in our own supposedly model economy, there is an accelerating breakout from this theoretically internalized and permanent system of competition-based limits. The competition is won, and the winner gets stronger; lost, and the loser gets weaker. Power condenses in the hands of steadily smaller, steadily more integrated and collaborative victor groups. And the federal government, not so very long ago the American businessman's arch enemy, now becomes his delighted and delightful partner. Without the federal government's Special Forces and Marines, United Fruit could not dominate Guatemala. Without AID and the World Bank and the supportive hands of the Commerce and State Departments, the corporations could not multinationalize themselves. Without the federal government's sugar subsidies, the sugar companies could not maintain their lethal grip on the economies of small states from the Caribbean to the Central Pacific. Without the State Department's cold war sales campaign and the active support of the Defense Department's weapon hucksters, General Dynamics could not continue to fatten on arms sales to Europe. Without big government, big business would be lost.

Will someone claim that the appetite for dominance which stimulated the growth of this corporate state will restrain itself when it goes on foreign cruises? David Rockefeller may very well exhort his fellow businessmen to "demonstrate [to Latin Americans] that a new brand of capitalism has evolved, based on the concept of a fair profit for free enterprise combined with social responsibility to the community as a whole."[14] And he may very well hope that someone takes his advice, for the businessman who does so, this same Rockefeller will crush. The idea of capitalism is that the "fair profit" will not have to be determined by a Christian capitalist alone with his morality. It will be set through his act of competing with *other* capitalists. Then where are the competitive capitalists of the Third World? And how are they to be produced? And who is to produce them?

Nothing the American businessman can see in past, present, or future will persuade him to forgo whatever commercial advantages may come to hand. *And for him, the Third World is a commercial advantage.* The Third World is that exposed, unprotected gold mine where his investment dollars fare better than anywhere else. Why should he want to change that? The United Fruit Company may be "enlightened," may (sometimes does, sometimes does not) build roads, houses, schools, and hospitals in model company towns on its plantations in the "banana republics." But why should it want to surrender its privileged position there, all in the name of some fuzzy humanitarian ideal? Or why should it rejoice to see the emergence of local capitalists who may some day get strong enough to give it some competition? Since when is the capitalist his colleague's keeper?

As ordinary, intelligent men giving the rest of the world a look, the American corporatists can see the truth as well as anyone else. They can even be concerned about the bloody implications of what they see,

233

Moral Argument and the War in Vietnam

and they might even have an ideological, impersonal preference for a Third World, in the best sense, Americanized. But to build that "American" Vietnam, that dynamic free-enterprising Brazil, that middle-class Guatemala—if that indeed is what these countries want—that is the job of independent, unharassed, unmanipulated Vietnamese, Brazilians and Guatemalans; it can no more be the job of American capitalists than the building of the American nation could have been the job of British mercantilists. For matters to stand otherwise, the Yankee free-enterpriser would for the first time in his life have to work for his competition. He would have to recognize a difference of interest, a dual economic good, and take sides against himself. He would have to supplant his money ethic with a social ethic. He would have to change entirely his style of thought and action. In a word, he would have to become a revolutionary socialist whose aim was the destruction of the present American hegemony. I see no reason to suppose that such a metamorphosis is about to transfigure this Yankee.

The agents of change in this world are today, as they have always been, those whose battered lives stand most in need of change. The entrepreneurs of social progress are those whose condition requires it. And at bottom, this revolution is nothing but the emergence of competitors who employ the only means of competition available to them. Revolution is the collective free enterprise of the collectively dispossessed.

. . . . If cold war anticommunism is most basically an ideological mask for Free World imperialism, then one should be able to show somehow that the issue of the Vietnam War is not Western freedom versus Eastern slavery but foreign versus local control of Vietnam—to show, that is, that the war is being fought to determine how and by whom the Vietnamese political economy is going to be developed. And since the United States has committed itself so unreservedly to Vietnam's Free World salvation, this line of analysis is also obliged to show that Vietnam is somehow crucial for the security and growth of the American commercial state.

It is precisely on this point that the imperialism theory confronts a simple, serious objection: Are American commercial interests in that very poor, very backward part of the world so substantial as to justify so dangerous and unlimited a war? The war is now costing Americans upward of $20 billion a year. How many years will it take for a "saved" Vietnam to start paying dividends on that kind of military investment?

. . . But probe the case more curiously. We shall find that America's Vietnam policy does not merely illustrate American imperialism, it is a paradigm instance of it; and that in its fusion of imperialist motive and anti-Communist ideology, the war is not only exemplary, it is also climactic.

There are four important points, argued below in ascending order of importance.

First, a direct American commercial interest in Vietnam exists. For the most part it is potential. That makes it no less real.

In its issue of January 1, 1966, *Newsweek* ran an essay called: "Saigon: A Boomtown for U.S. Businessmen." A similar piece by Edmund K. Faltermayer appeared in the March 1966 issue of *Fortune* under the title "The Surprising Assets of South Viet-Nam's Economy". . . . "A South Viet-Nam preserved from communism," Faltermayer wrote, "has the potential to become one of the richest nations in Southeast Asia." He notes that the country could become an exporter of sugar and cotton, both of which it now imports; that it exported a record 83,000 tons of rubber in 1961, and could easily surpass that record under normal conditions; that the Mekong Delta, the "rice bowl" which now produces about four million tons of rice annually, could produce 12 to 15 million tons. It is not by magic that the rice, the rubber, the sugar, the cotton—and the promising industrial crops, jute, ramie and kenaf—will come leaping from the ground into the holds of cargo ships. That will require capital, whether the socialist or the capitalist kind.

The capitalist pioneers are already staking their claims Chase Manhattan and the Bank of America have opened branch offices in Saigon.The New York firm of Parsons & Whittemore holds 18 percent interest in a $5-million American-managed paper mill at Bien Hoa. Foremost Dairies of California has controlling interest in a new condensed milk plant and half-interest in a new textile mill. Another textile mill has been partly financed by the Johnson International Corporation. The American Trading Co. and Brownell Lane Engineering Co. are selling and servicing heavy equipment—bulldozers, tractors, trucks, and railroad locomotives—and averaging 20 to 30 percent returns on their investments.[15] . . . .

"Never before," said *Newsweek,* "have U.S. businessmen followed their [*sic!*] troops to war on such a scale.". . . .

All new frontiers need their Paul Bunyans. Faltermayer offers a strong candidate in a New York entrepreneur named Herbert Fuller, head of an investor group which since 1958 has been promoting a $10-million sugar mill for the coastal city of Tuy Hoa:

> When the troops arrive to clear the area, as they sooner or later must, the American capitalist will literally be one step behind them. "I am in it for the money," Fuller says. "We could get back our investment in two years." Like all entrepreneurs, Fuller once again is pushing ahead with his plans because he assumes the U.S. is now committed to saving Vietnam.

But so what? Why is it so wrong for our businessmen to be right behind "their" troops? There is nothing strange about the pursuit of profit and opportunity, and that the businessmen should at once occupy, settle on. and begin to develop the ground just cleared by our troops does not mean that it is for them that the troops are there. Does it?

Moral Argument and the War in Vietnam

We encounter a problem of vision. It is hard to see these particular businessmen as being in any way crucial to the Vietnam drama. Their appearance in it seems incidental—important perhaps, but not especially significant. The war would be the same with or without them. It is being fought for freedom or to hold back the Communists. It is not being fought for this Herbert Fuller, "American capitalist."

No doubt. If Fuller decided the Tuy Hoa project was a bad bet and went back to New York, another coastal city, no one thinks the Marines would forgo the conquest of Tuy Hoa. But what do we suppose "freedom" means? And what is the real purpose of keeping the Communists back? Our functional definition of a free country is clear from our behavior. The definition says that a country is free when Americans like Fuller are free to do business in it if they have the skill and the drive to do so. It is free when there are native counterparts of Fuller. It is free when there is free enterprise. When there is *no* free enterprise, the country is Communist. It cannot be doubted that Vietnam's importance lies far more basically in its geographical and *historical* position than in its inherent commercial potentials, whether immediate or long-term. But, as we shall see, that is only because Vietnam is imagined to be the key to larger areas—areas whose commercial accessibility is important to us, and which will or will not themselves be "free," depending on the possibility of our doing business in them. . . .

Second, the militarized economy demands a militarized politics; a militarized politics demands a militarized economy. Vietnam, as conflict colony, helps turn this wheel.

Those who argue that the Vietnam War *must* have been forced upon us since it is so uneconomical do not grasp the economics of state capitalism. The economic effects of the war are anything but unambiguous. The war generates very real fiscal management problems and disturbing anomalies in the pattern of foreign exchange. But over all, the war is good for the economy because the economy is addicted to federal subsidy in general and to military subsidy in particular. It appears that we *have* to spend, because what a high-employment economy produces has to be vended. Whether it goes into the sweet life or the limbo of government silos, the product has to go some place and it has to be paid for. Consider, then, a key economic fact about the defense product: *It is not produced at the expense of recognized domestic necessities.* It is not as if Americans are standing in queues to purchase automobiles, which, for the sake of tanks, are going unbuilt. The opposite comes closer to being the case: If it were not for the tanks, the planes, the submarines, the missiles—where would the economy be? Which is very much like asking: If it were not for the heroin, where would the junkies be? Obviously: in hospitals undergoing very painful therapy. Perhaps even of a revolutionary nature.

One does not claim that the Vietnamese War was escalated only to cheer up an overblown, dour economy with that "external" and "expanded" market which it could not otherwise procure. But what if the Vietnam War ended and China said, Have it your way? What if the cold war faded and faded until one day someone noticed it had disappeared? What would become of the gargantuan Lockheed with its $500 million in research and development contracts alone? What would become of the intensively specialized scientists, engineers, technicians, administrators, and line workers it employs? Or of the tens of thousands of shopkeepers, middlemen, leaders, and suppliers their salaries keep in business? Where are the concrete plans, the great Congressional debates, the enabling legislation on the management of defense-to-civilian industrial conversion? Who is hammering out the answers?. . . .

Look at Europe, where there is no claim that the "threat" is increasing. The reverse is true: more trade with East Europe and the U.S.S.R., moves on both sides of the Curtain (of which de Gaulle's in the West and Ceausecu's in the East are only the most dramatic) to bring Europe toward accord and integration. Yet in this atmosphere of calm and confidence, after several years of the preaching and the apparent practice of coexistence, what is America's policy on European militarization? Over the past fifteen years we have given or sold to other countries some $35 billion worth of military equipment. Since mid-1961, military export sales have run to more than $9 billion, and the profit to American defense suppliers totals about $1 billion—nicely concentrated in the hands of three big and highly influential firms, General Dynamics, Lockheed, and McDonnell. Overseas military sales for 1965 were about $2 billion and, let the cold war thaw as it pleases, they will run on at that high rate into the foreseeable future.[16] Why does this happen, if the threat is diminishing? It happens because our military sales abroad represent one of our major handles on our chronic balance-of-payments deficit. These sales are actively promoted by the Pentagon, which seems to care little more about the buyers' need and ability to pay for guns than any ordinary used-car salesman: The goodness of the guns is a good enough need, and if the price seems high, never mind, another part of our government will put up an easy-term loan. The number-one salesman—the Pentagon calls him a "negotiator"—is Henry J. Kuss, Jr., Deputy Assistant Secretary of Defense for International Logistics Negotiations. In May 1965, in recognition of his section's "intensive sales effort," Kuss was awarded the Meritorious Civilian Service Medal.[17] . . .

So it goes. Apparently we are not really proud of this sort of thing, but what can we do? There stand the bright weapons in a row. Behind them stand their engineers. Behind the engineers, the executives, who serve on presidential committees and travel often to the capital. Behind the executives, the booming system for which they work, for which they speak, in which they have their being. The system must boom, the executives must have their being, the military engineers must design, the riveters must rivet, and the shining bright weapons must therefore

Moral Argument and the War in Vietnam

be *marketed*. And that marketing is easier if there is a certain uneasiness in the world, a little tension and anxiety. Who could market aspirin if there were no headaches? Yet what is more antiheadache than aspirin? Preventive aspirin, these sleek fighter aircraft. But the world should not forget what a headache is. So to go with that conceptual beauty called "preventive war," we have preventive *threats*, just big enough to put an edge on things and keep the system from coming unstuck. . . .

Sad to say, we have had to watch Russia's glory fade, her power to inspire our capitalism decline. Besides, when we have put 7,000 long-range nuclear rockets in West Europe alone,[18] we have perhaps began to saturate a good market. But we are in luck, for new Russias keep entering the cold war market. Today we have China—and therefore Vietnam. And in the wings, tomorrow's starlets—Guatemala? the Philippines? Iran?—are even now trying on their black-pajama *campesino* costumes and rehearsing their most splenetic Marxist curses. And the Third World is crawling with CIA and Special Forces talent scouts.

Third, the strategic heart of the matter.

Increasingly from the turn of the century, American policy has been preoccupied with the problem of pacifying the global commercial environment. As early as the mid-1890s we had already become the world's leading manufacturer and therefore internationalist in spite of ourselves. It had become critical to us that our foreign markets should not be disturbed. How were the required stability and freedom of access to be won? . . . .

We were steadily trying, that is, with a really remarkable constancy, to establish that political integration of the Big Powers which finally *was* established—at least temporarily—as one of the chief results of World War II. De Gaulle's France portends change today, and perhaps (it is debatable) Gaullism represents genuinely different ideas about how European power should be arranged and what its fundamental goals should be. But at least well into the mid-sixties, the postwar world was dominated by explicit or implicit alliances that linked the United States, Britain, France, Germany, and Japan into one another's economies, all our partners sharing our belief in a democratic-liberal political philosophy, and all of them more or less willing to accept and support our views on the Communist threat.

This system has two separate but integrated domains, the Atlantic and the Pacific. As Germany is the pivotal state of the Atlantic domain, Japan is the pivot of the Pacific. It is the situation of this Japan which we shall now examine more closely.

The first point is that Japan is a traditionally vigorous trader, one which has long been important to the commerce of the United States. . . .

The second point is that a healthy, westward-looking Japan is just as crucial to the containing of China as containing China is to the health and Western-orientation of Japan. To understand the essentials of this

238

dynamic, we have to unpack the meaning of this concept "containment.". . .

What is the nature of the Chinese Communist threat? As should be perfectly clear, the threat is not basically military. No real threat ever is. China's power to aggress against her neighbors is not to be doubted. But two other things are also not to be doubted. One is that she would be all but defenseless against the kind of strategic nuclear attack which a clear act of aggression would surely provoke. The other is that she has never attacked for spoils, nor without provocation. (The Korean "invasion" came only after repeated U.S. bombings of Manchuria, the Tibetan "invasion" only after a clear mutiny of the theocracy, the Indian "invasion" as a result of a very plain border dispute in which she had by no means the worst of the argument.)

The threat is political. And as with any political threat, the guts of it are economic. It has long been a statesmanly wisdom in the West that any China which could organize herself would be a China indeed. Only recall Napoleon's words about the slumbering giant who will awaken to shake the world, Lenin's observation that "for world communism the road to Paris lies through Peking and Calcutta." She has the people, the resources, the energy, and the ingenuity to be—what? Given equity in what time can purchase, what time will inevitably bring, China could become the peer of America, Europe, and the U.S.S.R. What she lacked for centuries was order, a sense of national unity, and positive control over her inherent resources. The people—industrious—and the land—rich—have been there all along, waiting for some iron-minded Johnny Appleseed. . . .

To dare to say anything conclusive about China's economy one would have to base it on a lengthy analysis, and a major reason for its lengthiness would be the need to explain why nothing exactly conclusive could be said. But we need not be so technical here. What is important is that no one denies that for the first time in centuries there *is* such a thing as a Chinese nation, that it *has* an economy, and that this economy has established contact with the intrinsic potential of the land and the people. That potential, plagued as it is with natural and political difficulties, is as great as it needs to be. Reflect then, as our statesmen surely must on the China of a hundred or even fifty years from now. Imagine a world in which creative action—economic, political, cultural—is no longer so densely and disproportionately concentrated in the North Atlantic global core—a world, that is, in which an independent and dynamic Asia *exists*.

Our response to the mammoth fact of Chinese revolution—something which has nothing at all to do with communism, but rather with the independent organization of China and her acquisition of modern fire—has not been exactly pragmatic. First we chose to believe that it was not happening. . . . China was still there, however, coming on like a freight train.

Moral Argument and the War in Vietnam

And there sits Japan in the very beam of the Manchurian industrial headlamp, *quite powerless to move.* (A roughly comparable situation would be one in which England found herself politically misallied against a Europe united to the Urals, a battering ram.) What are Japan's options? Isolationism vis-à-vis China was never even thinkable. Whether coerced by future political apprehensions or lured by present commercial opportunities, Japan is already China's foremost trade partner,* surpassing even the Soviet Union (with which, adroitly enough, Japan's businessmen are also arranging increased commerce.) It is not as if Japan could pretend that China is just not there. It would be strange economics, politics, and history if she tried to. The only questions that are at all open are how much, when, and on what terms. Most specifically: Will Japan contrive to maintain her present pro-American political bias? Will she submit to world history's commonest law that the Higher Economics determines the Lower Politics and so cast in with Peking? Or will she try instead the Greek way of golden-meansmanship and make of herself a bridge between the two supergiants, well knowing (as one Japanese has remarked) that bridges get walked on?

It will be clear what the United States expects Japan to do. . . .

We now ask: Does Vietnam bear materially on this drama? The key facts would seem to be the following: (1) Two of China's principal import needs are rubber and rice, improved access to which will in some measure accelerate her rate of development and thus her overall power. (2) The two principal export commodities of a normalized South Vietnam will be rubber and rice. (3) Japan's unemployment figure is an irreducible one percent. Increased industrialization will draw more workers from the farm to the factory. Urbanization of labor will reduce yield of unmechanized farms at the same time that the resultant higher purchasing power will raise demand. (4) Japan is traditionally a food importer, and she is becoming a greater one, her food imports being on the rise both proportionately and absolutely. Of 1962's total $5.6 billion imports, $700 million (12 percent) went for food; of 1963's $6.7 billion total, $1 billion (16 percent) went for food; of 1964's $7.9 billion total, $1.3 billion (17 percent) went for food.[20] (5) Japanese are the world's foremost shipbuilders and among its strongest steelmakers and textilers. They need markets. China needs ships, steel, and textiles. A developing Vietnam will want steel certainly and probably ships, but may be inclined to protect her textile industry.

Let us join a final fact with a professional observation. The fact is reported by the Indochina scholar Bernard B. Fall:

DRVN [North Vietnamese] trade with Japan, after a period of coolness when

---

* Japan's sales to China, $245 million in 1965, are rising annually at a rate matched only by her purchases from China. Exports (and imports) from her China trade from 1960 through 1965 are as follows (in millions of U.S. dollars): 2.7 (20.7); 16.0 (30.9); 38.5 (46.0); 62.4 (72.6); 152.8 (157.8); 245.3 (224.7).[19]

Japan decided to pay war reparations to South Viet-Nam only, has reached important proportions that might well provoke concern in the United States. Trade rose from about $10 million in 1959 to more than $40 million in 1961-62 and involves such items as chemicals, machinery of all kinds, and four seagoing 5,000-ton cargo ships and one of 2,000 tons; for these, North Viet-Nam pays in raw materials, notably coal.[21]

We can simplify this.

What the West faces in the Pacific is the formation of a regional economic system (*a*) whose potential and power are inherent in the Pacific situation itself, (*b*) which must include Japan, and (*c*) which would quite naturally be dominated by China. This is the "threat." America feels it most keenly because among the Western powers she now enjoys the dominant economic position in the Pacific, because her postwar Asian investment in blood and treasure is steep, and because she is by any measure the most international of the international states. Our purpose, then, is to frustrate the drawing together of this geoeconomic system by imposing political and military barricades between its elements and by holding out the alternative of other economic configurations. Thus, the struggle to hold South Vietnam. . . .

The *fourth* point—for its powers of commentary on our culture, it seems to me, much the most important—is coiled up in a not very puzzling puzzle. . . .

The military solution to the problem of Vietnam is not working; the attempt to achieve such a solution worsens and may begin to cripple our political position in Asia; and the really important and defensible eastern salients of the Western world—India, Thailand, the Philippines, Korea, Japan—drift every day a bit closer to that distinctively Oriental future which our policy-makers can hardly fail to see.

The government's computers have been no guard against a loss of control which may very well be unparalleled. Why does this happen?

This happens because the ideology that demanded and vindicated this "necessary" act of war continues to demand and vindicate the act even after it has overreached its necessity and become, on its own terms, *irrational.*What Western power opposes is the anti-imperialist social revolution of the poor. But in a time in which Western liberals have oversold themselves on their own slick humanism-*cum*-realpolitics, that position is not easy to sloganize. We have ourselves lately cursed imperialism—the more primitive imperialism of others; have ourselves once glorified revolution—our own. Perhaps because of this, America's leaders seem to have doubted that their subjects had the stomach for a repressive counterrevolutionary and imperialist war. Such a war, since it had to be fought, would have to be sweetened with a different name. Imperialism is thus rechristened as anticommunism, and our foe is instantly transformed from a human being into a pawn, a dupe, or an outright hard core agent of that International Communist Conspiracy

Moral Argument and the War in Vietnam

whose ultimate objective (so we are guaranteed) is the conquest of America.

This theory of the International Communist Conspiracy is not the hysterical old maid that many leftists seem to think it is. It has had an intimate affair with reality and it has some history on its mind when it speaks. There *is* a revolution which *is* international—one only has to count the perturbations and look at a map to see as much. In some less than technical sense, this revolution is "communistic," if by that we mean that it will probably not produce capitalist economies,that it will probably create autarkic and controlled economies, authoritarian central governments, programs of forced-march wealth accumulation, and the forcible dismantling of rich elites. And if not by any means melodramatically conspiratorial, the several national liberation movements, in their early stages especially, *do* make an effort to coordinate themselves; they do so, pathetically unadept, because they consider their enemy to be internationally coordinated himself—a view which is entirely correct. And the extent to which this revolution aims at terminating the masterdom of the rich, an aim which automatically implicates America, the revolution *does* aim itself at America—it aims itself, rather, at an America which most Americans have forgotten about: Rockefeller, Englehard, U.S.A. There is just no use being deluded about that. But what is added on for pure political effect is that ugly edge of clandestinity, pointless and merciless ambition, that cloud of diabolism which has nothing to do with the sustaining force of the revolution itself. And what is *subtracted* from the reality—much more important—is the *source* of the ferment, the *cause* of the anger, the supreme question of the *justice* of the rebellion. What this theory gives us is a portrait whose outlines are not unreal, but whose colors have been changed from human blacks and browns and yellows into devil's red, and whose background has been entirely erased. Thus, the theory wildly disorganizes and mismanages the very real history that allows it to survive. And if it lies within the power of an idea to pervert a nation's generosity and curse its children, then the widespread American acceptance of this view of revolution may forecast a bitter future for us all.

It is through the ideology of cold war anticommunism (a cynic might abbreviate it to CWAC and call it "cwackery") that the masters of American power have rationalized and quite successfully dissembled their opposition to the Third World's diffuse and uneven movement for independence, in the long bitter period between the Civil War and World War II. After years of perfection, and applied now to a remote world familiar to Americans only as the well-controlled mass media see fit to make it so, one has to say of this ideology that it is more effective now than ever. It entirely rearranges the moral terms of the encounter between the rich and the poor, and in one stroke deprives the revolutionary of the very right to name and explain himself. He stands already named—a criminal; already explained—an enemy. He is *not* the revolutionary which he pretends to be. The *real* social revolutionaries it seems, are ourselves. This other one is a fraud, whether willingly so or not; and, whether or not *he* knows it, *we* happen to know that he is an imposter, an intruder on the scene of social change whose real hope, real demand—is the destruction of our country. Whatever he may think, we know that he will never be satisfied with Moscow or Peking, Havana or Algiers, Caracas or Saigon. He is out to get us—Kansas City, Birmingham, Washington, D.C. So it follows that the inner, central, driving theme of the drama being acted out in Vietnam's jungles is nothing less than the question of our own national survival. This is the theory by which the war has been explained to us.

If it is a good theory, then it is good *absolutely*. If it is correct to say that our national well-being requires the defeat of the NLF, then the NLF will have to be defeated. The explanation will remain correct regardless of how hard it might be to carry out its implicit commands. Preserving the well-being of the nation is an overriding and transcendent objective. It is not possible to imagine that such an objective can be qualified or repealed *even for one moment* by any other objective. It is an imperative. The awesome consequence of this is that *any struggle that is rationalized in its name is one from which we cannot withdraw.*

Notes

1 Quoted in Maurice J. Goldbloom, "The Fulbright Revolt," *Commentary*, September 1966.

2 Wilfred Burchett, *Vietnam, Inside Story of the Guerrilla War*, International Publishers, New York, 1965, esp. pp. 109-194.

3 Bernard B. Fall, *The Two Viet-Nams*, Frederick A. Praeger, New York, 1963, rev. eds. 1964, 1966; Pall Mall Press, London, 1963, p. 318.

4 *The New York Times (NYT)*, August 10, 1966.

5 Gary Porter, "Globalism—The Ideology of Total World Involvement," *The Viet-Nam Reader*, eds., Marcus G. Raskin and Bernard B. Fall, Random House (Vintage book), New York, 1965, p. 322.

6 *Political Science Quarterly*, April 1965.

7 *NYT*, February 1, 1966.

8 John Gerassi, *The Great Fear in Latin America*, The Macmillan Company (Collier book), New York, 1965, p. 275.

9 *Ibid.*, p. 28.

10 *Fortune* magazine, June 1966.

11 *Economic Affairs*, June 1, 1966.

12 Gerassi, p. 263.

13 *Wall Street Journal*, May 12, 1965.

14 David Rockefeller, "What Free Enterprise Means to Latin America," *Foreign Affairs*, April 1966.

15 *Newsweek*, January 1, 1966.

16 Eugene J. McCarthy, "The U.S.: Supplier of Weapons to the World," *Saturday Review*, July 9, 1966.

17 *Ibid.*

18 *NYT*, September 18, 1966.

19 International Monetary Fund, *Direction of World Trade* (monthly). For an expert analysis of such trade figures, see Alexander Eckstein, *Communist China's Economic Growth and Foreign Trade*, McGraw-Hill Book Company, New York, 1966, pp. 200-212.

20 *Direction of World Trade*.

21 Fall, p. 194.

We Cannot Accept A Communist Seizure of Vietnam*

by Robert A. Scalapino

No doubt, it was easier for the United States, two decades ago, to assume major responsibility for the defense and development of Western Europe than it is to undertake a similar role in Asia today. We were, then, fresh and idealistic—and, above all, "our world" was at stake.

"Europocentrism" and "spheres of influence" have been the two central elements shaping American foreign policy in the recent past. It is not surprising that many Americans, including a significant proportion of our intellectual community, find it difficult—even painful—to adjust to a rapidly changing world in which these themes are no longer sufficient.

We face a challenge in Asia similar in its proportions to that which we faced in Europe twenty years ago. In this sense, the Asia-Pacific area is unique. Only in this region are we confronted with the immediate necessity of joining with others to create a political equilibrium—participating in the establishment of a balance of power if peace is to be underwritten. Latin America and Africa present complex problems affecting their peoples and the world, but neither continent contains the combination of factors which made Europe in its time—and Asia today—so crucial to global peace.

With this background in mind, let us look briefly at current trends in Asia. At the outset, I am prepared to make an embarrassing confession. In a period when being a fervent disciple of gloom is "in," I must admit to cautious optimism. I would assert that the broad events unfolding in Asia over the past several years warrant hope, and are themselves eloquent testimony to the importance of an American presence in Southeast Asia during these crucial times.

What are the most significant developments? First, a growing number of non-Communist Asian leaders are becoming alert to the responsibilities of this era—social, economic and political. In many Asian societies, one can detect a transition of major significance. Passing from the scene is a first-generation revolutionary élite that was strongly politicized, deeply ideological, and often possessed of striking charismatic qualities but very limited technical skills or interests. Emerging is a

---

* Reprinted in its entirety, by permission of the author and the New York Times Company, from the *New York Times Magazine*, December 11, 1966. Copyright 1966/1968 by the New York Times Company.

Moral Argument and the War in Vietnam

second-generation (or even third-generation) élite—more pragmatic than ideological, more administrative than charismatic, and infinitely more trained in, or committed to, the mechanics of social and economic engineering. If this transition continues and takes hold, it might well represent the most important development of this age.

Second, the economic progress achieved in certain parts of non-Communist Asia is impressive. The miracle of Japan has long been acknowledged, but recent economic trends in South Korea and Taiwan also deserve recognition. In Southern Asia, such states as Malaysia and Singapore, Thailand, and the Philippines—if political stability can continue—should be able to score striking economic gains in the years that lie ahead. Technical breakthroughs into population control, food production and industrial development, imaginatively used, could enable progress and freedom to go together in Asia. Meanwhile, non-Communist Asia can not only tolerate economic comparison with Communist Asia in many respects, but welcome it—a fact that shocks our die-hard pessimists.

Third, political trends can also be viewed as encouraging. A number of small Asian states have not only survived the first critical years after their birth, but managed to gain legitimacy in an increasing measure. In Indonesia, moreover, a shift of far-reaching significance has taken place. The leftist swing and the alliance with Peking, so threatening to other Southeast Asian states, have been reversed, and a new effort to make moderate politics is under way.

At the same time, the Communists of Asia have never before been so fragmented. Mainland China is in the midst of an upheaval involving top party and army circles. The party itself is split wide open. The Sino-Soviet cleavage, far from being healed as a result of the Vietnam conflict, as was predicted, has grown wider, partly because of that conflict.

Moreover, the small Communist states and parties of Asia have in some cases denounced *both* Moscow and Peking, seeking to form an alliance of the "small" against the "large" Communists. Currently, the North Koreans and the Japanese Communists are open members of that alliance, and some North Vietnamese are no doubt flirting secretly with the idea. Each of these parties, however, is split internally and, at least with the Korean and Japanese Communists, numerous purges have taken place.

Only the most rash man would attempt to predict the outcome of the Chinese internal struggle at this point, but its immediate impact upon the rest of Asia has been nothing less than disastrous for the Chinese Communist image. The purge of scores of intellectual, military and political leaders, together with the relentless pursuit of nuclear weapons, has drastically altered the "lovable China" myth so assiduously cultivated in the days of Bandung.

No leader in Asia today is unaware of the problem of China. And

few non-Communist leaders—if any—fail to recognize the critical importance of building some balance of power, containing economic, political
and military components, against the long-range threats confronting
them. In this task, they assign the United States a vital but by no means
exclusive role. The age of Western domination of Asia is ending. That
of partnership may have just begun.

Some critics have argued that if the Communists were allowed to
win in Vietnam, or possibly throughout the region known as Indochina,
Ho Chi Minh would become another Tito. Ironically, at the moment,
the chances for that seem far better if the Communists lose the struggle
to conquer South Vietnam by force, and are caused to live in the midst
of a true power balance, as was the case in Europe when Titoism
emerged. Neither Chinese hegemony over continental Asia, nor an
expanding Vietnamese Communist empire in the southeast (certain to
be bitterly resisted and therefore heavily dependent upon external support) is a promising route for the real independence of Hanoi.

Vietnamese Communist independence will be meaningful only if Chinese power to the north is counterbalanced by some other power to
the south, and if Hanoi is prepared to accept and work with a complex
power relationship among Moscow, Peking and Washington. A pledge
by the United States and its Asian allies to accept the sovereignty of
North Vietnam and to allow Hanoi to benefit from broad economic
developments within the Southeast Asia region, while receiving economic and technical assistance directly from the Soviet bloc, may be
the only method of assuring Hanoi's independence from Peking in the
long run. Surely, to count upon Peking's comradely benevolence in
the absence of any balance of power in this area is naive, especially
in view of China's attitudes and actions toward other Asian Communist
movements.

Naturally, there will be reverses in the future in Asia, as there have
been in the past. Even where trends are broadly favorable, much progress will occur in a zigzag pattern. Some essential changes will come
with painful slowness. Massive challenges lie ahead—particularly in
societies like India and Indonesia. It is time, however, to demand that
the pessimists at least face up to the evidence that contradicts their
prognosis of unalleviated gloom and doom.

There are some Americans who believe that our decision to make
a major commitment in Southeast Asia had nothing to do with these
developments. I am not one of them; more important, neither are the
overwhelming majority of non-Communist leaders in Asia. It is no exaggeration to assert that at present not a single non-Communist Asian
government wishes the United States to withdraw from Southeast Asia
or to be defeated in Vietnam. Cambodia's Norodom Sihanouk, in his
famous letter to *The New York Times* of June 4, 1965, put the critical
issue bluntly and in terms understandable to every leader of a small
Asian state. "I have never had the slightest illusion," he wrote, "on

Moral Argument and the War in Vietnam

the fate that awaits me at the hands of the Communists, as well as that which is reserved for 'my' government, after having removed from our region the influence, and especially the presence, of the 'free world,' and the U.S.A. in particular." Do we need stronger evidence, when such words can be written by one of our most bitter critics?

It is more meaningful to assert that our recent commitments in Asia have produced certain strains in our relations with Europe. Some articulate Europeans have feared that our preoccupation with the Pacific would reduce our interest in the Atlantic. Others have worried lest the Russians take advantage of the situation. Basically, however, non-Communist European leaders—Socialists included—have understood the reasons for our Vietnam policy, and supported it. Contrast their attitudes, for example, with those of Asian leaders two decades ago, when we were widely condemned throughout the non-Western world for upholding "rotten Western imperialist states."

A certain gap does exist between informed leaders and the common citizen in Europe. And this gap is produced in major part because the public, as in the United States, gets the TV-press treatment of the war in the American style. The Vietcong are notoriously uncooperative in allowing Western cameramen to shoot pictures of eye-gouging or throat-slitting ceremonies, or in permitting newsmen to attend briefings on marketplace terrorism. Most horror and sensationalism must thus be drawn from the non-Communist side.

To all of the above, France is a partial exception. Paraphrasing General de Gaulle, however, I think that old allies can afford to be frank with one another. Many French still harbor deep grievances against the United States for policies that appeared to them to abet the dismantling of the French Empire, and they suffer great anguish over the possibility that our policies might succeed in areas where French policies failed. Our understanding of these emotions does not require our acceptance of the judgments that flow from them.

In truth, our image in Europe and elsewhere will depend heavily upon one critical fact: can we succeed? It has been asserted by individuals who should know better, that we are big enough to accept defeat gracefully, and that our greatest contemporary problem is an arrogance of power. Such statements illustrate the powerful guilt complex that operates in some branches of American society, but they scarcely accord with the facts. The issue is not whether *we* can accept defeat but what the repercussions of our defeat would be for Asia and the world at this point. Our major problem in recent years, moreover, has not been an arrogance of power, but the uncertainty as to how best to use the massive power which we possess.

Our policy, and that of the South Vietnamese government, must rest fundamentally upon two premises. First, the Vietcong movement is solidly controlled by the Communist party and that party in turn is dominated by the North. These points have now been virtually conceded by the Communists themselves (see, for example, the September, 1966, issue of *Hoc Tat*, the North Vietnamese party organ), so they should be removed from the debate. Any victory for the so-called National Liberation Front, therefore, would be a victory for the Communists—and, in the long run at least, for the *Northern* Communists. Korea provides an analogy. The Southern faction of the Korean Communist party was ultimately overwhelmed by the Northerners because they controlled the apex of power; indeed, the Southern leader, Pak Heun Yong, was executed by the Northerners during the Korean War, with his followers being relegated to obscurity.

The second essential premise must be that many elements currently in the National Liberation Front, especially those who are not hard-core Communists, may well have become disillusioned in recent months, and under the proper political circumstances might be separated from the movement. Concerning these crucial points and their policy implications, we shall have more to say later.

Neither of the above facts, to be sure, directly answers two questions advanced by certain critics. Granted that the National Liberation Front is largely a creature of the Communists, and that without Northern Communist leadership, organization and support this movement would not have been initiated in the form that it took, and might now collapse, is the Vietnamese conflict still not in essence a civil war? Moreover, is it not possible, despite their recent reverses, that the Communists have won the support of a majority of the South Vietnamese people, casting us in the role of thwarting the democratic will?

Of course, the Vietnamese struggle can be defined as a civil war in certain respects. Vietnamese are fighting against Vietnamese, and there are Northerners and Southerners on both sides of the conflict. To analyze the struggle merely in these terms, however, is profoundly to misunderstand the nature of our times. Divided states everywhere—Germany and Korea as much as Vietnam—represent a precarious balance involving regional and international interests as well as internal political divisions. In all cases, these divided states are a result of complex history and imperfect agreements. To attempt to change them by force at this point, however, represents far more than civil war. Whether in Europe or in Asia, it represents a direct challenge to the political equilibrium of the entire region, and hence to world peace.

There are good reasons to believe, moreover, that the attempt to bring South Vietnam under Communist control does not represent the desire of a majority of the Vietnamese people. On every recent occasion when the National Liberation Front has elected to test its political strength, it has suffered a major defeat. Its calls for general strikes in October and December, 1965, were almost completely ignored. Its attempts to block the municipal elections of 1965 and the Sept. 11, 1966, Constituent Assembly election were ignominious failures. And, perhaps of greatest significance, it was unable to seize control, or even play a commanding

Moral Argument and the War in Vietnam

role, in the Hue and Danang uprisings of early 1966, when the authority of the central government was at a low ebb.

None of this is to assert that the political problems are unimportant. On the contrary, the Vietnam struggle will ultimately be decided as much by political as by military considerations. A revolutionary movement dedicated to violence does not need to have majority support in order to be victorious. When even 10 percent of the population is committed to such a movement, and able to neutralize the great majority of the people, most governments can be placed in grave jeopardy. Given our political culture, Americans naturally assume that threatening movements must have a majority on their side, but, in fact, deeply committed minorities prepared to employ any means to achieve power often hold the key to the politics of our times—unless they are resolutely and intelligently opposed.

A reasonable estimate of the broadest political divisions in South Vietnam would probably assign the N.L.F. some 15 to 20 percent support and opposition to the Communists 35 to 40 percent, with the remaining citizens essentially apolitical, prepared to accept the winners. Any such bald assessment, of course, is misleading because it cannot measure the fragility and infinite gradation of political commitment on various sides, and the relative importance of local and regional political leadership. No objective observer would deny, moreover, that South Vietnamese politics constitute the Achilles heel of those attempting to prevent a Communist takeover, and pose the central challenge of the immediate future—*not* because the Communists are so strong, but because the opposition is so divided.

The politics of South Vietnam have been those of minority militance, majority disunity and public confusion. Serious regional, religious, political and personal differences—given considerable rein in an atmosphere where the government does not, probably cannot, rule firmly—continue to plague the non-Communist cause. It is nonsense to define the present South Vietnamese government as "Fascist." True, its efficiency has been low. It has been insufficiently representative. It has been unable, and often unwilling, to conduct badly needed reforms (and this is a crucial test that lies ahead, with improving security conditions now removing one major barrier). All of these problems are commonplace throughout the new world and naturally they are exacerbated when the Communists decide to inject terrorism and guerrilla warfare into the scene. The fact is, however, that a considerable amount of free expression—including strong criticism of the government—takes place in South Vietnam every day—far more than is possible in Hanoi or, for that matter, in Rangoon.

It is also inaccurate to imply that the Communists have captured the Vietnamese nationalist movement. Indeed, it is extraordinarily important that none of the prominent Buddhist, Catholic, Cao Dai, Hoa Hao or Dai Viet leaders—many of them fervent nationalists—have joined the

N.L.F., whatever their grievances and divisions. They know the character of that organization, even if some foreigners do not.

The gulf between the Communists and ourselves is fundamentally over whether Vietnam shall be a unified Communist state or one divided into a Communist North and a non-Communist South. In this connection, the often-repeated thesis that the Communists could have won nation-wide elections in 1956 should be closely scrutinized. What kind of elections? And won what? The Geneva agreement of 1954 was defective, if not fraudulent, in positing a Vietnam solution through "free elections." Every action of the Vietnamese Communists after 1950, including their assassination of scores of non-Communist nationalist leaders, made it clear that *their* concept of "free elections" did not include the right of any real opposition to organize, or, indeed, to survive in areas where they had military control. The idea that an International Control Commission could establish freedom merely by supervising the mechanics of elections under these circumstances was scarcely worthy of world statesmen.

And if one chooses to believe in Utopia, what would truly free elections have demonstrated? Under no duress of any kind and with every group having full opportunities for campaigning, Vietnamese citizens in all probability would have voted overwhelmingly on the basis of religion, personalities and regional identifications. No political party would have come close to winning a majority of seats for a National Assembly. Undoubtedly, Ho Chi Minh would have been one of those elected, and quite probably he—as an individual—would have received the largest, single number of votes. That would have not signified, however, that most Vietnamese wanted a dictatorship of the Communist party.

Up to date, the Vietnamese Communists have continued to demand unconditional surrender as the price for ending the war. The so-called Four Points of Hanoi and the Five Points of the National Liberation Front, together with the embellishments added to them, constitute precisely this demand: All military opposition to the Communists by us should cease, and all American and other non-Vietnamese forces should be withdrawn from South Vietnam. All equipment given by us to the South Vietnamese military forces should also be removed. The National Liberation Front should be recognized as the sole legitimate representative of the South Vietnamese people. Its program, based upon a step-by-step unification of Vietnam under Hanoi's Communist regime, should be adopted.

The Communists are prepared today, as they have always been prepared, to negotiate with us on how these terms should be carried out. Matters of timing and priority are open to discussion now as they were in 1964 and 1965, providing we accept their basic conditions. They are perfectly willing to help us save face, just as they sought to perform this service for the French at Geneva. Up to the present, however, they have not been prepared to accept any formula which would allow the

Moral Argument and the War in Vietnam

non-Communists of Vietnam an alternative to Communist rule. When these facts are understood, much of the debate about our willingness to negotiate becomes irrelevant. The central issue is and always has been, are we prepared to accommodate ourselves to a total Communist victory?

Some critics insist that we too are demanding unconditional surrender, but this is not accurate. The United States does not insist upon a unified, non-Communist Vietnam, nor is it committed to a rollback of Communist governments elsewhere in Asia. Those individuals who want to live under Communism in Vietnam could have a Northern sanctuary. We are prepared, moreover, to withdraw American forces from South Vietnam when and if a political solution can be reached.

Indeed, there is nothing in the current American position that would bar the neutralization of the entire area under firm international security agreements. We are even prepared to see North Vietnam share in certain economic and political regional undertakings if the Hanoi Government chooses to do so. Are these the terms of unconditional surrender?

We are simply not prepared to accept a Communist seizure of power under the Hanoi-N.L.F. formula. Neither are the non-Communists of South Vietnam, who may be divided on many things, but who show unprecedented unity in rejecting current Communist terms.

Some observers believe that the Vietnamese Communists are being forced into a fundamental reconsideration of policy for the first time since 1959-60. Their heavy military losses, the growing disenchantment with Peking and increased Soviet influence in Hanoi, and the war weariness of the North are cited as key factors. The only evidence currently in the public domain is more ambivalent. French authorities have told us that Hanoi no longer believes that military victory is possible, but is prepared to conduct a holding operation rather than negotiate at this time.

Why? One might suppose that negotiations would now be extremely attractive, especially in view of our concessions. What if the Communists took advantage of all U.S. pledges with respect to military deescalation in the event of negotiations, but entered the sessions intending to make absolutely no concessions? Could they not regroup and resupply their bone-weary, battered troops, and prepare them for future activities if necessary? It is legitimate to question whether our preparations for negotiations are adequate and whether our concessions in this connection have been wise.

Why have the opportunities not been tested by Hanoi? First, the North Vietnamese cannot rid themselves of the illusion that the United States is France, and that internal political crisis, combined with global pressures, will force an American surrender.

Hanoi also continues to count upon the political disintegration of South Vietnam, perhaps its most realistic hope. There is now evidence, moreover, that fairly intensive Communist efforts are underway to penetrate certain non-Communist groups, notably the so-called militant Buddhists.

The greatest barrier to negotiations, however, is probably a psychological one relating to the Communists themselves. For years, all Communist leaders beginning with Ho Chi Minh himself have ceaselessly proclaimed that they are prepared to settle for nothing short of total victory, even if the struggle takes five, ten, or twenty years. Belief in total victory, indeed, has been made into an article of Marxist-Leninist faith, a touchstone of loyalty. Compromise, therefore, would be a traumatic experience for leaders and people alike, and possibly one with dangerous ramifications for the Communist party.

Thus, although the situation may change dramatically, the present prospects for negotiations are cloudy, and American policies for the immediate future must be based upon the assumption that the war will continue. Two related issues therefore continue to be of paramount importance. Are further concessions in an effort to induce negotiations in order, or should additional military escalation be undertaken for that purpose?

First, let us look very briefly at the past. Some critics charge the Johnson administration with deliberately using peace overtures to camouflage its planned escalations. To me, this is a vulgarization of an enormously complex, difficult problem. The plot thesis upon which it rests is simple, psychologically satisfying—and incorrect. We are not ruled by diabolically wicked men. To imply this is to obscure the true issue: What policy is most appropriate in dealing with opponents who often mistake concessions for weakness and who have very different rules for the political game? Is there a better method than a policy which simultaneously offers a broader set of opportunities for moderation and a set of rising penalties for extremism?

Earlier, we debated the enclave concept. As it was usually advanced, that concept had certain fatal weaknesses in my opinion, and it was correctly rejected. It would have destroyed all hope of any viable political alternative to communism in South Vietnam. It thus would have separated us totally from the non-Communist Vietnamese nationalists, and supported the false thesis that our interests lay only in military bases and the retention of American power—or the saving of American face—in Asia. In sum, the charge of imperialism would have been unwritten by American policy itself.

Moreover the enclave policy would have guaranteed no negotiations, because it would have given the Communists explicit indication of both the limits and the desperate nature of our commitment. Never have the Communists been willing to negotiate under such circumstances except to extract total surrender—and if that were our intent, there were less painful ways to effect it. Even from a military standpoint, the enclave proposal raised the gravest questions. The defense of fixed bases and separate garrisons, particularly if clogged with vast numbers of refugees,

Moral Argument and the War in Vietnam

requires scarcely fewer men than a more mobile strategy, and it gives the enemy enormous psychological advantages.

The argument for unilateral American concessions currently centers on proposals for the cessation of Northern bombing. The issue of Northern bombing has always been a thorny one. Strong arguments against it were advanced at the outset—the effect on world opinion, the dangers of further escalation, the likelihood of increased Communist rigidity.

At least weighty considerations were advanced on the other side. Why should the Communists be able to transport men and equipment safely to the borders of the "enemy," enjoy the immunity of their own military facilities from attack, even be allowed to deny any involvement (as the North Vietnamese have consistently done)?

There is no question that the bombings have hurt the North, and hurt it badly. The Communists themselves have admitted this. They have acknowledged weariness, food shortages and even a creeping defeatism, which they insist is restricted to a small segment of the people. They have also admitted that some "counterrevolutionary" elements exist in the North, elements affected by recent developments. Southern morale was unquestionably bolstered by the knowledge that South Vietnam was not the sole target of a war in which Hanoi played such a critical role.

Moreover, the physical condition of Northern infiltrators and the amount of supplies they can bring with them are additional evidences of the effect of the bombings. Incidentally, the Northern bombings led the Soviet Union back onto the Vietnamese scene and served to reduce Chinese influence, because only the Russians could provide the sophisticated anti-aircraft equipment needed once the bombings began.

These factors cannot be ignored, nor balanced by the simple assertion that the bombings have not stopped infiltration. We have stated that if there were signs—public or private—of an interest in negotiations or a willingness to engage in some reciprocal act of deescalation, our bombing of the North would cease. Thus far, the campaign for an immediate, unconditional, permanent cessation of these bombings on our part has failed to answer two related questions of major importance. Is there anything to indicate that a reduction of military pressure upon the Communists would induce compromises on their part, or would they merely take advantage of such a situation, as they have done on previous occasions? If so, how long could any administration justify a return to the "privileged sanctuaries" position while American casualties mounted? To put it bluntly, is not a unilateral cessation of Northern bombing certain to lead to major escalation unless the Communists respond favorably within a matter of months at most, and does it not give to the Communists the real initiative in determining the escalation issue?

Sometimes it is asserted that South Vietnam cannot be saved if it is physically destroyed in the process. Such a statement conjures up a false image. There is no need to minimize the suffering and destruction taking place in Vietnam today in order to challenge terms like "annihilation" and "genocide." In fact, destruction in Vietnam at this point has not approached the level suffered by certain countries in World War II, nor that endured by Korea in the aftermath of an earlier "national liberation" effort by the Communists. Indeed, the major cities have been relatively untouched in physical terms and the Vietnamese population—both North and South—is currently rising, not falling. Moreover, in no other conflict in history has there been so much sensitivity to the suffering of innocent people. A number of Americans lie dead today because we have sought to reduce noncombatant casualties even at grave risks to our own men.

None of this is to indicate joy over this war, nor is it to minimize the costs being borne by Vietnamese society. They are serious. It is time, however, to call a halt to emotional outbursts that grossly distort the facts. Furthermore, certain basic questions must be faced by those who imply that the responsibility for the killing lies with the non-Communists. Who is committed to the thesis that violence is an indispensable instrument of attaining power? Who categorizes all those opposing communism as "enemies of the people"—legitimate targets for liquidation? And what would happen to those "enemies" if the Communists were to win in Vietnam? Does anyone seriously believe that an American withdrawal would end the killing or the suffering in Vietnam? If we ever reach a position where our legitimate concern about the miseries of war enables any aggressive force to use violence with impunity, will we then deserve to be called moral?

What course of action should now be pursued? First, if the arguments against unilateral deescalation are powerful, so are the arguments against any massive escalation. To take steps, for example, that would threaten the obliteration of North Vietnam or involve us directly with either China or the Soviet Union would be to take actions unwise from any standpoint. Vietnam, above all, is a test of the American capacity to respond in measured terms to a threat that is important but not terminal. The Vietnam struggle must always be kept in its larger context, and to do so is to reject all extreme solutions.

With respect to the military arena, it is now time to define our function more specifically, and that act in itself can do much to prevent uncontrolled escalation. Our primary military task, and that of our non-Vietnamese allies, should be to prevent or to reduce to a minimum Northern infiltration into South Vietnam. No limit should be placed upon the number of troops necessary for this task, and the bombings of the North should be related specifically to this goal. Further escalation, thus, should not be contemplated unless the character of the infiltration changes.

We should make it clear, moreover, that we are prepared to reduce

Moral Argument and the War in Vietnam

the level of our attacks on Northern infiltration declines, without any necessity for formal negotiations. Meanwhile, we, together with our allies (especially the Koreans), should concentrate upon the speedy training of new South Vietnamese officers and the revitalization of the South Vietnamese Army forces, so that they can ultimately take up the primary task of coping with the Vietcong.

It is impossible—and it would be unwise—to attempt any rigid line of demarcation at this point between the tasks of dealing with Northern infiltration and handling the Vietcong. The objective, however, and the policy thrust should be strongly in this direction.

Our task is that of providing a military umbrella under which the process of building a nation can take place. It is also clear, however, that we cannot afford to stand aloof from the vital socioeconomic and political problems which South Vietnam faces. The so-called pacification program is not going well. The war cannot be lost militarily, but it can be lost politically. It can also be won—in the sense of seeing an evolution not dissimilar from that which has taken place in South Korea. Three basic conditions are necessary.

First, military security must be guaranteed, in order for villages to have any confidence that their allegiance will not be their death warrants.

Second, a social revolution in the countryside must be sponsored by the South Vietnamese government as its top political priority, with the full force of American influence being directed toward this end. In Japan, we conducted one of the most successful social revolutions ever undertaken in modern Asia. In Korea, we provided an environment for a much more modest evolution to take place. Vietnam demands an American policy between these two, but closer to the Japanese model. Corrupt and inefficient officials must go. Programs like land reform (on a much broader scale than previously attempted) must come—and now. This is more important—and more possible—than instant democracy, Western style.

Third, our general political support in Vietnam should be oriented less around a man, and more around a pattern of political evolution. The immediate thrust must be toward a mixed military-civilian government, a working coalition of moderate elements from which can be drawn acceptable leaders and, eventually, a dominant party that can enlist support sufficient to allow both stability and some degree of openness. It is particularly essential to get more Southerners into the government at all levels.

A formal coalition government involving the Communists is neither wise nor feasible. It has not worked in Laos, Burma or any other nation of Asia, and it would not work in South Vietnam. A generous amnesty for ex-Vietcong elements, however, and the inclusion of some persons previously associated with the National Liberation Front in the government as individuals may be both practical and desirable. The political evolution of South Vietnam is certain to be complex, with a number of crises lying ahead. Our stake in this evolution requires that our influence be felt.

Any Vietnam policy, to be effective, must be encased in a broader policy toward Asia that is at once subtle, flexible and forward-looking. With respect to the Communist states, we must advance policies that offer an extensive structure of opportunities for moderation, on the one hand, and a set of firm, explicit deterrents to extremism on the other. Toward other Asian states, including our allies, we must increasingly solicit opinions and cultivate an atmosphere of partnership and mutual responsibility. Nothing is more important in this age of nationalism than the psychological relations between states, including the patterns of style and behavior that are established.

Vietnam is a major test of American institutions and American political behavior. Can our people endure a long, complicated, intricate game which must not be played at either 0 or 100? Can they adjust to playing at 46, and being willing to go to 63—but no more? Or down to 8, but no lower?

In an age where the peace of the world depends upon establishing some political equilibrium in Asia, and fostering the type of socioeconomic programs that will make that equilibrium viable, do we have the patience and the sophistication to take a leading (but not solo) role? And, finally, are our political, communications and intellectual élites capable of providing the blend of maturity, balance and wisdom that is essential if these challenges are to be met? Upon the answer to these questions hinges our future, and that of many other peoples.

The Vietnamese and Their Revolution*

by John T. McAlister, Jr., and Paul Mus

"Prologue: Politics and Revolution in Viet Nam"

Revolution in Viet Nam has seen an unending repetition of some now familiar patterns of politics. Events and people have changed but the patterns have remained virtually the same. These patterns are the modern form taken by an age-old factional struggle for power among the Vietnamese—not just for power itself but for the way power will be held and shared. Though foreign powers have tried to separate the factions into different regions, this division has been largely artificial, because the essence of the struggle is not so much between regions as it is between segments of society. Since power has been so diffuse and difficult to organize by any of these factions, the struggle has already endured for a quarter of a century and is unlikely to be resolved soon. Underlying this struggle and producing its repetition of familiar political patterns are values common to all Vietnamese. Despite the turbulence of twenty-five years of revolution these common values have persisted, although they have not gone unchallenged. Indeed, the competition to change the values by which the Vietnamese live is what the revolution is all about. . . .

New communities require new values to link people together in a bond of common purpose. In Viet Nam, a confirmation of new values is being sought by two competitor governments, one in Hanoi, the other in Saigon, each of which hopes to become *the* modern leader for all Viet Nam. Their search is not an act of contemplation but a struggle to win commitment through political rewards proportional to performance in organizing power on the basis of new values. The struggle is far from over; human values rarely change quickly, and the experience of Viet Nam is no exception. . . .

. . . In the relationship between the three-fourths of the Vietnamese

*From the Harper Torchbook of this title (New York: Harper and Row, 1970). Copyright 1970 by John T. McAlister and the estate of Paul Mus. Reprinted by permission. Mr. McAlister has written the "Prologue" and "Epilogue" sections of the excerpts which appear here. The other sections are his translation and thorough rewriting of the late Mr. Mus's *Viet Nam: sociologie d'une guerre*. The passages here are from pages 1-4, 6, 26-27, 78-80, 82, 88-92, 95-96, 111-114, 123, 125-127, 116-119, 128-132, 138-141, 143-146, 148, 150-157, 160-166.

who live in bamboo-encircled villages scattered throughout the rich green-brown deltas and the governments encased in the tree-shaded, yellow stucco cities there have been few changes. This basic dichotomy between the life of the cities—outposts of modernity in an alien world of archaic tradition—and the life of the village is the focus of attention of this book. Across the gap of time, space, and culture separating the countryside from the cities, pro-Western urban governments have tried to project their strength through programs of political control and counter-guerrilla military operations. Despite the determined efforts of a quarter of a century none of these programs has been successful, nor have these discredited techniques even been changed very much in their essential characteristics from one era to another. Just like the French in the late 1940s, the Americans in the late 1960s boasted unjustifiably of the results of "pacification" programs designed to bring the countryside under government control.

This struggle by pro-Western urban-oriented governments to gain control over the countryside from village-based revolutionaries has been the most basic recurrent pattern of the twenty-five years of warfare in Viet Nam. The struggle has persisted because few rural people have felt any real stake in the activities of the urban governments. Yet at the outset of revolution in 1945 almost all rural people were uncommitted to any faction. They lived lives limited by the social horizons of their native village as well as by the routine of growing rice in the irrigated fields nearby. Their lack of commitment was not, however, a congenial mode of life; Vietnamese seem instinctively to feel the need to be a part of a larger cultural community than the village. Perhaps this longing is due to the loneliness of rural life or its uncertainty, but whatever the source, the result is that Vietnamese consider the creation of new communities not as political acts but as spiritual ones. The explanation, therefore, of why a peasant people with a deep sense of spirituality would become committed to mass participation in a national movement that was more overtly political than any in their previous history is the story of revolution in Viet Nam. . . .

The spirit or mentality of the Vietnamese—the three-fourths of those who continue to lead lives rooted in the traditions of the village—is the essential untold story about Vietnam. The reason for telling this story is not to rekindle the fight for the countryside or to lay the basis for any particular set of policy recommendations—it is to emphasize that the participation of peasants in a revolution to create a modern state is the story of most of Asia in this century. No one thought that the march of peasants into modern lives would be a peaceful event, but few realized that this transformation of a rural people's role in their society would become confused with communism—or rather with a view of communism as an international conspiracy orchestrated from world centers. . . .

. . . The most essential missing aspect of this revolution in the public

debate over the conflict during the past twenty-five years [is] the underlying attitudes and values of the Vietnamese peasants, why they have
been unwilling to accept the legitimacy of pro-French and pro-American
urban-based governments, and why they have steadily moved toward
the Communist-led revolutionaries in every area of Viet Nam. . . .

"The Political Consequences of Vietnamese Concepts of Society"

Viet Nam is a certain way of growing rice, of living in common on
a rice diet, and of asking heaven to protect your harvest just as it did
your ancestors'. Viet Nam is a piece of luck, solicited, administered,
and experienced in common. It is a country that presents us with a
dual paradox, because for the Vietnamese everything is religion down
to the simplest acts; yet they seem to have no religion in our sense
of the word. Magic, religion, ethics, temporal power: our categories are
not theirs; for them one sole fact is involved. This unity of life the
Vietnamese call "common fortune," and to them it means that which
makes them Vietnamese.

Within Viet Nam's former traditional society this whole system of
beliefs was embodied in the emperor, whose ritual acts symbolized the
spiritual feelings of the Vietnamese. For example, the emperor was the
Prime Plowman who each year used to "deconsecrate" the precious
rice land by opening the first furrow. This annual ceremony was preceded by an imperial procession into the rice fields, all of which gave
the village people a sense of the spiritual significance of their travail.
Government in traditional Viet Nam was thus inseparable from religion;
together they were formed in accordance with the human geography
required to cultivate rice. Indeed, government was the spiritualization
of this human rhythm of growing rice. . . .

The rice lands of the Mekong Delta in southern Viet Nam, which were
opened up to cultivation during the early part of the twentieth century,
do not fit into this traditional state religion and sociology. By contrast
the religious sovereignty of Hué, which became the imperial capital in
1802, was still appreciable in central Viet Nam in the years before 1945,
and even enjoyed vestigial prestige in the north. But such a sense of
spiritual identity ceased to be strong in Cochin China (southern Viet
Nam) after it fell under French control during the years 1863-67. The
principal reason for this spiritual decline was the emergence of a new
pattern of land tenure. Through the enterprise of French hydraulic
engineering vast new tracks of previously uncultivatable land were
opened up for rice growing in the delta of the Mekong River. Yet, instead
of being made available as small plots to individual peasant producers
in the traditional manner of Vietnamese migration into new areas, this
land was sold to large landowners as a means of rapidly recouping
the cost of hydraulic engineering projects. As a result of this decision

Moral Argument and the War in Vietnam

an upper class with wealth based on vast landholdings arose for the first time in Vietnamese society.

. . . The consequence of this wealth was that the new lands of the Mekong Delta were cultivated by a half-proletarianized labor force that had no title to the land it worked. . . .

Why has the Mekong Delta developed in a way that is so out of character with the rest of Viet Nam? The answer is to be found in the fact that the virgin lands of the delta were salty and, in order to become usable, required a complicated and costly irrigation system, which only French hydraulic engineering was capable of constructing. . . .

Because this system resulted in a different kind of settlement pattern, in which the village and its institutions were relatively less cohesive units than in previous Vietnamese migrations, the principal social consequence of the opening up of new land was not only to create a new class of extremely wealthy landowners but also to produce a rootless and restless peasantry. While the landowners were inevitably staunch supporters of French rule, the root peasants were not, and when their chance came they expressed their protest in a violent uprising in 1940-41. This Communist-led revolt was but a precursor of the more lasting effects of the unusual settlement of the Mekong Delta. . . .

The Vietnamese concept of society is not simply that of a contract between men; society does not gather individuals together according to the logic of Rousseau. The Vietnamese social contract is an agreement between heaven, the land, and the ancestors, whose spirit was thought to be embodied in the living generation. The state was the ultimate instrument of the contract: the emperor, the image of heaven, in his capital; the governors in their provinces; the heads of families in their houses, were all one sole entity who were in harmony with the reason of the universe. Through conformity with this hierarchy the contact with the supernatural was direct and assured. Natural calamities were regarded as proof that contact with the supernatural had been lost and that conformity to the social contract had been violated. Individuals had to function within the system; there was no reality for the individual apart from the social contract. There was no individual property; there weren't any individual rights. People were simply an element in social integration except when they achieved positions of authority. Such positions didn't mean, however, that their share of existence was any more individual; it was the heavenly mandate that had come upon them and that had made them a replica of itself.

Everywhere the concrete facts corresponded to these concepts of society. They were reinforced by all the ways of seeing, speaking, and writing which constituted Sino-Vietnamese civilization. The individual was situated within his family; the families were defined by the village, and when they became rich their assets inevitably reverted to the collectivity. When the French quantified the individual by giving him both a civil status and the idea of individual rights and duties, they destroyed a qualitative harmony made up of exchanges and compensations. They made the individual his own capital and gave him rights that could be opposed to his own family and his village; they armed him, theoretically, against them. But a society is not that easily reformed. In traditional society the individual has only relative rights, but they were fulfilled because, on an average, the system assured everyone a piece of land, and the communal assets helped the village erase the most glaring inequalities.

In the Mekong Delta, however, where the pattern of land tenure and social structure broke with long-standing tradition, the individual who was provided with absolute rights by the West found himself faced with empty rights from the viewpoint of customary values. He had the rights of a salaried man and this, according to Vietnamese civilization, does not constitute a person. These individual rights have no juridical value because they are not a function, a responsibility, or a replica of the heavenly mandate, and they cannot represent the will of heaven because, as one realizes immediately, they benefit only the very few. Riches now are placed in bank accounts and have left the community; the rich people live in cities and the villages encounter only the managers. The circulation of assets, which had once been assured within a closed circle by the community spirit, no longer takes place. "Face" is elsewhere: Western individualism passed that way, creating cities and a new world.

One cannot expect these simple people who live in the villages of southern Viet Nam to be able to make a correct economic analysis of the situation that the French colonial administration had created. For example, they cannot see that in the opening up of new lands in the Mekong Delta there was a requirement for machines and capital which traditional Vietnamese culture could not have provided. Instead they see themselves as dispossessed; emptied of substance. They see what for them are fabulous fortunes building up at their expense and beyond their reach. Although more exasperated, the attitude of the village communities toward such fortunes is the same as that toward village families who claim to be rich on their own account. There is a deep-rooted conviction that such behavior can never bring luck and that the vengeance of heaven is on its way. . . .

If it is true that the whole conflict began against France because of the individual Vietnamese's instinct for a recovery of social cohesion, then what is the meaning of possible choice for the future? Considered from a traditionalist point of view France's action in the virgin lands of the Mekong Delta has incurred two serious reproaches. France made the individual into a political principle to the detriment of collective groups; in French theory it was the individual and no longer the collectivity that became the legal and economic unit. Yet at the same time France dispossessed that individual of everything the collectivity had once put at his disposal, thus the only ones who benefited from this

Moral Argument and the War in Vietnam

fallacious emphasis on the rights of the individual were a few clever people who became French clients, the rich upper classes. Moreover, the resulting proletarianization, which is the most obvious characteristic of the system and the one most open to criticism, was due directly to France's failure to recognize the religious functions of communal unity. In Confucian society the ritual order, good behavior, and conformity to the past—that is, to the cosmic structure—within families and within the state regularizes the order of the seasons, the sun, and the rain. Seen in this way a society is a vast and perpetual incantation of the universe. Man does not act. He officiates—well or badly, and certainly badly if he is not enlightened. The classical and canonical books were his code, and in them he found the conduct each one was to follow so that the individual might be in harmony with his family and village and that the empire might be at peace. . . .

In traditional Vietnamese society every individual act carried out in a collective unit—family, clan, village, etc.—was governed and evaluated by relatives and neighbors. They judged a person's behavior on the basis of his "sacralization" or "deification" of life. Within the norms of the collective unit the individual always had his assigned part to play. During celebrations of the change of seasons, events in the calendar of agricultural labor, and family events, the purpose of traditional rituals was to consecrate the mundane passage of life. Every ritual action of the performers was preceded by an announcement, spoken aloud, of the gestures they were about to make. This was like an oracle predicting in advance the behavior prescribed to achieve harmony with the supernatural: through appropriate behavior there would be a good harvest, a prosperous year, a successful life. Through the behavior of its members each collectivity sought to establish harmony between itself and the divine power of nature; thus each village, each clan, each family continually prompted the individual's mind and governed his actions.

The problem for the individual was *to know* what was expected by the collectivity. The approval of the group was the invariable condition for action, and this was not just superficial approval arising from some whim or impulse but an expression of constitutional approval, as it were. When disapproval was incurred, it carried a power effective enough to maintain the basic character of the collectivity. When there was approval, the sanction of opinion became the very reason for individual existence: an individual had achieved harmony with nature and his fellows, he had been integrated into the world, and he could expect good luck.

For those who did not achieve this harmony there was death, a religious and civil death. The French were constantly surprised at the number of cases in which loss of face resulted in murder and, even more, in suicide. This violence occurred because "face" is not just another word for vanity or social pretension; it is the very character of one's being. . . .

Can Ethics, Ideology, and History Meet?

"Marxism and Traditionalism in Viet Nam"

What is the Communist solution for Viet Nam's political dilemmas? As a fundamental point in their revolutionary program, the Communists have decided to confiscate large landholdings, especially the estates amassed during French rule, and redistribute them as small plots to landless peasants. Here is a technique that the Communists, following the experience of the party in China, could have been expected to adopt, because it destroys the power base of those identified with the prevailing order and usually wins a popular commitment to a new form of political community. The party's name itself indicates that its ideal is communal, and, in an agricultural society, one of the most conspicuous ways to put such an ideal into practice is by providing land to those who have none. But this traditionalistic Vietnamese mind has had different ideas than those normally held by Marxists about what a communal link should be. According to Vietnamese beliefs, contracts between men and only between men are no foundation for a community.

Since a community in Viet Nam is felt to be a replica and an incantation of the universe, it must be a spiritual community or it doesn't exist. Such a sense of community takes form only through an agreement with heaven and earth, and it must include the symbolic participation of the ancestors whose spirit will permeate the group. When these conditions are unfulfilled there may be a coalescence of different interest groups but no society; there may be an enterprise but no mission. When they do not form a community no more can be expected of such Vietnamese groups than from our own Western forms of organization in Viet Nam. . . . Therefore, if the Communists, or any other modern political leadership, were to create a government capable of succeeding to French rule over all of Viet Nam, they clearly would have to adapt their concept of politics to the traditionalist expectations of the Vietnamese peasants. . . .

Obviously, the Communists could not merely style themselves as a dynastic successor to the French and pretend that they were engaged in a struggle for power along purely traditionalist lines. . . . But how could any revolutionary leadership adapt itself to the traditionalist expectations of the peasants, or rather, adapt itself with the effectiveness required to lead the peasants into the modern world, where the politics of mass mobilization and mass participation in political demonstrations and military operations have become the norm? The answer has been found in the traditional concept of "virtue," which is the sign that a prevailing regime enjoys the mandate of heaven, enjoys legitimacy in traditionalist terms.

Proof that a revolutionary regime has the mandate of heaven is the emergence of a new political system that is a complete replacement

Moral Argument and the War in Vietnam

of the preceding doctrines, institutions, and men in power and that shows itself to be in complete command of the society. Of course, such a stiff test of legitimacy merely indicates that the Vietnamese expect there to be little uncertainty about an insurgent's capacity to govern before there is popular recognition of his being endowed with the mandate of heaven. Since few competitors can fulfill these criteria all at once, the Vietnamese have usually taken a "wait-and-see" attitude toward challengers of the prevailing order. But being gamblers at heart, the Vietnamese have known that they cannot wait too long; otherwise, they may lose their chance to be identified with the winning side. In the critical task of making their choice they look for a sign or an intimation of legitimacy, and the Vietnamese call that sign "virtue."

An effective competitor for legitimacy in an internal conflict in Viet Nam must, therefore, have a program which anticipates and plans for a complete change in the way politics is conducted; which is to say, it must have a new "virtue." The practical necessity of such a requirement lies in the minds of the Vietnamese peasants. In times of turmoil, they look for signs that a new regime has a well-defined concept of order against which they might measure their prospects for local order in the countryside, and consequently, their hopes for personal security. . . .

One of the classic examples of a revolutionary competitor trying to respond to these traditionalist expectations occurred in 1945, when the Indochina Communist party gave clear evidence of how important it considered the influence of the wait-and-see attitude. In a stunning move it relinquished its name as a Communist party in favor of a socialistic formula that was more to the local taste, while at the same time it maintained its party structure. . . .

Without the Europeans apparently even noticing, the name of the Indochina Communist party expressed, paradoxically, an imperialist and Communist ideal. In 1945, while the traditional name of the country, Viet Nam, was hailed everywhere as the promise of a new future as an independent nation, the name of the Indochina Communist party . . . bore the name of Indochina, which was a creation of French colonialism from disparate traditional states along the Mekong River that were organized into the kingdoms of Laos and Cambodia. . . .

In dropping its name the Indochina Communist party sought to reassure traditionalist sentiment, which was inclined to see communism as a devilry left behind by the occupation of Westerners. Give and take: we must understand that the temporary elimination of the party's terminology at the moment of its great triumph in 1945 was not as small or even as deceitful a sacrifice as we might think. Of course, we realized that the masses traditionally consider the competition of candidates, organized groups, or peoples as a game of destiny. This explains the importance attached to the fact that while the game is being played out, a person can easily withdraw his bet.

Since the stakes of the game are the people's adherence to a doctrine, everything must be started over again from scratch and thus the long way around must be taken. Under the circumstances this meant that the Communists had to institute a moderate program of socialization to reassure the peasants. They achieved this by making rules against any interference with the rights of property, drawing up a constitution which, for the French, was unexpectedly moderate, and, finally, having representatives of the old order of things in the provincial councils or in the government. Of course, the Communists took care to keep the key posts in the government assigned to their staunchest adherents.

It is easy to say that in 1945 the Communists were dropping the shadow for the substance. But this view overlooks how essential and how definitive the Indochina Communist party was for the Vietnamese popular imagination. In the historic light in which the Democratic Republic of Viet Nam was launched by the August Revolution of 1945, the Communist party was little known except for its revolutionary victory. In effect, the party was renouncing its immediate rights over the masses by giving up its name. According to a rule of the game—a game it had no more control over than the French did—it realized that while having been a factor in its emergence, the word of heaven did not yet point specifically to the Communist party. At the very most the party was commending itself to a future opportunity to receive the mandate of heaven.

Such comments are in no way a disguised apologia for the party and should not be taken as a rationalization. Indeed, this explanation contains some bitter truths which the French did not comprehend. In view of Vietnamese public opinion—which, although it often eluded the French, exists nonetheless and is sovereign in its own way—Ho Chi Minh through his policies during that critical period from August, 1945, to March, 1946, secured a strong bond between the non-Marxist nationalists and the Communist party by withdrawing doctrinally. Instead of staking everything on the "trick" by which he had won power through a *coup d'etat* in August, 1945, Ho decided to make a change. He thus held his own against all comers, avoiding any clashes and allowing "heaven"—in other words, the situation at hand—to be disposed in his favor. . . .

On many occasions in Viet Nam, newcomers from France were surprised to realize that they were closer to the Communist Vietnamese than to other local political groups when talking about the nature of society. These Communists spoke the French language of society, even though it was in a Marxist dialect, and, despite obvious differences, their terminology and their logic blended in with that of the West. Consequently, both the French and the orthodox Vietnamese Marxists faced the same problem when they tried to communicate with the mass of the people, who had been trained in traditions as distant from the tenets of Vietnamese Marxism as they were from Western democracy. Above

Moral Argument and the War in Vietnam

all, the Marxist leaders have had a very hard time dealing with the effect of a cultural and linguistic situation in which modern expressions must first be expressed in Chinese in order to be incorporated into the Vietnamese language. But words chosen from Chinese to express a scientific and political concept are, when introduced into Viet Nam, permeated with local implications that are foreign to China. One can easily sense the consequences of such a shift.

For example, with what kind of rhetoric can a revolutionary platform be best presented to the half-proletarianized . . . tenant farmers of the Mekong Delta? "To socialize" and in particular to socialize landed property is expressed as *xã hôi hóa:* "to put in common." Social and political coloration is greatly dependent on the first word, *xã.* In it we find the Chinese *she:* "society, commercial company, community"; used with *hui* (in Vietnamese *hôi)*—meaning "union, assembly, society"—it corresponds in all its uses to our word "society"; *she-hui-hs"ueh,* for example, means "sociology" in Chinese. Together with a word designating a political party, the pair *xã hôi is the usual equivalent of "socialism."*

. . . The whole moral and social structure of a village takes shape around a spiritual cult. The cult sums up the life of the village by expressing that irreducible element of Vietnamese spiritual identity in terms of philosophical formalism borrowed from China. Within such a tradition the modern program of "socialization," when expressed in a familiar idiom, does not give small landowners, either actual or potential ones, the impression of a break with their past. At their level of information and judgment it would appear, on the contrary to be a new fulfillment of their traditions, which has been weakened by a French regime that had allowed the establishment of large landholdings in violation of customary law.

In the consciousness of the Vietnamese masses the word *xã* has a central value. It unfolds a landscape—not a physical landscape but a sociological landscape. Yet we have observed that the physical landscape of Viet Nam reflects the pattern of the country's society and that within this society the village or *xã* comes before all else; one belongs to the village before one belongs to oneself. Anywhere the village does not exist in the country's territory Viet Nam has yet to come into its own against the forests, the Chams, or the Cambodians; the national soil was constituted in exactly this way.

In the Mekong Delta the obstacle to establishing villages along traditional lines was the large landholdings resulting from French colonial policies, which prevented the creation of communal land and the maintenance of local village cults. By observing these cults men acknowledge the spirits of their ancestors as the authentic owners of the land. In a society that knows far better than those in the West do that life is made up more of the dead than the living, rights were thought to come from observing the wishes of one's ancestors. In the Vietnamese mentality, life is merely a brief transit, and the foundation for living remains beneath the nobility of people.

A socialization of the land defined by the words *xã hôi hóa* thus suggests not a spurious adventure and the disorder of social innovation, but the traditionally communal values that are most reassuring to the masses. The verb *hóa* completes this Confucian imagery. Far from denoting an anarchic convulsion, it applies specifically to the action in depth by which the "mandate of heaven," through its trustees, the imperial rulers, civilizes a country. This action brings out what man's social nature potentially contains everywhere in Viet Nam: a patriarchal organization at least partially collectivized (remember that in central Viet Nam, a traditional land, 26 percent of the fields were communal property) and based on the ancient model in accordance with the decree of heaven. . . .

"The Marxist World View and Revolutions in Modernizing Countries"

What meaning can militant Marxism—fashioned as it is on the complexities of life in the Western world—have for Vietnamese villagers whose life is so elementary? The answer is simple. In the 1940s and 1950s as well as today, Marxism had meaning only to the extent that it was known to be associated with the nationalist government against foreign rule. . . .

Since a capitalist economy has existed only within enclaves in their countries, capitalism has not been completely understood by colonial and postcolonial peoples. And because so few of them had been a part of this alien economy or shared its rewards, they opposed it. But their opposition was a nationalistic one and not a class antagonism, because class distinctions among the approximately three-fourths of the people who are peasants have been slight and, overall, less important than considerations of a national political identity in motivating revolutionary commitment. Consequently, when revolution broke out in Viet Nam in 1945, it was a nationalist manifestation. Yet, from the very beginning the Communist party stood at the center of the coalition that was seeking independence through revolution. Many observers regarded this Communist presence as a Trojan Horse. But weren't these Communists simply using nationalism as a pretext for overthrowing French rule so that they might then eliminate their Vietnamese adversaries and achieve total control over the country? Was the revolution begun in 1945 a genuine nationalist movement or was it surely a Communist plot?

These questions are too important to risk giving an emotional answer. First, one must acknowledge that Marxists will often cooperate with other revolutionaries if it serves their own purposes. Of course, it is a very natural defensive reaction to see such a tactic as an example

Moral Argument and the War in Vietnam

of Marxist treachery. Yet this reaction may obscure an underlying element of the situation which is bound up with the Communist methods we are trying to discern. For our own benefit it is necessary to examine more closely and dispassionately the attitude of Marxist leaders in modernizing countries with regard to their nationalist allies. In doing so one must keep in mind the local "revolutionary" circumstances which are so foreign to the economic and political framework of social revolution in the West.

Because of local circumstances the Asian Marxists—when they unite with antitraditionalist or anticolonialist nationalists—are not, as we have thought, so sure that their temporary allies are wrong. On the contrary, the educated militant Marxists believe that the nationalists are right at their own level—that they are even righter than they think. What characterizes the authentic Marxist is not only that he knows the mistakes of his allies and therefore prepares to do away with them as soon as possible, but also that he knows their truth and what they represent better than they do. For this reason the Asian Marxist considers himself called upon to go beyond his nationalist allies;he feels he must take charge of their revolutionary movement because they do not recognize what is valid in it.

This distinction may seem too subtle for non-Marxists, but for Marxists such distinctions between phases of revolution are essential. These distinctions are especially relevant to revolution in modernizing societies, since their level of development is so different from the conditions on which Marxist theories were originally focused. In circumstances where class antagonisms are a less significant source of political discontent, Marxists must relate their doctrines to the revolutionary situation as it actually exists or else their influence over the course of a revolution promises to be minimal indeed. But by acknowledging that revolutions in modernizing societies must initially go through a "nationalist" phase, in which there is a consolidation of national leadership by the elimination of colonial rule or archaic traditionalist rule, the Marxists anticipate succeeding revolutionary phases in which far-reaching social change can, indeed must, be brought about. Here the Marxists reap their doctrinal advantage, since those who are struggling with only the "nationalist" phase in mind tend not to realize the full dimensions nor, therefore, the total requirements for revolutionary change.

These Marxist distinctions about phases of revolution may seem purely arbitrary or even artificial; they might appear to be designed only for subverting Marxist competitors rather than assessing the underlying nature of a revolutionary situation. Such an appearance of artificiality, however, could only arise when one thinks in discursive patterns of thought—that is, patterns that are linked by analogies. But in dialetic thought—that is, patterns of thought which develop by "overcoming," or coming to grips with, contradictions and reconciling them—there is no artificiality about these phases of revolution and the action required to achieve them. To quote Hegel, from whom Marx borrowed the principle, "Woe unto anyone who cannot deal with contradictions!" Ignoring or denouncing the strangeness of this Marxist pattern of thought is not enough. If one is to understand the revolutionary action that springs from this Marxist method of thought, one must follow it to its roots.

Marxists do not sit around constructing an imaginary "future city" the way socialists do. Marxism believes that its ideal must emerge from the existing state of human society. Such is the "contradiction" that it has to overcome in order to exist. Such is the servitude of Marxism with regard to the society it destroys. It must come to grips with the reality of that society in order to move out of it. We have not always realized just how unimaginative and undiscursive the militant doctrine of Marxism is meant to be. What we in the West build up with imagination and discursive logic the Marxists consider mere superstructure. The real society, they believe, emerges only from a real foundation. In other words, it emerges from the authentic previous conditions.

. . . In Marxist strategy a revolution is not supposed to destroy the previous conditions of society but, instead, to actualize it and consequently to realize its social potential. . . .

The cosmology of Marxism has, therefore, influenced revolution in Viet Nam, as well as in other modernizing societies, in two important ways. Through its adaptation to the traditional cosmology of the Vietnamese peasants the Marxist cosmology has laid the basis for a political community in which village people have found—in an idiom familiar to them—a new rationalization for participation in national politics. Not only have they risen up in response to a sign of a new mandate of heaven, but these villagers have, in the process, also become participants in a revolutionary movement which offers them a means of sharing in national political power and in gaining access to the attributes of modern life. . . .

Closely related to these modernizing influences of the cosmology of Marxism has been an operational, or strategic, influence. The total assessment the cosmology makes of the underlying nature of the revolutionary process has led Marxist leaders to look beyond the "nationalist" phase of revolution. With this perspective they have realized that the replacement of colonial or traditionalist rule by a cohesive nationalist leadership is not an ultimate goal but merely an initial step. Consequently, Marxists believe that revolutionary change requires the total participation of a people and not just the raising of a force powerful enough to overthrow an incumbent regime. By acting on this perception, the Marxists went beyond their competitors in preparing to mobilize the Vietnamese for revolution, a preparation which catapulted them into the vanguard of revolutionary leadership as the most vocal and effective advocates of Vietnamese nationalism.

Any contradiction between their commitment to Marxism and their championing of Vietnamese nationalism was apparent only in the eyes

Moral Argument and the War in Vietnam

of their adversaries and not in the minds of this Marxist revolutionary leadership. Quite the contrary, it was precisely because of their cosmology of Marxism, with its total assessment and awareness of revolution, that the Marxists were able to outperform their nationalist competitors and take charge of the revolutionary movement in Viet Nam. Their effectiveness was not so much a result of the insidiousness of Marxism as it was attributable to the comprehensiveness of their strategy of revolution. And if the revolution begun in 1945 in Viet Nam really has been a Communist plot, it has succeeded more from its profound understanding of revolutionary politics than from its ruthless execution.

"The Possibilities For Modernization in Viet Nam" . . .

Our whole analysis in this study has been founded on the basic element of Vietnamese social structure: the village. Our major point has been that the village's traditional equilibrium, which has tended to make the Vietnamese secure in their rights and duties, was unable to withstand the impact of French colonial policies. The most significant of these policies was the introduction of money taxes, which demolished the traditional system that was based on an economy of consumption and short-range barter. Significantly, a pamphlet that introduced the young Ho Chi Minh under his early pseudonym, Nguyen Ai Quoc, entitled *Proces de la colonisation francaise (French Colonialism on Trial)*, contained a harsh denunciation of the sudden and crushing manner which the French used to raise taxes in Viet Nam. . . .

The taxes levied were probably not excessive in proportion to the demands placed on a modern economy; they were indicative of the needs of a state in which the big general departments—public works, communications, education, woods and forests, health, etc.—had become public organizations that required governmental financing. . . . But . . . the real objection to such a system is that it did not put enough coined money at the disposal of the peasants who were being asked to become taxpayers. Since the problem still exists long after the departure of France from Viet Nam, the solution is not to reduce taxes but to end the dual economic system in which demands are conceived in the modern sector of the economy and satisfied in the peasant sector.

While France's allies credited colonial administrators with an understanding of traditionalist social forces, they were showing their understanding of the economic conditions France had introduced into Viet Nam. They did not appreciate how hard it was for the Vietnamese peasant to earn cash from his traditional agriculture. With the most praiseworthy of human intentions France's representatives as well as its local allies approached Vietnamese society from a point of view that was more ideological than economic.

. . . The society [the villager] belonged to had a profound sense of community, and it is this village society which a century of French occupation has gutted. There are now urban concentrations everywhere; the big landowners have disappeared from the villages and have left everything in the hands of managers; the important families are in the cities or possess dwellings there. The local equilibrium and sense of community is lost and nothing will restore it. . . .

In describing Vietnamese society during the last years of French rule, Pierre Gourou strongly emphasized the sense of community that pervaded the lives of the people in the countryside:

> In the Tonkinese [northern] villages the inhabitants get together and form district associations, associations for intellectuals or for military mandarins, clubs for the aged, for wrestlers, singers, for tradesmen, for fans of cockfighting, for whistling-bird breeders, for students of a particular professor. There are even associations made up of people born the same year! Each of these associations has its meetings and banquets and to cover their expenses many of them use the income from landed property that was either a gift or that was bought. Such villages hide a strenuous social life behind a mediocre exterior; the peasants find thousands of opportunities to talk, to discuss, to scheme, to manage their common business and to lead the busy life of men burdened with social obligations.

Such was the real civic training of traditional Viet Nam. This perspective from the description of Gourou shows rather well that the Vietnamese peasant's sense of patriotism and civic competence goes far beyond his concern for his bowl of rice despite superficial opinions to the contrary. "This club spirit," concludes Pierre Gourou, "proves, on the other hand, that in Viet Nam conditions are favorable to cooperative associations. If they are organized in conformity with village traditions they will provide a good solution to the difficulties created by the recent introduction of a monetary economy in the rural areas."

Setting up a new economic system in the Vietnamese countryside is not so easy as one might imagine. Essential to such an undertaking would be to have in hand an economic network of both production and consumption. But in the first place one must eliminate the heretofore inhibiting influence of economic intermediaries, the Chinese money-lenders and rice merchants, who have had a powerful organization for monopolizing the fruits of peasant agriculture. Second, one comes up against the problem of choosing and controlling the elements of management in which there have been some previous endeavors to solve the managerial problem by recruiting personnel from the cities and even from among the Europeans. Just the reverse policy should be adopted

Moral Argument and the War in Vietnam

in order to recruit people from the countryside for the tasks of a modern agricultural economy. Economic cooperatives should deal with self-conscious units that, within their limited scope, profit by the solidarity described by Pierre Gourou and are capable of developing leadership from within their own ranks.

A broad policy of economic and social reconstruction is needed in order to bring the Vietnamese peasantry into the modern world.The decentralization of industrial production by creating small factories in provincial areas is but one of the necessary conditions for bringing the village into line with a modern economy. Grouped together in industrial cooperatives, the peasant-workers would also become consumers and would, therefore, enter into a monetary economy. The differential profit which is now going into the hands of the Chinese middleman would be eliminated by closing the gap between the urban economy and the village one. But unless the small profits acquired by the projected peasant cooperatives are channeled into capital formation they may fall back into such traditional uses as usurious loans, which inevitably result, through foreclosure, in the accumulation of landed property and the expropriation of small cultivators. Moreover, the breaking of such a tenacious cycle of traditional usury requires means that are not foreign but actually are in harmony with the ethos of the countryside. . . .

Paradoxically, this program of economic and social development parallels closely the program openly demanded by the Communist-led Democratic Republic of Viet Nam. A maturation of *xã hội hóa,* or socialism, integrated into the history of the country is a direct contrast to both the sclerosis of conservatism and to the social formula of Marxism. And in demanding their own brand of socialism the Vietnamese Communists are not merely erecting a facade, they are expressing their recognition of the situation in Viet Nam for what it really is. Without continuity to the country's traditional ethos, a program for the future can produce few practical results. . . . For Vietnamese popular opinion there are two criteria in politics: heaven and man. Heaven has not yet come to a decision in Vietnam. As for man, what is there to say? One of the first points established in this study was the powerful and singular interest—divinatory more than moral—in any obvious signs of integrity and selfishness during periods of crisis. The French had everything to lose by overlooking the fact that the signs given by their conduct of war and politics worked against them. This is not to say that their client, the Bao Dai government, did not recruit upright men as well as many who died courageously alongside French soldiers: to .deny this would be to insult them as men. But one has only to turn to the rightist press or to foreign observers who were in favor of the French action in Indochina because of their anti-Communist views to realize what an unfortunate effect the spectacle of the war had on the Vietnamese. What matters most then and now is the people's reaction.

. . . The French denounced the Communistic tendencies of their adversaries as morally pernicious; they recalled the deadly effect these principles would have on the moral and sociological structures of Viet Nam. But let us not forget that they were speaking to a people whom the Chinese influence has made skeptical of any declarations made by a power that doesn't have total command of a situation. Everything the French said in the hope that the Vietnamese would become involved in the war appeared to them above all as being their own business. After all, who doesn't denounce his enemies? France began by declaring that the Viet Minh were no more than a "handful of escaped convicts," but likening political convicts to common-law convicts has rarely been a rewarding argument, especially when radical opposition is involved.

In Viet Nam saying such things about one's adversaries simply means that one doesn't get along with them, so it was natural that subsequent French denunciations of communism and its dangers were heard with the same skepticism. For the Vietnamese people the opposition in the Viet Minh ranks stood for no more than a program of moderate socialization. The people then told themselves, *If the Communists are as dangerous as the French make them out to be and if heaven doesn't declare in France's favor and against her adversaries, it must be because her adversaries are right in maintaining that they are not Communists.* The weak ingenuity of French propaganda stumbled here. . . .

France should have approached the Vietnamese with an eye not to her own fears and uncertainties but to theirs. The arguments of anticommunism which the French put forward no longer had much appeal for the Vietnamese in the 1950s even though they had been attracted to them at the outbreak of the conflict. The French felt that the priority they were giving to anticommunism would make the Vietnamese accept the human imperfections of French activities. Yet, in order to justify themselves in contrast to communism, they would have had to give signs of the ease of their achievements as well as an austere and exemplary rigor in their political, administrative, and personal behavior. The "mystique" that the French wanted to propose to Viet Nam could not, however, be fulfilled when the non-Communist Vietnamese were so largely uncommitted to broader identities.

For them to have been integrated into an intelligible world order an establishment "under heaven" of a single unified program of politics would have been required. During the whole period of colonial rule there was a hiatus in the moral order of the Vietnamese which took the form of apparent acceptance of French control. Such an acceptance may be explained by the Vietnamese expectation that a new moral order would appear once the French interregnum had run its course. The masses were taught to believe that this moral order would spring forth through a decree of fate, and here is where Tran Van Huu's magic wand would be needed. Up until the 1920s at least, the Vietnamese thought that the French had a secret and were keeping it from them.

As a result of two world wars the West had shifted its ground. In the process, East Asia became convinced that the Western world has not yet found the formula required for giving the modern era its justification and direction. What do the present circumstances tell us? First, the Communist countries form a continental Eurasian mass that is adjacent to and now merges with the old imperial Chinese world. The land routes of communication across this Eurasian mass have always been familiar to merchants and to revolutionaries, but they have not been the routes that brought the civilization of the Western world. Instead we of the West have come by way of the sea, which has given East Asians the impression we have originated in island civilizations which they feel are subordinate in status. "Never trust a man who was born on an island," an old Vietnamese once told me. The prejudice is not only political but moral. Islands are a dispersion of man and God: we therefore do not have one sole religion.

What we have learned about Vietnamese sociology will at least spare us the illusion that very religious peoples prefer several religions to none at all. What they seek and call religion is, with certain exceptions, not Christian grace in all its conflicting forms or any other spiritual revelation; it is an intelligible principle that can impose one sole discipline on the world. The rigor with which Marxism means to master all sciences, institutions, and man's works as a whole may therefore be taken from the Asian perspective as the traditional sign of a call to power and political order. In this respect, the Confucian state can be seen as a precedent: its place has never been taken by a European successor because of the Western world's inability up until now to unite and to unify, or even to see society as a whole. . . .

"Epilogue: The Meaning of Revolution in Viet Nam" . . .

The revolutionary struggle in Viet Nam is a conflict between two modern cultures created by antagonists who still share an old culture in common. Both sides in the struggle want the same thing: a new Viet Nam that is united, independent of foreign involvement, and modern in its economy and society. The differences between them over how to achieve this new Viet Nam are not, however, merely political in the sense of being a disagreement over short-run strategies and priorities. These differences are much more profound. They are cultural, which is to say that they are based on sharply contrasting conceptions of the way a modern society ought to be organized. They clash over opposing ideas about social status and social cohesion, over what a man's place in society should be and what values should link him to other men.

Too frequently, the values of a society have been regarded by Westerners, especially Americans, as the same thing as ethics and morality. Values and morality are, of course, inseparably intertwined. But values are more than principles for personal conduct; they are also sources of social cohesion and guides for social action. Without common values men find it difficult to work together toward common goals. They either don't trust each other or they don't understand each other. Words don't have the same meaning to people who have different values. Moreover, without the discipline derived from shared values the efforts of men lack force and can easily be dissipated by quarrelsome divisions among them. In a society like the one in Viet Nam, where old values are no longer relevant to the new lives men must live, conflict over values is not merely an ethical and moral controversy—it is also, and most conspicuously, a struggle over political power.

It is because they are so critical in determining the capacity of people to work together that questions of values are also questions of power. . . .

From the perspective of the role of cultural values in Vietnamese politics, the powerlessness over the past quarter-century of pro-Western, urban-oriented governments becomes easier to understand. These governments have, by and large, been limited to urban bases of power precisely because they have not had values relevant to the lives which village people have had to lead. The sharp dichotomy in culture between the cities, where about one-fourth of the Vietnamese live, and the countryside, where about three-fourths live, has been a barrier which these governments have not really been able to overcome. . . .

Generalizations about the numerous pro-Western governments that have come and gone over the past twenty-five years are admittedly risky. These governments have run the political gamut from a transparently colonial regime under the ex-emperor, Bao Dai, to a self-righteous dictatorship under Ngo Dinh Diem, to the rule of American-trained military officers under Nguyen Van Thieu. But despite their differences in style these governments have had a conspicuous common denominator: a dependence on foreign troops and foreign financing to keep them in existence.

. . . Among the many reasons for Communist success the most essential one is the relevancy of their values to the lives villagers must lead. This relevancy springs from a conception of society as a communal as distinct from a secular organization—a conception which offers a comprehensive explanation for a new sense of community in which rural people can participate.

The longing for a new sense of community has been no abstraction among village people. Their spiritual traditions have left them with the belief that men must be linked closely together in a bond of communal identity. But as a practical matter this spirituality has not offered values explicit enough to make this bond a reality. The need has been for values to replace the Confucian traditions which once linked the villagers to a larger community and gave them a sense of being able to acquire a status of recognized significance. The relevance of Communist values, therefore, has been in the possibility of using them to establish a new communal spirit guided by the traditions and forms of the past.

Relevant though they are, these values have not been adopted in the Vietnamese countryside without great violence and extreme coercion. The struggle over who is to govern in the villages of Viet Nam and how, has, certainly, been one of the most tragic examples of political violence since the end of World War II. Moreover, even if the Communist-led-revolution had not been opposed by the French, the Americans, and the anti-Communist Vietnamese, there still would have been violence—the rural people are unlikely to have accepted a new scheme of values through a peaceful mass conversion.

Rarely have the values by which people live been changed fundamentally without a fight. Even in their vestigial form the values which tenuously held Vietnamese villages together prior to 1945 conferred status on some villagers and denied it to others. A change in values meant, therefore, a loss of status to the privileged, and from the first days of the revolution village notables have, almost routinely, lost their lives. But a change in values has also meant an opportunity for an increase in status for villagers who otherwise would have led dreary lives of little consequence within a static village hierarchy.

Worse than the dreariness was the uncertainty—the lack of any really precise identity within a declining village community that also had lost its own identity. How did one establish his distinctiveness under such circumstances? There were no longer examinations in Confucian learning to set a standard for achievement. Also unlike earlier eras, there was no new land to be opened up in the south to which one could move from one's home village. There was only the limited horizon of the village—a village no more a part of a spiritually endowed kingdom but now the object of alien bureaucratic control. Then came the revolution. Along with the new ideas came a way to act upon them. There were a multitude of new organizations to be formed, all of them having a legitimacy as part of the revolution and conveying a new status for those who participated in their activities.

Although access to this new form of status has been open to everyone in the countryside—even landowners if they agreed to a redistribution of their lands—advancement to higher status positions of authority has been strictly based on performance. In much the same way that examinations testing a person's knowledge of Confucian traditions once determined who would be chosen as mandarins, a knowledge of the ideology of revolution has become the criterion for choosing the new, revolutionary cadre from the village people of Viet Nam. Written examinations, of course, are now archaic; the real test of a person's knowledge of the revolutionary program comes in action. If he is to be successful the beginning revolutionary will need not merely a spirit of daring but also a capacity to mobilize his fellow villagers and coordinate their actions within the larger scheme of revolutionary strategy. . . .

The popular responsiveness to these opportunities for participation has resulted in a revolutionary movement powerful enough to dominate northern Viet Nam and to stalemate a massive American force in the south for over five years. A major explanation of the motivation for this response is the relevancy of revolutionary values to Vietnamese traditions. But probably as important has been the feeling that within the revolutionary movement there is a predictability and equity in the access to power. At the lowest levels there seems to be a tested conviction that mobility to positions of authority comes to those whose performance is most notable. And throughout the movement a firm belief appears to exist in a kind of simple justice: the sharing of power on the basis of a mastery of the values and strategy of revolution.

Yet if there is a relevancy of the values of the revolution in Vietnamese traditions and if there is a sense of equity in the sharing of power within the movement, then why hasn't the revolutionary cause been adopted by all Vietnamese? Why has the revolutionary struggle gone on for so long? Why does a substantial portion of Vietnamese society still oppose the revolution? All revolutions have, naturally, been opposed by those who benefit from an existing regime as well as those who are uncertain about what a future regime might bring. But as protracted as revolutions usually are, few have endured as long as has revolution in Viet Nam. Foreign intervention has, of course, made a major difference by prolonging and intensifying the conflict through the commitment of troops to fight on behalf of pro-Western governments.

From this intensity have come deeper cleavages in Vietnamese society and an emphasis by both sides in the struggle on coercion in winning political allegiance. Terror and brutality have mounted as techniques for obtaining popular bases of power as the war has escalated. It is impossible and undoubtedly useless to attempt to assess which side has been the most brutal. Neither side has clean hands. Their conflict has made pawns out of fellow Vietnamese; the score is now kept by the number of their countrymen each side can claim to "control." But despite the inhumanness of this violence an assessment can be made about its consequences and, particularly, about its relevance to the meaning of revolution in Viet Nam.

The Communist revolutionaries have prided themselves on the selective use of terror. By carefully relating their terror tactics to specific political goals, they have sought to break down the resistance of vestigial village cohesion and to persuade the villagers to adopt their scheme of revolutionary values. Killing a rich landowner or an informer for the pro-Western governments has been their way of communicating both revolutionary goals and revolutionary power. . . .

Pro-Western governments in Viet Nam have never relied on tactics of selective terror. Their political goals have instead called for force to be used in occupying and controlling territory. . . . Without any values to master as a means of gaining access to power and without local-level organizations for participations in national politics, allegiance from the countryside has been lacking.

In the discussion of the alienation of the Westernized elite from Vietnamese traditions, this book has tried to suggest some of the reasons why Viet Nam's upper class has not been able to offer leadership to the countryside. Divorced from their country's past, these new mandarins have nevertheless expected and demanded the compliance that previous Vietnamese elites had gotten. Yet they have not realized that this earlier compliance was based on shared values. The old mandarins were respected because their intellectual achievement could be measured in terms that villagers understood and according to values by which villagers lived. These country people now share the values on which this new Westernized upper class is founded because for them they are unattainable. These values were obtained primarily through education in an alien scientific culture. . . .

. . . Despite the enormous scale of violence and the far-reaching changes in the country the most important aspects of the struggle remain the same. Pro-Western governments are still trying to wrest control over the countryside away from rural-based revolutionaries who have developed power by relating their strategy and values to Vietnamese traditions. The meaning of revolution in Viet Nam is that the opportunity for predictable access to political power by village people is a more potent form of power than a primarily military force arrayed against them. In Viet Nam, therefore, the technological power of the West has had its weaknesses exposed by the political power of a peasant people.

Notes On Contributors

David Little is Assistant Professor of Christian Ethics in the Divinity School of Yale University. His specialties are historical and social ethics. He is the author of *American Foreign Policy and Moral Rhetoric: The Example of Vietnam.*

Arthur Bud Ogle is completing his Ph.D. in American diplomatic history at the University of Virginia. He received a B.D. from Yale.

Jean Lacouture is a distinguished correspondent for *Le Monde.* He is author of *Vietnam: Between Two Truces* and of a biography of Ho Chi Minh.

John McDermott teaches at Old Westbury College of the State University of New York. Formerly, he was the associate editor of *Viet-Report.* He is author of *Profile of Vietnamese History.*

Jean-Paul Sartre is a famous French philosopher and writer.

Noam Chomsky is Professor of Linguistics at M.I.T. In addition to many books in linguistics, he is author of *American Power and the New Mandarins* and *At War with Asia.*

Gabriel Kolko is the author of *Wealth and Power in America, The Roots of American Foreign Policy,* and many other books. He has recently taught at the State University of New York at Buffalo.

Paul Ramsey is Chairman of the Department of Religion at Princeton University and author and editor of numerous books in the field of ethics and theology.

David Schoenbrun, former reporter for CBS News, teaches journalism at Columbia University.

Mary McCarthy is author of many books, including *The Group.*

D. Gareth Porter is a Ph.D. candidate in Southeast Asian Studies at Cornell University.

Len E. Ackland is a graduate student at Johns Hopkins School of Advanced International Studies and co-editor of *Why Are We Still in Vietnam?*

Henry Kissinger was Professor of Government at Harvard before becoming President Nixon's special advisor on national security affairs. He is the author of several books on foreign policy and military affairs.

Theodore Draper is a fellow in the Institute for Advanced Studies at Princeton. He is the author of *The Abuse of Power* and *The Rediscovery of Black Nationalism.*

Samuel P. Huntington is Chairman of the Department of Government at Harvard and author of *Changing Patterns of Military Politics.*

Alfred Hassler is national executive secretary of the Fellowship of Reconciliation. He was largely responsible for the formation of the U.S. Study Team on Religious and Political Freedom in Vietnam, which toured Vietnam in 1969.

Carl Oglesby was president of Students for a Democratic Society before being a Radical Scholar in Residence at Antioch College for several years. He has just published a book of poetry and edited *The New Left Reader.*

Robert A. Scalapino is Professor of Political Science at the University of California, Berkeley.

John T. McAlister is a member of the Center of International Studies, the Woodrow Wilson School of Public and International Affairs, Princeton. He was a close associate of the late Paul Mus and has authored *The Origins of Revolution in Vietnam.*

Paul Mus, the late French master of Asian studies, is well known for his many books in French on Indochina and Asia.

Paul Menzel has received a B.D. from Yale University and just recently a Ph.D. in philosophy from Vanderbilt University. He is presently teaching at Pacific Lutheran University. He is co-editor of a forthcoming book of essays on disobedience of law.